THE LIFE AND LETTERS OF
ALEXANDER WILSON

1. *Picus Auratus.* Gold-winged Woodpecker. 2. *Emberiza Americana.* Black-throated Bunting.

3. *Motacilla Sialis.* Blue Bird.

Drawn from Nature by A. Wilson.

Plate 3 from Alexander Wilson, *American Ornithology* (Volume I)

The LIFE AND LETTERS *of* ALEXANDER WILSON

EDITED BY

CLARK HUNTER

American Philosophical Society

INDEPENDENCE SQUARE · PHILADELPHIA

1983

WITHDRAWN
ITHACA COLLEGE LIBRARY

QL
31
.W7
W55
1983

Publication of this volume has been made possible in part
by the John Ross Delafield Foundation

Copyright © 1983 by the American Philosophical Society
for its *Memoirs* series, Volume 154
Library of Congress Catalog Card Number 81–68195
International Standard Book Number 0–87169–154–x
US ISSN 0065–9738

54 4703   23.99

Table of Contents

List of Illustrations

FIGURE 1. Alexander Wilson. Reproduced with permission of the Paisley Museum and Art Galleries. (*Figures 1 to 7 follow page 36.*)

FIGURE 2. Paisley Abbey in 1791. Reproduced with permission of the Paisley Museum and Art Galleries.

FIGURE 3. Paisley in 1767. Reproduced with permission of the Paisley Museum and Art Galleries.

FIGURE 4. Paisley in 1808. Reproduced with permission of the Paisley Museum and Art Galleries.

FIGURE 5. Auchinbathie Tower, Renfrewshire, Scotland. Photographed by the author.

FIGURE 6. Alexander Wilson's statue in Paisley.

FIGURE 7. The Low Church, Paisley.

FIGURE 8. View of Philadelphia from Kensington. From engraving by William Birch and Son in the Library of the American Philosophical Society. (*Figures 8 to 14 follow page 212.*)

FIGURE 9. Street plan of Philadelphia in 1807. From original in the Library of the American Philosophical Society.

FIGURE 10. High Street, Philadelphia, 1799. From engraving by William Birch and Son. From original in the Library of the American Philosophical Society.

FIGURE 11. Wilson's schoolhouse at Kingsessing. From Grosart's *Poems and Literary Prose of Alexander Wilson.*

FIGURE 12. Old Swedes Church, Philadelphia. From Grosart's *Poems and Literary Prose of Alexander Wilson.*

FIGURE 13. John Bartram's house, 1730. From original in the Library of the American Philosophical Society.

Figures 6 and 7 were photographed by Frank Hardy Studios; Figures 11, 12, 15a, 15b, and 19 were photographed by Tom Scott, Edinburgh; Figures 8, 9, 10, 13, 14, 15c, 16b, 17a, 17b, and 20 were photographed by James L. Dillon, Philadelphia; and Figure 16 was photographed by The Meriden Gravure Co. The maps were drawn by Mrs. Barbara A. Morris. Illustrations were engraved on wood by Thomas Bewick.

COLOR PLATES

all from Alexander Wilson, *American Ornithology*

Introduction

A MAN who is barely able to distinguish between a sparrow and a robin is not normally qualified to write a biographical narration of an ornithologist or to attempt the most complete collection possible of his letters. The justification is that Alexander Wilson was more than an ornithologist. In his forty-seven years he was a weaver, pedlar, poet, reformer, pioneering ornithologist, and remarkable traveler, not to mention artist and writer.

He was the archetypal "lad o' pairts," of many parts, famous in Scottish folk lore. Starting life with few advantages he was determined to make a name for himself, at whatever cost. He was virtually self-taught. This is demonstrated in his early letters to David Brodie, his weaving friend turned schoolmaster. These are little more than writing exercises, and the turgid prose seems much worse when read directly from the manuscripts written by a hand more familiar with throwing the shuttle than pushing a pen.

There was a gradual improvement in style and penmanship, but it was when he got to America that Wilson threw off the shackles.

1

The affectedness vanished and his letters took a narrative form, except for a reversion in his letters to Charles Orr. As his character developed, so did his ability to express himself; it came to maturity in his travelog letters, especially those written on his way to New Orleans in 1810, and in the text of the *American Ornithology*. Good as his travel letters are, we are left with the regret that he did not fulfill his potential and publish a book of his journeys. All we have are these letters and the incidental narrations in his bird essays.

When searching for unpublished letters of Alexander Wilson, I found in private hands in Paisley his own copy of the 1791 edition of his poems. This particular copy was noted at Philadelphia in 1814, when George Ord had it before him as he wrote the sketch of Wilson's life later printed in the ninth volume of the *Ornithology* which he edited. Inscribed on an unnumbered page (iii) are these words:

I published these poems when only 22—an age more abundant in sail than ballast. Reader let this soften the rigour of criticism a little.

                                        ALEX WILSON
Gray's Ferry   July 6th,   1804.

There is a surprising error in the inscription. When the first edition was published in 1790 Wilson was twenty-four, not twenty-two. In the words quoted Wilson assesses his own volume of poetry fairly accurately. He attempted to display his craftmanship long before he had completed his apprenticeship. In doing so, he became one of the host of versifiers attempting to follow in the footsteps of Robert Burns who were carried away by the myth of Henry Mackenzie's[1] description of Burns as that "Heaven-taught ploughman." Wilson peeped out from the shadow of the great man with the anonymous publication of "Watty and Meg," but the poems that warrant him a place in the history of Scottish literature were "The Shark; or Lang Mills Detected," "The Hollander, or Light Weight," and "Hab's Door." These were the first poems prompted by the new

---

1. Author of "The Man of Feeling" (1771).

problems in human relations created by the Industrial Revolution. They earned him, not fame, but notoriety and the strictures of the law.

On 4 March 1801, at a celebration of Jefferson's first election to the presidency, Wilson delivered a splendid address in Milestown, Pennsylvania, entitled "Oration on the Power and Value of National Liberty," which was widely circulated. He had similar success with a song, "Jefferson and Liberty," set to the well-known Scottish air "Willie Was a Wanton Wag," which became a popular folk song. His excessively long poem "The Foresters," which described his expedition to Niagara in 1804, was published in the leading Philadelphia literary magazine, *The Port Folio*. As a descriptive poem it is far too long to be appreciated today. Its length conceals its merit as an early traveler's account of spectacular territory, when very few had Alexander Wilson's observant pen. The poems he wrote in America appeared in many influential newspapers and periodicals. His name was probably as highly regarded as that of any contemporary poet, even if early nineteenth-century Americans could not yet boast with Dr. Samuel Johnson, "Sir, we are a nest of singing birds." Feathered variety, yes! Poetical, no!

It was Wilson's great good fortune to become schoolmaster at Gray's Ferry early in 1802, for there he quickly became acquainted with William Bartram (1739–1823), who revealed to him "a world of naturalists."[2] Burns inspired Wilson to poetry, and it was Bartram who not only inspired but instructed Wilson in ornithology and promoted his skill as a bird illustrator. Bartram had been well grounded in the natural sciences by his father, John Bartram (1699–1777), who, although untaught, was described by Linnaeus as "the greatest natural botanist in the World." The generous and friendly

2. *A World of Naturalists* is the title of a delightful book by Joseph Kastner (published in America by Alfred A. Knopf, Inc., with the title *A Species of Eternity*), which tells the adventures of these splendid eccentrics, the naturalists working in eighteenth- and nineteenth-century America.

Bartram gave Wilson the run of his library and brought to him almost a century of accumulated knowledge and disciplined observation of the American wilds. Through Bartram he got to know Charles Willson Peale, the founder of the internationally famous museum of natural history in Philadelphia. Wilson often used the museum as a studio and as a repository for his bird specimens.

When the first volume of the *Ornithology* came out in 1808, it was not the work of an untrained amateur but of a man who had equipped himself for the first scientific description and listing of American birds. In the preface to his first volume, Wilson described the state of ornithological records in America when he commenced his all-absorbing task. After doffing his cap to the earlier English artist/naturalists Catesby[3] and Edwards, he continued:

From the Writers of our country the Author has derived but little advantage. The first considerable list of our birds was published in 1787, by Mr. Jefferson, in his celebrated "Notes on Virginia," and contains the names of a hundred and nine species. . . . The next, and by far the most complete that has yet appeared, was published in 1791, by Mr. William Bartram, in his "Travels through North and South Carolina," etc., in which two hundred and fifteen different species are enumerated, and concise descriptions and characteristics of each added in Latin and English. Dr. Barton, in his "Fragments of the Natural History of Pennsylvania," has favoured us with a number of remarks on this subject; and Dr. Belknap, in his "History of New Hampshire," as well as Dr. Williams in that of Vermont, have each enumerated a few of our birds. But these, from the nature of the publications in which they have been introduced, can be considered only as a catalogue of names, without the details of specific particulars, or the figured and colored representation of the birds themselves.

3. Mark Catesby traveled in the southern states and the Caribbean for more than a decade before returning to England to publish the first volume of *The Natural History of Carolina, Florida and the Bahama Islands* in 1731. In it there were 100 plates depicting birds and botanical specimens. Working almost a century before Wilson, he was the earliest significant ornithologist in America.

In the nine volumes of the *American Ornithology* there were individual essays on 293 birds and 315 were portrayed in the 76 plates.

The fierce arguments about the respective merits of Wilson and J. J. Audubon are now in the past. We have to accept that Audubon was able to complete his masterpiece while poor Wilson died with his great work incomplete, but nothing can take away from Wilson the magnitude of his endeavors and achievements over ten years from the conception of his idea "to make a collection of all our finest birds" until his death.

In his drawings the flamboyant Frenchman sought dramatic effects and succeeded wonderfully well while the cannier Scotsman aimed for facts and accurate delineation. Audubon and his splendid engraver Robert Havell, whose skill added an extra dimension to the finished plates, used Wilson's book as a standard guide, and there is no reason why Audubon should have pretended otherwise. It would not have diminished Audubon to give credit to the long-dead Wilson for his groundwork, just as Wilson made acknowledgment to Bartram. Wilson cleared the ground and planted the seed while Audubon reaped the crops.

Wilson was not a religious man in the sense of church affiliation, and perhaps his philosophy is best summed up in these words by Albert Einstein: "Enough for me the mystery of the eternity of life, and the inkling of the marvellous structure of reality, to-gether with the single-hearted endeavor to comprehend a portion, be it never so tiny, of the reason that manifests itself in nature."[4]

In the account of Wilson's life accompanying the letters, I have tried to be true to him and to avoid the dramatics dear to his follower, Audubon. My chronicle should be treated as explanatory notes to enable the letters to serve as Wilson's autobiography.

4. From Albert Einstein, *The World as I See It* (London: Bodley Head Ltd., 1935).

The first biographical sketch of Wilson's life was written by his friend George Ord, who saw the eighth and ninth volumes of *American Ornithology* through the press after Wilson's death. This memoir appeared in the ninth volume which was published in 1814, and it included a few letters. It was rewritten by Ord and substantially augmented with the inclusion of many more letters for the three-volume octavo edition plus a folio volume of plates of the *American Ornithology* issued by Harrison Hall in 1828–1829. The *Sketch of the Life of Alexander Wilson, Author of the American Ornithology*, was also published separately in Philadelphia in 1828.

Between the dates of these two accounts of Wilson, two useful monographs were published in Scotland. The first, entitled "Life of the Author," appeared in *Poems Chiefly in the Scottish Dialect by Alexander Wilson*, printed by J. Neilson, Paisley, in 1816. The name of the writer was not given but the 1844 Belfast edition of Wilson's poems, supported by local evidence, establishes that the work was commenced by Dr. Whyte who, because of his profession, was acquainted with Thomas Crichton, Wilson's friend and governor to the Town's Hospital for the Poor. Dr. Whyte died with the work unfinished but it was taken over by his medical colleague, Dr. Robert Watt, author of the monumental, posthumously published *Bibliotheca Britannica*, who wrote the Life. Both doctors had the advantage of source material from Crichton and it was he who, under the pen-name Senex, published in 1819 *Biographical Sketches of the Late Alexander Wilson*. The volumes of 1816 and 1819 contain passages from a few of Wilson's letters to friends in Scotland of which these extracts are the only record.

Two later editions of *American Ornithology* in 1831 and 1832 added a little to the understanding of Wilson, but no more letters. That of 1831, edited by Robert Jamieson and published in Edinburgh, contained a fairly mundane life by the Rev. W. M. Hetherington. The next Edinburgh publication in 1832, with notes and a life by the eminent naturalist, Sir William Jardine, benefited from information given to Sir William by Wilson's sister, Jean.

The Poetical Works of Alexander Wilson published by John Henderson, Belfast, in 1844 included an interesting preface and a memoir of Wilson. The unnamed editor had some personal knowledge of Wilson's life in Scotland and the preface is noteworthy for its details of the early editions of his poems.

In 1863 Allan Park Paton produced *Wilson the Ornithologist: A New Chapter in His Life*, published by Longmans, Green of London. The "new chapter" was the near farcical account of an amour in Milestown from which Wilson was probably fortunate to escape with no other injury than to his dignity. The interlude was revealed by Paton when he printed a series of letters from Wilson to Charles Orr, written mainly between 1800 and 1801. In accordance with the conventions of the age Paton deleted names, and these letters are here printed for the first time without deletions from the originals which are preserved in the National Library of Scotland, Edinburgh.

There followed in 1876 what has been the most complete collection of Wilson's correspondence, *The Poems and Literary Prose of Alexander Wilson*, edited in two volumes by the Rev. Alexander B. Grosart. Some of Wilson's letters are known to us only from Grosart's book, and all later students of Wilson's life and work have been indebted to Grosart for his primary research. As a minister of religion he was probably more inhibited than Paton by contemporary social and literary standards and he made many excisions from the texts.

Grosart appeared to have scooped the pool and for many years afterwards new material was scarce and desultory, confined to the publication of a few items in journals such as *The Auk* and *Penn Monthly*, etc. Then in 1951 came Elsa G. Allen's *The History of American Ornithology before Audubon* in the *Transactions of The American Philosophical Society*. Dr. Allen rescued Wilson from the all-enveloping dominance of Audubon and returned him to his rightful place in the history of American ornithology.

Exactly a decade later the first penetrating investigation of Wilson's life and character was made in the pages of Robert Cantwell's

Alexander Wilson: Naturalist and Pioneer. Cantwell brought to us a much fuller picture of the man and a great deal of new information. The book is also valuable for the pen portraits of many of Wilson's contemporaries. The account of Wilson's difficulties with the law involving his poem "The Shark; or Lang Mills Detected," difficulties which only culminated when he emigrated to America, is by far the best and most enlightening that has been printed. However, he apparently did not note that the National Library of Scotland, Edinburgh, contained the records of an earlier Wilson court case concerning his poem "The Hollander, or Light Weight." The negative outcome of this case almost certainly influenced his subsequent actions resulting in the later prosecution. The papers of "The Hollander" case are here printed for the first time. This and a few other errors of omission or commission by Robert Cantwell must be looked upon as relatively trifling when set against the importance of his biography.

In this compilation there are some forty-two letters from Wilson not included in Grosart and fifteen more with significant additions to previously published texts. Several letters to and from Thomas Jefferson are included. The publication of an edition of letters is often the means of uncovering lost letters, diaries, and other papers. The present editor would welcome details of any of Alexander Wilson's writings which may come to light.

I am very pleased to have this opportunity to thank the following institutions which made available to me the originals, transcripts, or photocopies of Wilson letters in their care: the Academy of Natural Sciences and the American Philosophical Society in Philadelphia; Rare Books and Manuscript Library, Columbia University; Edinburgh University Library; Houghton Library and the Museum of Comparative Zoology of Harvard University; Haverford College

Library; Historical Society of Pennsylvania (Philadelphia); The Paisley Museum and Art Galleries (Renfrew District Council); The Library of Congress (Washington, D.C.); The Library Company of Philadelphia; Trustees of the National Library of Scotland (Edinburgh); The Charles Patterson Van Pelt Library of the University of Pennsylvania; Tracy W. McGregor Library of the University of Virginia; The Beinecke Rare Book and Manuscript Library of Yale University.

Very little Wilson material is privately owned, so I appreciated all the more the kindness of Miss Leckie of Paisley in giving me the extended use of her unique 1791 edition of Wilson's poems, Wilson's own copy with notes.

From the Paisley Burns Club I received the full transcript of a letter which Grosart printed only in part. For this, and much encouragement from various members of that venerable club, my sincere thanks. It was Mr. Henry Herron, one of the members and formerly procurator fiscal in Paisley and latterly Glasgow, who penetrated for me the Scottish legal mists and complexities of the court records of Wilson's conflict with the law over his poem "The Hollander, or Light Weight." It is an interesting coincidence that, almost 200 years after his predecessor became entangled with Wilson, a more recent procurator fiscal should unravel the story.

Mr. David R. Shearer, Chief Curator of The Paisley Museum and Art Galleries, gave me full access to the early Wilson letters in that museum and to other Wilson material. In this and other ways Mr. Shearer and his staff rendered me every assistance that lay in their power.

I am also grateful to Mr. J. D. Hendry, Chief Librarian of Renfrew District Library Service, to Mr. Kenneth W. Hinshalwood of Paisley Central Library, and to Mr. John B. Hood, formerly Senior-deputy Librarian in Renfrew District and now Chief Librarian to Clydebank District Council, for the use of the fine collection of Wilsoniana in the Paisley Central Library.

The maps were drawn by Mrs. Barbara Morris, Cartographer, Department of Geography, Edinburgh University, but I take full responsibility for Wilson's routes traced on the maps.

When the book was almost ready to go to print, Mr. Humphrey A. Olsen, editor of the *Snowy Egret*, Williamsburg, Kentucky, offered to make available Wilson material he had been collecting for a number of years. I am indebted to Mr. Olsen for drawing my attention to seven Wilson letters I did not have and for enabling me to collate a further four. I have also referred to a Wilson article he published in the *Snowy Egret* (spring 1981). I hope that Mr. Olsen may yet publish in book form some of his own material and opinions concerning Wilson's life in America.

Dr. Charles Cullen, editor-in-chief of the *Papers of Thomas Jefferson*, has kindly made available letters of Wilson in the Jefferson collection at The Library of Congress.

Dr. G. Scott Wilson, formerly of Hutchesons' Grammar School, Glasgow, and now teaching English at Warwick School, England, has taken an interest in this work from its earlier days. From time to time his suggestions regarding bibliographical sources relating to Wilson have been most helpful. He has also corrected the script for my idiosyncrasies of grammar and his charming wife, Rita, has typed, with great care, a very difficult manuscript. Dr. Scott Wilson has also been kind enough to perform the unenviable task of preparing the index. It is doubtful if *The Life and Letters of Alexander Wilson* would ever have been completed without the aid of Dr. and Mrs. G. Scott Wilson.

In the introduction and the chronicle of Wilson's life I have used four short quotations which I gladly acknowledge and express my thanks to the copyright holders of the following publications: Joseph Kastner, *A World of Naturalists* (London: John Murray, 1978); Albert Einstein, *The World as I See It* (London: Bodley Head Ltd., 1935); Francis Hobart Herrick, *Audubon The Naturalist*, 2 vols. (New York: D. Appleton & Co., 1917); Ernest Earnest,

John and William Bartram, Botanists and Explorers (Philadelphia: University of Pennsylvania Press, 1940).

Both in Scotland and in the United States, I am beholden to the many friends, and even mere acquaintances or correspondents, who have helped me in their various ways to make possible this collection of the letters of Alexander Wilson.

In particular I should like to acknowledge the assistance given and care taken, when preparing this manuscript for the printer, by the members of the editorial staff of the American Philosophical Society. Their guidance has been invaluable. My thanks are also due to all members of the staff of the American Philosophical Society for information provided and other help over nearly a decade.

Paisley, October 1982   CLARK HUNTER

PART ONE

The Life of Alexander Wilson

CHAPTER I

Childhood: "A Bird of Passage"

W HEN the parliaments of Scotland and England were united in 1707 it was with very great misgivings, at least in Scotland, and these misgivings were not confined to any one section of the population. There were riots or disturbances in many Scottish towns, notably Glasgow, Edinburgh, and Dumfries, and contemporary writings convey the distinct impression that a majority of the people of Scotland were against the Union. One such contemporary account was given by Daniel Defoe, then operating as an English spy in Edinburgh, when he reported picturesquely, if fearfully, to Robert Harley, Earl of Oxford:

I had not been Long There but I heard a Great Noise and looking Out Saw a Terrible Multitude Come up the High street with A Drum at the head of Them shouting and swearing and Cryeing Out all scotland would stand to-geather, No Union, No Union, English Dogs, and the like.

In the end a handful of able and determined men succeeded where, from Roman times, armies had failed. Perhaps they did not make the best bargain they should have made, perhaps personal gain was of more importance to some than a vision of the future, but the Union provided the great stimulant that Scotland needed.

During the century from 1700 to 1800, although the population of Scotland increased only from 1,000,000 to 1,600,000, the revenue increased 51 times! Glasgow and Paisley particularly benefited from the Union; Glasgow started the eighteenth century with a population of 12,500 and entered the next century with 77,000, poised to overhaul Edinburgh. Paisley, Wilson's birthplace, grew from little more than a village of 2,200 souls nestling round the Abbey Kirk to be the third largest town in Scotland with a population of 31,000.

Majorities, even in the best of democracies, are not infallible in their political judgments and the mob in Glasgow drove out the Provost, John Aird, and plundered his home, while in Dumfries a similar mob was burning the Articles of Union at the Cross. But in Paisley all was peace and quiet and the Union was not even mentioned in the Town Council minutes. The inhabitants were apparently too busy preparing themselves, not to attack supporters of the Union, but to attack the vastly increased market for their textiles; and this they did with dramatic success.

There were only 87 looms in the little township in 1695, possibly about 100 in 1707, and by 1744 there were 867 looms and 93 thread mills. The town produced and attracted weavers of great skill so that even Robert Burns's witch in "Tam o' Shanter" was proud to wear her "Cutty Sark o' Paisley harn." These men adapted with changing fashions and commercial needs from fabrics of homespun linen and wool to lawn, cotton, muslin, silk and gauze. It was then, the last quarter of the eighteenth century, that the Paisley weavers acquired the technical skill and aesthetic appreciation which survived after Adam Smith's division of labor had become a tenet of industrial belief and the invention of mechanical and powered appliances had reduced their status as artist craftsmen. The final flowering came with the production of the famous Paisley shawls in the nineteenth century, when designs originating in Kashmir were copied by French and English weavers and adopted and embellished in Paisley, and the market cornered by virtue of quality and price.

One of the immigrants to the thriving, energetic town was Alexander Wilson, father of the ornithologist, and generally bynamed Saunders in the couthy, Scottish way. He was born in Campbeltown in 1728 although the family had originated in Renfrewshire, and it was from Lochwinnoch that the grandfather had gone to Campbeltown. Wilson is one of the most common of Renfrewshire names; when the Poll Tax Roll was prepared in 1695, some 5 percent of the population of Paisley, or 23 out of the 467 families, were called Wilson. In those happy days when spelling was a matter of personal choice, however, they were recorded as Willsune or Wilsoune.

Later Saunders Wilson and his family lived for some years in or about the parish of Lochwinnoch. Early in the next century, when many who had known the Wilsons were still alive, a crippled doctor, Andrew Crawfurd of Johnshill, occupied his time collecting all the local records and gossip he could unearth, preserving them, almost verbatim, in forty-six volumes of manuscript called the *Cairn of Lochwinnoch*. The Wilsons had been well known, if not notorious, in the area—young Alexander because of his skill as a "dabbler in poetry" and auld Saunders because of his skill as a distiller of whisky, a skill which he had no doubt obtained in Campbeltown, at one time a hive of distilleries. He had also appeared before the court in Renfrewshire as a smuggler and been penalized for being found out!

The births, deaths, marriages, weather reports, tales, and local scandals in the *Cairn* are written mainly in the homely language of the Renfrewshire-Ayrshire border just as Andrew Crawfurd took them down from his informants. He provided a wonderful outlet for the local gossip-mongers, and, because of this, the *Cairn* has to be treated with caution as the gossips in Lochwinnoch were no more accurate than elsewhere, and there was the occasional dash of spite to add flavor. It does, however, offer a mine of information to the delver about Alexander Wilson and his family during the years they lived in the neighborhood.

The *Cairn* reveals the varied talents of Alexander Wilson, Senior. He is described as "Saunders Wilson the smuggler" and "a weaver and smuggler," and from it we learn of the additional skill he acquired in Campbeltown: "Auld Saunders was an illicit distiller of Whisky." Then we get an unflattering portrait: "Auld Saunie was a scraggy wee body, verra sair pockmarked. He was a soldier after he married." Here the little dash of spite shows, for the unprepossessing description came from the son of Saunders's landlord, John Craig, and was perhaps repayment for an even more unflattering portrayal of his father by Wilson, Junior, in one of his poems. Another contemporary of Saunders describes him thus: "In personal appearance he is said to have greatly resembled his son, being tall, vigorous, inclining to the slender rather than the athletic and having a marked intellectual expression of countenance."

There is reason to believe that the reference to Saunders as a soldier "after" his marriage should read "afore he married," because his movements from the time of his first marriage are fairly well documented and the three children of Saunders Wilson and Mary McNab who survived beyond infancy appear all to have been born when he was in his thirties. We cannot be precise about the time of Wilson, Senior's, career as a soldier, but we can be certain that, although he was a jack of all trades, it was as a weaver that he was attracted to Paisley with its thriving textile industry, and it was to the Seedhills of Paisley that he brought his young wife, Mary McNab from Rhu. Their home and weaving shop was one of a little row of weavers' cottages at right angles to the White Cart Water just above the Seedhill Craigs, where a picturesque waterfall, better known to Paisley "buddies" as the Hammils, tumbles playfully, perhaps amused at finding itself in the center of a busy industrial town. A little lane beside the cottages led to stone steps at the river's edge; the lane was eventually to take its name from Saunders's and Mary's famous son and be known as "Wilson's Place."

Alexander Wilson the younger was born on 6 July 1766 within what had been the walled garden of Paisley Abbey, and there spent the first ten years of his life. A print of Paisley in 1767 shows a pleasant sylvan spot at the dawn of the Industrial Revolution, with a landscape attractively featured by the wooded hills of Oakshaw and Camphill. Nearby the hills of Saucel and Hunterhill sloped gently down to the White Cart Water on its way to meet its twin and then its bigger brother. Of it Daniel Defoe had written only forty years earlier:

The Abbey of Pasely is famous in History, and to History I refer the Enquirer; it lyes on the West Side of the Clyde, over against Glasgow, the Remains of the Building are to be seen, and the Town bears still the Marks of being fortify'd. When I tell you this was one of the most eminent Monasteries in Scotland; that the Building was of a vast Extent, and the Revenue in Proportion; you need not ask if the Soil was good, the lands rich, the Air healthful, and the Country pleasant. The Priests very seldom fail'd to chuse the best Situation, and the richest and most pleasant Part of the Country wherever they came; witness St. Albans, St. Edmond's-Bury, Glastenbury, Canterbury; and innumerable other instances in England, and also many in Scotland; as St. Andrew's Holy-Rood, Pasely, and others.

Four days after his birth, the infant Alexander Wilson was christened by the minister of the local kirk, Dr. John Witherspoon. Both the minister and the babe in his arms were to become notable citizens in the as yet unborn United States of America. Almost exactly ten years later Witherspoon, now president of the College of New Jersey, was the only minister of religion or educator to sign the Declaration of Independence.

Wilson was to be no churchman, but Doctor Witherspoon's influence upon him was considerable, if indirect. The power exerted by this man of character and standing in nurturing the seeds of revolution which resulted in the burning of his effigy by British soldiers and led to Horace Walpole's comment, "Daughter America has run away with a Presbyterian parson," helped to create the conditions in Scotland, in America, and in Alexander Wilson's life which eventually drove him to America in 1794, the year that Dr. Witherspoon died.

The first ten years of Wilson's life were the happy, uneventful years of a normal childhood in a "bien" (comfortably prosperous) and close-knit family. His favorite playground was at the Hammils or among the ruined portions of the Abbey. The depredations of time had created the ruins, assisted to no small extent by the Earl of Dundonald who had used the site as his private quarry. John Parkhill described it, with a bit of a moral lesson, in his quaint *History of Paisley*:

The Earl of Dundonald, who lived in the old palace of the Abbot, was a wild and reckless young nobleman, and sunk in dissipation. His greatest associates were the young lads of the town; he learned them to drink and fight; and, in short, to make them as big blackguards as himself, with them he would go to the neighboring fairs, and fight with all they met.

The choir, the transept and several other parts of the Abbey were in ruins; these ruins contained excellent building stones; these he sold to raise money, and when this quarry was exhausted, he proceeded to take down the ruins which were still standing; and after taking down a good portion of the North transept he began to take down the building that was above the arch of the main window of the transept (perhaps one of the finest windows of any abbey in Britain), all to get possession of the asheler stones of the arch; the heritors however interdicted him. Thus ended my Lord Dundonald's exploits in Paisley; he immediately went off as a captain in the army to America, taking about forty of his old friends with him, and was killed whilst leading the forlorn hope at the siege of Louisburgh, July 26, 1758. There were not above three of the lads he took with him ever returned. It was rather a melancholy story, but the result was quietness to the countryside.

From his earliest years Wilson, who was a well-built, wiry, bright youngster, began to develop a wanderlust; his later and peculiarly apt self-description was that he was "a bird of passage," although his childish wanderings took him only to nearby woods like Oakshaw Hill and then, as he grew a little older and bolder, to the Gleniffer Braes, a paradise of glens, waterfalls, lochans, and rickles of stones and earthenworks—the relics of prehistory.

His parents sent him to Paisley Grammar School, and he even had the privilege of some additional tuition from a Mr. Barlas—perhaps with the aim of preparing him for what was then the summit of Scottish ambition, the ministry—but, as he came to the end of the first decade of his life, there was a quick succession of happenings which had their effect on his future life.

With Saunders and his wife, Mary McNab, the family now numbered five, including Mary, the elder daughter; Jean; and young Alex. There is conflicting evidence about whether or not Jean was older than Alex, although it is generally assumed that Alex was the youngest of the family. As a family they were outgoing and had no lack of friends; included among them were their near neighbors, the Witherspoons, one of the many families of incomers to Paisley, but unrelated to Dr. John Witherspoon.

Now came a climacteric in young Alex's life. His mother became ill and died sometime before his tenth birthday. Then, on 4 July 1776, came one of the watersheds of history, the American Declaration of Independence, that great statement of ideals so stirringly set forth by Thomas Jefferson. These ideals, stated with a frankness impossible in eighteenth-century Scotland, became Wilson's philosophy of life and the achievement of American independence was to provide him with the place and environment in which he could best flourish. Two days later, on 6 July 1776, there was a proclamation of another kind in Paisley, the marriage banns of Saunders to "Catherine Brown or Urie, a widow," who brought to the family two children and provided another—a daughter, Janet—so speedily that there must have been some raised eyebrows in the Seedhills, when she was baptized in February 1777. The war with America cut off trade with the colonies and brought hardship to the Paisley weavers. The elder Wilson with a family of eight took Alex from the Grammar School and sent him to work as a herd boy for Hugh Stevenson at Rakerfield Farm on the Ayrshire-Renfrewshire border. The farm overlooked the Lochlands or Lows, as the district, part of which is now a reservoir, is known to this day. There are some inaccuracies in the dates of the Wilson family movements in the *Cairn*, which appear to indicate that Saunders and family were at Lochlands while young Alex was a herd boy a quarter of a mile further up the hill at Rakerfield; but, as the father's address on his son's apprenticeship certificate (dated as beginning on 31 July 1779) is shown as the Seedhills, Paisley, this must be taken as still the family home at that date.

Despite the difficult times in weaving Alex was apprenticed as a weaver with his brother-in-law, William Duncan, his eldest sister having married young, and served for three wearisome years. Sometime during this apprenticeship period, Saunders moved his home and weaving shop out to the Lochlands which was convenient and yet remote enough for the smuggling trade with the colonies and for his "wee still," to both of which Saunders Wilson was driven by necessity, and drawn by inclination.

This was an era in Scotland's history when smuggling and illicit distilling were given respectability by many well-known Scottish families, who laid the foundations of their fortunes at the time. The famous "The Glenlivet" whisky did not allow itself to become "respectable" until 1824, though even then much to the indignation of other Highland malt distillers. David Daiches put the situation succinctly in his lively and authoritative book, *Scotch Whisky*:

Men of the highest moral character, including highly religious men and even ministers (though some ministers deplored the consumption of whisky) regarded illicit distilling and smuggling as proper and even necessary activities. The necessity lay in the fact that since tenant farmers found their rent money from the produce of their farms, it was often only by converting their barley into whisky that they could find enough money to pay their rent. Again and again, in reading through the Statistical Account of Scotland (that invaluable economic and social survey of Scotland produced in the 1790s, parish by parish by the parish minister) we find this point made.

His apprenticeship completed, young Wilson celebrated his release with his first verse which he endorsed on the indenture:

> Be't kent to a' the warld in rhime
> That wi'right mickle wark and toil
> For three lang years I've sert my time
> Whiles feasted wi' the hazel oil.

The reference to the hazel oil indicates that the birch rod had been used liberally to keep young Alex's hands at the shuttle and his feet on the treadle; the flights and fancies of his thoughts, however, roamed free. His ambitions were to soar beyond the flying shuttle but the skill which he acquired was to stand him in good stead over the years.

CHAPTER II

Weaver, Packman, and Poet

WILSON'S apprenticeship certificate was the passport which led to his wanderings, but to begin with he was happy enough. Released from his bondage, he worked at his craft in Paisley, and enjoyed long, stimulating walks most weekends over the Gleniffer Braes to visit his family at the Lochlands, which now, in addition to Janet, included another half-sister, Margaret, and a baby half-brother, David. There was the pleasure of seeing and telling his family of all that was going on in Paisley and the world beyond, of the new mills springing up, and of the radical talk among the young weavers. Then there was the delight he got from identifying and studying the birds and wildlife that made each walk over the wild Renfrewshire uplands a new adventure.

Early in 1783 Saunders heard that the Tower of Auchinbathie, overlooking what is now Rowbank reservoir, was available for rent, and that, in addition to his other activities, it would be a very suitable place for a whisky still. We learn from the *Cairn* that he moved

24

there at Beltane [May] 1783, and that John Craig was his landlord. The steading was built round the ancient tower, which had historical associations with the family of Sir William Wallace of Elderslie, the Scottish patriot, right up until at least 1398. It had been mentioned by Blind Harry in his metrical history of Sir William Wallace:

> Malcolm Walys hir gat in marriage,
> That Ellerslie then had in heritage,
> Auchinboth and other sindrie places;
> The second oe[1] he was of guid Walys.

At first sight the place appeared more romantic than practical, but in fact it was ideal for a whisky still. Saunders distilled both for himself and for the neighboring farmers. The tower was also suited to the smuggling traffic, which probably included contraband materials for the gauze and silk weavers. Strangely enough, the ancestors of Humphrey Fulton, who introduced silk weaving to Paisley in 1759, had at one time owned the lands of Auchinbathie and there was still a branch of the family farming at nearby Spreulston. They were good neighbors and helped Saunders by carting stones for the building of the stillhouse.

Saunders now had one or two weavers working for him and with smuggling, distilling, and weaving Auchinbathie was a busy scene of cottage industry. Young Alex was soon brought home to work at a loom. Alexander, Senior's, activities, while illegal in the eyes of the government in London and of the excisemen, were not such as to bring any disgrace or ill-repute in the west of Scotland. Indeed, his whisky still, his ability to secure scarce materials by devious channels, and his sociability (as the *Cairn* puts it, "Old Saunders was a great talker and greatly amused the folk about Auchinbathie with his cracks") all combined to make him a well-known and well-liked member of the community. The American War of Independence, too, had ended in 1783 and business was prospering.

1. For this and other Scottish words and phrases, see Glossary.

Now came one of those apparently trivial events that can alter a life and which, in young Wilson's case, was to drive him away from home again. His stepmother hired a young handmaid, Meg Duncan, who proved to be both a tart and a tartar. The fact that she was retained and that she came from Paisley makes one wonder if she was related to Alexander's brother-in-law, William Duncan. She soon revealed herself, at age fifteen, to be both amorous and avaricious, eyeing with different forms of desire not only Alex or any other personable young weaver but also the seventy-five-year-old landlord, John Craig. Kate Wilson took prompt evasive action to defend her stepson and yet not offend the landlord, for she was fond of the lean, intelligent young lad; and he was found a job and lodgings in Lochwinnoch as a weaver in Matthew Barr's shop, known as the "Dowcot" or Dove Cote because of its tall, narrow shape. The looms were on the ground floor and living accommodations above.

Meg Duncan quickly trapped old John Craig into marriage much to the disgust and annoyance of his sons, the eldest of whom, Robert, took the brunt of his father's anger for making his displeasure too obvious. Meg bore a son in February 1785, an arithmetically respectable number of months after the marriage, but few in Lochwinnoch gave any credit to John Craig for this and a hastily scribbled note in the "gossip columns" of Dr. Andrew Crawford's *Cairn* reads: "Auld Fauldheads [said] this son was not his begetting frequently, altho' he had to father it." While Meg Duncan was no inspiration to Alexander Wilson, she and her ancient husband were the subjects of one of his earliest poems, "Elegy on the Long Expected Death of a Wretched Miser." Here are eight verses out of the twenty in the version of the poem which later appeared in the first edition of Wilson's poems in 1790.

> "A Wife! a curse!" (quo' John, in rage,
>   Soon as his tickling heat abated,)
> "A black, bare whore, to vex my age!"
>   He said, he girn't, swore an' regretted.

His dearie, glad o' siccan routh,
    To mill a note was aye right ready:
Aft she wad kiss his toothless mouth,
    While John keen ca'd her his ain lady,

When in the bed, (whare a' fouks gree)
    An' John laid soun' wi' Venus' capers;
She raise—lowst frae his breeks the key.
    Slade up the lid, an' poucht the papers.

This pass't a wee, till rous'd he ran,
    He visited his cash,—his heav'n;
He couldna see, but trem'lin' fan'
    A yearly income frae him riv'n.

O then what tortures tare his soul!
    He groan'd, he spat, he Glowrt, he shor'd out:
Then rais't a most tremendous growl,
    Sunk by the box, and desperate roar'd out:

"My soul—my all—my siller's fled!
    Fled wi' a base confounded limmer!
O grief o' griefs! alake, my head!
    My head rins roun', my een grow dimmer.

Oh! had I ta'en but Rab's advice,
    By clean an' fair my *daft thing* stuing.
It's torn my heart in mony a slice,
    An' now, at last, it's been my ruin.

The Jade, since e'er we met, ilk night,
    Wi' wabsters rows amang the heather,
Has born a *get*, an' tho' untight
    She kens my pith, ca's me its father."

John Craig's "long expected death" did not occur until he was eighty-six, by which time Meg had been banished, leaving him blind and in his dotage. The last we see of old John Craig is this vignette: "They had a great facht to get his corp through the snaw of 1795."

A nice safe matronly woman, Peggy Orr,[2] was found as Alexander's pirn-winder[3] in Lochwinnoch but in fact he was not interested in the type of wench who hung about the weaving sheds. It was to be a year or two yet before he met a young woman who could inspire and attract him. His circle of friends began to increase; one was John Allan, also a weaver in the "Dowcot," quiet, dependable, but slower and less alert than Wilson, a lad who liked nothing better than to trail after Wilson on his rambles among the hills and glens of the parish. When Wilson began to gain some local reputation as a poet, Johnnie kept coaxing him, for some macabre reason, to write an epitaph, until at last he dashed off this quatrain:

> Below this stane John Allan rests;
> An honest soul, though plain;
> He sought hale Sabbath days for nests,
> But always sought in vain!

Other friends were Robin Barr, brother of the owner of the "Dowcot," and Johnnie Gilmore, but closest of all was David Brodie, who, like Wilson, had ambitions beyond the weaving shop and was later to become a schoolmaster in the Quarrelton, near Johnstone, ten miles away from Lochwinnoch.

There seems to have been something in the work of handloom weavers which raised these craftsmen above the common run of men. Perhaps it was the sense of working for oneself induced by piecework, or maybe it was the creative pride of seeing a pattern or diaphanous length of muslin or silk gauze beneath the rhythmic

2. The name Orr was even more common in Lochwinnoch than Wilson was in Paisley; it seems to have originated in Renfrewshire, being first mentioned in 1296 when one, Hew Orr, rendered homage to Edward I of England. There were even four Peggy Orrs in the tiny village of Lochwinnoch and they were given secondary names, Lochside Peggy, Gentle Peggy, Pirn Peggy and Gospel Peggy. One of Wilson's friends John Orr, a fellow-weaver in Matthew Barr's "Dowcot," was another member of the clan, and it was with his brother, Robert, that Wilson boarded in Lochwinnoch.

3. The person who wound the yarn on the shuttle bobbin.

movement of the flying shuttle. Whatever the cause, the weavers as a body, and nowhere more so than in Paisley, were unusually liberal —in the political sense—forward-looking men. They do not seem to have been worn down by the burden of drudgery which made so many men and women old before their time in the early days of the Industrial Revolution. We read constantly of their interest in natural history; of the establishment of floral societies, circulating libraries, and the like; and when the clacking looms were silent, of their meeting together to discuss and argue the topics of the day. Although Wilson was rather harshly remembered by at least one contemporary as "a lazy wabster," it was in the weaving sheds of Paisley and Lochwinnoch that his character was molded and his horizons widened.

It is difficult to be precise about where Wilson was working at any given time during this period of his life. He certainly moved about, and there are well-authenticated records of his working in a two-loom shop in Paisley with David Brodie and for James Clark, heddle twine manufacturer in Cotton Street, Paisley, father of the founders of Clark & Co. Ltd., who, with Coats, later made Paisley the world's largest producer of sewing thread. Despite the difficulty with dates, it is clear, from the *Cairn* and other sources, that at least a year and a half of Wilson's early working life as a journeyman weaver was spent at Lochwinnoch.

With his friends he roamed the Renfrewshire countryside and over the border into Ayrshire. One favorite walk was up the deep Calder Glen or over the Glen and up the shoulder of the aptly named hill, Misty Law, but that was rough going and not to be attempted unless the weather was fine. Every other weekend or so he would take the long climb past Beltrees, one-time estate of that poetic branch of the great Sempill family which had produced the Scottish classic "Habbie Simpson, the Piper of Kilbarchan," and over the Braes to the Tower of Auchinbathie, where there was always a cheery welcome from Kate, Saunders, and the children. There would be the occasional argument about religion with his father, who was a traditional Presbyterian, but it was Kate, herself described as an "independent in religion," who kept the peace and saw that no ill feeling was left to mar the day. As for Alex, religion or church connections appear to have had no influence on his life, and for him the open countryside and the wind on his face brought spiritual well-being.

In his walks up the Calder Glen Wilson became acquainted with an Irishman named Robert Carswell, known to country folk as Tippeny Robin because he never accepted more than twopence for a day's work, except at harvest-time, when he allowed the sum to be doubled. He lived hermitlike in a crude bower he had fashioned with materials that lay at hand. Wilson had his own name for the hermit—"The Solitary Philosopher"—and the man and his setting made such a strong impression upon him that some years later, he sent a pen portrait with that title to the editor of *The Bee*, a transitory publication of the time.

In spring 1786 some subscription sheets dated 14 April 1786 were circulated among a number of people in Ayrshire, the friends and acquaintances of Robert Burns. They were headed with these words: "PROPOSALS, for publishing by subscription, SCOTCH POEMS, by Robert Burns. The Work to be elegantly Printed in One Volume, Octavo, Price Stitched Three Shillings." On 31 July 1786, John Wilson of Kilmarnock produced 612 copies of the "elegantly Printed" volume. In Burns's well-known autobiographical letter to Dr. John Moore he wrote, "I threw off six hundred and fifty of which I had got subscriptions for about three hundred and fifty . . . ," but in less than a month the entire edition was sold and copies were being eagerly passed from hand to hand. Considering the primitive means of communication in the Scotland of the eighteenth century, it is amazing how quickly the literary world in Edinburgh got to hear of the little book of *Poems, Chiefly in the Scottish Dialect* by an obscure "Ayrshire Ploughman." In the autumn a re-

view of the poems appeared in *The Edinburgh Magazine*, followed by
another in *The Monthly Review*, and then came the most important of
the early reviews, that in *The Lounger* of December 1786 by Henry
Mackenzie, author of "The Man of Feeling." Mackenzie was what
today we would call a trendsetter and his article was the authoritative intimation that a new star had risen in the west.

Not only the intelligentsia of Edinburgh were reading Robert
Burns; the weavers in Paisley had their own informal circulating
library and when the greatly enlarged first Edinburgh edition of the
poems was published 21 April 1787, there were ninety subscribers
from Paisley, among them the youthful Alexander Wilson, a subscriber for two copies.

Wilson was already known as a poet in both Paisley and Lochwinnoch, although some of his friends thought he should be spending more time throwing the shuttle and less wielding a pen. Years
later the widow of John Allan, his shopmate at Lochwinnoch, was to
tell Dr. Andrew Crawfurd that "Wilson spent the most of his time
musing and writing poems upon his loom." He gradually built up
his stock of verses and David Brodie, now teaching at the Quarrelton village near Johnstone, encouraged him to persevere. Another
good and helpful friend was his boyhood neighbor Tom Witherspoon and it may have been Tom who recommended that he seek the
advice of Thomas Crichton, governor of the Town Hospital in Paisley, who had some local reputation as a man of letters, a reputation
which he later enhanced when he published useful monographs
about Alexander Wilson and John Witherspoon.

Thanks to Tom Witherspoon, the stimulation of an attractive
and intelligent girl's friendship enriched his life when he was introduced to Martha McLean. Martha was the sister of Tom's wife,
Jean, and Alexander and Martha became instant friends. How close
the friendship became is now difficult to gauge, because with Wilson's wandering habits their courting was carried on mainly by
correspondence, and none of their letters survives. Reading between

the lines of Crichton's account of Wilson, we gather that many letters passed between Martha and Alex, starting off as friendly exchanges and warming into what may have become love letters; she
probably destroyed them when she eventually married after the
"bird of passage" had winged his way to America. Crichton appears
to have been the go-between and to have read the letters, for he
described them as touching, high-minded, and revealing deep affection, but he did not recall any mention of marriage. This appears to
have been almost the only time in Wilson's poetic years when fondness, perhaps even love inspired his poetry, although Martha's
name was never used directly, and we can but regret that the letters
no longer exist to throw light on this and another episode yet to
come, when his radical views and actions ultimately drove him to
America and away from Martha McLean. His immediate journey
was rather shorter; driven by his wandering urges he traveled to
see his favorite sister, Mary, who had moved with her husband,
William Duncan, to Queensferry on the River Forth, where he
worked at the loom assisting Duncan, preparing more poems and
writing letters to the girl he was growing to love in Paisley.

Typical of Wilson was his next venture as a pedlar or packman,
but less typical was the fact that he had a companion on some of his
trips—his brother-in-law and former taskmaster, William Duncan.
We learn a little more about Wilson from the first of his extant
letters, one to David Brodie from Edinburgh dated 23 April 1788.
This earliest recorded letter is strangely artificial and appears almost to be a writing exercise meant to impress his schoolmaster
friend with a picture of involvement in the literary life of the capital.
Nor does it reveal the keen observation or the unforced narrative
language which was to make his American travel letters so interesting. Like the summer swallow Wilson returned for a season to the
west and the encouragement of his friends "where Cart rins rowin
to the sea"[4]—Paisley. He was resolved to strike for publication of a
book of verse—and fame.

4. From "The Gallant Weaver," by Robert Burns.

It was probably Crichton who introduced him to John Neilson, the town's leading printer, who quickly acquainted him with the facts of publishing life. The only hope of publication was by subscription, but by now Wilson was being driven to publish by the compelling urge, ambition, madness (call it what you will) which affects poets, and in that frame of mind he was ready to publish and be damned to poverty. Another spell at the loom raised sufficient money to pay Neilson to print some subscription sheets and copies of a lively little poem, a declaration of intent and appeal for subscribers. Wilson had now convinced himself that he had sufficient friends in the west to raise a few hundred subscriptions, and with his packman's bag on his shoulder, he would fill his subscription sheets as he did his rounds in the east of Scotland with his brother-in-law. It was not to be as easy as that. First he had to borrow some money from James Kennedy, his dilettante friend in Edinburgh, to stock his pedlar's pack with goods. Kennedy had a prosperous little business and was able to indulge his literary flights without the hardships which attended Wilson's excursions.

Wilson told the story of his expedition in search of subscribers in his "Journal as a Pedlar," which was printed in his volume of poems when it appeared in 1790. The "Journal" also contained the ingenious little jingle or "Advertisement Extraordinary" with which he introduced himself to his customers:

> Fair Ladies, I pray for one moment to stay,
>   Until with submission I tell you,
> What muslins so curious, for uses so various
>   A poet has here brought to sell you.
>
> Here's handkerchiefs charming, book-muslin like ermine,
>   Brocaded, strip'd corded and check'd
> Sweet Venus they say, on Cupid's birth-day,
>   In British-made muslins was deck'd.
>
> If these can't content ye, here's muslins in plenty
>   From one shilling up to a dozen;
> That Juno might wear, and more beauteous appear,
>   When she means the old Thund'rer to cozen.

Here are fine jacconets, of numberless sets,
    With Spotted and sprigged festoons;
And lovely tambours, with elegant flow'rs,
    For bonnets, cloaks, aprons, or gowns.

Now, ye Fair, if ye choose any piece to peruse,
    With pleasure I'll instantly show it;
If the Pedlar should fail to be favour'd with sale,
    Then I hope you'll encourage the Poet.

One other extract from the "Journal" must suffice and that only because it contains one of the earliest spontaneous references to the game of golf, then very much a game of the east coast of Scotland:

SEPT. 18—Departed from Edinburgh, designing to cross over to Fifeshire; changed my resolutions, and proceeded forward to Musselburgh, beneath a most oppressive load. Arrived at this place late in the evening —MUSSELBURGH (so called from the vast quantities of mussels that are found along the shore) is a small, though a neat town, six miles east from Edinburgh, stretching along the Frith of Forth, which, at this place, may be ten or twelve miles broad. The streets are wide and well paved; its inhabitants numerous, a great many of whom are butchers, which appears by the numberless carcases of sheep, calves, cows etc., that are to be seen suspended in rows at almost every door. Edinburgh is their market, to which, every morning, their stores are conveyed. This day saw several troops of dragoons reviewed, which made a formidable appearance, on an extensive level green, that spreads along the shore, where the game of golph is much practised by parties of gentlemen; and is, in my opinion, a more healthy than entertaining amusement.

The French Revolution had erupted on 14 July 1789 and trade was in the doldrums; so, too, was Wilson. With neither sufficient sales to repay Kennedy nor sufficient subscribers to please Neilson, the young pedlar came back to Paisley via Edinburgh. We know he was in Edinburgh because of two letters—one of which is noted in a letter-book of Robert Burns's correspondents prepared for Dr. James Currie, Burn's biographer. The letter-book is, unfortunately, badly damaged by dampness and all that remains is the name of the sender, date, and place, "Alex. Wilson. 8th November 1789. Edinburgh," and these few words, still extant, of the précis of contents, "A youth—A stranger—Expresses in. . . ." The other letter, dated 10 November 1789, was to his friend and supporter David Brodie. It was in the same flowery language as his earlier letters to him and makes clear that he had been less successful than he had hoped in adding to his list of subscribers.

Wilson returned to Paisley with but 12s. in his pocket; his only other article of value was a watch. His fortunes were in one of the deepest of the constant series of financial troughs in which he was engulfed during the remainder of his life in Scotland. Penury, however, was only an incidental worry; his real concerns were his inability to refund Kennedy's loan and the obstacle to the printing of his poems—lack of subscribers.

Neilson advised him to seek a patron, a man of note, whose name on a subscription sheet would encourage other people of substance to add their names. The only man of quality within Wilson's ken was the "Mr. M'D." mentioned in his letter to Brodie. This was William McDowall of Garthland and Castlesemple, five times member of parliament for the county of Renfrew, over whose estate Wilson had rambled many times. McDowall, a bachelor, was the third McDowall of Castlesemple, where the splendid mansion and estate were a symbol of wealth. Forty-four years earlier the town council of Paisley had sought the aid of Mr. McDowall's grandfather, Colonel William McDowall, when Bonnie Prince Charlie's secretary, John Murray, imposed a fine of £500 upon the inhabitants for their loyalty to the Hanoverian cause. McDowall was looked upon as a philanthropist and his involvement with the splendid new cotton mills of Houston, Burns and Company in Lochwinnoch had added to his popularity. These mills had brought many jobs and, in eighteenth-century terms, good working conditions. Wilson carefully penned an introductory letter to Mr. McDowall and set off to deliver it himself. The account of his visit to Castle-semple, where he was courteously received, is told in a letter to James Kennedy dated 26 January 1790. A footman led Wilson into the library, which McDowall entered from the adjoining dining-room, where he was entertaining the Earl of Eglinton. The poems were still in manuscript and the member of Parliament studied them carefully for an hour and a half, paying particular attention to the poem "Lochwinnoch," with its flattering references to himself. He asked Wilson a great many questions about the verses, his background, birthplace, and the like. Twice they were disturbed by the Earl of Eglinton who came into the room in search of pictures. Finally, McDowall gave Wilson some words of encouragement, asked for two proposal forms, and promised to get him some subscribers. The interest, if not the patronage, of William McDowall was the turning point for Wilson, and Neilson agreed to publish.

Although Wilson had already built some local reputation as a poet, his first poem to have any extensive circulation was "The Hollander, or Light Weight," and it was almost certainly the earliest piece to appear in print with a few copies thrown off by Neilson. Possibly Neilson and Wilson felt that the humorous attack on a well-known silk manufacturer, William Henry, would stimulate interest in the volume of poems which they planned, and it certainly aroused amused attention in some quarters and concern in others when it began to be widely circulated in February 1790.

At a parochial level "The Hollander" reached its targets, but it also reached out further for, in its way, this was one of the first poems to comment on the factors associated with the social transformation inherent in the Industrial Revolution which led to the formation of trade unions. To William Henry the poem was defamatory and inflammatory, particularly dangerous in the growing

FIGURE 1. The original, fairly primitive, oil painting of Alexander Wilson
by James Craw, from which the frontispiece of Grosart's book was engraved.

FIGURE 2. Paisley Abbey as it was in 1791 and as it was known to Wilson. The building has since been fully restored. Wilson's birthplace was nearby.

FIGURE 3. Paisley seen from the east in 1767, the year after Wilson's birth. The tall spire in the middle is that of the Tolbooth, where Wilson was later imprisoned.

FIGURE 4. Paisley in 1808 showing the White Cart River. The waterfall on the left is known locally as The Hammils.

FIGURE 5. The ruin of Auchinbathie Tower, Gleniffer Braes, Renfrewshire. Associated with Sir William Wallace, the Scottish patriot. The adjoining ruin is what was the Wilson family home for a number of years. The illicit distillery was on the other side of the ruin.

FIGURE 6. Alexander Wilson's statue on the grounds of Paisley Abbey.

FIGURE 7. The Laigh Kirk (Low Church), Paisley, built in 1736. Here Dr. John Witherspoon ministered for ten years before emigrating to New Jersey. Here, too, Wilson was christened by Dr. Witherspoon.

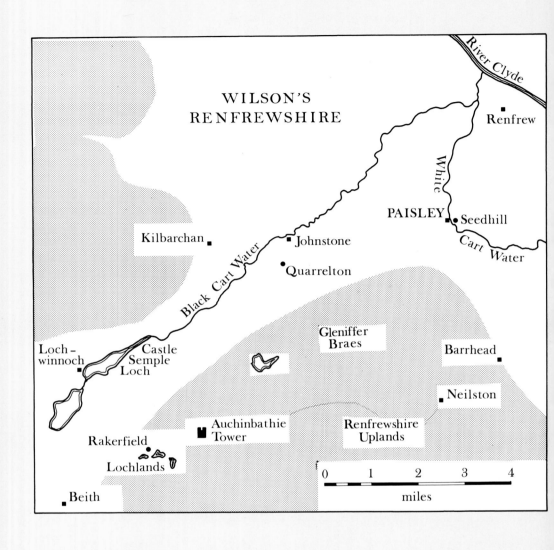

WILSON'S
RENFREWSHIRE

River Clyde

Renfrew

White

PAISLEY • Seedhill

Cart Water

Kilbarchan ■ ■ Johnstone

Black Cart Water

• Quarrelton

Gleniffer
Braes

Barrhead ■

Loch–
winnoch Castle
Semple
Loch

Neilston ■

Rakerfield

Auchinbathie
Tower

Renfrewshire
Uplands

Lochlands

0   1   2   3   4

miles

■ Beith

manufacturing town, but his immediate reaction was to ignore it. Wilson, however, quickly became something of a folk hero to the weavers. That—together with the continuing frightening news from France; pressure, no doubt, from other manufacturers; and the realization that almost everyone in Paisley and its environs had read or been read the poem—now prompted Henry to take action, and he sought the aid of the law.

On 10 June 1790 with the concurrence of the procurator fiscal, Henry took out a summons against Wilson for criminal libel and incitement to unrest.[5] The summons asked for penalties of £50 sterling as damages and assythment (legal compensation or atonement) to the private prosecutor, for an apology in open court and a fine of £10 to the procurator fiscal as a deterrent, and for payment of the expenses of the process. The twenty-four year old Wilson fortunately realized that he needed legal assistance. After one or two formalities John Craig, a Paisley solicitor, answered for him on 1 July 1790 and denied that the poem referred to William Henry. Craig asserted that even if it did, it was not libelous. Craig particularly suggested that the very title of the poem proved that it could not be intended to mean Henry since the designation "Hollander" was an epithet applicable only to a person born in Holland.

Henry and his solicitor, Edward Jamieson, had no difficulty in demolishing Wilson's defense, pointing out that "for some years previous to the pursuer's settling in Paisley he had resided in Holland and for those good many years past he had carried on a very considerable manufactury in the town of Paisley." They maintained that William Henry must surely be the only manufacturer in Scotland, and certainly in Paisley, who had a son named "Jock," had strong Dutch connections, and served as an elder of the "Auld Kirk" all counterparted in the poem. They noted, finally, that Wilson "does not seem to deny that he is the author of the poem."

5. The court papers are in the National Library of Scotland. See below, Appendix 1.

If Wilson believed that any publicity was good publicity for his forthcoming book of poems, he had certainly taken steps to produce the desired result. On 6 August 1790 he sent the first published copy of his poems to James Kennedy in Edinburgh with a covering letter in which he mentions that 600 copies had been printed for nearly 400 subscribers, but that these were so widely scattered in different parts of Scotland that the collection of the subscriptions might leave him worse off than before. He sought Kennedy's assistance to provide him with a pack, which he hoped would make the economics of selling his poems profitable, allow him to achieve fame and happiness, and enable him to repay his debts to Kennedy.

On 10 August 1790 Sheriff Orr issued an interlocutor ordering Wilson to "lodge duplies[6] and therein to set furth whether he admits or denies the composing, uttering or promulgating the paper complained of." By the time it was issued, however, Wilson had already departed to Edinburgh and the Lothians. The collection of money from 400 subscribers proved dishearteningly difficult and when Wilson had finished his collecting he had sold no more than 200 copies. Many of the people who some months earlier had been ready enough to sign an undertaking to buy were now reluctant to the point of rudeness to pay hard cash for his book. Despite his lack of success Wilson gave a commendably honest account of his second trip as a chapman and bookseller in a continuation of his journal, the first part of which was included in his volume of poems.

Unlike their reception of Burns's book four years earlier, literary circles in Edinburgh showed no flicker of interest in Wilson's verses. Whether or not the market could stand more than one vernacular poet, the literati of Edinburgh could not, and there were no enthusiastic reviews for Wilson. His venture was a failure, he felt humiliated, he was in debt to Kennedy and Neilson, and to make matters worse he contracted a serious chest infection. The illness

6. A reply to a rejoinder.

was probably a symptom of his depression, and he returned to the only place he could call home, the Tower of Auchinbathie, where the sheriff's interlocutor awaited him.

Recovery was slow but in due course family care and his own toughness helped him overcome the illness. Before resuming his role as the poetic pedlar, he arranged with John Craig to send duplies to the sheriff, which was done on 23 September 1790. This argued that it was for the prosecution to prove the charge and not for the accused to admit anything and thereby incriminate himself. There was a further petition by John Craig on Wilson's behalf dated 21 October 1790, withdrawing the duplies but reiterating Wilson's denial of the charges. This petition is much less recalcitrant in tone than the earlier papers, stating that Wilson would have signed the petition but for his absence in "the east country" and would do so upon his return.

The final court paper is an interlocutor by Sheriff Orr dated 16 November 1790, agreeing to the withdrawal of the duplies and appointing 23 November 1790 as the date of the trial. The trial never took place, and we are left to conjecture upon the reason or reasons. We know that at the relevant period Wilson was back in the east of Scotland trying to sell his book, and there are letters postmarked from Haddington on 2 and 21 November which confirm his whereabouts; but no warrant to apprehend him for failing to appear on 23 November seems to have been issued. Had John Craig convinced Henry and the court that Wilson was penitent and in any event quite impoverished and unable to pay any fines that the court might impose? Wilson's poverty almost certainly precludes any suggestion of an out of court settlement. Whatever the reasons, the action appears to have been allowed "to go to sleep," and with no evidence to the contrary we may put this down to the generosity of William Henry and the court.

It is curious that no hint of Wilson's problems resulting from the printing of "The Hollander, or Light Weight" is given in any of his

known letters, although these were to such old friends as David
Brodie, James Kennedy, and William Mitchell (to whom three
epistles were addressed in his volume), and his newer, highly respected friend Thomas Crichton. Discretion was not one of Wilson's virtues during this period, and it may be that any incrimina-
tory letters were destroyed or withheld by Wilson's friends or by
later Victorian editors in the fashion of the time.

For an unknown impoverished versifier to sell a book of poetry in
the shadow of the colossus Burns and in competition with a host of
Burns's imitators, such as Lapraik, Sillar, Tait, and Shirrefs, was a
daunting task, even if his verses did contain merit those of others
lacked. As we have already seen, Wilson had sent progress reports
to his friends Crichton and Brodie and to William Mitchell, who
was to prove a friend he could have done without. His first letter to
William Mitchell, dated 21 November 1790, saluted him "Dear
comrade." This letter and three poems to William Mitchell give the
first record of Wilson's friendship with one who was later to be
known as a reformer; it was an association which was to have a profound influence upon his life.

Back in Paisley again he wrote to his father at Auchinbathie on 25
January 1791, where the mention of "little Peggy's misfortune"
refers to a crippling illness which had befallen his half-sister. It is
heart-warming to learn of Wilson's concern for Peggy and of the
strong ties within the Wilson family, which contrasts with the
earthy crudity of the comment on her disability in the *Cairn*, received at second-hand from John Craig, son of the "wretched Miser": "He does not know how many wanes Auld Saunie had by Kate
Brown, only of yin whase members were decrepid."

In Paisley Wilson received an interesting letter from James Kennedy telling him about a contest to be held in the Pantheon, Edinburgh, where the candidates would debate in verse or prose the respective merits of Allan Ramsay and Robert Fergusson, or more precisely, "Whether have the exertions of Allan Ramsay or Robert Fergusson done more honour to Scotch Poetry?" Kennedy suggested that this might be an opportunity for Wilson to gain a little fame and thus promote the sales of his book; he even offered to serve as his deputy and read his essay or poem for him. Wilson replied rather cautiously on 10 March 1791, having already been humbled by the public's continued lack of interest in his book. In the meantime, however, resilient as always, he sent off to *The Bee* his tale of "The Solitary Philosopher."

Wilson borrowed a copy of Fergusson's poems from David Brodie and there and then decided to speak up for their author. Within a week he had woven 40 ells (50 yards) of silk gauze at Lochwinnoch, to pay for his venture, visited his family at Auchinbathie, and written and memorized his poetical address of over 200 lines, "The Laurel Disputed." Not a bad week's work for a "lazy wabster"!

Wilson delivered his address on Thursday 14 April 1791, before a large, fashionable crowd of almost 500 persons, who were also the judges; it was both a success and a failure. First prize was won by one Robert Cumming, an Edinburgh man of whom it was widely believed that he had arranged and paid for about forty of his supporters to be present. He won the contest by seventeen votes over Wilson; Wilson's friend Ebenezer Picken was third. Wilson was acclaimed a moral victor, and although it would be an exaggeration to say that he was lionized, as Burns had been in Edinburgh, he did gain a little fame. Encouraged by this modest success, he arranged for Peter Hill, a well-known Edinburgh bookseller, to bring out a new edition of his poems. In truth, it was a reissue of the unsold copies of the 1790 edition, considerably improved by cancellations and by additions, including "The Laurel Disputed," intended to attract the fashionable and influential audience which had appreciated it at the Pantheon. The reissue was much more successful than the original printing, and Wilson's name began to be noised abroad.

In March 1791, Burns's masterpiece, "Tam o' Shanter," had appeared in *The Edinburgh Magazine* and *The Edinburgh Herald*, and soon after the Pantheon contest Wilson sent a critical review of the poem to Dr. Anderson, editor of *The Bee*, who had just published his essay "The Solitary Philosopher." Dr. Anderson, however, rejected the review. Wilson then sent it, with a covering letter, to Burns, who liked it even less than Dr. Anderson. There was a brief exchange but the letters are now lost, and all we have is evidence of a tetchy interchange between poets. The damaged précis-book of Burns's correspondents preserved at the Burns Cottage Museum, Alloway, contains a few phrases of a letter addressed this time from Paisley and dated 7 September 1791, in which Wilson expresses his admiration of Burns. The evidence that Burns replied, and possibly even once met Wilson, is contained in George Ord's "Life of Alexander Wilson," first printed in the ninth volume of *American Ornithology* published by Ord after Wilson's death:

Wilson, in common with many, was desirous of becoming personally acquainted with the poet Burns, who was now in the zenith of his glory; and an accidental circumstance brought them together. The interview appeared to be pleasing to both, and they parted with the intention of continuing this acquaintance by correspondence. But this design, though happily begun, was frustrated by an imprudent act of the former, who, in a criticism of the tale of "Tam O'Shanter," remarked of a certain passage that there was "too much of the brute in it."

The paragraph alluded to is that which begins thus: "Now, Tam, O Tam! had thae been queans!" Burns in reply observed: "If ever you write again to so irritable a creature as a poet, I beg you will use a gentler epithet than to say there is, 'too much of the brute' in anything he says or does." Burns's reply rings true, and the few words from the précis above appear to confirm Ord's tale. It would have gladdened the heart of Wilson to know that Mrs. Dunlop, the patron, friend, and correspondent of Burns, wrote to him on 25 January 1792 with liberal praise for Wilson's book and that Burns replied on 3 February 1792: "Wilson's book I have not seen; but will be much obliged to you for a sight of it."

There can be little doubt that it was the influence of "Tam o' Shanter" which made Wilson try a narrative poem, "Watty & Meg," his best known but not his best. The two poems have little in common apart from the characters of the nagging wives. Wilson's was published anonymously and was believed by many to be by Burns. It may even be that it was published anonymously in the hope that it would be mistaken for the work of Burns. Many thousands of copies of the poem were sold with little or no profit accruing to Wilson. The first and many of the succeeding printings were by Neilson, who had been tolerant of Wilson's difficulties in paying for the printing of his first edition; Wilson repaid his generosity with such profit as was earned by "Watty and Meg."

With Wilson's constant coming and going his friendship with Martha McLean never developed beyond the beginnings of love. He became more and more involved with the reformers of the time, of whom Paisley had its fair share. The forces which had led to the French Revolution were playing on Alexander Wilson and that sensitivity which he expressed in verse responded to the radical ideas which were widespread in Scotland. He was quite a good violinist and flautist and it was perhaps because of this that he had first become friendly with the two musical brothers in Paisley, James and William Mitchell—the same William Mitchell mentioned earlier, to whom Wilson wrote a letter on 21 November 1790. The brothers became leaders of the radical faction in Paisley and William Mitchell led the Paisley delegation to a convention of Friends of the People in Edinburgh on Tuesday 30 April 1793, where "J.B.," a government agent, faithfully reported to London that the delegates from Paisley were William Moodie, Wm. Mitchell, James Kelly, Archd. Hardie, John Taylor, John Tannyhill,[7] and William Wood. Then he continued, "Mr. William Mitchell of Paisley was called to the Chair, Mr. Fortune having left it upon completing the roll." With Wilson now well known as a poet and writer of some skill, the brothers Mitchell made full use of his abilities. Parkhill, the homespun Paisley historian we have noted earlier, wrote:

We have heard the late Mr. Paterson, who was coeval with Wilson, state, that Wilson was the most expert writer of reports and resolutions that he ever witnessed, and that too in a style of elegance most astonishing to his compatriots; his companionship with these men [the reformers, in particular the two Mitchells] was the true cause of his emigration.

7. Probably the uncle of Robert Tannahill, poet.

CHAPTER III

"The Friend of Liberty and Reform"

THOMAS PAINE'S *The Rights of Man* appeared in 1791 with its doctrine of individual responsibility and rights, which in essence meant electoral reform, or one man–one vote. The Home Office papers in the Public Record Office, London, contain reports from government agents in Scotland together with copies of resolutions, advertisements by the Friends of Reform, and so forth. Among these papers is one entitled "A Declaration of Rights and An Address to the people. Approved by a number of the Friends of Reform in Paisley"; written about the same time as Paine's, this Scottish "bill of rights" summarized the Paisley reformers' interpretation of *The Rights of Man*:

I. The Government of this Realm, and the making of Laws for the same, ought to be lodged in the hands of King, Lords of Parliament, and the representatives of the *whole body* of the free men of this realm.

45

II. Every Briton (infants, insane persons, and criminals only excepted) is of common right, and by the laws of God, a *freeman*, and intitled to the full enjoyment of *liberty*.

III. A Briton's liberty, or freedom, consists in having *an actual share*, either in legislation, or in the *appointing* of those who are to frame the laws; although they ought to protect him in the full enjoyment of those absolute rights, that are vested in him by the immutable laws of nature, may yet be fabricated to the destruction of his person, his property, his religious freedom, family, and fame.

IV. It is the right of the commons of Britain to *elect* a new house of parliament once at least in every year: because, when a parliament continues for a longer term than *one Session*, thousands, who have attained to man's estate since it was elected, and are therefore entitled to enter into possession of their best inheritance, the actual exercise of their elective franchise, are, in that case, unjustly *denied their right, and excluded from freedom.*

Alexander Wilson was undoubtedly influenced by Paine's writings and, like him, was a constitutionalist, not an extremist. He was recognized as a skilled writer of reports and resolutions, and, while these had to be written in secrecy, an example may be contained in a report which appeared in *The Glasgow Advertiser* under the dateline 8 February 1793. There is no proof that it was written by Wilson, but the signature of his friend James Mitchell as secretary, Wilson's acknowledged expertise in these matters, and the expression of the principles of *The Rights of Man*, of which he was an enthusiastic advocate, leave little room for doubt. If it is indeed the work of Wilson, his reputation was well founded![1]

It took courage to press for parliamentary reform when the smell of revolution was wafting over from France and Henry Dundas, the Home Secretary, was nurturing a network of spies and agents in Scotland, especially since Wilson had been lucky to escape punishment for the publication of a contentious poem like "The Hollander." Paisley seems to have been one of the centers of disaffection,

1. The report dated 8 February 1793 printed below in Appendix 2.

and there are many references in the Home Office records by the reporting agents:

The bad news from the Continent has been received in this Place [Edinburgh] and in the West Country, by the disaffected with as sincere joy as we lament them and I am sorry to say from the information received that Paisley and its neighbourhood are in a very unpleasant situation.

In a letter concerning the idea of militia in Glasgow and Paisley John Dunlop warns that it would be "highly improper to trust arms in the hands of the lower classes of People here and in Paisley."

It was against this background that Wilson appears to have committed the most foolhardy act of his life. The circumstances were so out of character that one wonders if he was the tool of others with more extreme views than his own. One of his early biographers, Allan Park Paton, writing when some who had known Wilson and the facts were still alive, thought so. The real folly was not the "libellous stanza" but an accompanying letter demanding money by threats. The sorry story is told in the following pages.

On Tuesday 22 May 1792 William Sharp, manufacturer in Paisley and owner of the Long Mills, received this letter:

Sir,

The enclosed poem, by particular circumstances, has fallen into my hands. The author, I can certainly assure you, is on the eve of concluding a bargain for the MSS. The offered price is five pounds.

If you know any person who will advance *five guineas*, the manuscript from which I copied the enclosed, shall, with the most solemn regard to justice and secrecy, be immediately destroyed and buried in perpetual oblivion. If not, three days shall publish it to the world.

I give you *three hours* to deliberate on the offer, by which time I expect a final and determined answer, addressed to A.B., to lie in J. Neilson's bookseller, Paisley, till called for. If the *price* or *copy* is not received by four o'clock this present afternoon, I can no longer prevent the author from proceeding with this production as he may think proper. I am, Sir, your well-wisher, A.B.

Tuesday, half-past 11 o'clock, A.M.
[Addressed] Mr. William Sharp, Manufacturer, Paisley.

The poem was "The Shark; or Lang Mills Detected," and at any other time than in the shadow of the French Revolution it would have been ignored and thrown in the fire. Although written on a parochial level, this poem, with "The Hollander" and "Hab's Door," is among the earliest poems directed against the system which had evolved with the Industrial Revolution. In this kind of protest, although the thought probably never occurred to him, Wilson was an innovator.

The Shark;
or Lang Mills Detected

Yes, while I live, no rude or sordid knave
Shall walk the world in credit to his grave.
POPE

Ye weaver blades! ye noble chiels!
  Wha fill our land wi' plenty,
And mak our vera barest fiels
  To waive wi' ilka dainty;
Defend yoursels, tak sicker heed,
  I warn you as a brither;
Or Shark's resolved, wi' hellish greed,
  To gorge us a'thegither,
        At ance this day.

In Gude's-name will we ne'er get free
  O' thieves and persecution!
Will Satan never let abee
  To plot our dissolution!
Ae scoun'rel sinks us to the pit,
  Wi' his eternal curses,
Anither granes,—and prays,—and yet
  Contrives to toom our purses,
        Maist every day.

A higher aim gars Willy think,
  And deeper schemes he's brewin';
Ten thousan' fouk at ance to sink
  To poverty and ruin!
Hail mighty patriot! Noble soul!
  Sae generous, and sae civil,
Sic vast designs deserve the whole
  Applauses of the devil
        On ony day.

In vain we've toiled wi' head and heart,
  And constant deep inspection,
For years on years, to bring this art
  So nearly to perfection;
The mair that art and skill deserve,
  The greedier Will advances;
And saws and barrels only serve
  To heighten our expenses
        And wrath this day.

But know, to thy immortal shame,
  While stands a paper-spot,
So long, great Squeeze-the-poor! thy fame,
  Thy blasted fame shall rot;
And as a brick or limestane kiln
  Wi' sooty reek advances;
So grateful shall thy mem'ry still
  Be to our bitter senses,
        By night or day.

Lang Willy Shark wi' greedy snout
  Had sneaked about the C-n-l,
To eat his beef and booze about,
  Nor proved at drinking punch ill;
Till, Judas-like, he got the bag,
  And squeezed it to a jelly;
Thae war the days for Will to brag,
  And blest times for the belly
        Ilk ither day.

The mair we get by heuk and cruk
   We aften grow the greedier;
Shark raiket now through every neuk
   To harl till him speedier;
His ghastly conscience, pale and spent,
   Was summoned up, right clever;
Syne, wi' an execration sent
   Aff, henceforth and for ever,
            Frae him that day.

This done, trade snoovt awa wi' skill
   And wonderfu' extention;
And widen't soon was every mill,
   (A dexterous invention!)
Groat after groat, was clippet aff,
   Frae ae thing and anither;
Till fouk began to think on draff,
   To help to haud thegither
            Their banes that day.

Now round frae cork to cork he trots
   Wi' eagerness and rigour,
And "Rump the petticoats and spots!"
   His Sharkship roared wi' vigour;
But, whan his harnishes cam in
   In dizens in a morning;
And a' grew desolate and grim,
   His rapture changed to mourning,
            And rage that day.

Thus Haman, in the days of yore,
   Pufft up wi' spitefu' evil,
Amang his blackguard, wicked core,
   Contrived to play the devil;
High stood the gibbet's dismal cape,
   But little thought the sinner
That he had caft the vera rape
   Wad rax his neck, e'er dinner
            Was owre that day.

Wha cou'd believe a chiel sae trig
   Wad cheat us o' a bodle?
Or that sae fair a gowden wig
   Contained sae black a noddle?
But Shark beneath a sleekit smile
   Conceals his fiercest girning;
And, like his neighbours of the Nile,
   Devours wi' little warning
         By night or day.

O happy is that man and blest
   Wha in the C-n-l gets him!
Soon may he cram his greedy kist
   And dare a soul to touch him.
But should some poor auld wife, by force
   O' poortith scrimp her measure,
Her cursed reels at P—y Corse,
   Wad bleeze wi' meikle pleasure
         To them that day.

Whiles, in my sleep, methinks I see
   Thee marching through the city,
And Hangman Jock, wi' girnan glee,
   Proceeding to his duty.
I see thy dismal phiz and back,
   While Jock, his stroke to strengthen,
Brings down his brows at every swack,
   "I'll learn your frien' to lengthen,
         Your mills the day."

Poor wretch! in sic a deadfu' hour
   O' blude and dirt and hurry,
What wad thy saftest luke or sour
   Avail to stap their fury?
Lang Mills, wad rise around thy lugs
   In mony a horrid volley;
And thou be kicket to the dugs,
   To think upo' thy folly
         Ilk after day.

Ye Senators! whase wisdom deep
    Keeps a' our matters even,
If sic a wretch ye dare to keep,
    How can ye hope for heaven?
Kick out the scoun'rel to his shift,
    We'll pay him for his sporting,
And sen' his mills and him adrift
    At ance to try their fortune
                Down Cart this day.

Think, thou unconscionable Shark!
    For heaven's sake bethink thee!
To what a depth of horrors dark
    Sic wark will surely sink thee—
Repent of sic enormous sins,
    And drap thy curst intention;
Or faith I fear, wi' brislt shins,
    Thou'lt mind this reprehension
                Some future day.

It was not the poem but the covering letter with its element of
blackmail which was so uncharacteristic of Wilson. Twenty years
later he wrote to his father, "In youth I had wrong ideas of life.
Imagination too often led judgement astray"; but the poem and the
letter in particular were errors of judgment to the point of absurdity
while "The Hollander" affair still hung over his head. It appears
that the court's leniency had been wrongly interpreted by Wilson.
He undoubtedly believed that the weavers were being cheated and
persecuted by their masters under the new industrialized system
which was so alien to their independent character. In his youthful
indiscretion he saw no reason why he should not use the only weapon
available to him to make at least one employer pay. At this stage,
however, Wilson had not admitted to being author of the poem or
letter.

Sharp hurried off to see his lawyer, and the following day James
Orr, sheriff substitute in Renfrewshire, received a long, wordy peti-

1. *Corvus cristatus*, Blue Jay. 2. *Fringilla Tristis*, Yellow-Bird or Goldfinch.
3. *Oriolus Baltimorus*, Baltimore Bird.

Drawn from Nature by A. Wilson. 1 Engraved by A. Lawson.

Plate 1 from Alexander Wilson, *American Ornithology* (Volume I)

tion which asked for Wilson's apprehension and stated that he was well known for his productions of the kind, "some of which are at this moment the subject of enquiry." The petitioner went on to affirm that, impressed most seriously with thoughts of personal and public safety, he sought "the discovery and punishment of the author of these highly libellous, incendiary and dangerous publications."

The sheriff promptly granted a warrant for Wilson's arrest.[2]

On the morning of 23 May Wilson had gone off to Glasgow and Sheriff Orr, thinking, no doubt, that Wilson had gone into hiding, issued a further warrant prohibiting publication of the poem and calling on all sheriffs, magistrates, and justices of the peace in any other county to apprehend him. Unaware of the legal pitfall which awaited him, Wilson had no intention of fleeing, and when he returned to Paisley, he was arrested and taken before the sheriff.

Wilson admitted that the letter was in his handwriting, but claimed he had sent it with the poem at the request of the poem's

2. This and other documents connected with the case are printed at large in Robert Cantwell, *Alexander Wilson* (Philadelphia, 1961), pp. 268–276. I found a copy letter, *not in Wilson's hand*, in an unpublished manuscript account of the trial at the Manuscript Dept. of the National Library of Scotland. It bears the bracketed comment (copy of a note to the Sheriff Substitute of Paisley). The note reads:

To Mr. James Orr Sherrif Subst of Renfrewshire.

[*5 February 1793.*]

Mr. Orr,

Sir, On the moment of dispatching the Petition I received 2 copies by the hands of a Person unknown to me. I request you will be pleased to give orders that the time may be immediately appointed for destroying them according to the Interlocutor which part of it I am ready to perform. I am with the most sincere respect

Sir, your Most Obed. Sert

ALEX. WILSON

author. He refused to name the author or to answer many of the questions put to him: "and being interrogated, if he knows at whose instigation, or by whose desire, the said poem was written? He declines answering the interrogatory."

Wilson's second statement was naive in the extreme and a reversal of his previous evidence; he now admitted having written the letter and poem but asserted that it was quite wrong to believe that it was intended as a lampoon on William Sharp, for whom he had the greatest respect. He, or his lawyer, put it as follows:

The gross acts of injustice, avarice, and oppression, imputed to the hero of that poem, are so opposite to the known character of the complainer, so contradictory to the defender's own opinion of that gentleman, and so remote in every particular from his reputation in public, that he is astonished the complainer should for a moment have entertained the least idea of being the person meant in the above poem.

Sharp's lawyer had no difficulty in demolishing Wilson's case by pointing out that it was to William Sharp the poem and demand had been sent, and by also noting the affinity between the names "Shark" and "Sharp," the use in several verses of the appropriate Christian name of "Will" or "Willy," and the identification of "Shark" as a town councillor, as was William Sharp.

Wilson and Sharp submitted further pleas and on 27 June 1792 the sheriff principal of Renfrew, Allan Maconochie, pronounced judgment. The sheriff granted damages of £50 sterling and directed that Wilson "appear in open court, and beg pardon of God and the complainer, and confess, acknowledge and declare, that the said incriminations thrown out against the complainer's character; in the foresaid libel, are scandalous and injurious." Wilson was also to pay £10 sterling to the court to deter others from similar crimes, to be imprisoned until payment of the sums was made, and to pay the costs of the case.

Off on one of his usual wandering journeys, Wilson failed to appear in court. When he next came to Paisley on 11 August 1792 he was imprisoned and fined £10 Scots (at this time worth one-twelfth of £1 sterling) and he had to get his brother-in-law, William Duncan, to stand security under a bond of 100 merks or Scottish marks. In a petition to the court on 30 August he said he had no wish to offend it and that he had asked "a person of the law" to speak for him who had neglected to do so. He asked to be excused of the fine totally or in part. There is no record that the court showed him any leniency.

Between his court appearances, Wilson roamed off again to Glasgow, Falkirk, Callander, and Edinburgh. In a letter to David Brodie from Edinburgh, dated 23 November 1792, he referred vaguely to "now earning more in a sphere which you shall be made acquainted with hereafter." As a reply had to be directed to him via James Kennedy, manufacturer at the High School, Edinburgh, the likelihood is that Kennedy had something to do with his new-found employment. In Callander Wilson made a brief attempt to improve his arithmetic. He purchased a slate and enrolled in the town school. On the third day he cut his losses, paid his lodgings, and left for Edinburgh. It is little wonder his arithmetic lessons were unsuccessful, for as he recounts in his letter:

There are two teachers in the school at Callander,—one teaches Latin and French, the other English, Writing, and Arithmetic. As for the first, I am not a proper judge of his merits, further than that he seemed totally devoid of all sentiments of humanity in correcting. The latter surprised me very much, and must undoubtedly be a genius, as he teaches a language he has not yet learned to speak (being a Highlander), and writes about as well as your humble servant did in our Gordon-Ionian cell. Upon the whole, I found them a couple of morose, unsociable Highland pedants,—sullen, because they had nothing to say; and reserved, because they were afraid of exposing their mighty ignorance.

On 22 January 1793 we find the sheriff substitute, James Orr, giving another ruling. Wilson had allowed the poem which had caused all his troubles to appear in print, despite the court's ban. He was ordered to be incarcerated in the Tolbooth of Paisley, "therein to remain for space of fourteen days, and ay, and until he finds good and sufficient caution, to the extent of three hundred merk Scots, for his good behaviour for two years to come." From this wording it looks as though the court was becoming a little impatient with Wilson's repeated appearances and disappearances. He was also required to burn in the Market Place of Paisley all the copies of the offending poem he could find. On 6 February 1793, two copies of the poem were burnt by him on the steps of the Tolbooth.

The final episode of this unhappy case occurred on 14 May 1793 when the sheriff substitute, James Orr, awarded further damages to Sharp and to the procurator fiscal because of the way Wilson had aggravated the charges. The awards were for small amounts and the clerk of court was given authority to alleviate or remit the fine if Wilson, within eight days, in a letter to the private complainer, made suitable acknowledgment of the wrong done him. Sharp and the court seem to have been treating Wilson with considerable tolerance—or did they now know that any meaningful damages would be beyond his empty purse? On 21 May 1793 Wilson wrote to David Brodie from the Paisley jail thanking him "for the token of friendship which you sent me, which I will repay as soon as Providence shall open the door for my release from this new scene of misery, this assemblage of wretches and wretchedness. Being perfectly unable to pay the sum awarded against me, which is *in toto* £12.13.6d.," Wilson continued, "I yesterday gave oath accordingly, and had the comfort to be told that Mr. Sharp was *resolved* to punish me though it should cost him a little money." There is confirmation here that arithmetic was not Wilson's strong point for the sum of the sheriff's award was £11.7.6d., not £12.13.6d. Two days of arithmetic from an inarticulate Highlander had not been enough!

Apart from this mention in his letter to Brodie of Sharp's resolve to punish him, Wilson makes no reference to the Sharp court case in any of his letters. The transcripts of the court proceedings make nonsense of the statement that he was the "tool of others." The related examples of his contempt of the court show a man who was being as difficult and awkward as possible. The only reason Wilson gave for his aggravation of the original case appeared in Sheriff Orr's judgment when Wilson was again before the court for printing "The Shark" in violation of the court's ban: "He admits his having consented to the publication of this poem, in consequence of what he is pleased to call the foolish and determined severity of a rigorous prosecution."

What began as an understandable objection to the new society which the Industrial Revolution was creating (what handloom weaver could be blamed for disliking the factory system?) and was encouraged by his involvement with the reformers, particularly the Mitchell brothers, ended as an episode from which Wilson takes no credit. The honest, if radical, aims of "The Friend of Liberty and Reform," of the disciple of Thomas Paine, were devalued by the spiteful and foolish acts associated with sending "The Shark; or Lang Mills Detected" and its covering letter to William Sharp.

❀

Throughout Wilson's ordeal of fines, imprisonments, and cautions his friends stood by him; his character and sense of humor sustained him and, no doubt, entertained them. He showed his resilience in the following mock petition:

The humble petition of A.W. humbly sheweth that your petitioner is, and has been for some time past, grievously afflicted with a want of pecunia; the want of which has brought him to such low circumstances that no person ever experienced but himself. He therefore flatters himself that the charitable disposition which always shows itself in you, on like occasions, will also distinguish itself in the relief of your poor petitioner, and your petitioner shall ever pray.

A.W.

Wilson walked a tightrope between his friends—reformers on one side and those happy with the status quo on the other. In the end it was his loyalty to the reformers and respect for the others which created the conflict that compelled him to start a new life.

On 4 January 1794, Wilson was again in jail. The alleged crime as stated in the bail bond was that of

being concerned in framing and industriously circulating an advertisement addressed to "The Friends of Liberty and Reform." Calling a General Meeting of the friends of Reform to have been held this night in
Falconer's Land, Stories Street at five o'clock. Said to be by order of a
committee and of having John Neilson Printer in Paisley to print the
said advertisement.[3]

Almost a year earlier, the sheriff substitute had pronounced an in-
terim interlocutor requiring caution of 300 merks for his good be-
havior for two years, and his old friend Thomas Witherspoon,
Martha McLean's brother-in-law, had on 5 February 1793 bound
himself to ensure that Wilson kept the public peace for that period.
Wilson had now created an impossible situation for his friends, yet
nowhere in local records or legend do we find any criticism from
them—only the recurring theme that Wilson was taking the blame
for others.

To get bail Wilson had to find another guarantor; this time it was
one of the many Paisley Wilsons, William, a weaver in Williams-

---

3. Some of the sentences passed on reformers found guilty of treason and
sedition at this time were horrible. In Hector's *Judicial Records of Renfrewshire*, 1876, a chapter entitled "The Fate of a '93 Reformer" tells of transportation. One sentence for high treason passed at Edinburgh was ". . . to be
drawn upon a hurdle to the place of execution there to be hanged by the neck;
but not till dead, for you are then to be taken down, your heart to be cut out,
and your bowels burned before your face; your head and limbs severed from
your body, and held up to public view." See Cantwell, *Alexander Wilson*, p. 216,
which prints a slightly different version of the petition. This had the effect of
making it appear that the alleged crime had been committed six months earlier.
There are other minor differences.

burgh near Paisley. This was the third acquaintance to stand security for him; of the other two, William Duncan was in no position to stand security for anyone now, and Thomas Witherspoon was already sufficiently burdened. The petition for bail reads:

The Petition of Alexr. Wilson present Prisoner in the Tolbooth of Paisley Humbly Sheweth

That your Petitioner is incarcerated by virtue of a Warrant raised against him at the Instance of the Procurator Fiscal under suspicion of having circulated certain Hand Bills calling a meeting of Reformers. That however innocent I am of the crimes laid to my charge I would wish to be admitted to Bail which I am ready to produce.

May it therefore please your Lordship to allow your Petitioner to be admitted to Bail and give orders to the Clerk of Court to grant liberations to that purpose.

According to Justice
ALEX. WILSON

When we consider the date of the incident, 4 January 1794, when the Reign of Terror in France was at its height, the court seemed to handle Wilson with kid gloves. The authorities had no desire to have a ready-made martyr on their hands and with the bail bond in their pocket they were happy to proceed no further with the prosecution. They had him cornered and that is exactly how Wilson felt!

Between 4 January and May 1794, there is no record of Wilson's movements or whereabouts. He may have been peddling, or weaving, and living with the Duncans or the Witherspoons. He may even have been in Edinburgh occupied in that mysterious sphere where he could earn more. Wherever he was, he was working hard and subsisting, as he told friends later, on one shilling per week to save as much as possible. He had decided that the vast country across the Atlantic, with its newly won freedom, was the place for him and there he would try to wipe out the mistakes of the past.

Not only Alexander Wilson but his sister Mary Duncan and her husband, William, had thoughts of going to America, that new world with the wonderful, if impossible, dream of equal opportunity for all. The same thought had already occurred to his reforming friends, James and William Mitchell. Eventually it was decided that his sixteen-year old nephew, William Duncan, would accompany him, and when he and William were firmly placed, the rest of the Duncans would follow.

There were few arrangements to be made and very few belongings to pack but there were farewells to be said and his father had still to be told. From Sir William Jardine, that early editor of the *American Ornithology*, who had the benefit of biographical information direct from Alexander Wilson's sister Jean, we learn what Wilson told his father: "I am bound now, and cannot ruin Thomas Witherspoon, and I must get out my mind."[4]

He had also to see the closest and most loyal of his friends, David Brodie, Thomas Crichton, and, of course, Tom Witherspoon, the dearest friend of all. At least he would be able to assure Tom Witherspoon that he would no longer need to stand security for him. In effect he had given himself a self-imposed sentence of transportation for life, but to America, not Botany Bay.

Because of his precarious situation Alexander had ceased to correspond with Martha McLean some months previously and he bade her no farewell. Many years later Crichton, in his monograph about his friend, said that he had been privileged to read some of the letters that passed between Alex and Martha. Crichton seemed to think they were the letters of friends, not lovers, but the statement may have been out of consideration for Martha's family because fairly soon after Wilson's departure she married and had a large family. It is likely that Wilson either destroyed Martha's letters or returned them through Thomas Crichton. Whatever happened to them, Crichton's version of the nature of the letters appears to be contradicted by his own verse tribute to Wilson with which he ended the biographical sketch he published under the pen-name Senex. Here are two of the verses:

4. Wilson's way of saying that he must get these things off his mind.

Friend of his youth, the pride of swains,
    Young Damon was, I knew him well;
Him mourn'd the bard in plaintive strains,
    When call'd to take his last farwell.

There too, he sung Matilda's charms,
    A lovely maid who flourish'd fair,
But snatch'd by fortune from her arms,
    His dreams of bliss dissolved in air.

Surely Matilda and Martha were one and the same person?

We know from Crichton that Wilson and he met for the last time on a beautiful evening in mid-May. He had no previous knowledge of Wilson's plans and as they strolled together along the banks of the Cart, Wilson confessed that many of his actions had been foolish. While he regretted them, the beliefs which motivated them had been right and he would continue to think them right. He feared the results of any further involvements on his part in radical schemes, although even these were now in inner conflict as the horrors of the Reign of Terror in France unfolded. It was not so much fears for his own safety as the consequences for his friends, like Tom Witherspoon who had stood bond for him.

Early the following morning Alexander Wilson and sixteen-year-old Billy Duncan began their long journey. They walked or "cadged" lifts to Portpatrick, where there were regular sailings to Belfast. In Belfast a disappointment awaited them; the *Swift*, the vessel they planned to sail in, already had a full complement of passengers. Wilson found that only if they were prepared to sleep on deck would the *Swift* take them. The Atlantic crossing was hazardous enough without having to spend the entire voyage on deck, but Alex Wilson and Billy Duncan had no difficulty in making a decision—they did not have enough money to maintain them until the next transatlantic sailing. They had enough to pay for their passage and no more. They set sail from Belfast, bound for Philadelphia, on Friday 23 May 1794 and during the crossing Wilson celebrated his twenty-eighth birthday.

CHAPTER IV

The Schoolmaster: "That Painful Profession"

WILSON and his nephew set foot in the United States on 14 July 1794. They landed at Newcastle on the Delaware River, at that time a landing place for Philadelphia. The story of their journey and first eleven days in the New World is recounted in a letter Wilson wrote to his father and stepmother on 25 July 1794; it is a simple narrative which is all the more effective for its lack of exaggeration. The hardships and perils of an Atlantic crossing at the end of the eighteenth century are well illustrated by the following extracts:

We had 350 passengers—a mixed multitude of men, women and children. Each berth between decks was made to hold them all, with scarce a foot for each. At first sight I own, it appeared to me almost impossible that one half of them could survive; but, on looking around, and seeing some whom I thought not much stouter than myself, I thought I might have a chance as well as the rest or some of them.

The next sentence seems to be a matter of fact rather than anything unexpected: "Till the 17th of June we had pretty good weather, and only buried an old woman and two children.'' Then he describes a sighting of icebergs: "On the 18th we fell in with an amazing number of islands of ice; I counted at one time thirty four in sight, some of whom that we nearly passed were more than twice as high as our main-top gallant mast-head, and of great extent.'' A fearsome Atlantic storm is covered in two sentences:

On the 20th we had a storm of wind, rain, thunder and lightning beyond anything I had ever witnessed. Next day a seaman dropped overboard; and, though he swam well and made for the ship, yet the sea running high, and his clothes getting wet he perished within six yards of a hen-coop, which we had thrown over to him.

When they came ashore at Newcastle the two young Scotsmen were almost penniless. Their entire wealth was a few shillings loaned to them by a kindly fellow passenger named Oliver, sufficient to set them on their way to Philadelphia. Newcastle is some 65 miles from the Atlantic, and Philadelphia a further 33 miles up the Delaware River, then America's main commercial artery. Philadelphia in 1794 was not only the capital but the largest city in the United States. Indeed, before the Revolution it had been the second largest English-speaking metropolis in the British Empire.

No correspondence apparently survives from the time of Wilson's arrival in 1794 until 22 August 1798, when he wrote his father again.

Dear Father, if I were to judge of my friends in Scotland by their cold silence to all my letters these two years, I might perhaps wrong them but I will be more generous with them, and conclude that they all wrote me ten or twelve times a piece, and all miscarried; so now we are on good terms again.

We are mainly indebted to George Ord, who was to be Wilson's friend, defender, and editor, for information about the four-year gap as Alex and Billy strove to establish themselves. There was a dearth of weaving opportunities in both Wilmington and Philadelphia, but the two young men were ready to turn their hands to anything. A fellow Scot, John Aitken, a copperplate printer, offered Wilson employment, which he gladly accepted. The two kinsmen began to find their feet and their way around and soon met Joshua Sullivan, another Scot, whose home and weaving mill were on Pennypack Creek about ten miles north of Philadelphia. Wilson started working on one of his looms. Meanwhile Billy obtained employment as a weaver with another prospering Scottish connection, James Robertson, brother-in-law of John Finlayson of Paisley, who had signed Wilson's apprenticeship certificate.

There now followed a necessary period of settling in, but once Wilson was sure that Billy Duncan's employment was secure, he began to look for the means to better himself. Discovering that aid was being offered to settlers in Virginia he moved to Shepherd's Town, New Virginia. This proved to be an unhappy venture, however, for he liked neither the people nor the place. He was also forced to resume weaving to maintain himself and as quickly as he could he returned to Philadelphia and to his old place at a loom at Sullivan's mill. He celebrated his departure with this verse:

> Farewell to Virginia, to Berkley adieu,
> Where, like Jacob, our days have been evil and few!
> So few—they seemed really but one lengthened curse;
> And so bad—that the Devil only could have sent worse.

Wilson had no intention of exchanging the "seat tree" of a loom in the Old World for one in the New, and in the autumn of 1795 he filled a pedlar's pack and headed for New Jersey. This was not only a successful but a profitable undertaking—which, for him, was a new experience. According to George Ord, Wilson kept a journal of his trading expedition, in which he recorded more about the ways of people, quadrupeds, and birds than about the state of trade. The journal is now lost, but Ord's extracts from it are interesting because they contain the first mention of the observations which were to make Wilson famous.

Wilson never again returned to weaving and he now opened a school near Sullivan's house and weaving shop. He appears to have stayed there for only a short period, possibly one term, before moving in 1796 to a school at Milestown, some 20 miles from Philadelphia, more or less on the road to Trenton and New York.

The five years that Wilson spent at Milestown, while not shrouded in mystery, do contain elements of a mysterious amour. For this period of his life we have to rely upon a series of letters to Charles Orr, a Paisley man, described as a "writing-master," then living in Philadelphia. Wilson's first letter to Orr is dated April 1799, and the last 15 July 1802; shortly afterwards Orr seems to have returned to Scotland. These letters first appeared in *Wilson the Ornithologist: A New Chapter in His Life* by Allan Park Paton, published in 1863. Wilson's reticence with names and the discretion of early editors in omitting letters and parts of letters have created difficulties in unveiling the details and extent of Wilson's infatuation. The rediscovery of most of the original letters in the National Library of Scotland lifted no more than a corner of the curtain.

Wilson settled in Milestown, teaching the pupils and himself as he went along. Billy was now joined by his sister Isabel, and all was well until the summer of 1798, when the dreaded yellow fever, then a recurring summer hazard, returned to Philadelphia. According to Wilson, the epidemic carried off some 4,000 persons, and what with deaths and flight to more healthful places, it reduced the population at the height of the outbreak from some 65,000 souls in midsummer to not more than 8,000 by the autumn. Wilson was reasonably safe out in the healthy country air at Milestown. In November he wrote to his father:

Isabel and William are both in good health, as well as myself. William and I have these two years been planning out the purchase of a piece of land in some healthy and fertile part of the country, convenient to a market for the disposal of produce. In the State of New York there is a tract of perhaps the richest land in the United States, situated about 270 miles to the north, or north and by west of Philadelphia, lying between the Senica and Cayuga lakes . . . after consulting together, about two months ago, William set out on foot to see the country and learn further particulars. He travelled it in eight days, and remained there nearly a week. The soil is rich beyond any land he had ever seen and the situation exceedingly healthy. . . .

With the aid of a substantial loan from Joshua Sullivan, Wilson's former employer who probably told him of the opportunity, the land was purchased. In Wilson's view William Duncan was now safely settled, a base had been established for any of the family who might want to follow them to the United States, and he was free to go his own road.

Wilson earned the respect of the community at Milestown as a conscientious and worthy schoolmaster. He also taught himself surveying and added to his income by surveying for farmers and others in the neighborhood. As always he was restless. He complained of illness on one or two occasions. He even resigned from the school for health reasons and the trustees interviewed a replacement, but Wilson disillusioned him about the potential income, and the episode ended with the trustees granting Wilson another week of sick leave, glad to have him stay on. His popularity and standing in the little community continued to grow and reached new heights when on 4 March 1801 before the townspeople he delivered an "Oration on the Power and Value of Natural Liberty," to celebrate the election of Thomas Jefferson as third president of the United States. The speech was printed and reprinted in newspapers and periodicals, and brought a kind of reflected glory to Milestown.

During one of the sickly Philadelphian summers Wilson made a trip on foot to the family farm at Ovid, Cayuga County, New York, where William was working hard to carve fields out of the woods. William, too, was talking of following in his grandfather's footsteps by setting up a still to make whisky. We learn from George Ord that Wilson covered almost 800 miles in 28 days, which suggests that his illness was rather more mental than physical.

By the spring of 1801 his time at Milestown was coming to an end. There had been a hint the previous summer of the direction in which his instincts were driving him at the age of thirty-four. He wrote to Orr on 23 July 1800:

It was about the middle of last May, one morning in taking my usual rounds, I was delighted with the luxuriance of nature that everywhere smiled around me. The trees were covered with blossoms, enclosing the infant fruit that was, at some future day, to give existence to others. The birds, in pairs, were busily engaged preparing their nests to accommo-date their little offspring. The colt pranced by the side of his dam; the bleating of lambs was heard from every farm; and insects in thousands, were preparing to usher their multitudes into being. In short, all nature, every living thing around me seemed chearfully engaged in fulfilling that great command, "Multiply and replenish the earth," excepting my-self. I stood like a blank in this interesting scene, like a note of discord in this universal harmony of love and self-propagation; everything I saw reproached me as an unsocial wretch separate from the great chain of nature, and living only for myself. No endearing female regarded me as her other self, no infant called me its father, I was like a dead tree in the midst of a green forest, or like a blasted ear amidst the yellow harvest. Full of these mortifying reflections, I wandered homewards and entered my lodging; there my landlord and his amiable spouse were playing with their children and smiling on each other with looks of mutual affec-tion and parental pride. "O despicable wretch," said I to myself, "what is all thy learning, books, or boasted acquisitions, to a companion like that, or innocents like these whom thou could'st call thine own? By all that's good"; cry'd I, "I shall share these pleasures though ten thousand unseen distresses lurk among them." To you, Mr. Orr, who know me as well, it is unnecessary to add that these resolutions were soon forgot in study and abandoned for some algebraic solution or mathematical pursuit. But I have to ask you, is it not criminal to persist in a state of celibacy?

The landlord and landlady to whom he referred were Mr. and Mrs.

Isaac Kulp, one of the many German families settled in the locality.

His next letter to Orr, on 6 August 1800, was almost entirely a variant of this theme, and it was datelined "Milestown Monastery." What exactly happened next we do not know; only that following spring Wilson suddenly left Milestown without telling any of his friends where he was bound. Only his letters to Charles Orr partially reveal the cause. The first we know of Wilson's troubles is in a letter to Orr dated 1 May 1801:

> I am indeed much obliged to your friendship, and request that you would come out this evening and stay with me till Sunday evening. I have matters to lay before you that have almost distracted me. Do come, I shall be so much obliged. Your friendship and counsel may be of the utmost service to me. I shall not remain here long. It is impossible I can. I have now no friends but yourself, and *one* whose friendship has involved us both in ruin or threatens to do so. You will find me in the schoolhouse.

The letter is a strange mixture of caution and concern that care be taken not to mention the name of *"one* whose friendship has involved us both in ruin or threatens to do so."

The next letter, dated 12 July 1801, is from Bloomfield, near Newark, New Jersey, where he told Orr, "I keep school." He had been in New York apparently to look up the Mitchells, his former reforming friends.

> From every person who knew the Mitchells I received the most disagreeable accounts of them, viz, that James had by too great a fondness for gaming and sometimes taking his scholars with him, entirely ruined his reputation and lost his business and from his own mouth I learned that he expected jail every day for debts to a considerable amount. And William is lost for every good purpose in this world and abandoned to the most shameful and excessive drinking, swearing, and wretched company. He called on me last Thursday morning in company with a hocus pocus man for whom he plays the clarinet.

The reformers of Wilson's youth were badly in need of reformation! Then he goes on with the meat of the letter:

I have lost all relish for this country, and, if Heaven spares me, I shall soon see the shores of old Caledonia. . . . I request you, my dear Orr, to oblige me in one thing if you wish me well. Go out on Saturday to Davidson's and try to get intelligence how Mr. Kulp's family comes on, without letting anyone know that you have heard from me. Get all the particulars you can, what is said of me, and how Mrs. Kulp is, and every other information, and write me fully. I assure you I am very wretched, and would give me the greatest satisfaction. Davidson will tell you everything, but mention nothing of me to anybody on any account.

In the following months of 1801, he wrote frequently to Orr with remarks such as:

As to the reports circulated in the neighborhood of Milestown, were I alone the subject of them they would never disturb me, but she who loved me dearer than her own soul, whose image is for ever with me, whose heart is broken for her friendship to me, she must bear all with not one friend to whom she dare unbosom her sorrows.

Again to Orr,

I entreat you to keep me on the rack no longer. Can you not spare *one* day to oblige me so much? Collect every information you can, but drop not a hint that you know anything of me. If it were possible you could see *her* or anyone who *had*, it would be an unspeakable satisfaction to me.

Previous editions of Wilson's letters have encouraged the view that he had fallen in love with a married woman and that discovery, or the possibility of it, had led to his flight. Wilson had certainly fallen in love and Dr. Elsa Allen refers to this in her authoritative "The History of American Ornithology Before Audubon" (1951), but is careful to point out in a footnote (p. 555), "According to Wilson's commentators, this woman was married, although there is not definite proof of this. Wilson in some letters refers to a 'Mrs.——,' but we should not assume from this alone that this woman was the one in question." The discretion in omitting the name of "this woman" was not of Wilson's doing. In the particular sequence of letters, Allan Park Paton in 1863 and the Rev. A. B. Grosart in 1876 had deleted the name of Mrs. Kulp, Wilson's landlady, which is clearly and openly written in Wilson's hand in the original. His uninhibited references to "my landlord and his amiable spouse" are surely proof that his landlady was not his lover. More likely his amour was one of the "clusters of dimple-cheeked, soft-eyed females" he mentions, perhaps the maidenly daughter of a local personage, the kind of man who might use every influence to discredit the thirty-five-year-old dominie and expose his unsuitability as a son-in-law. Whatever the pressures they were sufficiently strong to drive Wilson from his sweetheart and Milestown.[1]

The school at Bloomfield was 6 miles north of Newark, New Jersey. Wilson soon took a jaundiced view of the populace which he described as "canting, preaching, praying, and sniveling ignorant Presbyterians. They pay their minister 250 pounds a year for preaching twice a week, and their teacher 40 dollars a quarter for the most spirit-sinking laborious work, six, I may say twelve times weekly."

After a few months he returned to Philadelphia and settled there on 25 February 1802. He had the great good fortune to obtain a position at a school at Gray's Ferry on the Schuylkill River, with a much better income of $100 per quarter. He quickly began to recover from the depression of the Milestown misadventure and the uncongenial interlude at Bloomfield. He even said, "My harp is new strung," and talked of publishing another edition of his poems. But

---

1. Mr. Humphrey A. Olsen has made the tentative, but interesting, suggestion in the *Snowy Egret* (Spring 1981) that the lady-love was Nancy De Benneville, daughter of Dr. George De Benneville, physician in the Milestown neighborhood. He bases this identification mainly on a gossipy book by the doctor's granddaughter, Annie De Benneville Mears, *The Old York Road and Its Early Associates of History And Biography* (New York: Harper, 1890). He also states, "Wilson inscribed 'Nancy De Benneville's' in large script on a sheet of paper with 'Milestown School House' and 'Sept. 14, 1797' in the lower corners. She was then 14 and may still have been a student at 18 when Wilson (then 35) was forced to leave town."

there was another heartening feature to his new school, the Union School, Kingsessing (his letters at this time are variously datelined Gray's Ferry, Union School or Kingsessing); this was Bartram's Garden, a botanical garden which had been established in 1728 by John Bartram (1699–1777), described by Linnaeus as "the greatest natural botanist in the World." It still exists as part of the system of public parks in Philadelphia. John Bartram was succeeded in owner-ship of the farm by his son John and in his botanical work by his son William (1739–1823), who as a lad accompanied him on explora-tions. William Bartram's major work, *Travels through North and South Carolina, Georgia, East and West Florida* (1791), told of his travels in these states; it brought him considerable fame, not only among naturalists, but among the romantic writers in Europe, for example, the English poets Blake, Wordsworth, and Coleridge. Bartram was one of the earliest American ornithologists and his list of some 215 American birds suggested to Alexander Wilson where his life-work might lie.

By the autumn of 1802 Billy Duncan's mother and the rest of his family excepting his father had joined him on his New York farm. Mary Duncan found the accommodation primitive—lacking even a proper fireplace. Wilson constantly encouraged his nephew to im-prove both their house and the land, his letters showing concern for his sister and the discomforts of the backwoods. He also was anxious that Billy should do everything possible to see to the education of the young ones. Wilson even suggested that if his health were equal to it, he would gladly give up the school and join them. But he hoped to accumulate $200 by the following spring, and this would go a long way towards covering their indebtedness on the farm.

In midwinter, Wilson was able to tell Billy, "I succeed tolerably well; and seem to gain in the esteem of the people about. I am glad of it, because I hope it will put it in my power to clear the road a little before you." One of the people whose esteem he gained was Wil-liam Bartram; the two men began a friendship which lasted throughout the remaining decade of Wilson's life. Bartram was the first man of more than local reputation with whom Wilson became intimately acquainted. The association revealed new horizons. Bartram's list of native birds roused Wilson's interest and the more he studied, the more Bartram's records filled him with a kind of creative enthusiasm. He had known Bartram but a few months when he wrote on 1 June 1803 to one of his old Paisley friends about his new goal. "I am now about to make a collection of all our finest birds." The way ahead was now set.

CHAPTER V

Collector of "All Our Finest Birds"

A T GRAY'S FERRY Wilson served his apprenticeship in
the study of ornithology. No one assisted him more than
William Bartram, who could also answer his queries on
many aspects of natural history. He gained more than technical
knowledge from Bartram; he absorbed a romantic view of nature.
The sensitivity, but not sensibility, with which Wilson had reacted
to radical ideas in Scotland responded creatively to the romantic
revolution. *American Ornithology* is a classic example of the changing times, the realism of the past changing to romanticism: the
honest, unsophisticated realism of his bird drawings—anything
more was beyond his untaught skill—contrasting with the sensitive
descriptions of birds and scenes in his prose.

The four years Wilson spent at Union School, Kingsessing, were
among the happiest and least complicated of his life. He was constantly knocking on Bartram's door or submitting letters and drawings with requests for critical judgments. With Bartram's niece,

73

ITHACA COLLEGE LIBRARY

Nancy Bartram, who looked after her uncle, Wilson formed a class of two who studied under the venerable man. All the while his own native gift for observation was being refined as he stored the knowledge collected in his excursions through the avian paradises around him.

Ten years had raced past since Alexander Wilson's arrival on the American continent. Now at the age of thirty-eight he had come to realize that he was an American despite the ties of family and heritage that would always link him with Scotland. On 9 June 1804 he presented his petition to become a citizen of the United States. He satisfied the court as to his good character, renounced allegiance to the "king of the United Nations of Great Britain and Ireland," and became an American citizen.

His whole life was now geared to the collection of material for his study of American ornithology. Encouraged by the example of William Bartram, he planned a journey into the wilds aiming for that natural wonder of the North American world, the Falls of Niagara. The journey was to take him past Ovid and so enable him to see his sister Mary and others of the family there. When Billy Duncan learned of his uncle's plans, he had to go too. Billy was well equipped for the difficult journey, toughened as he had been by several years of hard farm work. The third member of the expedition was young Isaac Leech, of whom little more is known other than what appears in Wilson's mammoth poem, "The Foresters," which recounts, in over 2,200 lines, their journey of over 1,200 miles. As a poem this epic work suffers from its length. It is hard reading but is worth study, and is as good as any verse being written in America at that time.

Wilson set the scene as the little party began its journey from the banks of the Schuylkill:

> The sultry heats of Summer's sun were o'er,
> And ruddy orchards poured their ripened store;
> Stripped of their leaves the cherry av'nues stood,
> While sage October ting'd the yellow wood,

> Bestrew'd with leaves and nuts the woodland path,
> And rous'd the Katydid in chattering wrath.

He then described the three bold travelers in an admirable pen-picture:

> Three cheerful partners: Duncan was the guide,
> Young, gay, and active, to the Forest tried;
> A stick and knapsack, all his little store,
> With these, whole regions Duncan could explore;
> Could trace the path to other eyes unseen,
> Tell where the panther, deer or bear had been;
> The long dull day through swamp and forest roam,
> Strike up his fire and find himself at home;
> Untie his wallet, taste his frugal store,
> And under shelbury bark profoundly snore;
> And, soon as morning cheered the forest scene,
> Resume his knapsack and his path again.

> Next Leech advanced, with youthful sails unfurled,
> Fresh on his maiden cruise to see the world;
> Red o'er his cheek the glow of health was spread,
> And oilskin covering glittering round his head;
> His light fuzee across his shoulder thrown,
> His neat-slung knapsack full and glistening shone;
> Though unknown regions wide before him lay,
> He scorned all fear while Wilson shared the way.
> He next appeared, with glittering arms supplied,
> A double gun, a deadly dirk beside;
> A knapsack, crammed by Friendship's generous care,
> With cakes and cordials, drams, and dainty fare;
> Flasks filled with powder, leathern belts with shot,
> Clothes, colours, paper, pencils—and what not.

After the hardships of their journey, all carefully documented by Wilson, they drew near Niagara:

> Heavy and slow, increasing on the ear,
> Deep through the woods a rising storm we hear;
> Th' approaching gust still loud and louder grows,
> As when the strong north-east resistless blows;
> Or black tornado, rushing through the wood,

Alarms the affrighted swains with uproar rude.
Yet the blue heavens displayed their clearest sky,
And dead below the silent forests lie;
And not a breath the slightest leaf assailed,
But all around tranquility prevailed.
"What noise is that?" we ask, with anxious mien,
A dull salt-driver passing with his team.
"Noise! Noise!—why nothing that I hear or see,
But N'agara falls—Pray, whereabouts live ye?"

All look amazed! yet not untouched with fear,
Like those who first the battle's thunder hear,
Till Duncan said, with grave satiric glee,
"Lord, what a monstrous mill-dam that must be!"

Finally Wilson described the Falls:

High o'er the watery uproar, silent seen,
Sailing sedate, in majesty serene,
Now 'midst the pillared spray sublimely lost,
And now, emerging down the rapids tost,
Swept the gray eagles; gazing calm and slow,
On all the horrors of the gulf below;
Intact, alone, to sate themselves with blood,
From the torn victims of the raging flood.

The poem ends at the Falls. By this time long overdue back at
Union School (he was away almost two months—October to 7
December 1804), Wilson turned home by the quickest route with
all the speed he could muster, to the point of exhaustion—of the
youthful limbs of young Isaac Leech! On 20 November at Aurora on
the shores of Lake Cayuga he and Isaac parted from Billy Duncan,
who was returning to Ovid, and headed almost due east for Utica.
Up at five the next morning, Wilson set off at a great pace, carrying
Isaac's gun, to ease the lad's burden, but even so Isaac was soon
struggling to keep up. They covered 34 miles that day. Up again at
five the next morning over tracks worse than ever and covered in
deep snow, they were joined by a young traveler going part of their

route. Wilson led the way singing at the top of his voice to drown the chorus of lamentations from the two youngsters struggling in his wake. All the while, he found time and energy for his ornithological observations. Near Utica, for example, he shot a bird the size of a mockingbird, which proved to be one previously undescribed by naturalists. On the twenty-fourth, Isaac was struggling desperately to keep up without the consolation of his fellow sufferer; even Wilson admitted that the road was very bad. They covered only 24 miles that day. The dreadful day had its compensations, for Wilson shot three birds, all a species of jay which had apparently never been identified before. On the morning of 25 November they ploughed their way through deep mud and snow to within 15 miles of Schenectady, where the exhausted young Leech seized the opportunity of a boat coming down the river Mohawk to get on board, arranging to wait for Wilson in Schenectady. Wilson reached Schenectady the next day, several hours before Isaac arrived in his boat. Isaac Leech was now worn out. So too was Wilson's clothing; his pantaloons were in rags and his boots had little left but the uppers; but Wilson's energy was constantly restored by the excitement and wonder of the expedition. So the travelers took the stage coach to Albany, where they stayed two days. From there they took a sloop down the Hudson River to New York, where they arrived on 1 December. It cost Wilson $12 to replace his pantaloons and boots, which left him enough to get back to Philadelphia—if he walked! He arrived at Gray's Ferry on Friday 7 December, having covered between 1,200 and 1,300 miles, mostly on foot, in two months. On the last day he covered 47 miles to Gray's Ferry and in the evening visited friends. The wife had given birth to twins, a boy and a girl, and the parents had named the boy after him, so with his blessing he handed over $6.00 for his infant namesake, bought some firewood, and was left with seventy-five cents to his name!

The expedition to Niagara had convinced Wilson that ornithology was his vocation, and every hour he could spare from his school duties was spent increasing his knowledge of birds and perfecting his skill as an artist. In all of this he had a willing tutor in William Bartram. Bartram, too, was the means of introducing him to President Thomas Jefferson by sending the president a covering letter with one from Wilson presenting drawings of the bird finds he had made. The friendly, courteous reply dated 7 April 1805 revealed that the president was no mean ornithologist himself; he thanked Wilson for "the elegant drawings of the new birds you found on your tour to Niagara."

Another benefit from the trip to Niagara had been the reunion with Billy Duncan. His fatherly feelings and sense of responsibility to the younger man were strengthened as he began to realize that William Duncan, despite his earlier intentions, had deserted Billy's mother and would not join his family in America.[1]

Fortunately the farm venture was beginning to succeed; not only that, the price of good land in the area was rising. But Wilson had unwittingly unsettled his nephew. To Billy, Wilson was both a father figure and a hero; and so he decided that he would be a schoolmaster like his uncle, and he found a position at Wilson's former school in Milestown. Soon after Billy's arrival at the school, he urged Wilson to come and deliver a political lecture. To this invitation Wilson replied 26 February 1806:

I have not the smallest ambition of being considered an orator; and would it not, by some, be construed with vanity, or something worse, for me to go all the way from this place to deliver a political lecture at Milestown? Politics has begot me so many enemies, both in the old and new world, and has done me so little good, that I begin to think the less you and I harangue on that subject the better.

The truth was that Wilson did not want to harm the good reputa-

1. In a letter to his father, 24 August 1806, Wilson explains that the elder Duncan had only traveled as far as Ireland where he chose to remain, living in "guilt, poverty, and infamy."

tion he had worked hard to establish in and around Philadelphia by flaunting himself in Milestown:

They have all heard me often enough on different subjects about Milestown, and as it would raise no new friends to you, but might open old sores in some of your present friends, I hope you will agree with me that it will be prudent to decline the affair.

About this time Wilson learned that Jefferson was planning to send an exploring party across the Mississippi. Once again he called on Bartram to forward a letter to the president. Wilson felt this expedition would offer a wonderful opportunity to widen his field of study to include "our southern wilderness." The territory to be explored would include the "Red River, Arkansaw, and other tributary streams of the Mississippi," and he offered his services on the expedition mentioning, by the way, that it would also allow him to procure ornithological specimens. Neither Bartram nor Wilson ever received a reply, and probably the letters were withheld from the president. Wilson told his nephew on 26 February, 1806, "either Mr. Jefferson expects a brush with the Spaniards, or he has not received our letters." It is perhaps fortunate for Wilson that he did not make this journey, for in April of that year, 1806, he secured a job as assistant editor to Samuel F. Bradford for a new edition in twenty-two quarto volumes of Rees's *New Cyclopaedia* which Bradford's firm was about to publish. The firm was one of the leading publishing houses in America, having set up the first printing press in Philadelphia in 1685, after William Bradford had emigrated from England with William Penn. The position was congenial and the salary of $900 per annum meant undreamed-of luxury. More than that, it placed him at the heart of the publishing business in Philadelphia and made it possible for him to commence work on his *American Ornithology* after all the years of preparation and training. He resigned from the Union School on 1 April 1806 and started work with Bradford on the twenty-sixth of that month.

Wilson entered into his new occupation with his customary enthusiasm. Very few of his letters between April 1806 and the autumn of
1808 survive, except, of course, for the regular letter to his father
and what one might call the continuing technical exchanges with
William Bartram.

When he told Bartram of his move to Philadelphia, he hinted that
in more ways than one it would enable him to proceed with his intended book on ornithology; he wasted little time in telling Samuel
Bradford of his aim to publish the most complete illustrated account
of the birds of America that had yet been attempted. He was able to
show Bradford some of his drawings. The honest skill and precision
of his work were patent because Wilson not only had benefited from
Bartram's help, but had also received coaching in drawing and engraving from Alexander Lawson, another immigrant Scot and a
trained engraver. Before Wilson took up the assistant editorship
with Bradford, he had suggested to Lawson that they might publish
his work on ornithology as a joint venture but the engraver felt that
the book would prove to be too expensive to recover the cost. An
edition of 200 sets of 10 volumes with 10 plates per volume would
mean hand-coloring 20,000 plates! Samuel Bradford saw it differ-
ently—as an opportunity to enhance his firm's reputation with what
could be the finest book yet produced in the United States; accordingly, he undertook that Bradford and Inskeep would finance an
edition of 200 sets on condition that Wilson obtain that many subscribers. Bradford was impressed by Bartram's obviously high opinion of Wilson; he also had seen some fine examples of the latter's
work and, convinced of Wilson's dedication to the task he had set
himself, he felt he was taking only a normal commercial risk.

That summer of 1806 was a good one for Wilson, working at one
job that earned him an adequate livelihood and at another which he
hoped would earn him fame. He was bubbling over with news when
he wrote to his father on 24 August that he had good prospects of
prosperity working for Mr. Bradford; Mary Duncan was living

comfortably at Ovid; William was doing wonderfully well as a teacher at Wilson's former school in Milestown. But not a word about his intention to publish his *American Ornithology*! Time enough when he had found the requisite number of subscribers, when the first volume was off the press and he had proved himself.

There was an occasional escape into the countryside around Philadelphia. Once he rose at dawn intending to shoot a nuthatch, but when he reached the confluence of the Schuylkill and Delaware he found there was hardly half an acre of wood left on the neck to offer the nuthatch cover. He returned soaked, bathed in perspiration and with wet feet; but, he told Bartram, he intended to repeat the experience as the exercise and fresh air had done him a world of good. "If I don't launch out into the woods and fields oftener than I have done these twelve months, may I be transformed into a street musician"—another job, incidentally, for which he would have been well qualified.

Wilson was now ready to put his work before the public. He had the encouragement and support of Bartram, who knew more than anyone in America about the native ornithology. A prospectus was prepared with great care; 2,500 copies were printed, and Samuel Bradford intended to bind some in at the end of the next half-volume of Rees's *Cyclopaedia*.[2] They planned to appoint an agent in every large town in the Union and to print the proposals in the principal newspapers. At the end of September Bradford sent Wilson off to New York to seek orders for both the *Cyclopaedia* and the *Ornithology*. He carried with him some specimen plates of his birds, but the principal booksellers, Brisbane and Brannan, declined to commit themselves until the first number was published, and he got only two or three subscriptions.

In September 1807, Wilson also called upon Robert Fulton who on 17 August commenced the first commercial steamboat service

2. The prospectus is printed in Part Two as letter XCV together with information about subsequent advertisements.

between New York and Albany. The reason for calling upon Fulton was to get him to check over the article about canals in the *Cyclopaedia*, a subject upon which he was an acknowledged expert following the publication in 1801 of his "Treatise on the Improvement of Canal Navigation." When Fulton told Wilson about the performance of the steamer, he recalled his own lengthy, hazardous crossing of the Atlantic and realized that sea or water transit would now be revolutionized. The *Clermont* had arrived from Albany the previous day after a journey of 160 miles in 27 hours carrying 60 passengers at $7 per head with their goods. He went to see it depart at ten o'clock in the forenoon into the teeth of a gale and he reported, "The wharves and vessels were crowded with spectators many of them dubious of her meeting such a sea but as soon as the machinery was put in action she shot through the water as steady and level as a line midst the shouts of the multitude." Wilson was delighted to get Fulton's name as a subscriber. Soon after he returned home, there was an order for a set of the *Ornithology* from the president, Thomas Jefferson, dated 9 October 1807 and on it written, "He salutes Mr. Wilson with great respect."

Other than working visits to Bartram's Garden, to which Bartram's niece brought the social graces in addition to practical help with the coloring of the master copies of some plates, his social life was encompassed within the houses of William Jones, his landlord, and of the Miller family into which Jones's son, Nicholas, had married. William Jones had also been his landlord at Gray's Ferry, where he had a second home; and, what neither of them knew then, Jones was going to be Wilson's landlord into eternity for it was in Jones's family burial ground at Old Swedes Church, Philadelphia, that he was finally laid to rest in 1813. Wilson became particularly friendly with Nicholas Jones's brother-in-law and sister-in-law, Daniel Miller and Sarah Miller, friendships which developed into high regard for Daniel and affection for Sarah.

In September 1808 the first volume of *American Ornithology* was printed. There were nine plates in volume one, not the ten promised in the prospectus, but that was the only expectation that was not fulfilled. Those who saw the book were perceptive enough to appreciate the integrity of both plates and letterpress. This was the first scientific treatment of American ornithology but there was also a charm and joy in nature about Wilson's book which lifted it far above the common run of scientific books. His first object had been achieved; now he had to fulfill the other part of the understanding with Samuel Bradford, to obtain enough subscribers to prove to him that continuation of the publication was, commercially, worthwhile.

In 1808, Wilson started on five years of the most intense physical and mental activity which, though securing his place among American naturalists, finally killed him. During this half decade he traversed every state in the union and some that were not yet in it, searching with equal vigor and determination for subscribers and birds. These travels were almost invariably made alone, often on foot. According to the introduction of volume one he intended to go over thousands of miles, "from the shores of the St. Lawrence to the mouth of the Mississippi, and from the Atlantic Ocean to the interior of Louisiana." He very nearly achieved all of it. Judged only as a traveler, his exploits were amazing when one remembers he was traveling in all weather, often through dense forests, swamps, across and along dangerous rivers, and, on occasion, through Indian territories alone.

The emphasis on Wilson's next journey was to obtain subscribers for his *American Ornithology*, and he suffered fewer of the hardships of travel than he was accustomed to face. He left Philadelphia by stage coach on 21 September 1808 for the northeastern states and planned to travel through Boston to Maine and back by way of Vermont and New York. He had hoped to study some birds en route but feared that he might find that few people would commit themselves to an outlay of $120 for ten volumes about American birds of which only one was in print.

Wilson found the stage coach journey most agreeable, although he was taking it only as far as Princeton. There was congenial company in the person of Colonel Simonds, known to Wilson. It is amusing to learn from Wilson's letters that whenever the coach stopped, which was often, to water the horses or for the driver to visit a hostelry, he and his friend got out and walked until they were sometimes several miles ahead of the coach. As he said, "By this method we enjoyed our ride!"

At Princeton, Wilson was welcomed by the president, Samuel Stanhope Smith, son-in-law of the late John Witherspoon, and his professor of natural history, Dr. McLean. He does not seem to have mentioned that he had been christened by Dr. Witherspoon or to have presumed in any way upon the Paisley connection. The doctors appeared to be impressed with the book, although Wilson was not impressed with the professor of natural history, but he left a specimen plate for Dr. McLean and departed with the hope that he might still prove to be a subscriber—a hope that was not fulfilled. On his trip he also visited Dartmouth, Columbia, Harvard, and Yale Colleges. The first two received him very well and both subscribed. Of the other two Wilson merely said, "I visited the university at Cambridge, where there is a fine library, but the most tumultuous set of students I have ever seen," and "The literati of New Haven received me with politeness and respect."

On this journey, too, he found time for a pilgrimage to Bunker Hill with two old soldiers and spent the evenings with them over a bottle of wine listening to their reminiscences. Perhaps the most interesting call was upon Thomas Paine in Greenwich, where he now lived ostracized and in poverty. The old man looked at Wilson's book with great interest and asked to be put down as a subscriber, but either poverty or his death the following year prevented his name from being listed among the original subscribers.[3]

Wilson was able to tell Lawson that many compliments had been paid to the book and this he put down to Lawson's skill as an engraver. The truth was that he had found only forty-one subscribers. So far as birds were concerned he had arranged correspondents throughout New England and he told a friend that "scarcely a wren or tit shall be able to pass along, from New York to Canada, but I shall get intelligence of it."

Wilson was no sooner back in Philadelphia than he was arranging another expedition. The information he had gleaned from Bartram about the bird life of the Carolinas, Georgia, and Florida was invaluable but he had to make his own field studies and get more subscribers. In preparation for this long and formidable journey Wilson had acquired a horse, and the first stage of his peregrination of some 2,000 miles took him to Baltimore. He remained a week in Baltimore before continuing by way of Annapolis to Washington. The 38 miles from Annapolis to Washington irked him—having just received a series of noes from the members of the legislature there who thought there was no such thing as a book worth $120. The irritation was increased by a series of gates he had to open, fifty-five in all; he saluted each new gate, he wrote to Daniel Miller, "with less Christian resignation than I ought to have done."

For the first time he noted and commented on the increasing numbers of Negroes he saw as he approached Washington, and their poverty and the loss of human dignity brought about by squalor troubled him. In Washington he called at once upon Jefferson at

3. A list of subscribers to volume one may be found in Cantwell, *Alexander Wilson*, pp. 277–305.

the President's House (not yet known as the White House) and upon sending in a note he was immediately admitted and received very courteously by the president, whose second term had but three months to run. Jefferson, an enthusiastic ornithologist, gave Wilson a letter to a contact in Virginia, Richard Fitzhugh, who, in turn, would introduce him to a third party, a Mr. Coffer, who "has spent his whole life in studying the manners of our birds." Jefferson had intended to see the man himself and make a record of his findings before they should die with him; he now entrusted the task to Wilson who promised to let him know the outcome. From Washington he traveled on to Georgetown, Alexandria, Richmond, and then Charleston which he reached in February 1809. The letters stemming from Wilson's earlier travels had always been informative, revealing a perceptive eye and mind, but on this and subsequent expeditions they took on a new dimension as though they were intended for publication.[4] (Some later letters did appear in newspapers or periodicals, but the majority were not printed until George Ord's biography augmented later in Grosart's *The Poems and Literary Prose of Alexander Wilson*, which appeared in two volumes in 1876 and has, for a hundred years, been the only reasonably complete publication of Wilson's writings. Unfortunately Ord's and the Rev. Alexander B. Grosart's editing resulted in the omission of some letters and serious deletions from others.)

From Charleston Wilson sent a long letter to Daniel Miller, and when he finally reached Savannah after nearly losing his horse and his life in the flooded Savannah River, there were further narrative letters to Miller and William Bartram. In his letter to Bartram of 5 March 1809 he wrote, "There is a Mr. Abbot here, who has resided in Georgia thirty-three years, drawing insects and birds. I have been on several excursions with him. He is a very good observer and paints well. . . ." Abbot, an Englishman, became one of Wilson's

4. *The Poems and Literary Prose of Alexander Wilson*, ed. Rev. Alexander B. Grosart, 2 vols. (Paisley: Alexander Gardner, 1876).

most important helpers and, to him, Cantwell devoted two and a half pages remarking that "At the Declaration of Independence he migrated with a few Virginians into Georgia," because he was not prepared to fight against his king. After the outbreak of war he changed his allegiance and fought with his adopted countrymen. His services were recognised by a land grant.[5] There are many references to John Abbot throughout the *American Ornithology* and he continued to send Wilson specimens, drawings, and notes right up until at least 1812 when we have the record of a letter from Wilson to Abbot dated 23 January 1812.

In another letter to Bradford dated 8 March 1809 Wilson commented again about the Negroes and the inordinate number of them in the southern states and that this had brought about an indolence and dissipation among the wealthy planters which was contemptible. This letter reveals examples of Ord's and Grosart's editing, referred to earlier. The omissions are italicized.

Everything must be done through the agency of these slovenly blacks *and a gentleman here can hardly perform the services of Cloacina without half a dozen negroes to assist him.* These, however, are not one-tenth of the curses slavery has brought to the Southern States.

In the same letter,

The negro wenches are all sprightliness and gayety; and if report be not a defamer *on them are lavished, in secret, those caresses, from the first dawnings of manhood to impotent old age* that render them callous to all the finer sensations of love and female excellence.

Wilson thought of returning by land but he was running out of money and had caught a fever which weakened him. He felt unenthusiastic about returning by the same route. He was delighted with the result of his efforts on all counts, strenuous as they had been, for he had signed up 250 subscribers and thus more than met Mr. Bradford's target. He was anxious to get home to convince Mr. Bradford

5. Cantwell, *Alexander Wilson*, p. 183.

that the printing should be increased to 400 sets. He had virtually guaranteed the financial success of the book; he had greatly widened his knowledge of the bird life in the southern states from personal observation; and he had established reliable correspondents, the most important being the worthy John Abbot. Spring was already well advanced in Georgia with temperatures between 70 and 78 degrees when he sold his horse and boarded a vessel bound for New York—reaching it on 22 March 1809. There he "found many parts of the country still covered with snow and the streets piled with ice to the height of two feet."

The remainder of 1809 was spent on his editorial work for Mr. Bradford and on preparing the ornithological riches he had brought back from the southern states. For the second volume he had a wealth of material and in it he crammed fifty birds on to nine plates. Working steadily, by 4 August he was able to tell Bartram that the second volume was almost ready to go to press. In five months he had drawn in detail fifty birds, given the colorists master copies to work from, and written, with a warmth and vivacity new to ornithology, the accounts of forty-two different species, some of which were here introduced to the world of natural history.

Earlier in the summer Wilson had written to his father telling him, with some pride, that he was sending him the first volume of his *American Ornithology* and that he would send him the remaining nine volumes, the number then intended, as they appeared. He claimed that in producing this work he had expended all the savings he had made since arriving in America fifteen years ago; he had visited every town within 150 miles of the Atlantic coast from the St. Lawrence River to St. Augustine in Florida. The rest of the letter was full of news of the growing American branch of the family and of other acquaintances like William Mitchell who was now "living and in good health at New Orleans—as a common soldier." There was a wistful inquiry about Tom Witherspoon, once his particular friend, who, he supposed, had quite forgotten him.

All the while there were exchanges with Bartram, the more stimulating when he stayed at Bartram's Garden and they could talk into the small hours, but when he could not prize himself away from his desk in Philadelphia his letters were full of queries and comments: "Let me know if you have ever seen the nest of Catesby's Cowpenbird. I have every reason to believe that this bird never builds itself a nest, but, like the cuckoo of Europe, drops its eggs into the nests of other birds." Again, "Thanks for your bird, so neatly stuffed, that I was about to skin it. It is the Rallus Virginianus of Turton, and agrees exactly with his description." Another time, "What bird do you mean by the little chocolate breasted Titmouse?" and in the same letter, "Do you know anything relative to the mode of building, eggs etc. of the small Pigeon Hawk . . . or of the Small Hawk, commonly though improperly called the Sparrow Hawk."

Wilson was now almost one of the family at Bartram's Garden and William sponsored him as though he were his son, while Nancy (Ann) Bartram seemed an admiring younger sister. Another warm relationship had developed with Robert Carr who was printing the *American Ornithology* for Bradford and Inskeep. As a result of his common interest with Carr in establishing high standards for the engravings and Nancy Bartram's assistance in the constant problem of hand-coloring, Wilson had been close enough to both to observe something more than friendship grow between them. Unfortunately, when the wedding day came, he had been marooned in Savannah while he awaited a vessel for Philadelphia or New York; thus he missed the wedding of two people high in his esteem.

His friendships in the Old and New Worlds were remarkable for a man variously described as quiet, withdrawn, self-contained, and with the appearance of "a congregational minister in his black dress."

In the United States his acquaintances ranged from the most important man in the land, the president, Thomas Jefferson, to William Mitchell, a "common soldier" in New Orleans. Between these poles his friends and acquaintances covered a remarkable range which included William Bartram; Charles Willson Peale—painter, father of painters, and founder of America's first natural history museum; John Abbot; Meriwether Lewis; Samuel Bradford, his publisher; Robert Carr (later Colonel Robert Carr), his printer; Thomas Paine of *The Rights of Man*; Robert Fulton, inventor of the first commercial steamship; William Dunbar, the Scottish-born scientist and Mississippi planter; and many other worthy individuals who in differing degrees helped to create confidence and pride in the young country. He even brought out the best in the infamous General James Wilkinson, soldier and adventurer, betrayer of many trusts but a subscriber to the *Ornithology*. There was also a host of personal friends beginning with his nephew William Duncan, then Daniel and Sarah Miller, Joshua Sullivan, John Finlayson, his landlord, William Jones, his engraver, Alexander Lawson, and those countless people whom he met in his travels over thousands of miles of North American territory. He was never a "hail fellow, well met" character. Yet only a man of fellow-feeling and understanding with a gift for responding to others could arrive penniless and unknown on a vast continent and in fifteen years fashion such a circle.

Despite the hopes expressed in his letter of 4 August, the appearance of the second volume was delayed; the coloring of the plates seems to have been the main problem and this meant further outlays by Samuel Bradford's firm. Because of Wilson's success as a salesman, 500 copies of volume two had to be printed, plus the extra copies of volume one. With 9 plates per volume, 4,500 plates had to be hand-colored for this second volume, and as a result the publication date was pushed further back. Fortunately the long-term profitability of the *American Ornithology* was now virtually assured and Samuel Bradford's worries on this score can only have been on whether Wilson would retain the health and strength necessary to complete his work. The second volume was eventually published on 1 January 1810 if we accept the dateline to Wilson's preface, and he began the final preparations for his longest and most spectacular expedition.

The recent journey to Florida had persuaded Wilson that if his book were going to meet his own standards and fulfill the expectations of subscribers, then a journey to the vast hinterland of America was essential. Such was the influence of his personality and his powers of friendship that he almost talked the seventy-year-old Bartram into accompanying him—a journey that would surely have killed the old man, for Wilson had decided that to travel on foot into the wilds was the best mode for a scientific observer and naturalist.

Wilson put all the determination and single-mindedness into the venture which other men have expended for their country on territorial expansion or conquests, but he did it in the name of that most inoffensive of sciences, natural history. In the preface to his second volume he gave a statement of purpose which formed an admirable introduction both to the book and to the journey he was about to begin:

. . . in ransacking our fields and forests, our sea shores, lakes, marshes and rivers; and in searching out and conversing with experienced and intelligent sportsmen and others on whose information he can venture to rely, he pledges himself, that no difficulty, fatigue or danger, shall deter him from endeavouring to collect information from every authentic source.

The first stage of his journey took him to Lancaster, to Columbia, across the Susquehanna—almost impassible with ice—and on to York. Next he traveled to Hanover, to Chambersburg, and over the Allegheny Mountains and then descended to Pittsburgh where the

Monongahela and Allegheny rivers combine to form the Ohio. When Wilson saw the rivers that day in February 1810 they were a churning mass of ice which had just begun to break upriver. The white of the ice contrasted with the black pall from the glass works, blacksmiths, breweries, forges, and furnaces which presented a re-markable scene of industry. Pittsburgh had already become a city for making fortunes, as Carnegie, Frick, and Mellon were to find later. The city also had its early philanthropists from whom Wilson benefited to the extent of nineteen new subscribers!

Wilson's plan was to purchase a rowboat and sail to Cincinnati or beyond; he had suggested this river voyage as long ago as 1806 in letters to Bartram and Jefferson. By this means he could be close to nature while transporting himself some hundreds of miles on the way to Louisiana. Some of the river folk thought he was foolhardy to attempt the journey on his own and that he should hire a rower. When putting the proposal to William Bartram he had estimated "with strict regard to economy," as he put it, that the journey might cost them one dollar a day each and the expense of a rower was beyond his purse. He purchased a small skiff, named it the *Orni-thologist*, and as the weather had turned warm and fine with the river like glass except for miniature icebergs dotting its surface, he loaded his baggage and set off on 24 February 1810.

He arrived in Louisville, Kentucky, on 17 March after a voyage of 720 miles, as he estimated it, in an open rowboat—an average of about 33 miles per day. Indeed on the first day he had covered 52 miles by nightfall, but in fact there were many side trips on foot or up tributaries by skiff, and he was constantly being turned aside by the enthralling interest of the country through which the Ohio River passed. When he eventually wrote Alexander Lawson a long letter on 4 April from Lexington, Kentucky, he was still bubbling over with the wonder of it all. It is told with such wide-eyed enthusiasm that only a reading of Wilson's own letter can convey adequately a voyage which began in warm, still weather, even if there were some ice floes to steer clear of, and continued (with no chances of taking a wrong turn!) through a storm of wind, rain, hail, and snow to the haven of Bear-Grass Creek at Louisville. He had been warned of the dangers of the falls on the Ohio River near Louisville and, with night coming on, had turned into the creek when, with still no sign of the lights of Louisville, he heard the noise of the rapids, which appeared to be getting uncomfortably near. The following day he went along to look at the renowned rapids and see what he had missed. He saw two Kentucky arks and a barge run the falls with ease and he was confident that he could easily have negotiated them in his skiff. Having no further use for his rowboat he sold it for half the original cost to a waterside character who inquired why he had given it such an outlandish Indian name as the *Ornithologist*.

At the time of Wilson's sojourn in Louisville where he remained until 23 March, another man was living there who was to surpass him as a bird artist but not as an ornithologist or pioneer—John James Audubon. That they met was confirmed by Audubon and alleged by George Ord but is not mentioned by Wilson in his long letter to Alexander Lawson covering that period. In Ord's life of Wilson written for the final volume of the *Ornithology* in 1814, there is a brief extract from what he described as Wilson's journal referring to his visit to Louisville which reads,

Packed up my things which I left in the care of a merchant here, to be sent on to Lexington; and having parted with regret, with my paroquet, to the gentleman of the tavern, I bade adieu to Louisville, to which place I had four letters of recommendation, and was taught to expect much of everything there, but neither received one act of civility from those to whom I was recommended, one subscriber, nor one new bird; though I delivered my letters, ransacked the woods repeatedly, and visited all the characters likely to subscribe. Science or literature has not one friend in this place.[6]

6. Here I must make atonement for Wilson's criticisms of the people of Louisville. I have received many kindnesses there and I gladly pay tribute to those friends who have redeemed, for this Scotsman, the good name of Louisville.

The parts of Audubon's famous *Birds of America* began to appear in London in 1827, seventeen years after Wilson's Louisville visit, and in 1828 another three-volume edition of the *American Ornithology* edited by George Ord was published which included an extended extract from Wilson's journal. Apparently, Wilson lodged at the Indian Queen Tavern where Audubon and his family lived and the journal, as printed by Ord, reads that he saw "Mr. ——'s drawings in crayons—very good. Saw two new birds he had, both Motacillae." According to the printed account Wilson went out shooting on 20 March and wrote "no naturalist to keep me company." On the following day he noted, "Went out shooting this afternoon with Mr. A. saw a number of Sandbill Cranes. Pigeons numerous." Then follows the paragraph which was dated 23 March and which Ord had published as early as 1814. Wilson's journal, or diary, has not been seen since it was in the possession of George Ord, nor was it included in his library willed to the College of Physicians in Philadelphia when he died in 1866. It would be difficult for anyone to invent the details given, which do not conflict with Wilson's carefully worded letter of 4 April, 1810 to Alexander Lawson, although I have noted one discrepancy between the extract for 23 March, 1810 and the account of the Carolina parrot in the *American Ornithology* (see below, note 10). The journal probably comprised spontaneous reference notes never intended for other eyes, and which more studied reflection amended, but we have to accept that there may have been some injudicious editing by Ord.

The matter should have rested there: with Wilson the observant pioneer, whose drawings—in all the honesty of what is today called the primitive or naive style—are brought alive by the artistry of his commentary; and the more sophisticated Audubon, whose brilliant drawings built upon the work of Wilson. What followed was a hornet's nest disturbed by Audubon himself when in 1831, twenty-one years after Wilson's visit to Louisville and seventeen years after Ord's biography, he began to publish his *Ornithological Biography*.

It was printed in five volumes between 1831 and 1839 in Edinburgh and described in F. H. Herrick's bibliography[7] as "An Account of the habits of the Birds of the United States of America; accompanied by descriptions of the objects represented in the work entitled 'The Birds of America,' and interspersed with delineations of American scenery and manners." In the first volume appears Audubon's version of his meeting with Wilson in 1810.

In the episode referring to Kentucky, Audubon said that Alexander Wilson, of whom he had never heard until that moment, walked into his counting-house in Louisville one morning in March 1810. Wilson carried under his arm the first two volumes of his book. He was seeking subscribers. Audubon turned over a few of the plates and was about to sign his name in favor when his partner Ferdinand Rozier interrupted and said in French, "My dear Audubon, what induces you to subscribe to this work? Your drawings are certainly far better, and again you must know as much of the habits of American birds as this gentleman." At that Audubon changed his mind; or, as he put it, "I did not subscribe to his work, for, even at that time, my collection was greater than his." Audubon was known as an artist and, as Audubon confirmed, was lodging in the same house as Wilson who then asked if he had many drawings of birds. At this point Audubon produced a large portfolio, much to the surprise of Wilson, who is alleged to have said that he had no idea anyone else was forming such a collection and asked if he had any intention of publishing. Audubon replied, "When I answered in the negative, his surprise seemed to increase. And truly such was not my intention; for, until long after, when I met the Prince of Musignano in Philadelphia, I had not the least idea of presenting the fruits of my labours to the world." Audubon went on to say that Wilson inquired if he could borrow some of the drawings during his stay, to which Audubon agreed. He also said that he introduced Wilson to his wife

7. Francis Hobart Herrick, *Audubon the Naturalist*, 2 vols. (New York: D. Appleton and Co., 1917).

and friends and tried to help him procure the specimens he wanted, took him shooting, and obtained birds for Wilson that he had never seen before. He added that he offered Wilson the results of his researches and his services as a correspondent to which Wilson made no reply. This last sentence seems extraordinary in view of Wilson's known enthusiasm to have reliable correspondents throughout America, particularly when he had Audubon's confirmation that he had no intention of publishing himself. Audubon also referred to another meeting in Philadelphia where in his own words,

he received me with civility, and took me to the Exhibition Rooms of Rembrandt Peale, the artist. . . . Mr. Wilson spoke not of birds or drawings. Feeling, as I was forced to do, that my company was not agreeable, I parted with him; and after that I never saw him again. But judge of my astonishment some time after, when on reading the thirty-ninth page of the ninth volume of American Ornithology, I found in it the following paragraph. . . .

Then followed the extract from Wilson's journal in Ord's biographical sketch of Alexander Wilson in the final volume of the *Ornithology* published the year after Wilson's death. It is doubtful if the particular paragraph concerned Audubon in the least, but the extended version published by Ord in 1828 clearly did sting him and the brickbats flew between the Wilson faction and Audubon and his supporters from then on.

The charges of plagiarism against Audubon have a much stronger basis than the belated criticism of Wilson by Audubon. Unfortunately the Wilson faction overreacted, especially George Ord and Charles Waterton, a fearless if capricious English naturalist. This caused a backlash in Audubon's favor.[8] Audubon's claim that in 1810 his collection of birds was greater than Wilson's is highly unlikely for two good reasons: first, by 1810 Wilson had covered very much more of America from the Canadian border to Florida for

8. See, for example, Ord's statement before the American Philosophical Society, *Proc. Amer. Phil. Soc.*, vol. 1 (1840), pp. 272–273.

the specific purpose of ornithological study; second, Audubon did not then have the technical support available to Wilson from the active help of important observers of the caliber of William Bartram, Meriwether Lewis, and John Abbot.

How much better would the good name of both men have been served if Audubon had been more generous in his tributes to Wilson. In 1966 the original Audubon drawings were published instead of the Havell engravings of the drawings. These confirmed that Ord's charges had a factual basis, but some of the arrows should have been aimed at Robert Havell, Junior, the brilliant London engraver whose contribution to *The Birds of America* was immeasurable, for Havell borrowed from Wilson in one or two notable instances. If only Audubon had acknowledged what the passage of 150 years would indicate to be Wilson's due—that at the very least he made Audubon's task easier and that the meeting in Louisville was probably the inspiration which led from *American Ornithology* to *The Birds of America*.

Wilson left Louisville on 23 March and walked to Shelbyville and thence to Frankfort, the capital of Kentucky, where he stayed a few days before moving on to Lexington which he reached on 29 March and there awaited his luggage. During the period of Wilson's journey through Kentucky the townships were just emerging from the backwoods, the territory having been opened up for settlement only in 1774 and admitted to the Union as a separate state in 1792. Before that it had been inaccessible country beyond the barrier of the Allegheny Mountains.

On the trek to Lexington Wilson had been told that it would be worth his while to take a detour between Shelbyville and Frankfort where there was an immense pigeon roost over forty miles in extent. There he saw a forest which was a fantastic scene of devastation now abandoned by passenger pigeons, who had moved to another roost sixty to eighty miles away towards Green River. He observed that in many trees there were the remains of more than ninety nests. Altogether, he told Alexander Lawson in his next letter, it was the most incredible thing he had seen since leaving home. As he neared Frankfort an immense flight of the pigeons passed overhead and by rough measurements of the length and width of the column and the time it took to pass he calculated, in his account of the passenger pigeon for the *American Ornithology*, that more than two thousand million pigeons were in the convoy flying over that afternoon.[9]

Louisville had proved to be a disappointment, but Lexington was more congenial and he thought the general air of tidiness and evidence of a growing prosperity a tribute to the hard work and enterprise of its people. He had his criticisms, too, but they were muted when one middle-aged man told him that within his memory there had been only two log cabins where the town then stood, surrounded by a wilderness inhabited by dangerous Indians. Now the frontier had retreated from Lexington and the symbols of civilization were there—schools, a public library, and even a college. Formerly part of Virginia, Kentucky had inherited slavery although this was alien to a society of predominantly small farms, and when Wilson went to the horse auction in Lexington to purchase a mount for his journey to New Orleans he saw, to his horror, a Negro woman and boy being sold for $325. In the privacy of his journal he wrote, "Damned, damned slavery! This is an infernal custom the Virginians have brought into this country."

His failure to find subscribers or anything else in Louisville had been abundantly compensated for in and around Lexington, and by the time he left on Saturday 14 April he had gained fifteen names. He made leisurely progress to Nashville for there was much to captivate him on the way: a family with its covered wagons, cattle, and

9. Man's inhumanity is not confined to man. The last passenger pigeon died at the Cincinnati Zoo in 1914.

horses making for the Cumberland River; an exhausted soldier on foot, who said he was from New Orleans and had been robbed by Choctaw Indians; an excursion into the vast caves which are Kentucky's great natural spectacle. He stayed with a kindly landlord, Isaac Walton, for a few days where he gave Walton's daughters a few lessons in drawing and was rewarded on leaving by the landlord who said, "You seem to be travelling for the good of the world; and I cannot, and will not charge you anything."

In Nashville, Tennessee, Wilson spent eight days preparing drawings with appropriate descriptions to enable Lawson to start work on another series of plates and these were sent with a long letter dated 28 April 1810. This was one of Wilson's letters which was written with publication in mind and when it appeared in *The Port Folio* it occasioned some hostility from one of the inhabitants of Lexington who, a bit piqued by Wilson's attempt at an objective representation of the town, wrote to the editor. In a reply to the editor, Wilson acknowledged his respect for the people of Lexington, "But," said he, "they would be gods, and not men, were they faultless."

The letter of 28 April, as we know, got safely to Lawson but the parcel of drawings was lost and with it not only the eight days of work that Wilson had put into them but much of the invaluable data on which the drawings were based. A few days after his letter to Lawson he sent Sarah Miller a friendly, chatty one which was not intended for publication, for it indicated that Sarah was coming to mean more to him than simply the sister of his friend Daniel Miller. He concluded by presenting his compliments to her mother and father and asking kindly for the rest of her family, as is the way with prospective suitors!

On Friday morning 4 May 1810 Wilson left Nashville bound for Natchez en route to New Orleans. He had been well warned in Nashville not to attempt the journey alone on account of natural obstacles and human dangers: the swamps, impassible rivers, and wild Indians, not to mention other less specified horrors of the imagination, but he now traveled with the confidence of one who had, almost certainly, seen more of the American wilds than his advisers and possessed a sense of mission and of his own invulnerability.

The story of Wilson's ride to the Mississippi Territory is carefully documented as far as Natchez in his letter to Lawson from there dated 18 May 1810. He reached Natchez, after surviving a debilitating attack of dysentery on the way, thanks to his own toughness and that of his Kentucky horse. He took a detour to visit the scene of the mysterious death, the previous year, of Meriwether Lewis, explorer and later governor of the Louisiana Territory. Wilson had become acquainted with Meriwether Lewis through their common interest in Peale's Museum, Philadelphia, and Lewis had authorized him to make full use of any of the ornithological specimens that he required, as Wilson explains in the notes to Plate XX of the *American Ornithology*:

It was the request and particular wish of Captain Lewis, made to me in person, that I should make drawings of such of the feathered tribes as had been preserved, and were new. That brave soldier, that amiable and excellent man, over whose solitary grave in the wilderness I have since shed tears of affliction, having been cut off in the prime of his life, I hope I shall be pardoned for consecrating this humble note to his memory until a more able pen shall do better justice to the subject.

Jefferson had assumed that Lewis committed suicide although the possibility that he was murdered has never been quite eradicated. Wilson's is the first independent account of his death although he merely repeated the story told him by Mrs. Grinder, the landlady, whose husband was away from home at the time of Lewis's death. But Wilson's letter raises questions. What kind of woman left a dying man for two hours before fetching his two servants; could the two servants have failed to hear two pistol shots in the still of the night, at a distance of 200 yards, as estimated by Wilson, from where they were sleeping in a barn? Wilson paid Grinder to erect a

1. *Cedar Bird.* 2. *Red bellied Woodpecker.* 3. *Yellow throated Flycatcher.* 4. *Purple Finch.*

Drawn from Nature by A. Wilson.

7

Engraved by G. Murray

Plate 7 from Alexander Wilson, *American Ornithology* (Volume I)

stout fence round the grave to protect it from hogs and wolves and today a monument marks the spot.

The remaining 300, and more, hazardous miles to Natchez were through Indian country, but he had more trouble from the swamps and a hurricane than from the Indians. He described the water in the swamps as being like poison—the probable cause of "something like dysentery"—and he developed a raging thirst which was assuaged during the hurricane as he stood in the rain for half an hour enjoying "the most profuse heavenly shower bath," albeit with branches of trees flying past and other trees being torn out by the roots around him.

He stayed in Natchez from 17 to 23 May and obtained twelve subscribers. He also received a most friendly and welcoming letter from William Dunbar, a Scottish-born scientist and Mississippi planter, the discoverer of Hot Springs, Arkansas, and the man who in drawing the boundary line in 1798 insured that Natchez was in United States territory. He was in the last months of his life but was established as one of America's scientific pioneers, having also set up an astronomical observatory, explored the Mississippi delta, and published botanical and wildlife studies of the territory. The dying man wrote to Wilson on 20 May:

Sir, It is very unfortunate that I should be so much indisposed as to be confined to my bedroom; nevertheless, I cannot give up the idea of having the pleasure of seeing you as soon as you find it convenient. The perusal of your first volume of Ornithology, lent me by General Wilkinson, has produced in me a very great desire of making your acquaintance.

I understand, from my boy, that you propose going in a few days to New Orleans, where you will see some small cabinets of natural history that may interest you. But, as I presume it is your intention to prosecute your inquiries into the interior of our country, this cannot be done better than from my house as your headquarters, where everything will be made convenient to your wishes. My house stands literally in the forest, and your beautiful Orioles, with other elegant birds, are our court-yard companions.

The bearer attends you with a couple of horses, on the supposition
that it may be convenient for you to visit us to-day; otherwise, he shall
wait upon you any other day that you shall appoint.

I am respectfully, etc.
WILLIAM DUNBAR.

It is interesting to see the name of the rascally General Wilkinson
turning up again with a kindly action to aid Wilson. Wilson gladly
accepted Dunbar's offer and on 23 May rode the 9 miles to his forest
house, appropriately enough named the "Forest."

With the exception of the date of his departure from New Orleans
on his return journey, Wilson's precise movements, until his ultimate return to Philadelphia, are not well documented and, surprisingly, no narrative letter has been found similar to those to Alexander Lawson at earlier stages of his journey. Even the date of his
return to Philadelphia is contradicted by his own letters of 2 September 1810 to William Bartram and 4 March 1811 to James Gibb.

He was undoubtedly made very welcome by Dunbar and his wife
and family of seven children, as is confirmed by his letter of 24 June
from New Orleans when he set sail for home. Despite the fact that
Dunbar was confined to his room, he introduced Wilson to all the
notables of the region so that, in addition to the twelve subscribers
he had signed up in Natchez, a further sixty-four were obtained
between there and New Orleans. He traveled from plantation to
plantation presenting the introduction, exploring the forests and
bayous, and discovering new birds almost as readily as he was finding subscribers. This was the happiest and most rewarding part of
his journey which possibly explains that he had little time for letter
writing. We know from George Ord, who had the benefit of Wilson's journals and diaries, that he reached New Orleans on 6 June.

There are few records of Wilson's eighteen-day stay in New Orleans and none of his journey from Dunbar's estate some 250 miles
along the Mississippi to that city. From the evidence of the names of
the subscribers in the territory, it appears that he took full advan-

tage of Dunbar's recommendation and visited planters, government officials, and traders mainly along the east bank of the Mississippi. In a note to his *Sketch of the Life of Alexander Wilson*, George Ord wrote:

The editor of Wilson's Poems, which were published at Paisley in 1816, gives what he states to be an extract from one of our author's letters to his father, wherein it is said that he had travelled through West Florida to New Orleans [see the letter to his father of 25 February 1811] and had "sailed thence to East Florida, furnished with a letter to the Spanish governor."

This passage needs explanation. Wilson was never in either East or west Florida (except a small part of the latter province, through which the road to New Orleans passed). but, in the event of his going thither, he had provided himself with a letter of introduction from Don Luis de Onis, the Spanish ambassador to the United States, to Don Enrique White, governor of East Florida, and another to Don Vincente Folche, governor of West Florida. In his passage from New Orleans to New York, he merely landed, for a few minutes, upon one or two desert islands lying in the Florida Gulf.

He departed from Philadelphia on the thirtieth of January, 1810; and returned on the second of August of the same year. It is stated in his diary that the total amount of his expenses, until his arrival in New York, was the sum of four hundred fifty-five dollars. This particular is given as proof of how much may be performed, by a good economist, with slender means.

There are incidental references to the homeward journey in *American Ornithology* in his descriptions of the stormy petrel and the Carolina parrot. A Carolina parrot, now an extinct species, had been Wilson's companion since he captured it, slightly wounded, at Big Bone Creek on the Ohio River, but the sea trip home, far from being good for its health, was its undoing:

. . . she had learnt to know her name; to answer and come when called on; to climb up my clothes, sit on my shoulder, and eat from my mouth. I took her with me to sea, determined to persevere in her education;

but, destined to another fate, poor Poll, having one morning, about day-break, wrought her way through the cage while I was asleep, instantly flew overboard and perished in the Gulf of Mexico.[10]

The euphoria of Wilson's return to Philadelphia quickly vanished when he found that Lawson had never received the packet of drawings and bird data posted from Nashville. As a result the third and fourth volumes of *American Ornithology* were disastrously behind schedule and, therefore, not yet generating the income from sales needed to please Samuel Bradford. With feverish intensity Wilson set to work to replace the lost drawings. He pushed himself to complete the letterpress and drawings for the third volume only to find that Lawson and the colorists were not impelled by a similar driving force. Some instinct seemed to urge him to keep working while his health still permitted. Wilson had to wait until 12 February 1811 before he could add the date to the preface of the third volume, but this delay was put to effective use with an expedition to Cape May and the Great Egg Harbor area of New Jersey, a journey he was to make six times over the next two years to study water-birds.

In the summer of 1811, having given up his editorship of Rees's *Cyclopaedia*, Wilson spent much of his time at Bartram's Garden in the home of his mentor relaxing with congenial company and in the peaceful surroundings. There he made a survey of the nesting birds in the eight-acre garden, recording fifty-one pairs representing the

10. The account of the Carolina parrot from Big Bone Creek is at odds with Ord's extracts from the missing diary appended to letter CXXXVI. Wilson is alleged to have written that he had "parted, with great regret, with my paroquet to the gentlemen of the tavern" in Louisville. In the *Ornithology* he specifically refers to his experiences with the paroquet between Nashville and Natchez, at Mr. Dunbar's, and when he arrived at New Orleans.

nests of nineteen different species. He thrived on Bartram's encouragement and succeeded in convincing Alexander Lawson that the
engraving of the plates for the *American Ornithology* would benefit
his fame and fortune. The result was that volume four appeared later
the same year under the date 12 September 1811. This was a propi-
tious period for Wilson and his reputation grew with the realization
of the seminal nature of his work.

That summer, too, Wilson became personally acquainted with
that strange character, George Ord, who, more than a decade after
Wilson's death, when the first parts of Audubon's *Birds of America*
began to appear, formed a pro-Wilson faction in Philadelphia that
tended to act more like an anti-Audubon society. It is assumed that
Ord communicated with Wilson after he read the appeal in the
preface of the third volume:

To gentlemen of leisure, resident in the country, whose taste disposes
them to the pleasing and rational amusement of natural history, and who
may be in possession of facts, authentic and interesting, relative to any
of our birds which have not yet made their appearance in this work, the
author respectfully addresses himself . . . for the direction of those who
may be disposed to honour the Author with their correspondence, the
following list is subjoined; containing the common popular names of the
most interesting of our Land Birds, whose history we have yet to detail,
and of whose manners any authentic particulars will be gladly received.

It is unfortunate that today Ord is mainly remembered as the
acrimonious anti-Audubonist rather than for his collaboration with
Wilson. Human relationships were an insoluble problem to Ord; for
him there could be no easy, comfortable fellowship and to incur his
displeasure was to come up against a wall of unwavering hostility.
Wilson was one of the few people who penetrated the inner court-
yard and entered into his friendship. He married the daughter of a
wealthy Swede and, with the added support of his own ship chan-
dlery business, he applied himself to the compilation of a lexicon of
archaic words which led only to a quarrel with Noah Webster, of

dictionary fame. Then as a disciple of Alexander Wilson he came to his life's vocation, the study of the natural sciences. Ord's life, to a considerable extent, was blighted by the death of his only daughter in infancy and the subsequent derangement of his wife, who spent the rest of her life in a mental institution. He had a son who survived to become an eminent portrait painter.

Ord accompanied Wilson on at least two of his expeditions to Cape May which brought this tribute from Wilson in his description of the Cape May warbler (*American Ornithology*, vol. 6):

This new and beautiful little species was discovered in a maple swamp, in Cape May County, not far from the coast, by Mr. George Ord of Philadelphia, who accompanied me on a shooting excursion to that quarter in the month of May last. Through the zeal and activity of this gentleman, I succeeded in procuring many rare and elegant birds among the sea islands and extensive salt marshes that border that part of the Atlantic; and much interesting information relative to their nests, eggs and particular habits. I have also at various times been favoured with specimens of other birds from the same friend, for all which I return my grateful acknowledgements.[11]

An interesting feature of 1811, the forty-fifth year of Wilson's life, was a reaffirmation of his links with Scotland. He sent letters to his father, to his half-brother David Wilson, to his half-sister Janet and husband, and, after a break of seventeen years, to his old confidant Thomas Crichton. The letter to Crichton was in response to one from him giving news of his former friends and in his reply

11. Alexander Wilson, *American Ornithology* (Philadelphia: Bradford and Inskeep, 1808–1814), vol. 6, p. 99. The Cape May warbler was seen for the first time outside the New World on 17 June 1977, and it is, surely, extraordinary that this sighting should have occurred in Paisley. The bird was observed for some five hours in the Glen, a local beauty spot and nature trail about 1½ miles from Wilson's birthplace. Among the handful of observers was Mr. Hector Galbraith of the Department of Natural History, City of Glasgow Museums and Art Galleries, Kelvingrove, who recorded the event with an article in *British Birds*, vol. 73, no. 1 (January 1980).

Wilson made kindly references to Neilson, Kennedy, Picken, and Brodie, but, strangely, there was no mention of his friend from boyhood days, Thomas Witherspoon. Crichton asserted that they corresponded throughout Wilson's life but this was patently not true as is manifest from the letters to his father of 24 August 1806 and 15 June 1809 in which he inquired after Tom Witherspoon. There were also letters to David Brown (who on returning from America conveyed Wilson's letter of 15 June 1809 to his father together with a copy of the first volume of *American Ornithology*). These letters are now known only from snatches printed in the Life which prefaced the edition of Wilson's poems published in 1816 and in Crichton's monograph of 1819.

Many of Wilson's relatives and friends were encouraged by his successful example to follow him to America, although he made a point of never influencing them to do so. One of these, some years after Wilson's death, was Tom Witherspoon. As told by Crichton in the literary language of the time, ". . . and as this distinguished friend of the bard has now reached the Western shores of the Atlantic, may he find the evening of his life happy in a land of strangers." Nothing is known of Witherspoon's American life and he disappeared as effectively as if his ship had been lost in mid-Atlantic.

The beginning of 1812 found Wilson making rapid progress in the preparation of his book; the publication date of the fifth volume was 12 February and the scheme of work for the sixth volume was well advanced. In effect Wilson had produced three volumes in one year, the third, fourth, and fifth, a remarkable feat when one remembers his involvement in every aspect of the work from field research, writing, and drawing to supervision of the publication and ultimate sale of the book. Not surprisingly, Wilson felt physical and nervous strain which was increased by the threat of war between the United States and Great Britain. Though it was not a popular war it seemed to cause Wilson great personal concern. In addition, Samuel Bradford began to put pressure on him for a speedier return on his invest-

ment and some long-looked-for profit. Possibly the greatest stress
of all came from his own instinct that he was engaged in a race
against time.

He continued to reside at every opportunity with William Bartram where he could work undisturbed and to good effect. In May
he had the rewarding month-long expedition to Cape May with
George Ord; this, and subsequent trips to the same area of New
Jersey, provided much data for the remaining three volumes.

On 18 June 1812 the United States declared war on Great Britain. This was a period when the old country had its hands full with
Napoleon Bonaparte; indeed the series of Napoleonic Wars was
one of the causes of the War of 1812. Neither Britain nor France
was overly observant of the rights of neutrals, and the British
policy of stopping and searching American ships and impressing
American seamen was infuriating to the young country. This was
ideal fuel for the ambitions of the frontiersmen and the politicians
who wanted to extend the territories of the United States by annex-
ing lands from the Indians and British. After some injured pride on
both sides a peace treaty was concluded at Ghent in 1814. The
declaration of war did nothing for Wilson's peace of mind and the
business-like Bradford had visions of many subscribers defaulting,
particularly those in the maritime states where commerce was likely
to suffer from a British blockade.

Five volumes of *American Ornithology* had now come from the
press of Robert Carr and his brother, printers to the publishers,
Bradford and Inskeep, and Wilson's name was becoming widely
known in American scientific, literary, and artistic circles centered
in Philadelphia. The marriage of Robert Carr, the head of the printing firm, to Nancy Bartram, niece and heiress to William Bartram,

had further increased the interest of the Bartram ménage in Wilson's *Ornithology*. Earlier in the year Wilson had, at Robert Carr's request, written to the Hon. Samuel L. Mitchill in Washington recommending the name of "my particular friend," and asking Mitchill to support Carr's petition to the secretary of war for a commission in the military forces of his country in the approaching hostilities.

So far neither Bradford nor Wilson had made any profit from what was a very successful publication. The outlays, at this stage, were ahead of the cash returns and with five volumes now out and another on the stocks both publisher and author could see that any delays in receipts from subscribers could be fatal. They were so near the top of the mountain barrier and the valley of plenty lay on the other side! They were particularly concerned about the subscribers in the New England states which were so vulnerable to British counterattack now that war had broken out.

On 7 August 1812 Wilson wrote to Sarah Miller that he was going to have to make a long and expensive journey to collect what was due and that the only alternative was absolute ruin. He was annoyed by Bradford's attitude: "Mr. B. has positively refused to advance anything untill he receives it and I have as positively told him that I will proceed no further with the work untill I am paid for what I have done." This letter to Sarah indicates that she had settled into a relationship with Wilson which must have led to marriage between the forty-six-year-old ornithologist and the thirty-one-year-old sister of his friend Daniel had not death intervened.

Volume six, published five days after the date of the letter to Sarah, was evidence of Wilson's continued intense activity for it meant he had produced four volumes in the two years since his return from New Orleans. He announced in the preface to the sixth volume that he had completed his work on land birds with the exception of a few which would appear in a subsequent volume or appendix; the remaining parts of the *American Ornithology* would concentrate on waders and web-footed birds.

Three or four weeks later Wilson journeyed to New England. He sailed up the Hudson and crossed rugged country to Lake Champlain. On the next stage of his journey he "traversed a rude mountainous range to Connecticut River" down which he "coasted"—to use his own word—to Haverhill on his way to the maritime townships, but here he had an embarrassing misadventure. He had spent a day climbing a peak near Haverhill where he described the scene as "the most sublime and astonishing view that was ever afforded to me." An "immensity of forest lay below," spreading to the horizon with columns of smoke from burning timber pointing straight to the heavens. Upon his descent he was immediately arrested under suspicion of being a spy from Canada. He was, of course, a spy but the object was not to observe military maneuvers; it was information about the feathered battalions he was after. He was taken before the local magistrate who, upon being convinced of Wilson's peaceful pursuits, released him.

The immediate purpose of his tour was, as we know, the business affairs of his book, but in all Wilson's travels his overriding interest was ornithology and he gleaned useful material. Owing to the state of affairs in New England he probably had difficulty with his subscribers and in settling accounts with his agents. On 13 October 1812 he wrote to George Ord from Boston,

In New England the rage of war, the virulence of politics, and the pursuit of commercial speculations engross every faculty. The voice of Science, and the charms of Nature, unless those last present themselves in the form of prize sugars, coffee, or rum, are treated with contempt.

More important than his financial worries was his admission that several times he had suffered from violent palpitations. He spoke of trying a short sea voyage for the benefit of his health; this he probably managed homeward bound for Philadelphia by sailing from Boston to New York.

The winter of 1812–1813 was one of discontent for Wilson's colorists and they deserted him. This difficulty with colorists had plagued him from the beginning of the enterprise; 4,500 plates had to be individually hand-colored for each issue. To find people with the necessary skill and perseverance essential to maintain the high standard of color accuracy he had set was never easy. As winter yielded to spring, he was virtually housebound, working steadily with a minimum of assistance on the painstaking but important task. There was, however, another reason for his labors as a colorist; it was his only source of income at this time. George Ord's comments in his biographical sketch of Wilson are illuminating:

But the true cause of this extraordinary toil was his poverty. By the terms of agreement with his publisher, he was to furnish at his own cost, all the drawings and literary matter for the work; and to have the whole under his control and superintendence. The publisher stipulated to find funds for the completion of the volumes. To support the heavy expense of procuring materials, and other unavoidable expenditures, Wilson's only resource, as has been stated, was in colouring the plates.

He eventually signed and dated the preface to the seventh volume on 1 March 1813 but it was more than a month later, 21 April, before he could tell William Bartram that it would be published the following week. He confessed to Bartram that for months he had hardly left the house for more than half an hour at a time and he longed to breathe the good air of the countryside at Bartram's Garden. Proudly he told his old friend that he had been elected to membership of the American Philosophical Society, founded in 1743 with Benjamin Franklin as secretary—the first scientific organization in America. His election set the seal upon his achievement as the father of American ornithology.

When the seventh volume was off the press Wilson hurried to Cape May with George Ord to prepare for the penultimate volume, and there they worked for four weeks. Wilson hoped that the tonic of fresh air and the freedom of the open spaces away from the strains associated with the workaday problems of producing his book would restore his vitality, but a price had now to be paid for the years of unremitting work and the hardships of his earlier years in Scotland; his health was undermined.

Back in Philadelphia the awareness of his deteriorating health and the instinctive need, combined with the practical necessity, of completing his *American Ornithology* before ill health or financial forces brought it to a halt drove him to push on with the script and drawings for the next volume instead of following his self-prescribed remedy, a summer break in the agreeable surroundings of Bartram's Garden. It was all to no avail and in the fragment of a last letter to Scotland dated 6 July he wrote,

I am myself far from being in good health. Intense application to study has hurt me much. My 8th volume is now in the press and will be published in November. One volume more will complete the whole which I hope to be able to finish in April next.

The last written words we have from Wilson, apart from the signature to his will dated 16 August 1813, are these:

Undrawn August 13th 1813.

Gannet	Turkey	Tropic Bird
Young	Blue Hawk	Puffin
Frigate Pel.	Razor Bill	Black backed Gull
Cormorant	Crested Grebe	Skua G.
Brown Booby	Little G.	Kittiwake G.
Great White P.	Speckled Diver	Herring G.
Swan	Shearwater Petrel	Common G.
	Albatross	

That very day he suffered a sudden collapse in health and it appears from the accounts submitted to his executors, Daniel Miller and George Ord, that a Dr. Gallaher was called in to treat him at his lodgings in the home of his friend William Jones, where he had lived for many years.

Wilson was suffering from dysentery, but his body had no longer the powers of resistance which had enabled him to throw off a previous severe attack in 1810. His condition worsened and on the nineteenth his worried friends brought in Dr. Charles Caldwell, an eminent physician in Philadelphia. By now his illness was beyond the medical knowledge of the early nineteenth century and four days later, on 23 August, he died.

Wilson's will had been prepared hurriedly, when the serious nature of his illness became apparent, and although signed, had not been witnessed. On 25 September 1813 Henry L. Coryell and Susannah Jones[12] appeared before the Register of Wills and testified "that they did see and hear Alexander Wilson the Testator in the said Will named sign seal publish and declare the said Will as and for his last Will and Testament and that at the doing thereof he was of sound mind memory and understanding." He bequeathed two copies of the *American Ornithology* to his "honoured father" and one copy to his nephew William Duncan, who had accompanied him to America nineteen years before, and the remainder of the estate and all his rights and interest in the *American Ornithology* were willed to Sarah Miller. There is a statement attached, signed by Daniel Miller and dated 1 November 1816, showing a claim against the estate by the assignees of Bradford and Inskeep for $2,284.22 but there is a covering note which states, "The executors however are well assured that so soon as the remaining volumes of Ornithology which remain in the hands of the assignees shall be sold, & the full settlement takes place, there will be ample funds for the discharge of all legal claims." Wilson never received the financial benefits of his work. Had he survived a few more years, the first and succeeding editions, which he planned, would have earned him the reward and added greatly to the fame he worked so hard to attain.

Wilson was buried in the graveyard of Gloria Dei Church, known as Old Swedes. The minister made this entry in the records:

1813, August 24. Alexander Wilson, native of Scotland, but resident here for many years, author of *American Ornithology*, aged about 40 years, not married. He had for a long time lived with Mr. William Jones, last in Spruce Street near 7th, & was buried in his lot. The disease was flux.

12. The sister of Sarah Miller and daughter-in-law of William Jones.

PART TWO

The Letters of Alexander Wilson

EDITORIAL NOTE

In presenting the letters and other papers in Part Two, I have followed the original text and spelling as written by Wilson, or as given in the primary source quoted and I have endeavoured to maintain his fairly liberal capitalization. Wilson was largely self-taught and his letters disclose the constant and quite remarkable improvement in penmanship, grammar, and literary skill achieved through time and by diligence. Nevertheless, his letters were often hurriedly written under difficult circumstances, and punctuation suffered. I have been induced to render a little editorial first aid, by way of a few punctuation marks, where necessary. In the first letter to a recipient the original form of address has been retained. Thereafter, unless it is of special significance, it has been omitted. The place and date of writing, with few exceptions, have been standardized. The source from which each letter was obtained has been indicated by an abbreviation (see below). In a number of instances, where Grosart is given as the source, the letters were first published by Ord in 1814 or 1828, but it has been more convenient to cite Grosart, until now, the major record of Wilson's correspondence.

Abbreviations

The following abbreviations have been used when citing the locations of letters or, where the original letters have not been found, identifying the sources quoted.

ANS   Academy of Natural Sciences, Philadelphia.

APS   American Philosophical Society, Philadelphia.

BLC   Rare Book and Manuscript Library, Columbia University.

BLY   The Beinecke Rare Book and Manuscript Library, Yale University.

CRICHTON 1819   *Biographical Sketch of the Late Alexander Wilson,* Paisley, 1819. In a series of letters to a young friend by Senex [Thomas Crichton].

EUL   Edinburgh University Library.

WRF   Mrs. William R. Funck, Geneva, Ohio.

GROSART   *The Poems and Literary Prose of Alexander Wilson,* ed. Rev. Alexander B. Grosart. 2 vols. Paisley, 1876.

HC   Haverford College Library.

HCL (JARDINE)   Jardine Transcripts of Alexander Wilson letters in the Houghton Library, Harvard University.

HLH   Houghton Library, Harvard University.

HSP   Historical Society of Pennsylvania, Philadelphia.

LCP   The Library Company of Philadelphia.

LOC   The Library of Congress.

MCZ	Museum of Comparative Zoology, Harvard University.
NLS	National Library of Scotland.
ORD	Ord, George, *Sketch of the Life of Alexander Wilson, Author of the American Ornithology*, Philadelphia, 1828.
PBC	Paisley Burns Club.
PMA	Paisley Museum and Art Galleries.
POEMS 1816	*Poems Chiefly in the Scottish Dialect by Alexander Wilson*, 1816. With a Life.
PRL	Paisley Central Library, Reference Department.
THAYER	Scrapbook containing many Wilson letters. Property of Museum of Comparative Zoology, deposited at Houghton Library, Harvard University.
UOP	The Charles Patterson Van Pelt Library, University of Pennsylvania.
UOV	University of Virginia, Tracy W. McGregor Library.

PMA, HCL (JARDINE)

To Mr. David Brodie, Schoolmaster.
Quarrletoun, Near Paisley.

Edinburgh, 28 April 1788.

Dear Friend,

A poor inconsiderate mortal once known to you, but alas! long since lost from you midst the hurry and bustle of life, here takes the liberty of enquiring after your welfare. Many a scene has he passed through, and many a part has he acted; yet in all his lonely hours, you presented yourself to his view. And did that sooth his grief or heighten his pleasure? No alas, no more than the last bright glimpse of the setting sun gives to the traveller when he sees himself just about to be benighted in some lonely desert, and hears already the dismal howls and growls of ferocious animals surrounding him; or as the weeping sailor, when he takes his last long look of his native shore which contains all he holds dear. With what anguish do I reflect on past scenes, where all was harmony and love, except for a few visits that your humble servant had the dishonour of receiving from a certain tattered dame, whom, however, he did not much regard, but often laught her out of countenance. Oh! happy, happy scenes, ne'er shall ye return! and where or what have you left me? Why, nothing but a Poor Packman! Nay, stare not, my friend; nothing more or less, I assure you, is the personage that thus makes bold to address you. Here I should pause and stop, and let you ponder and wonder and laugh; but I will not, for I have more to tell you. Know then, that last week I passed almost a whole night in company with three poets. One was James Kennedy, Ebenezer Picken—who is publishing his works, and the last and most glorious was the immortal author of that well-known ballad, "The Battle of Bannockburn," "From the Ocean, &c." Blessed meeting! Never did I spend such a

119

night in all my life. O, I was all fire! O, I was all spirit! I had the honnour of being highly complimented by Bannockburn for a poem which I wrote in praise of his sublime song. Perhaps I may have the pleasure of sending a copy of it, if you please to answer my letter, with several other pieces which I have beside me. I have sent you here a few verses on a trifling circumstance, but the Poets resemble a spider—she spins a very extensive work from a small compass. Dear Sir, if you will favour me with a letter on receiving this, I shall account it one of the greatest honnours you ever did me. I have now a more deep regard for the Muse than ever. I have opportunity, and my views are more expanded than when I sung on the loom. Mr. Kennedy desires to be remembered to you. I would write more full to you, but perhaps I disturb you. If I have said anything amiss, pardon me. I know there are a great many wrong spelled words, which you will please look over. That you may long be happy in your noisy mansion to hammer wisdom through the dark walls of the blockheads' skulls; to teach the young ideas how to shoot; to pour instruction over the opening mind; to be a terror to evil-doers, and a praise to well-doers, is the sincere wish of

Sir,

Your humble Servant,

ALEXANDER WILSON

P.S. Please direct to the care of Alexander Leishman, West End of Falkirk, where I will be for three weeks to come.

[With this letter, there are 110 lines of verse which end thus:]

> Dear Friend and patron of my Muse's song,
> All she attempts does unto you belong;
> Vouchsafe the thanks she thus most grateful pays.
> Inspir'd by you she shot her infant rays,
> Dawn'd to the light, and glory'd in your praise;
> But cursed Fortune that still frowning slut,
> Rent us asunder from our peaceful hut.
> O happy dwelling! where my willing pen

Drew scenes of horror, or deceits of men,
In your kind face I saw encore or hiss,
Each smile was rapture, and each laugh was bliss.

P.S. If you should wonder at this short address,
Read the first letters of these lines, and guess.[1]

1. The first eleven lines of verse quoted form an acrostic, but it is the letter that poses the real problem, in fact two problems of identification. Who were the "tattered dame" and "the immortal author of that well-known ballad 'The Battle of Bannockburn' "? The "tattered dame" was certainly not Martha McLean. Robert Cantwell, the most recent American biographer of Wilson, who unearthed more about his life than any other biographer, believed that the "tattered dame" was Meg Duncan—and he may well have been right—although the proof is entirely circumstantial and rests on the facts that she worked at Auchinbathie Tower, that she was the anti-heroine of the "Elegy of the Long Expected Death of a Wretched Miser," and that she lived in Paisley after she left Fauldheads. But Paisley, like other places, would have more than one "tattered dame"! The "immortal author" at first glance might appear to be Robert Burns but the Ayrshire poet was in his native county throughout April 1788, which can easily be confirmed from his published letters, and, indeed, the writer possesses one addressed from Mauchline to Mrs. Dunlop on the very date that Wilson wrote to Brodie. The title given to "Scots Wha Hae" by Burns was "Robert Bruce's March to Bannockburn" but it was not written for another five years nor published until it appeared in *The Morning Chronicle* of May 1794.

Walter Scott's "The Battle of Bannockburn" formed part of "The Lord of the Isles" which was not published until 1815 and in any event Scott was only seventeen in 1788. I have recently found a long ballad poem entitled "Bannockburn" printed in 1810 by J. Hedderwick & Co., Glasgow. Neither the name of the author nor any indication if this is the first printing is given, and I have been unable to establish the identity of the author. Apart from Burns and of course Kennedy and Picken, the only other Scottish poet known to have any contact with Wilson was Gavin Turnbull, who is mentioned in Crichton's monograph. Turnbull published his only volume, *Poetical Essays*, in Glasgow in 1788 but it contains no "Battle of Bannockburn" and there is no "From the Ocean." However, Turnbull was well known to Burns who thought rather more of him than posterity, and in a letter to George Thomson dated 29 October 1793 Burns sent him three of Turnbull's songs and said, "By the by, Turnbull has a great many songs in M.S.S. which I can command if you like his manner. Possibly as he is an old friend of mine I may be prejudiced in his favour: but I like some of his pieces very much." There is therefore the possibility, however slender, that the

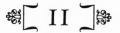

PMA, HCL (JARDINE)

To David Brodie.

Edinburgh, 13 August 1788.

Respected Sir,

I am very much ashamed to think I have used you so mean and dishonourably, after promising to leave the book; but

> O, place it not to blank regard,
> Nor disrespect insist;
> Ye ken yoursel' my hapless weird,
> The frail, the faithless chest!!

I have at length sent it to be conveyed to you from Paisley by Thomas Witherspoon. Mr. James Kennedy has his compliments to you. As for the little book, if you take the trouble to peruse it, let it be with the joint eye of a friend and a critic. I shall take it very kindly to hear your objections. I could have sent you another, but let this suffice for the present—as perhaps you have little time to spare.

> Now, tho' I did my promise break,
> An' gart you on my truth reflect;
> Believe me, sir, with true respect,
>   Though undeservin',
> While I can lift a pen or snek,
>   Your humble servin'.

ALEXANDER WILSON

_____

two poems may have been by Turnbull and there is some confirmation from Sir William Jardine, editor of the 1832 edition of *American Ornithology*, who had the benefit of biographical material from Wilson's sister Jean; he wrote, "We find him in frequent society with Gavin Turnbull, E. Picken and James Kennedy who formed part of his companions in his song of "The Group." Whoever the author was, he was not immortal and his work is long forgotten; his only immortality is this brief mention by Wilson.

⁂[III]⁂

PMA, HCL (JARDINE)

To David Brodie.

St. Andrews, Written on the last day, and last hour
of that last day, 31 December 1788.

Respected Sir,

Far distant, in an inn's third storey rear'd,
    The sheet beneath a glimmering taper spread,
Along the shadowy walls no sound is heard,
    Save Time's slow, constant, momentary tread.

Here lone I sit; and will you, sir, excuse
    My midnight theme, while (feebly as she can)
Inspiring silence bids the serious Muse
    Survey the transient bliss pursued by Man.[1]

Deluded Man, for him Spring paints the fields;
    For him, warm Summer rears the rip'ning grain;
He grasps the bounty that rich Autumn yields,
    And counts those trifles as essential gain.

For him, yes, sure, for him those mercies flow!
    Yet, why so passing, why so fleet their stay?
To teach blind mortals what they first should know,
    That all is transient as the fleeting day.

Short is the period since green smil'd the wood,
    And flowers ambrosial bath'd my morning path;
Sweet was the murmuring of the silver flood,
    And glad the bee roam'd o'er the empurpled heath!

With conscious joy, I hail'd the rosy scene;
    I join'd the music of the woodlan' throng,
Stretch'd on the hazel bank, or sunny plain,
    Where answering echo warbl'd all day long.

1. This verse is in PMA original but not in the Jardine transcript.

Delightful time! but, ah, how short its stay!
    Stript were the foliage, from each flower, each tree,
Grim tyrant Winter vail'd the joyless day,
    And roar'd imperious o'er the hail-beat lea.

Where now the fragrance of the howling wood,
    And what the pleasures we from morn can taste;
The snow-clad banks, the big brown roaring flood,
    The bleak wind whistling o'er the drifted waste.

'Tis thus, dear sir, in Life's delusive dream;
    We fondly sport till Youth's gay act is o'er,
Till Age, till Death, steal on in sullen stream,
    And worldly bubbles charm the soul no more.

Passing by a whole cart-load of Holy inferences which I had drawn
from these considerations, also overleaping the long train of admo-
nitions resulting from these inferences, let me tell you that nothing
but the hopes I have that you entertain most magnificent ideas of my
poems, (part of which I guess by your expressive silence) would
have induced me to have racked my brain at such a rate, and sitten
in such an uncomfortable situation, to give you a rhyme narration—
a hint of which uncomfortable seat you have in the following verses,
which I am obliged to give you just as they are broken off from the
cluster of a long prayer which I had inserted, but which, on account
of its enormous weight and vast extent, I omit:

But, sir, forgive the wandering of the Muse.
    To you, again, her sadd'ning strain she'll turn;
To you, to ask (and oh! remit the news)
    Why thus, with silence, all my warmth return?

It is because—but, hark!—the tempest blows
    Loud O'er my fireless dome it wildly heaves!
The wintry drop, prone from my drooping nose,
    Hangs dangling, limpid as the brain it leaves.

The frowning Muse has fled the frozen frame,
    The voice of Riot strikes my list'ning ear,

In sinking, mounting—sad, inconstant flame—
My candle's ending with the ending year.

Here you may perhaps stare up, and exclaim—"Why, what does the fellow mean? If he sat pining in that deplorable case, was it not his own fault? Was there no liquor in the house?" Aye; but my friend you don't consider that drinking is destructive to reason, and reason, in her purest state, is requisite when I write to you. And, moreover, drinking is the bane of frugality, and frugality is one of the essentials of a pedlar, and I am a pedlar; so you see no wonder I suffered patiently, when I suffered rightly. But to conclude—

Dear sir, adieu! may success, health, and peace,
Crown your each year, and every labour too;
And, sure, if virtuous worth claims human praise,
Fate yet in keeping holds a wreath for you.

Fraught with fresh blessings be this coming year;
And should some period of its fav'ring reign
Admit the pedlar joy's, he'll homeward steer,
And hail your mansion and his friend again.

I am,
Respected Sir,
Yours,
ALEXR. WILSON

IV

PMA

To David Brodie.

Edinburgh, 8 April 1789.

Dear Sir,

Presuming on the approbation you have been pleased often to honour my small performances with, I have here sent for your perusal a collection of the most noticeable that I have at present by me, requesting it as a most singular favour, that you would examine them with the severity of a discerning critic—without mercy; (or rather, in mercy) exposing what you deem improper or unharmonious, as no doubt, in spite of my studied particular care, numbers of such has escaped me. Wrong spelling, or a word or two neglected, I hope you will rectify. Such oversights are not strangers to the most carefull. As to the penmanship in which they appear, I'll say nothing about it. If you can read it, that's all I want; if not, I will join with you in calling it truly wretched. What of that! Genius often appears in rags, beauty in a hut; and why may not you disregard the garb when the author has alas! no better to give them. But I know you will.

I believe I may have as many pieces as finish the book with some themes only in view yet; and should you approve of it, I would soon curse the world with another poetical volumne; but Vanity, hence!

I have this some time fondly expected a letter from you; but have been disapointed. Involved amid the ceaseless murmur of a school, and your mind employ'd in hearing petitions, distributing learning and justice, stilling internal commotions and spreading a venerable awe over your tumultous subjects, is a task superior to thousands, and adequate to great parts. No wonder then that amid your political operations, you forget a Pedlar (removed to a distant country), despicable as the vanities he deals in. However, don't imagine I reflect on you. You know me too well for to think that; and I hope you will excuse the freedom I have taken, imputing it to that principle of impudence that every packman is essentially vested with. If after perusing the miscellany, they merit your praise, how will I exult! but as I am prepared for the worst, I shall be bold enough to read my fate in the following fable, which, as I have a little leisure at present, I relate for the sake of the striking likeness of the principal character to that of a certain pedantic genius well known to you:

> A Monkey who, in leisure hours,
> Was wondrous fond of herbs and flowers
> (For once he wore a gardener's chain,

But scap'd safe to his woods again),
Chose out a spot to show his parts.
Scratches the soil,—the flower inserts;
 Here stuck the rose,)[1]
 There placed the pink, }
With various blooms filled every chink.

Around him stole the mimic crew,
Amaz'd at the appearance new;
 The shrubs surveyed,)
 The nodding flowers;}
And, struck with wonder at his powers,
Pronounc'd him with applauding gape,
A most expert, ingenious ape—
"Knew humans what you thus inherit,
Unbounded gifts would crown your merit."
 He proudly boued,
 Aprov'd their taste,
And for the town prepares in haste.

A bee who flew from bloom to bloom
In vain, for food, thus fix'd his doom;
"What mighty fool! what senseless ass!
Has laid these gaudy nothings thus?
 Stalks placed in bloom,)
 Shrubs fix'd for fruit, }
And each without a trunk or root,
Fool that I was to ramble here,
I merit just the whole hives' sneer;
For they who patronize a fool,
Are meanest mankind's meanest tool."
He spoke, the burning noontide came,
They withring shrunk, and sunk his fame.

If such be my fate, "I'll break my reed, and never whistle mair."

I have sent you here a printed piece of a friend's, with a motto on the title page from the pen of the illustrious Alex, which I had inexpressible rapture of seeing in the *News*!!

1. These lines and their counterpart in subsequent stanzas are written as one line in Jardine and PMA.

Dear Sir, I hope you will, in a short time, remit a few lines to me by Thomas Witherspoon, or by the direction you have, as I don't know "what a day may bring forth"—some unavoidable though virtous misfortunes beginning to blacken over my head, and looking melancholy enough, yet for all that, it glads me to be your humble servant,

ALEXANDER WILSON

p.s. I have no other copy of the Essays save the one I send you having commited them to the flames. Some of the pieces are not finished for want of time, not for want of materials.

CRICHTON 1819

To David Brodie.

Edinburgh, 10 November 1789.

Dear Sir,

Among the many and dismal ingredients that embitter the cup of life, none affect the feelings or distress the spirit, so deeply as despondence. She is the daughter of disappointed hope, and the mother of gloomy despair, the source of every misery, and the channel to eternal ruin. Happy, thrice happy the man, whose breast is fortified against her insinuations, and towers above her tyranny. But, alas! what heart has not sunk beneath her melancholy frowns. To be snatched from the yawning jaws of ruin, raised on the wings of hope to the delightful fields of bliss and felicity—to have the enchanting prospect before us, or within our grasp, and in these flattering circumstances to be cruelly insulted, and unmercifully precipitated down the unfathomable gulph, is what would bring a sigh from the most insensible and hardened wretch in the universe. How much more then must it agonize that individual who trembles at the least prospect of disorder or misfortune. In every age the poet has been allowed to be possessed of finer feelings, and quicker sensations than the bulk of mankind. To him joy is rapture, and sorrow despair; the least beam of hope brightens, and the slightest shades horrify his tumultuous soul. Imagination points out the approaching storm, and anticipates that wretchedness which it thinks is impossible to be avoided. If such their state, may Heaven guard me from the wretched tribe. But what do I say? I have been hurried on by the irresistible tide of inclination until now, and at this moment I find myself enrolled among those very wretches, and a sharer of these express torments at which I start. Oh, my friend! why did you awake that spark of genius, which has now overspread my soul? Your smile called it to existence, and your approbation inspired its gathering flame. How greedily did I devour the tempting bait. Every look of applause lifted me a stage, till I gained the highest pinnacle of Hope and Expectation; and how dreadful my fall! Happy would I have been, had I scorned the offered incense of praise, and been deaf, resolutely deaf, to the bewitching accents; then had I still been buried in the dark cobweb recesses of some solitary hut, launching the murmuring shuttle, or guiding the slender thread; all my care a trifle to satisfy my landlady, and all my joy John's[1] grim-like smile; and my highest hope, a good web. Transporting thought, 'delightful period.' These were the times of joy and plenty, the reign of uninterrupted content. Were they? Ha! where is my mistaken fancy running? "The reign of content, the times of plenty." Conscience denies the lying assertion, and experience shakes her expressive head. She says no such times were they. Toil was thy abhorrence. Want hovered over thy loom, and poverty stalked with thee as thy shadow. True, my faithful guide, true is your accusation. I own I grovelled in obscurity, no hopes to inspire, nor muse to soothe my struggling

1. A well-known manufacturer in Paisley (note by Crichton).

breast, till you, my dear friend, saw the glimmering spark, blew it to a flame, and rescued the buried muse from oblivion. How often has she soothed my troubled mind, and enabled me to breathe forth my melancholy plaints, dissolved me to joy, or swelled me to rapture; and shall I blame you for this? No, my dear Sir, your name inspires her theme, and her best services shall be at your feet.

Since I left Paisley, I have met with some encouragement, but I assure you, Sir, that my occupation is greatly against my success in collecting subscribers. A *Packman* is a character which none esteem, and almost every one despises. The idea which people of all ranks entertain of them is, that they are mean-spirited, loquacious liars, cunning and illiterate, watching every opportunity, and using every low and mean art within their power to cheat. When any one applies to a genteel person, pretending to be a poet, he is treated with ridicule and contempt; and even though he should produce a specimen, it is either thrown back again, without being thought worthy of perusal, or else read with prejudice. I find also that a poet's fame is his wealth. Of this the booksellers to whom I applied with proposals have complained, saying "it was a pity I was not better known." I think therefore it will be my best scheme to collect the manuscripts in an orderly manner, and send them to some gentleman for correction. Since I saw you, I have finished several pieces in English verse, particularly a poem entitled "Lochwinnoch," in which I hope I have drawn the character of Mr. M'D. so as to please you, and perhaps himself, yet after all you cannot conceive the difficulties which at present involve,

Dear Sir,
Your humble Servant,
ALEXANDER WILSON

PRL

To Mr. James Kennedy.
Morroco's Close, Edinburgh.

Paisley, 26 January 1790.

Mr. Kennedy,

   Your letter is now before me. To say I am sorry at its contents is but a faint expression of that grief which the perusal of it has involved me in. If I have wronged you, which I own I have, and that deeply, my intentions were very honest. To collect subscribers so that I might have it in my power to recompense my first loss to you was always what I wished for. And as no scene of life was seemingly more promising for the purpose of travelling, encouraged by your offers I again attempted what I never would have followed but for the same reasons. Every week that passed I found myself sinking deeper into debt; little regarding my employment, I often confined myself writing pieces whole days, or sought the acquaintance of those who professed themselves admirers of poetry, hoping to make them my friends, and by their means have soon more in my power than barely to pay my debts. It was these considerations that hurried me to the West Country, expecting nothing from the merchant way; but, rather finding myself diminishing, I almost disregarded it, save only as the means of ensuring a quantity of subscribers sufficient to recompense my loss, so that I, here before God and my own conscience, declare that I often scarce raised as much money as bore my charges, and when I (unable longer to bear the thoughts of going about to ruin you and myself) sent back my goods, what money I had amounted to twelve shillings, and a watch. These to defend me from extreme poverty till my book would be published, I own I kept, and but for that little triffle should have experienced it in its severest rigours. Yet hard as my circumstances may be, I'll a thousand times rather bear approaching misery than hazard your friendship forever; You will therefore receive (and I would have sent them sooner had I received the letter sooner) the watch and the two bills at the date desired from me this week by the first opportunity. This is all I can do at present. I have told you the truth, and rely on your goodness only. If you are determined to punish, I submit; nor shall I ever accuse your cruelty though my ruin should be the consequence when, to your appearance it is not your friend but a villain you crush and extirpate. But if you can believe that the unfortunate writer of this letter has the strongest inclinations, but wants the power to put it in his reach to pay you, I say, if you can believe this, I beg leave to address you in another strain with which were your interest not connected I should never have presumed to mention. Know then that I, having wrote out a fair copy of the most part of my MSS. made myself as decent as possible, and after taking Mr. Neilson's advice on the letter I wrote, I sealed it and set out for Castlesemple. At my arriving to the house I sent up the letter which was immediately read, and I was desired by the footman to follow him, who introduced me to a little room crowded with piles of books, and opening another door that led to the diningroom, made a signal to Mr. M'Dowal; on his entering the footman disappeared, and he desired me to sit down, asked a great many questions, and on my pulling the MSS. out of my pocket, eagerly took them, and sitting down with the deepest attention, read them for the space of an hour and a half; and as I sat nearly behind him I could observe him more than ordinary engaged with Lochwinnoch, though twice disturbed by the Earl of Eglinton and Cassils, who came into the room seeking pictures. After reading, he asked me what education I had got, where born, and where I staid? Having told him, he said by what he had seen they seemed not amiss; bade me push prudently on and he was my friend; and sought two proposal papers from me, and said he would get me some subscriptions. Now the number of subscribers I believe amounts to about 400, and I am convinced that scarce a genteel family in town but will purchase a copy for the sake of Hab's Door, and as Neilson refuses to print Hab's Door, could you recommend it to any friends in Edin.? Neilson's refusal of Hab's Door would be occasion enough for me dropping him, and I am persuaded the book would take none the worse of being done in Edin. I have collected the greatest part of the names and MSS., and revised them greatly. I send you this, not expecting on my account, but in regard to your interest, you will please to favour me with your sentiments upon it. If you comply with the above, you will enable me to unburthen my mind, repay you every farthing, and prove myself your grateful friend.

ALEXANDER WILSON

Gabriel Watson will give you the articles.

PRL

To James Kennedy.[1]

Paisley, 6 August 1790.

Sir,

Along with this you will receive a copy of my poems, which are now happily completed. Although I am sensible that I have wronged you, and am at present totally incapable of giving you your own, yet I don't wish, Mr. Kennedy, that you should consider me as unworthy of your acquaintence, or that our friendship and correspondence should henceforth cease. From the first moment on which I found myself declining in your debt, the distant view of a publication flattered me with hopes of soon being able to reimburse the difficiency,

---

1. "Morroco's Close, Lawn Market, Edinburgh."

and but for that consideration you never should have had occasion to suspect me of dishonesty. That long-looked-for period is at length now arrived, but, alas! hath still brought its difficulties. I am possessed, indeed, of 600 neat copies, near 400 of which are subscribed for; but these are so scattered up and down through different places in Scotland that were I to take a route through them, with no other business but that of delivering the volumes, my perigrinations would be distressed by numberless disadvantages, and I at the end might be no richer than now. I therefore once more solicit your assistance with boldness and sincerity not to satisfy an inclination of travelling; not to have honour of trudging with a pack, but from hopes of becoming able to repay my creditors, make myself more known, and perhaps procuring a more independant situation for life. These are my motives, and I believe it to be in your power to enable me to accomplish these designs with interest to yourself, and with fame, honour, and happiness to me. My scheme is therefore as follows: I would wish only for a little assortment of goods. I would advertise the publication in some of the Edinburgh papers, declaring the station of the author, and of the method he was taking to dispose of his works. If this were not convenient for a newspaper it could be done in the Review. I would have a number of proposals thrown off, such as I published last; these I would leave with the different friends I became acquainted with in my travels. In the meantime I would have a genteel copy always along with me that subscribers might know what they were signing for. After taking a circuit for twenty or thirty miles I would return, pack up the number of volumes subscribed for, and proceed to the delivery of them making it my business to address every literary character I found out. This would not much hinder the sale of my goods, and perhaps in some cases assist it: and I have not a doubt but that in two months I could dispose of every copy. If these proposals are agreeable to you I shall immediately prepare myself for the business. If not, I have no other hopes to rely on, nor the prospect of anything but misfortune, poverty, and obscurity (if the inhabitant of a jail may be said to live obscure). I hope you will favour me with an immediate answer to this, and either seal the ruin or inspire the hopes of, sir, your sincere and humble servant,

ALEXANDER WILSON

P.S. I have sent you the first finished copy and shall, if health permit, be in Edinburgh on Wednesday or Thursday first, which may prevent you the trouble of writing.

 [VIII]

CRICHTON 1819

To Thomas Crichton.

Tower of Athenbathy, 20 September 1790.

Dear Friend,

It undoubtedly requires a greater degree of fortitude, and a firmer constitution for a feeling mind to struggle with adversity, than is often their lot. Under the pressure of virtuous misfortunes, thousands pine in secret till disease settles on their frame, and consumes the little of life they have left, while others are unhappy only in the eyes of the world. Blessed with hearts unsusceptible of feeling the past, or fearing the future, they only endure the present sufferings, which hope dissipates with endearing smiles and ceaseless promises. A sensibility under misfortune gives every new distress innumerable stings, but when once hope takes her residence in the heart, their numbers diminish, their terrors disappear, and, though under real suffering for the present, we forget them in the anticipation of future scenes of approaching happiness.

Such, my dear Sir, are the thoughts that for ever revolve through my breast—such the melancholy reflections of one lost to every beam of hope, and such, amid the most dismal, the most complicated horrors of distress. Driven by poverty and disease to the solitudes of retirement, at the same period when the flush of youth, the thirst of fame, the expected applause of the world, and the charms of ambition, welcomed him to the field. Had I but one hope more left of enjoying life and health, methinks I could cheerfully suffer the miseries that now surround me; but, alas, I feel my body decay daily, my spirits and strength continually decrease, and something within tells me that dissolution, dreadful dissolution, is not far distant. No heart can conceive the terrors of those who tremble under the apprehension of death. This increases their love of life, and every new advance of the king of terrors overwhelms them with despair. How hard, how difficult, how happy to prepare for eternity; and yet how dreadful to live or to die unprepared. Oh! that I were enabled to make it my study to interest myself in his favour, who has the keys of Hell and of Death. Then all the vanities of life would appear what they really are, and the shades of death would brighten up a glorious path to everlasting mansions of felicity.

My dear Sir, you will no doubt be surprised to hear me talk in this manner, but are not you more surprised that you found me so long a stranger to these things? They are the sincere effusions of my soul, and I hope that through the divine aid they shall be my future delight, whether health shall again return, or death has lifted the commissioned dart.

My health is in a very declining state. The surgeon believes my disease to be an inflammation of the lungs. I intend to stay some time longer in the country, and to hear from you would be acceptable to the unfortunate.

ALEXANDER WILSON

P.S. Excuse this shift for want of paper, and direct to me, care of William Ewing, Innkeeper, Lochwinnoch, who will get your letter conveyed to me, or write by the bearer, who returns to-morrow.

CRICHTON 1819

To Thomas Crichton.

Haddington, 2 November 1790.

Dear Friend,

I have no doubt, but by this time, you are anxious to hear what has become of me; and as I am at present disengaged, and have experienced much of your sympathy, I shall not think my time altogether lost to inform you of my situation—not that I can cheerfully assure you that all my miseries are sunk in oblivion, and all my sorrows vanished like a vision. No, alas! that happy period, that long-looked-for time has not yet arrived, but my miseries seem lengthening with life. I look upon myself as a traveller who, fond of variety, has left the beaten track to explore the recesses of some wood, whose tempting borders had drawn him from his way. Eager to contemplate the surrounding scenes, and captivated by the gaudy flowers that everywhere bend beneath his feet, he wanders on, forgetful of his journey, hunts through every new thicket, rushes through the thickening shade, till at length he finds himself involved amid a labyrinth of perplexing branches, and harassing brambles. Forward, ten thousand distresses present themselves, and backward, he is unable to trace the path. Night approaches, the tempest roars among the trees, and the relentless savages of the forest howl around the distressed wretch, who now too late sees his folly, and reflects with a tear on those happy times when he cheerfully pursued his journey.

In this poetical wood, I am at this moment lost. There, the brambles and briars of poverty harass, and there is heard the growl of creditors. O that I could roll back the tide of time, and place myself in the same circumstances I was a few years ago. Then all the charms of Fame, the insinuations of ambition, the applause, renown, and

admiration of the world, would in vain display their united glories
to tempt me to one line of verse. But you will perhaps say, Why do
you not adopt this laudable design, and put it in immediate practice?
Alas! Sir, I fear I cannot, and this alone makes me to tremble. From
repeated experience, I can here solemnly declare, that I have found
poetry, however pleasing and delightful for the present moment, to
be productive of nameless miseries, and in reality the source of all
my sorrows. It has consumed much of my fleeting time, that might
have been employed to unspeakably better purposes in actions and
necessary designs, that would have secured me the esteem of my
friends, and conveyed pleasure in the reflection. By diverting my
mind from the essential interests of life, it has plunged me into the
depths of poverty, there solitary to languish, pained by the bitter
reflection of being my own destroyer. In a word, it has sunk me in
sickness, in debt, in disappointment, and in all the gloom of despondence; has embittered the comforts of life, and veiled from my view
all the hopes of religion. And shall I still attend its dictates? Shall I
nourish this deluding, this murdering enchantress, in my bosom?
No, Heaven forbid. The smiles, the promises of Hope, shall never
again deceive me, since all these once-expected laurels of fame and
honour, and the treasures of wealth, are as distant from my view as
ever. Let me, therefore, learn to despise them all; for what are all
their glories but shadows, bubbles, and poisonous potions that cor-
rupt the heart, disorder the judgment, and continually blast, and for
ever banish that inestimable and best of blessings, *peace of mind.*
But where am I going? I sat down to give you an account of my
present situation, but have distressed you with a melancholy detail
of my past misfortunes. Pardon the digression, my dear friend, and
consider that it is to the friend alone, that the burthened heart ven-
tures to pour forth its sorrows. You know the little success I received in Paisley made me to tremble to think in what manner I
should reveal my unfortunate circumstances to Mr. N[eilson]. To
leave the place without making an apology for the past, or explana-

tion of the method I intended to follow for the future, would, I considered, justly expose me to his displeasure and suspicion, and also be highly ungrateful in return for all that kindness he had all along shown me. I therefore went and explained matters as they stood, with the deepest regret for being unable to give him any money arising from the few copies I had sold. His goodness I shall never forget. He freely excused me on account of the circumstances in which I had been placed; but recommended it to me to be industrious in getting the rest disposed of, and that from whatever place I sent for copies, he would remit them. This was kind, exceeding kind, but alas! where was I to dispose of them? However, necessity urging, I gave my landlord one guinea, and an account, which I hope, by this time, has produced him another; and taking leave of all my friends, departed from the confines of that town where, in the short place of seven months, I had experienced all the combined horrors of sickness, poverty, and despondence. In two days I arrived at Edinburgh, and immediately paid Mr. —— a visit. Unwilling to be looked upon as a burthensome guest, I hired a small room in the other end of the town, and five or six times a-day (by desire) attended this elevated gentleman's Levee. To give you a particular account of the distant and strange reception I met with from this quarter, would be unnecessary. After staying two weeks, Mr. —— all on a sudden told me that he meant to take a jaunt through part of Scotland with goods, and invited me to assist him. To this I immediately consented, in expectation of selling my books. We have already been in Dalkeith, Musselburgh, Prestonpans, and are come to this place, and although I have used every scheme I could invent, none seem to regard the author or to encourage his performance. How long I will continue in this state is uncertain. When at leisure write me, and you shall not fail in return to hear from the most unfortunate of poets, pedlars, and men, who, notwithstanding, is with the most sincere esteem,

Your affectionate Friend, while
ALEXANDER WILSON

MCZ

To Mr. William Mitchell.
Williamsburgh, Near Paisley.

Haddington, 21 November 1790.

Dear Comrade,

I now with much pleasure sit down to let you hear from me—Indeed I have but little fortunate intelligence to communicate, yet I know by experience that the relating of our misfortunes to a friend, lightens the load of misery, and conveys a secret tranquility to the Relator. But think not that I mean by my uncomfortable epistles to involve you in perpetual melancholy. To a heart so susceptible of others woes as yours is it were the most extreme cruelty to harrass your feelings with distressing narratives—No! Let us sport beneath the little sunshine we enjoy.

"Hopefull that the storm Tho' hung in blackest frowns may soon disperse or Roll unbroken O'er our peaceful heads."

By a letter which I received yesterday from our friend Clark, I have the agreeable news that your pupils are increasing. This is no more than I have long since expected. Your merits in the musical way have long been my secret pride and public boast and I now rejoice to think that they will yet shine forth in their genuine splendour to the eye of the world. I have sent you here for your amusement what was wrote merely for my own. Viz—A simple tho' real Narrative of my reception in the East. I wrote Thomas Wotherspoon[1] last week but have as yet been favoured with no answer—It

---

1. Wilson usually spelled his friend's name Witherspoon, if not consistently so after the date of the Wotherspoon spelling above. The name given when he was cited as a witness in the "Hollander" case was Thomas Witherspoon. The latter spelling gradually fell out of favor and now there is not a single Witherspoon in the Glasgow/Paisley telephone directory, while there are about one hundred Wotherspoons.

is uncertain how long I may continue in this way. Several circumstances occur to make me dislike it and my Poetical expectations are
all disappointed. I hope to be in Edinburgh about the middle of next
month, and I may surely expect to hear from you there—nothing
will be more welcome, and by directing to the care of J. Kennedy
back of the fountain well, Edinburgh I will safely receive it. I have
just one thing more to observe, which in case we should never meet,
I earnestly entreat you to remember. Depend little upon the encouragement of the World, which, let Merit be ever so worthy, seldom
rewards it till its possessor is *no more*. And rather practice your
favourite study as an Amusement, than rely on it as the means of
subsistence, by which precious maxim you will be more independent
—preserve that invaluable blessing *Peace of Mind* and escape the
solitary state of him who shall ever remain.

Your true friend
A. WILSON

P.S. Present my kind respects to your Brother James. Was he and
two or three more to bid adieu to Paisley, I should consider my
solitary native [place] like a body without its soul, nor even express
one wish to visit the deserted and unfriendly Town. Remember me
to John Mathers, I will shortly acknowledge the receipt of his jocose
letter.

XI

PMA, HCL (JARDINE)

To David Brodie.

Paisley, 5 January 1791.

Sir,

Were you to see the situation in which I am while writing this
letter, I can't for my life say whether mirth or sorrow would be
most predominant in your mind; whether a burst of uncommon

laughter would convulse your nerves, or the tear of pity steal from your cheek. All the stories you have read of garrets, tatters, unmerciful duns, lank hunger, and poetical misery, are all sadly realised in me. The neglect of an unrewarding world has blasted all those airy hopes that once smiled so promisingly, and I find the decree of my fate running thus—Renounce poetry and all its distracting notions, descend to the labourer's vale of life, there attend the dictates of prudence, and *toil or starve.* The enclosed narrative I send you for your amusement, as a small return for the kindness you have often showed

Your humble Servant,
A. WILSON

GROSART

To Alexander Wilson, Sr.

Williamsburgh, 25 January 1791.

Dear Father,

I am very sorry that the uncommon coarseness of the weather, and a perplexity of affairs, has entirely prevented me from coming out to see you. I was determined, Sunday was a week, to have paid you a visit, but was taken badly, and scarcely able to move for four days, by running, one stormy night, from Paisley to Glasgow and home again, without intermission, on a particular affair. I was much concerned, on coming from the east country, to hear of little Peggy's misfortune. I have spoken to several persons who have experienced the like disorder, and have been perfectly recovered by the simple means of a cold bath, rubbing, and exercise. I would sincerely advise you to disregard the foolish prescriptions that every old wife is ready enough, on occasions of this kind, to recommend. The simplest remedies are always the most successful, and, considering her age, I have great hope of her recovery. When in Paisley, I shall speak to Dr. Cleland, with whom I am acquainted, and what in that case he prescribes or advises shall cost you nothing. I am happy to hear that you are both in health yourselves. When blest with this invaluable treasure every enjoyment has a sweeter relish, and the ills of life are more easily supported, but deprived of health, the greatest dainties disgust, and the slightest misfortunes sink us in despondency. As soon as the weather will permit, I hope to see you, but as I am not yet quite strong, I am unwilling to venture out amid such weather. However, I wish you the comfort of the season, a prosperous new year, and more happiness than at present seems to attend you. This is the sincere wish of

Your affectionate Son,
A. WILSON

NLS, HCL (JARDINE)

To David Brodie.

Paisley, 7 [?] 1791.

Sir,

As Alexr. Wilson has some new scheme in view you will please send in any letters of importance or value you may have received from him at any past period which will in a few days be thankfully and carefully returned.

I remain
Yours sincerely[1]
A. WILSON

Give these to the carrier as he passes, or if you be coming in yourself, be yourself the carrier.

1. NLS says written for Wilson—not in his hand.

PRL

To James Kennedy.[1]

Paisley, 16 March 1791.

Mr. James Kennedy, Sir,

Thanks for the information you were kind enough to communicate me, which, however, I could wish to have received sooner, your letter and translation having only reached me about ten minutes ago. I shall, though with some reluctance, venture a few lines on the question and remit them by the carrier. Not through any foolish hope of being successful, or of inviting contempt but rather through a consciousness of the truth of what I have often heard you declare, viz. that—"In great attempts 'tis glorious even to fail."

With much esteem, I remain, sir, your obliged servant.

A. WILSON

PMA, HCL (JARDINE)

To David Brodie.

Edinburgh, 23 November 1792.

Dear Sir,

As a few leisure moments, at present, are at my disposal, I willingly devote them to your service. And as anything that relates to those we esteem never fails to interest, I hope, on receival of this, you will oblige me in your turn. I left Paisley on Thursday's night,

---

1. "Back of the Fountain Well, Edinburgh."

slept in Glasgow, and next morning travelled to Falkirk, where I was kindly received by Picken, who presented me to his wife, a *decent enough woman*, and prevailed on me to stay with him till Monday. I was agreeably informed that he had engaged to go to Carron (about a mile distant), there to enjoy a yearly salary of £50, for the trouble of teaching the English, French, and Latin Languages, Writing, and Arithmetic. For this purpose, they have built him a little genteel kitchen, with a parlour and two bedrooms, or closets, greatly enlarged the schoolhouse, and promise to do their utmost for him. I have not a doubt but Picken may please them. He has so much of the tongue, and such a quantity of the pedant in him, that what little abilities he possesses, will appear to the vulgar ten times greater than what they really are. It was fortunate this place started, as he told me he was in danger of starving in Falkirk. He was to remove Monday was eight days. From Falkirk, I went to Callander —a town on the border of the Highlands, about 28 miles distant. I was half resolved to stay here, and study Arithmetic; and for this end, sent for the town-schoolmaster. (I should have informed you that there is a large Academy here under the inspection of Mr. Robertson, the minister, and patronised by Drummond of Perth.) Well, he came, and I told him my intention. "Very well," says he, "you can come whenever it is agreeable." I had a little money with me, and I foolishly believed it would serve me till I should make considerable proficiency in arithmetic. I accordingly went, purchased a slate, and set seriously about it. Two days elapsed, I persevered; but the *third* I gave it up. I began to consider the *costs*, which would soon have consumed my little all; so paid my lodgings, and decamped. I reached Stirling about 7 at night, and went forward to St. Ninians, a mile farther where I lodged all night. I set out for Edinr. next morning, where I arrived about twilight.

There are two teachers in the school at Callander, one teaches Latin and French, the other English, Writing, and Arithmetic. As for the first, I am not a proper judge of his merits, further than that he seemed totally devoid of all sentiments of humanity in correcting. The latter surprised me very much, and must undoubtedly be a genius, as he teaches a language he has not yet learned to speak (being a highlander), and writes about as well as your humble servant did in our Gordon-lonian cell. Upon the whole, I found them a couple of morose, unsociable highland pedants, sullen, because they had nothing to say, and reserved, because they were afraid of exposing their mighty ignorance. Indeed, it is all one to the minister what sort of men they may be, as the longer their pupils are in finishing their learning, the longer they are his boarders, 13 or 14 of them at least, and this consideration, without doubt, makes the reverend rogue wink at their shallowness.

At Edinr., I passed several days without having [MS. torn and mutilated] enough to determine on anything. At length the [MS. mutilated] of my last half-crown roused me from my lethargy, and I am now earning more in a sphere which you shall be made acquainted with hereafter. The only thing left for me to tell you is that on Thursday last I went to the Pantheon, resolved to deliver my sentiments on the night's debate. The house was uncommonly crowded. In the course of debating, a long and languid pause occurred. I seized the wished-for opportunity; and with a melancholy phiz, delivered the enclosed speech, and was crowned with the most *unbounded applause.*

I am,

Dear Sir

Yours sincerely,

A. WILSON

P.S. Direct to the care of Mr. James Kennedy, manufacturer, at the High School, Cannongate, Edinburgh.

 XVI

PMA

To David Brodie.[1]

Paisley Jail, 21 May 1793.

Dear Sir,

When I last wrote you, nothing but absolute necessity would have prevailed on me to make the requisition I then did, and sorry I was that *that* necessity should ever had cause to exist. I sincerely thank you, sir, for the token of friendship you sent me, which I will repay as soon as Providence shall open the door for my release from this new scene of misery, this assemblage of wretches and wretchedness. Where the rumbling of bolts, the hoarse exclamations of the jailor, the sighs and sallow countenances of the prisoners, and the general gloom of the place require all the exertions of resolution to be chearful and resigned to the will of fate, particularly those who have no prospect or expectation of liberty. Being perfectly unable to pay the sum awarded against me, which is *in toto* £12 13s. 6d., I yesterday gave oath accordingly, and had the comfort to be told that Mr. Sharp was *resolved* to punish me though it should cost him a little money. However, I shall know after a little more confinement of two days or so. Meantime, to have a line or two from you would be an additional favour to,

Dear Sir,
Your obliged servt.
A. WILSON

1. "At Mr. Campbell's Mill, Johnstone."

❧⟦ XVII ⟧❧

HCL (JARDINE), GROSART

To his Father and Mother.

Philadelphia, United States, 25 July 1794.

Dear Father and Mother,

You will see by this that I am at length landed in America, as is also my nephew, William Duncan—both in good health. We sailed in the ship "Swift," from Belfast Loch, on Friday the 23d of May, about six in the morning, at which time I would have wrote you; but, hoping we would have a speedy passage, and feeling for the anxiety I feared you might be under in knowing we were at sea, I purposely omitted writing till our arrival in America. I fear that by this conduct I have given you more unhappiness than I am aware of; if I have, you will forgive me, for I intended otherwise. We had 350 passengers—a mixed multitude, men, women, and children. Each berth between decks was made to hold [them all],[1] with scarce a foot for each. At first sight I own, it appeared to me almost impossible that the one half of them could survive; but, looking around, and seeing some whom I thought not much stouter [than myself], I thought I might have a chance as well as the rest of them. I asked Willie if he was willing, and he saying that he was, we went to Belfast immediately for our clothes; and in two days after we got on board, she sailed. We were very sick four days, but soon recovered; and having a good, steady, favouring breeze for near a fortnight, had hopes of making an excellent passage. On the third day, and just as we lost sight of land, we spoke the Caledonia of Greenock, a letter of marque, bound for the Bay of Fundy; and on the Monday follow-

---

1. The words set off in brackets in this letter are omitted in the Jardine transcript.

Drawn from Nature by A. Wilson. 1. Cardinal Grosbeak. 2. Female & egg. 3. Red Tanager. 4. Female & egg. Engraved by A. Lawson.

Plate 11 from Alexander Wilson, *American Ornithology* (Volume II)

ing, Dr. Reynolds, who was tried and condemned by the Irish House of Lords, was discovered to be on board, and treated all the passengers and crew with rum-grog, which was drank to the confusion of despots, and the prosperity of liberty all over the world. Till the 17th of June we had pretty good weather, and only buried an old woman and two children. On the 18th, we fell in with an amazing number of ice islands; I counted at one time thirty-four in sight, some of whom that we nearly passed were more than twice as high as our main-top gallant mast-head, and of great extent; we continued passing among them, with a good breeze, for two days, during which time we ran at least five knots an hour. On the 20th we had a storm of wind and rain, thunder, and lightning, beyond anything I had ever witnessed. Next day a seaman dropped overboard; and, though he swam well and made for the ship, yet the sea running high, and his clothes getting wet he perished within six yards of a hen-coop, which we had thrown over for him. On the 11th July we could plainly perceive land from the mast-head; but a terrible gale of wind blowing all night from the shore, it was Sunday before we had again the satisfaction of seeing it, scarcely perceptible through the fog; but a pilot coming on board, and the sun rising, we found ourselves within the Capes of the Delaware—the shore on each having the appearance of being quite flat, and one perpetual forest of trees. About seven at night, having had a good breeze all day, we cast anchor at a place called Reedy Island, where [one of] the cabin passengers, and the first man who leapt ashore from the long-boat, was drowned on his return to the ship. We arrived at Newcastle next day about mid-day, where we were all as happy as mortals could be; and being told that Wilmington was only five miles up the river, we set out on foot through a flat woody country, that looked in every respect like a new world to us, from the great profusion of fine fruit that everywhere overhung our heads, the strange birds, shrubs, &c., and came at length to Wilmington, which is on the side of a hill, about a mile from the Delaware, and [may be]

about as large as Renfrew, or perhaps larger. We could hear of no
employment here in our business, though I saw two silk looms
going, and some jennies preparing for establishing some little manufactory of cotton cloth; but they proceed with so little spirit that I
believe it may be some years before half a dozen looms can be employed. From Wilmington we proceeded to Philadelphia, twenty-
nine miles distant, where very little of the ground is cleared; the
only houses we saw were made of large logs of wood, laid one over
another; and what crops we could see, consisted of Indian corn,
potatoes, and some excellent oats. We made free to go into a good
many farm-houses on the road, but saw none of that kindness and
hospitality so often told of them. We met with three weavers by the
way, who live very quiet, and well enough, but had no place for any
of us. At length we came in sight of Philadelphia, which lies something like Glasgow, but on a much flatter piece of ground, extending in breadth along the Delaware for near three miles. Here we
made a more vigorous search than ever for weavers, and found, to
our astonishment, that, though the city contains from forty to fifty
thousand people, there is not twenty weavers among the whole, and
these had no conveniences for journeymen, nor seemed to wish for
any: so after we had spent every farthing we had, and saw no hopes
of anything being done that way, we took the first offer of employment we could find, and have continued so since.

  The weather here is so extremely hot, that [even though] writing in an open room, and dressed—according [to the custom]—in
nothing but thin trousers and waistcoat, and though it is near eleven
at night, I am [wet with] sweat. Judge, then, what it must be at
[noon, with all] kinds of tradesmen that come to this country: none
[with less] encouragement than weavers; and those of that trade
would do so well to consider first how they would agree with the
spade or wheelbarrow under the almost intolerable [heat of] a
scorching sun. I fear many of them never think of this. Necessities of
life are here very high, owing to the vast number of emigrants from

St. Domingo and France. Flour, though you will scarce believe it, is near double the price to what it is in Scotland; beef, ninepence of their currency, which is about sixpence of ours; shoes, two dollars; and boarding in the most moderate houses, two dollars and a-half; while house-rents are most exorbitantly high. I was told yesterday, by a person who had come immediately from Washington, that that city does not contain above two dozen of houses, and if it come not faster on than they have done, it won't contain one thousand inhabitants these twenty years. As we passed through the woods on our way to Philadelphia, I did not observe one bird such as those in Scotland, but all much richer in colour. We saw great numbers of squirrels, snakes about a yard long, and some red birds, several of which I shot for curiosity.

Let John Findlayson know that I dined with his brother-in-law, James Robertson, and spent three hours in the woods with him in his own house. I was sorry there were some things I could not inform him of, but he will hear from himself soon. He lives in a very agreeable place, not far from where I was directed to seek him; keeps a cow, and has a decent family of children, the oldest girl may be about thirteen or more. He is very fond that one of us should come and work with him, as he has three looms and only one hand beside himself, and I believe Willie will go there next week. I offer my best wishes to Thomas Wotherspoon and wife, and would write to him, but the ship sails early to-morrow. I have wrote to both my brothers-in-law, and I hope you will write me as soon as possible. I am uneasy to hear if you are both well, or if you have lately heard any word from Robert, as it is reported here that Howe and the French fleet have had an engagement. I am sorry I have so little room. I beg once more you will write to me soon, and direct to the care of Mr. William Young, Bookseller, Chestnut Street, Philadelphia. And wishing you both as much happiness as this world can afford,

I remain, your affectionate Son,

ALEXANDER WILSON

[To a Paisley friend sometime after July 1794, probably 1795.]

But let no man who is stout and healthy, and has a mind to come to this country, be discouraged. If he is a weaver, and can't get employment at his own business, there are a thousand other offers, where he will save at least as much as he can in Scotland and live ten times better. Where I am at present, which is eleven miles to the north-east of Philadelphia, nobody could wish for a more agreeable spot. Fruit of almost every kind, peaches, apples, walnuts, wild grapes, I can pull at pleasure, by only walking a short stone's throw from the house, and these not enclosed by high walls, and guarded by steel-traps and mastiffs.

[To a Paisley friend.]   *[1796]*

Assure all my friends this is a good country. The transplanting a tree or flower checks its growth for a little, but let them persevere, and they will finally prosper, be independent, and wealthy, and happy, if they will. When I look round me here on the abundance which every one enjoys, when I see them sit down to a table loaded with roasted, boiled, fruits of different kinds, and plenty of good cyder, and this only the common fare of the common people, I think on my poor countrymen, and cannot refrain feeling sorrowful at the contrast.

[XX]

EUL

To Alexander Wilson, Sr.

Milestown, Bristol Township, Philadelphia County,
22 August 1798.

Dear Father,

If I were to judge of my friends in Scotland by their cold silence to all my letters these two years, I might perhaps wrong them, but I will be more generous with them, and conclude that they have all wrote me ten or twelve times a-piece, and all miscarried; so now we are on good terms again, and I shall write this with as real good will to their amusement as if I had received them all. This is the most unwholesome and sultry season in this western woody world. For two Months the heat has been intense, the Thermometer at noon in the shade always above 90, sometimes 96, and at one time 101, which is three degrees above blood-heat. The consequence has been that the Yellow Fever—that American pestilence—has broke out in Philada. with great mortality, and the inhabitants are flying to the country in all directions.

But a still worse scourge is likely to fall on us soon—that monstrous mother of almost every human evil—*War*. The French Directory, by their dishonourable conduct towards us, have utterly lost the esteem and good wishes of the Americans, and have, by their threatenings, raised such a spirit of union and military ardor among all our Citizens, and such a contempt for the French rulers, that nothing but their return to the principles of justice and true liberty, and restoration of our plundered property, will ever do away. Ships of war are building in every seaport, and every merchant vessel is armed. We can raise in two days an army of two Hundred Thousand foot and cavalry, and our internal resources of provisions, arms, & ammunition are inexhaustible. Yet I sincerely deplore the coming calamity. Gainers or losers, the effects of War are ruinous. It corrupts the morals of youth, and disseminates every species of vice over the Countries wherever it goes. But indeed it is needless to spend the little time we have in thinking on the badness of the times, for I am persuaded while the world remains there will be Tyrants and Freemen, Reformers and Revolutionists, peace and war, till the end of time; and he is only the wise and happy man who, in following a peaceful employment through private Life, intermeddles with politics as little as possible. Provisions have fallen greatly here within these twelve months, so have the wages of labour. Our crops of wheat almost universally failed, owing to the Hessian Fly, and in many places the Buck-wheat and clover have been stripped and eat up by the Grasshoppers; a circumstance never remembered to have happened, and looked on by the country people as an omen of some great calamity. I hope, however, that the greatest will be in the loss of the grain. I walked through a field last Evening, where at every step they rose in thousands.

The Family where I have boarded in nearly these three years, and two-thirds of the inhabitants, are Germans; a hardy, sober, industrious, and penurious race of people, lovers of money, and haters of Irishmen. The very sound of an Irishman's voice will make a Dutchman draw down his eyebrows, gather up his pockets, and shrink into himself like a tortoise. Their religion is a mixture of Presbyterian, Universalism, and Catholic; very ignorant of Books, and very superstitious; firm believers in astrology and necromancy. Many of them will neither kill a steer, let blood, cut hair, or draw a tooth, but in a particular time of the moon. All their cures are performed by Charms and Spells, and the greatest confidence is placed on the most ridiculous forms, words, and gibberish. I thought that the highlands of Scotland might challenge any place on earth for Witches, Ghosts, and supernatural agency, but those of our Neighbourhood are ten times more knowing, more numerous, and more obliging.

Before I could converse with them in their own language, or read their Books, I could not have believed them or any people so credulous, but I have read in some of their books such stuff as would make the gravest philosopher on earth laugh at their notions. However, they are sober and very punctual in their payments, and have of late begun to be very careful in educating their Children in the English language, and I have always experienced much kindness and esteem from them.

I should be happy, Dear Parents, to hear from you, and how my Brother and Sisters are. I hope David will be a good lad, and take his Father's advice in every difficulty. If he does, I can tell him he will never repent it. If he does not, he may regret it bitterly with tears. This is the advice of a Brother with whom he has not yet had time to be much acquainted, but who loves him sincerely. I should wish also that he would endeavour to improve himself in some usefull parts of learning, to read Books of Information and Taste, without which a man in any Country is but a Clodpole; but beyond every thing else, let him indulge the deepest gratitude to God, and affectionate respect for his Parents. I have thought it my duty, David, to recommend these amiable virtues to you, because I am your Brother, and very probably may never see you. In the experience I have had among Mankind, I can assure you that such Conduct will secure you many friends, and support you under your *misfortunes*; for if you live you must meet with them—they are the lot of Life.

Billy and Isabel were both well four days ago; he is mowing, and Isabel has gone to the Country with Mr. Dobson's family, till the sickness be over.

I have observed that William Duncan has a strong desire to come to America, and I don't wonder at it, while so many of his children are here. Were I persuaded that my Sister and him could reconcile their minds to be for ever removed from their Native Country, placed in a Country where the language, customs, and employment were totally different, where a labourer who works under a broiling sun will perspire at the rate of pints an hour; I have seen Billy myself, while a-mowing, take off his shirt and wring it every two Hours, I say where the language, the customs, and every thing that they had been so long accustomed to think right, would be laughed at, and they themselves looked on as unknown, and perhaps suspected Strangers. If they can reconcile themselves to these things, the great expense, and the uncertainty of the Climate agreeing with their Constitutions (for it has been, I fear, fatal to mine), I shall not advise them against it. I hope that they will not look upon this as unkind in me. Whatever others may think, I have spoken my opinion most openly, and beg they will think on it. There is no employment that would suit him here so well as weaving, and having a cow for his family, or land sufficient to raise his bread, 30 or 40 miles from Philada. and if he and my sister are resolved to attempt it, I doubt not but with health the boys and him might do very well. He, as well as my sister, will find two great assistants in their Son and Daughter, and nothing will be more rejoicing to me than to see them once more, and to give them all the assistance in my power.

Dear Parents, I request once more that you will write me by the earliest opportunity, that you will tell my old comrade, Thomas Witherspoon, that I should be most happy to hear from him and Jean; and remember me to William Duncan and John Bell and to Mall and Jean—to William M'Gavin and John Wright, my old bedfellow (I hear he has got a better one now)—to John M'Arthur, to whom I have frequently wrote, without one line in return since Sept., '96—to William Greenlees and Effy—most heartily to John Black and James Frazer; James minds me of one of the Priests—he is continually preaching up the glories of this New world to his neighbours, and sending them a-packing like so many pilgrims, but you'll never catch James on that Journey himself. When did you hear from Robert Urie and Bell? I have heard nothing of either of the two since the action of the 1st June, '96. James Robb is well. Mr. Orr, of King Street, Writing Master, is well. I never could get the least intimation of the Gentleman Mr. M'Gavin enquires for. I have not heard from James or William Mitchell these ten months. James Robertson and family are all well.

I refer you for our political Intelligence to your own newspapers. I am sorry to see such anarchy and bloodshed in Ireland. From Scotland I hear nothing. I have not seen it mentioned in the papers since the affair of Tranent. Every fresh piece of news from England is published here the moment it arrives, and flies from town to town with the rapidity of lightning; we have sometimes news here in five weeks, and often in six from England, but all Correspondence with France is suspended. Our Frigates and Sloops of War are at present out cruising in search of French privateers, but I have not heard of any prizes they have made except one. Our President, John Adams, is very popular at present. Washington has accepted the Commission of Commander in Chief, and they talk of him with enthusiasm as equal to any army of 100,000! This has always been the way of the people in all Countries, and of those whom they have idolized, angels or Devils—the Saviours of their country or Arch-traitor. Who would pass one anxious thought for the possession of such precarious popularity? I don't believe that Washington is one jot happier than I am, or than any poor man may be if he pleases.

In speaking of our Crops I forgot to mention that our Rye was good, our Indian Corn promises to be remarkable good and there never was a better show of Fruit. The Cyder presses are at work in all Quarters. There is a great emulation among our Farmers to improve the breed of Horses. One Man in the Neighbourhood, a Tavernkeeper, imported 3 Stallions this Spring from England. There is a small breed of Horses brought from Canada, I don't know if any of them have ever been in Scotland but they are the stoutest to the [indecipherable] of any. They are remarkably thick and short-necked and much esteemed among the Waggoners. There is also an immense quantity of Clover raised in Pennsylvania, formerly the Farmers confined themselves to the Meadows but since the use of

Plaister of Paris became general they have found their interest in sowing Clover for nothing tends more to enrich their Lands.

I must now bid you farewell, as my paper is almost done. May providence continue to bless you with Health, Peace, and Content, and when the Tragic-Comic scene of Life is over, may all meet in regions of Bliss and Immortality.

I am, till Death,

Dear Father,

Your truly affectionate son,

ALEXR. WILSON

GROSART

To Alexander Wilson, Sr.

November 1798.

I have in my former letters given so many particulars respecting this country that I think anything more on the subject would be superfluous. "Come and see" is now my motto.

It is probable that peace may still be preserved here yet. The French Directory have made professions to that purpose to us, and it is neither the interest nor inclination of Americans to declare offensive war against any nation. There is universal peace along our whole frontiers with the Indian tribes, and the Cherokees have lately, for certain considerations, ceded to the United States upwards of 800,000 acres of land. This country, notwithstanding the ravages of the French and yellow fever, is rapidly advancing in power, population, and prosperity. Our boundary is continually extending towards the West, and may yet, after some ages, include those vast unexplored regions that lie between us and the Western

Ocean. Men of all nations, and all persuasions and professions find here an asylum from the narrow-hearted illiberal persecutions of their own Governments, and bring with them [indecipherable] respective countries. So that it is not impossible that when Great Britain and the former enlightened countries of Greece [and Rome] will have degenerated into [their] ancient barbarism and ignorance, this will be the theatre of arts and science; the most populous and powerful empire in the world. My kind wishes, dear father, once more for your welfare and happiness, and that of your family and all enquiring friends; farewell.

ALEXANDER WILSON

November 20th—Since writing the within, this unfortunate city has been dreadfully afflicted. 4000 inhabitants have fallen victims to the yellow fever. The population of Philadelphia is calculated at 65,000 souls, and five weeks ago there were not more than 8000 in the city. You might stand half-an-hour at the most public square at mid-day, without seeing or hearing a human being, except the drivers of the death-carts; but, thank God, health is again restored, and the city looks as gay and as busy as ever. Isabel and William are both in good health, as well as myself. William and I have these two years been planning out the purchase of a piece of land in some healthy and fertile part of the country, convenient to a market for the disposal of produce. In the State of New York there is a tract of perhaps the richest land in the United States, situated about 270 miles to the north, or north and by west of Philadelphia, lying between the Senica and Cayuga Lakes, about 40 miles long and 6 to [indecipherable], and beginning to be well settled. After consulting together, about two months ago, William set out on foot to see the country and learn further particulars. He travelled it in eight days, and remained there nearly a week. The soil is rich beyond any land he had ever seen, and the situation exceeding healthy; and for game of all sorts remarkable, both of deer, bear, turkeys, and water-fowl in incredible numbers. The best of the land can be purchased for 5 dollars an acre, [*indecipherable*] advantage [*indecipherable*] probably in a few years be flourishing settlements. We have, therefore, come to the determination of purchasing 150 acres on the borders of Senica Lake, and removing there in the Spring; where, in a few years, if health still continue, we shall make the woods give place to fields of pasture and plenty, and see our little stock improving and multiplying around us, far from the noise and tumults of the world. Can there be a more independent life than this? Every individual that has gone there has prospered and nothing is wanting on our part to do so likewise, but perseverance. Had John Bell not been irresolute, he might have [joined] us, and even yet it is not too late; but if he is still doubtful or afraid I shall advise him no more.

 XXII

GROSART, NLS

To Mr. Charles Orr.[1]

April [May?] 1799.

Dear Sir,

   Will you please to call at Mr. Biggs, Mathematical Instrument maker, No. 81 Front street, & employ him to make me a Stile of Brass ⅛ of an inch thick, exactly corresponding with the enclosed Pattern. I suppose he may be able to finish it before Mr. Kulp leaves

---

   1. Grosart gave the addressee of letter XXII as Charles Orr, but the original in the NLS, which is frayed and incomplete, gives no such indication and Grosart's attributed date of April 1799 is probably incorrect since Wilson refers to a letter from his nephew, dated 28 April, who was then at Ovid, Cayuga County, some 270 miles away. Letter XXI tells of William Duncan taking 8 days to make the journey on foot. Letter XXIII to Charles Orr, dated 25 May 1799, suggests that that was Wilson's first letter to Orr.

Town, & who will pay you. I finished the other Dial completely to
my mind, and employed a clumsy Blacksmith to make me a stile,
who ruined the whole marble in driving it in, & I broke it to pieces.
If Biggs cannot finish it in time, I shall wait until you find an opportunity of sending it, or shall bring it out yourself. I had a letter from
my Nephew, Dated Ap. 28, at which time he was in excellent health,
sweeping away and burning down the woods. I am . . . ,

N L S

To Charles Orr.
At Mr. Dobson's Book Store,
Second Street between Market and Chestnut Street, Philadelphia.
                              Milestown, 25 May 1799.
Sir,
    Considering the short distance between this and Philada., the
many pressing invitations you have received to come & see me,
and the friendship and respect I most sincerely declare I have for
you, it is a matter of regret to me that you seem insensible to them
all nor ever do me the pleasure of one visit. Have I injured you? Am
I unworthy your acquaintance? Are you afraid of contaminating
yourself with the rusticity of my manners & address? I have lived,
to be sure, 5 years in the woods, pursuing a business the most apt of
any to render peevish & pedantic the best disposition in the world
& it were vain indeed in me to hope that I had escaped without a
touch of both the one & the other; but what of that? Have not we all
our failings and vanities? and ought we not rather to smile at &
forgive, than to be too sensible and feeling on these occasions? Come
out, Mr. Orr & see me; you shall find an open & frank hospitality

such as my Brother or best friend would receive. The sight of the green meadows the singing of Birds the fragrance of flowers & blossoms & the conversation of myself and the rest of our clod-hoppers will be an excellent contrast to the burning streets, the growling oystermen, the stinking sewers and polite company of Philada. You will receive from the bearer the money you paid for me to the Mathematical Instrument maker with my thanks for your trouble & if you are determined never to visit me, your good disposition I hope will not refuse to let me know by letter what I have done to deserve such neglect and Contempt, that I may correct myself for the future if I have done amiss.

I believe this is the first letter I ever wrote to you. You used to visit me, perhaps I seemed sorry to see you & happy when you went away. If so—May every soul that I visit spit in my face & kick me from their company. If otherwise (which your own heart must testify) may every friend I love receive me with as sincere pleasure as Wilson has received & *would* receive Orr.

I am with respect,
Sir your Obedt. Sert.
ALEXR. WILSON

⁙[XXIV]⁙

NLS

[*To Charles Orr.*][1]

23 July [1799], Half past 5 Morning.

Dear Sir,

I did not mention anything of the affair till last night when I paid them 4s & 6d for you which they accepted and said they did not think that we had gone off on Sunday so sudden and said that they

1. It can be assumed that letter XXIV is to Charles Orr although the addressee's name is not given in the NLS original. The year is, of course, 1799.

had no objection of your staying but mentioned no terms though I asked. In fact they seemed ashamed to ask. I told Kulp I thought myself ill used in him neglecting to give you or I any answer tho' we waited half the day & so I said no more of the matter. I have no doubt that they would object to your coming but they dont deserve to be so much honoured. However if you think of coming I shall be very happy. If not I beg you will let me know what you intend doing. I find that Westmoreland County is an immense distance from Gennesee at least 250 miles so our project would be I think not prudent. I believe I shall stick to my former plan of continuing till the latter end of Sept. & then going up to Gennesee & staying there a week or two and returning excercising myself in the meantime morning & evenings constantly. Please send by the Bearer the Stile for which he'll pay you

I am Dear Sir,\
Yours sincerely,\
ALEXR. WILSON

XXV

NLS

[*To Charles Orr*].[1]

Dear Sir,

I shall be very much obliged if you will please to make enquiry respecting the within mentioned affair today & send me out word this Evening. It is no transitory notion I assure you for I am determined & in health to prosecute the thing till I attain it which I think I can if I do not overate my Capacity. Give me a full Account of how Matters go & every thing else.

1. This incomplete and undated letter in the NLS collection is probably to Charles Orr. With it is a silhouette marked "WILSON" in pencil but not in a contemporary hand. It does not particularly resemble any of the known likenesses.

❧[XXVI]❧

HCL (JARDINE)

To Charles Orr.

Milestown, 11 June 1800.

Dear Sir,

The Bearer is Mr. Newman our News Rider, please to shew him some little attention on my account. Mr. Davidson and myself have often spoke to him of you. He was once a man of fortune but times are altered—I am with sincere esteem.

Your obedient Servant

From Milestowns fertile fields and meadows clear
I hail my worthy friend with heart sincere
And welcome—nay most pressingly implore
One friendly visit to my Cot once more
The fairest scenes that ever blest the year
Now Sir our lawns and woods and meads appear
The richest Harvests choak each loaded field
The fairest fruit our glowing orchards yield
The green and gold and Purple hues arrayed
The sweetest songsters chant from every shade
Such boundless plenty such luxurious stores
The Busy hand of nature round us pours
That every living tribe their powers employ
From morn to e'en to testify their joy
And pour from meadow, field and air above
One general song of gratitude and love
Even now emerging from their Caverns deep
Wak'd from their seventeen years of drowsy sleep
In countless millions to our wond'ring eyes
The long remember'd Locusts glad arise
Burst their enclosing tombs at Nature's call
And join in praise to the Great God of all

Come then, Dear Orr, the noisy town forsake
With me a while these Rural joys partake
Forget your books, your pens, your studious cares
Come see the gifts that God for man prepares
Here, as with me at morn you range the Wood
Or headlong plunge amid the sparkling flood
More vigorous life your firmer nerves shall brace
A sudden glow shall wanton on your face
A brighter glance reanimate your eye
Each anxious thought, each fretting care shall fly
For here through glades and every rustling grove
Sweet peace and Rosy health forever rove
For you my Vines their clustring fruit suspend
My pinks and Roses, blow but for my friend
For him who joins with elegance and art
The brightest talents to the warmest Heart
Come then, O, come, your burning streets forego
Your lanes and wharves where winds infectious blow
For deep majestic woods and opening glades
And shining pools and awe-inspiring shades
Where fragrant flowers perfume the air around
And bending arcades Kiss the flow'ry ground
And luscious berries spread a feast for Jove
And golden cherries stud the boughs above
Amidst these various sweets your rustic friend
Shall to each woodland haunt thy steps attend
His noontide walks, his Vine entwisted bowers
The old associates of his lonely hours
While friendship's converse generous and sincere
That mingles joy with joy and tear with tear
Shall fill each heart and give to memory's eye
Those native shores where fond relations sigh
Where war accursed and haggard famine howl
And Royal Dogs on prostrate millions growl
While ever alas! these mournful sounds retrace
In climes of plenty, liberty, and Peace
A mingled flood of joy and grief shall flow
For this so free, and that so full of woe.

Thus in celestial bowers the Heavenly train
Elate from Earth's dark ills and all its pain
—[See all our] scenes of suffering here below
And drop a tear of pity for our woe—[1]

I am Dear Sir,
Yours sincerely

XXVII

GROSART

To Mr. Wm. Duncan.

Milestown, 1 July 1800.

Dear Bill,

I had the pleasure of yours by the hands of Mr. P. this day; and about four weeks ago I had another, directed to Mr. Dobson's care, both of which were as welcome to me as any thing, but your own self could be. I am just as you left me, only my school has been thinner this season than formerly.

I have had four letters from home, all of which I have answered. Their news are—Dull trade—provisions most exorbitantly high—R's sister dead—the Seedhills mill burnt to the ground—and some other things of less consequence. . . .

I doubt much if stills could be got up in time to do any thing at the distilling business this winter. Perhaps it might be a safer way to take them up, in the spring, by the Susquehanna. But if you are determined, and think that we should engage in the business, I shall be able to send them up either way. P. tells me that his two stills cost about forty pounds. I want to hear more decisively from you before I determine. Sooner than live in a country exposed to the ague, I would remain where I am.

O. comes out to stay with me two months, to learn surveying,

1. See letter XXVIII, below.

algebra, &c. I have been employed in several places about this summer to survey, and have acquited myself with credit, and to my own satisfaction. I should not be afraid to engage in any job with the instruments I have. . . .

S. continues to increase in bulk, money and respectability; a continual current of elevenpenny bits pouring in, and but few running out. . . .

We are very anxious to hear how you got up; and well pleased that you played the Horse Jockey so luckily. If you are fixed in the design of distilling, you will write me, by the first opportunity, before winter sets in, so that I may arrange matters in time.

I have got the schoolhouse enlarged, by contributions among the neighbours. In summer the school is, in reality, not much; but in winter, I shall be able to teach with both pleasure and profit. . . .

When I told R. of his sister's death, "I expected so," said Jamie, "any other news that's curious?" So completely does long absence blunt the strongest feelings of affection and friendship. May it never be so with you and me, if we should never meet again. On my part it is impossible, except God in his wrath, should deprive me of my present soul, and animate me with some other.

❦[XXVIII]❦

N L S

To Charles Orr.[1]

10 July 1800.

From Schuykill's rural Banks o'erlooking wide
The glittering pomp of Philadelphia's pride
From Laurel shades that bloom for ever here

1. "Philadelphia."

I hail my worthy friend with heart sincere
And fondly ask nay pressingly implore
One friendly visit to my Hut once more
The fairest scenes that e'er adorned the year
Now o'er our vales and yellow planes appear
The richest Harvests choak our loaded fields
The ruddiest fruit our glowing orchards yield
In green and gold and purple plumes array'd
Sweet flow'r fed Humming Birds rove thro' each shade
At dawn of Day the lofty boughs among
The merry Mocks pours out his[2] song
The Thresher shrill, the artless Robin too
The strong pip'd Hanging Bird of yellow hue
The rattling Woodpecker with crimson crest
That digs from solid trunks his curious nest
The lonely Red bird too adorns the scene
In brightest scarlet through the foliage green
With many a Warbler more, a vocal throng
That shelter'd here these Joyous notes prolong
From the first dawn of dewy morning grey
In sweet confusion till the close of Day
Even when still night descends serene and cool
Ten thousand pipes awake from yonder pool
Owls, Crickets, Tree frogs, Kitty-Dids resound
And flashing Fire Flies sparkle all around
Such boundless plenty—such abundant stores
The rosy hand of Nature round us pours
That every living tribe their powers employ
From morn to night to testify their Joy
And pour from meadows, fields, and boughs above
One general Song of Gratitude and love
Ev'n now emerging from their prisons Deep
Wak'd from their nap of seventeen years of sleep
In countless millions to our wondering eyes
The long remember'd Locusts thick arise

2. Wilson has probably omitted a two-syllable word in this line; perhaps
"swelling," "limpid," or "trilling" would fit.

Burst their enclosing shells at Nature's call
And join in praise to the great God of all
   Come then, Dear Sir, the noisy Town forsake
With me awhile these rural Joys partake
Come leave your Books, your pens, your studious cares
Come see the bliss that God for man prepares
Here, as with me, at morn you range the wood
Or headlong plunge amid the chrystal flood
More vigorous life your firmer nerves shall brace
A ruddier glow shall wanton o'er your face
A livelier glance re-animate your eye
Each anxious thought, each fretting care shall fly
For here, thro' every field and rustling grove
Sweet peace and rosy Health for ever rove
My sheltering Bowers with Honey suckles white
My fishy pools, my Cataracts invite;
My vines for you their clusters thick suspend
My ruddy peaches glow but for my friend
For him who joins with elegance of Art
The brightest Talents to the warmest heart

Come then, O come, your burning streets forego
Your lanes and Wharves, where winds infectious blow
Where Sweeps and Oyster Men's eternal growl
Carts, Crowds and Coaches harrow up the soul
For deep majestic woods and op'ning glades
And shining pools and awe-inspiring shades
Where fragrant shrubs perfume the air around
And bending Orchards kiss the flow'ry ground
And luscious berries spread a feast for Jove
And golden Cherries stud the boughs above
Amid these various sweets, thy rustic friend
Shall to each woodland haunt thy steps attend,
His solitary walks, his noontide bowers
The old associates of his lonely hours
While friendships converse, gen'rous and sincere
Exchanging every Joy and every tear
Shall warm each heart with such an ardent glow

As wealth and pageantry can ne'er bestow
PERHAPS—(for who can Nature's ties forget?)
As underneath the flow'ry shade we sit
In this rich western world remotely plac'd
Our thoughts may roam beyond the wat'ry waste
And see with throbbing hearts in memry's eye
Those native shores where dear lov'd kindred sigh
Where War, and Ghastly Want, & terror reign
And dying babes to fainting sires complain
And gasping mothers sink to endless rest
The Infants clinging to their clay cold breast
While we, alas! these mournfull scenes retrace
In climes of plenty, Liberty and Peace
Our tears shall flow, our sighs and prayers arise
That Heaven would wipe all sorrow from their eyes

Thus in celestial climes, the heavenly train
Escap'd from Earth's dark ills and all its pain
Talk o'er the scenes of suffering Man below
And drop a tear in tribute to our woe.[3]

ALEX. WILSON

XXIX

NLS, GROSART

To Charles Orr.[1]

Milestown, Monday noon 21 July 1800.

Dear Sir,

You and I have often conversed together on the use and pleasure of Epistolary Correspondence, which is, in fact, nothing more than

3. See letter XXVI. It cannot be imagined that Wilson sent two versions of the same poem to Orr, on 11 June 1800 and then on 10 July 1800. It is likely that Jardine's transcriber had before him Wilson's first draft while the final version is that in the NLS in Wilson's own hand bearing the later date.

1. "Philomath."

artificial conversation; with this advantage, that we are in no danger of being interrupted by the person we are in conversation with, and are always certain to be listened to; whereas in verbal conversation it often happens that, through impatience to give vent to the ideas that strike us while our friend is speaking, or from something advanced by him that we think absurd, we can hardly hear him out, & so the dispute becomes a mere battle of *Words*, and instead of producing pleasure or conviction to either party, begets ill-will and bigoted obstinacy of opinion. Now, Mr. Orr, as you and I are both lovers of truth—as we are subject to the failings of Human Nature as well as others, and as we are both capable of giving & receiving information and advice to each other—why may we not avail ourselves of the advantages that this method of Communicating holds out? I, for my part, have many things to enquire of you, of which at different times I form very different opinions, and at other times can form no distinct decided opinion at all. Sometimes they appear dark and impenetrable; sometimes I think I see a little better into them. Now I see them as plain as broad day, and again they are as dark to me as midnight. In short, the moon puts not on more variety of appearance to the eye than many subjects do to my apprehension & yet in themselves they still remain the same.

I have also many things of a more interesting and secret nature which I will in confidence entrust to your examination that may at least afford you matter of diversion to laugh at, and an opportunity of laughing me out of them likewise.[2]

I have nothing more at heart at present than the propriety of pursuing a plan of economy, and of observing the strictest frugality for the future in all my proceedings. Tell me if you think my resolutions laudable, and what advantages I may expect to reap from a rigid adherence to them. You see I have only scrawled this hasty

2. The NLS original ends here, but the librarian believes that the letter was complete when seen by Grosart.

preparatory billet. Do you the same. It is the matter, not the manner, I care for.

I am, with sincerity,
Yours affectionately,
ALEXANDER WILSON

To Charles Orr.[1]
Dear Sir,

Please deliver the enclosed to Mr. Witherspoon immediately on receipt he will inform you of its contents. I hope you will let me hear from you as soon as possible in return and

I remain
Dear Sir
Yours sincerely
ALEX. WILSON

To Charles Orr.

Milestown, 23 July 1800.

Dear Sir,

We don't always feel in a mood for conversation. Just so it is in writing. Sometimes the sprightly ideas flow out irresistibly. At

1. "at Mr. James Robb's, Market Street, Philadelphia."

other times we sit scratching our stupefied noddles for some dull idea, which is dragged out like a thief to the gallows. This is the situation at this time with my pericranium. You will therefore forgive me if I trouble you no farther than just to acknowledge the receipt of yours of the 21st. I congratulate you, sir, on the specimen of Epistolary Correspondence with which you honoured me on Monday. The sentiments are just, well expressed, and perfectly correspond with my own. And that, you know, is a pretty handsome compliment from one like me, who thinks so much of my own self, my own performances, and my own opinions.

I troubled you yesterday with the subject of Frugality. I shall now ask your opinion on a still more interesting subject, and shall first relate the Circumstances that impressed this subject so strongly on my mind.

It was about the middle of last May, one morning in taking my usual rounds, I was delighted with the luxuriance of Nature that everywhere smiled around me. The trees were covered with blossoms, enclosing the infant fruit that was, at some future day, to give existence to others. The birds, in pairs, were busily engaged in preparing their nests to accommodate *their* little offspring. The colt pranced by the side of its dam; the bleating of lambs was heard from every farm; and insects, in thousands, were preparing to usher their multitudes into being. In short, all Nature, every living thing around me, seemed cheerfully engaged in fulfilling that great command, *"Multiply and replenish the Earth," Excepting Myself.* I stood like a blank in this interesting scene, like a note of discord in this universal harmony of love and self-propagation, everything I saw seemed to reproach me as an unsocial wretch separated from the great Chain of Nature, & living only for myself. No endearing female regarded me as her other self, no infant called me its father, I was like a dead tree in the midst of a green forest, or like a blasted ear amidst the yellow harvest. Full of these mortifying reflections, I wandered homewards, and entered my lodging; there Mr. Kulp and his amiable spouse were playing with their children and smiling on each other with looks of mutual affection & parental pride. "O despicable wretch," said I to myself, "what is all thy learning, books, or boasted acquisitions, to a companion like that, or innocents like these whom thou could'st call thine own? By all that's good," cry'd I, "I shall share these pleasures though ten thousand unseen distresses lurk among them."

To you, Mr. Orr, who know me so well, it is unnecessary to add that these resolutions were soon forgot in study and abandoned for some algebraic or mathematical pursuit. But I have to ask you, is it not criminal to persist in a state of celibacy? And how comes it, that those whom science allures in her train, and whose hearts are most susceptible of the finer feelings of the soul, are so forgetful of this first and most exquisite of all human enjoyments, the enjoyment of a virtuous wife and little innocents in whom they can trace their own features blended together?

I beg pardon for detaining you so long. I have been unintentionally led away into a train of speculation which I only intended to hint at & which all I can say in their favour is that they are absolutely sincere. I have only one thing further to observe, but this you must keep to yourself, that so resolved was I on contributing my mite towards this grand work of generation that I had determined, *marry or not marry*, to be the father of at least *one* of my own species, till the considerations of Interest and Character disuaded me from the attempt.

Excuse all blunders & believe me to be with great regard, yours sincerely,

ALEX. WILSON

XXXII

HCL (JARDINE), THAYER

To Charles Orr.

Milestown, Frid. Noon 25 July 1800.

Dear Sir,

I find it impossible to catch one moment to write to you as Intended. I hope you will excuse me till tomorrow & not impute it to want of inclination but to absolute impossibility which is really the case with

Dear Sir,
Yours sincerely
ALEX. WILSON

XXXIII

NLS

To Charles Orr.
Professor of Astronomy, Mathematics, Algebra, Geography,
History, Poetry, Criticism, &c., and practical Astronomy on
The School Green, Milestown,[1] 6 August 1800.

Dear Sir,

Time has always been accounted among wise men the most precious gift of God to man. And has been, generally speaking, received and used as the most worthless & despicable. O ingrateful return for such invaluable bounty! But let us, my friend, profit by our past prodigality and husband well this precious commodity, who knows how soon it may be taken from us!

1. At the end of this letter, Wilson indicates that he is writing from "Milestown Monastery."

I have been led to these reflexions by a retrospection of this day. Rose half an hour before day. Sauntered abroad, surveying the appearance of the fields, and contemplating the progressive advances of morning, the appearance of the moon, &c., without suggesting or hearing suggested one sentiment of gratefull adoration to the great Architect of the Universe, without learning one truth that I was before ignorant of. Wrought one solitary problem before breakfast. Composed 8 lines of rhyme at noon, and am now writing these observations near evening. Thus 14 hours have passed almost unimproved away, and thus has thousands of precious hours so perished! Not one prayer said, not one thought of matrimony entered my mind. An old Bachelor, verging to the gloomy regions of celibacy and old age and clusters of dimple-cheeked, soft-eyed females in every log hut around & sighing for a bedfellow—O shame! By the Immortal Gods, time & youth and opportunities were not given to be so thrown away. We must improve time. We must make advances in some one or all of these important duties which Mr. Sterne says, devoid of, a human being is undeserving the name of Man. That is, to write a book, plant a tree, beget a child (I ought to have said marry a wife first), build a house, and learn something every day that he did not before know. Without these done, Sterne won't allow us to lay claim even to the name of Man. But while I am thus reprobating the waste of time, I am guilty of a double crime this moment, in losing my own time to write, what perhaps you will consider also lost time in reading.

> Great Jove O assist us to husband our time
> To marry, gain knowledge and wealth in our prime
> To squeeze the sweet Charmers while youth is our own
> Ere old crazy Age with his wrinkles come on
> Let us taste every pleasure that life can afford
> And *Spark* now & then *thro' the help of the Lord.*

Excuse Blunders. I am, My Dear Friend, yours sincerely,

ALEX. WILSON

⚜[XXXIV]⚜

NLS

To Charles Orr.[1]

Milestown, 15 September 1800.

Dear Sir,

The day on which the Trustees were to meet arrived, but I said not a word to either of them, partly through shame & partly through pride. About 5 in the evening they assembled, accompanied by a candidate for the school; a very genteel young man. They spoke of me looking much better than I did a few days before. I talked with the Candidate about the average income of the school, which he had been told was at least 50 scholars a quarter. I told him what it had nearly averaged me, which never amounted to 40, one quarter with another. His own school contained at present 45, with a good dwelling-house. The Trustees said that I looked so well that, perhaps with a few days more relaxation, I might be able to begin again myself. I told them that I had twice given up the school from the same motives, want of health & if they could suit themselves with a person with a constitution better fitted to encounter the hard duties of a school, I was satisfied, but I was sorry still to part with them. I was attached to the children & to the people, and, if they would allow me one week more to ramble about, I would once more engage if I should die in their service. My request was immediately acceded to & I am once more the dominie of Milestown school.

I am most sincerely yours,

ALEX. WILSON

1. "Care of Mr. Dobson, Second Street between Market and Chestnut Street, Philad."

❦[XXXV]❧

N L S

To Charles Orr.

Milestown, 24 September 1800.

Dear Sir,

I take the opportunity of Mr. Kulp's going to town to write you a few lines by way of refreshing your memory, as I am afraid that you have forgot the mutual agreement we made, to correspond as often as convenient. I have begun the old way again, have about 30 scholars, which number may probably increase to 40 before the quarter is concluded. I study none & take my morning and evening ramble regularly. Our Debating Society commences again on Saturday first. The proposed question—"Is the cultivation of the vine an object worthy the attention of the American farmer?" will produce I think an agreeable debate. I am anxious to hear from you. Has Mr. Marache called on you for any new loan or otherwise? Do you spend any of your leisure hours with these puzzling fellows, Algebra, Trigonometry, &c., or are you wholly absorbed in the study of Mechanics? You must write me particularly. I think I shall take a ride 15 or 20 miles on Saturday. I find riding agrees better with me than any other exercise. I always feel cheerful after it & can eat confoundedly. Have you made any new discoveries in the Heavens above, or the Earth beneath, with your microscope or telescope? I expect to hear from Billy in less than a week, as 2 persons have gone up more than 3 weeks ago. Do not forget to write.

Your sincere & affectionate Friend,
ALEX. WILSON

❦[XXXVI]❦

HCL (JARDINE)

[To Charles Orr.]

Milestown, 29 September 1800.

Dear Sir,

I wrote to you last week and having heard nothing from you since shall trouble you with another memento. Marache it seems intends sending up his 3 Boys today to me during the winter and yesterday I had a letter from my Nephew per Joshua Sullivan in which after telling me of his welfare he recommends me to send the Stills up to [Easton] during the winter and as Sleds run there from [Wiomy] to [Easton] with wheat and return frequently without back load I can send them to [Wiomy] in that manner from whence, in the spring they and I can ascend the River. I approved his plan and shall act accordingly—I wish you would send me a line per the bearer—I have no great school but in 3 months expect it much better—Hope like a glittering vision dances eternally before us till in the unceasing pursuits we stumble into the grave.

I am

with regard

[ALEX. WILSON]

❦[XXXVII]❦

NLS

To Charles Orr.[1]

1 May 1801.

My Dear Sir,

I have received all the Orations. I am indeed much obliged to your Friendship, and request that you would come out this evening

1. "Writing Master."

and stay with me till Sunday evening. I have matters to lay before you that have almost distracted me. Do come. I shall be so much obliged. Your friendship and counsel may be of the utmost service to me. I shall not remain here long. It is impossible I can. I have now no friend but yourself, and *One* whose friendship has involved both in ruin or threatens to do so. You will find me in the School House.

I am, most affectionately yours,
ALEX. WILSON

❈[XXXVIII]❈

HLH

To Mr. S[olomon] Marache.
Corner of Walnut & Second Street, Philadelphia.

16 May 1801.

Dear Sir,

Since being in Town I find myself obliged to take a Journey which will occupy at least 3 weeks and I have Accordingly broke up School for 4 weeks from Monday first. If well I shall return at that period and request you to remit to the Bearer who is my Landlady the Amount of your Acct. I think it would be proper to send up a Chair or carriage for the Boys and their Books &c. I am with esteem

Dear Sir
Yours &c
ALEX. WILSON[1]

1. I am indebted to Mr. Humphrey A. Olsen, editor of *Snowy Egret*, Williamsburg, Kentucky, for sending me a transcript of this letter and informing me that it is inserted in the front cover of George Ord's copy of the 1790 edition of Wilson's *Poems*, in the Houghton Library, Harvard. There is a copy of this letter in the Paisley Museum.

XXXIX

N L S

To Charles Orr.

Bloomfield, near Newark, New Jersey,
12 July 1801.

My Dear Friend,

If this letter reach you it will inform you that I keep school at 12s. pr. Qr., York currency, with 35 scholars, and pay 12s. per week for board, and 4s. additional for washing, and 4s. per week for my horse. After I parted with Davidson, the Quakers not coming to any agreement about engaging me, I left Wrightstown & steered for New York through a country entirely unknown to me, visited many wretched hovels of schools by the way; in four days reached York, and from every person who knew the Mitchells, received the most disagreeable accounts of them, viz., That Jas. had by too great a fondness for gaming and sometimes taking his scholars along with him, entirely ruined his reputation and lost his business, and from his own mouth I learned that he expected jail every day for debts to a considerable amount. And Wm. is lost for every good purpose in this world and abandoned to the most shameful & excessive drinking, swearing, and wretched company—he called on me last Thursday morning in company with a Hocus Pocus man for whom he plays on the clarinet. New York swarms with newly imported Irishmen of all descriptions, clerks, schoolmasters, &c. The city is very sickly; Mitchell and all the rest to whom I spoke of you believed that your success here would be even more unsuccessful than in Philada., and related so many stories to that purpose that I was quite discouraged. Mr. Milnes attempted it there, but was obliged to remove and is now in Boston wandering through the streets insane. I staid only one night in York and being completely run out except about 3, 11-penny bits, I took the first school from absolute necessity that I could find. I live six miles north from Newark and 12 miles from New York, in a settlement of canting, preaching, praying & sniveling ignorant Presbyterians. They pay their minister 250 pounds a year for preaching twice a week, and their teacher 40 dollars a quarter for the most spirit-sinking laborious work, 6, I may say 12 times weekly. I have no company, and live unknowing and unknown. I have lost all relish for this country and if Heaven spares me I shall soon see the shores of old Caledonia. How happy I should be to have you beside me. I am exceedingly uneasy to hear from you. Dear Orr, make no rash engagements that may bind you for ever to this unworthy soil. I shall arrange all my affairs with Billy as expeditiously as I can. In the meantime I request you, my Dear Friend, to oblige me in one thing if you wish me well. Go out on Saturday to Davidson's and try to get intelligence how Mr. Kulp's family comes on, without letting any one know that you have heard from me. Get all the particulars you can, what is said of me, & how Mrs. Kulp is, & every other information, and write me fully. I assure you I am very wretched, and this would give me the greatest satisfaction. Davidson will tell you everything, but mention nothing of me to anybody on any account. Conceal nothing that you hear, but inform me of everything. My Dear Friend, I beg you would oblige me in this. I am very miserable on this unfortunate account. I shall write you more fully on a variety of things I have to inform you of next week or as soon as I hear from you. Direct as above dated. I shall try to get information from a friend in Albany how matters would do there.

I am, most sincerely, your affectionate Friend while

ALEXANDER WILSON

p.s. Mitchell got the letter I wrote, but was so swallowed up in extravagance, I suppose, that he never replied to it.

Let us contrive a plan to leave this country and try old Scotia once more in company.

The bones of a mammoth or some gigantic animal are digging up here, of which I shall send the particulars in my next. I shall superintend the whole process.

N L S

To Charles Orr.

Bloomfield, 23 July 1801.

My Dear Friend,

I received yours last evening. O how blessed it is to have one friend on whose affection, in the day of adversity, we can confide! As to the reports circulated in the neighbourhood of Milestown, were I alone the subject of them they would never disturb me, but she who loved me dearer than her own soul, whose image is for ever with me, whose heart is broken for her friendship to me, she must bear all with not one friend to whom she dare unbosom her sorrows. Of all the events of my life nothing ever gave me such inexpressible misery as this. O my dear Friend, if you can hear anything of her real situation, and whatever it be disguise nothing to me. Take a walk up to my Niece's perhaps she has called lately there, and go out to Davidson's on Saturday if possible. Let nobody whatever know that you have heard anything of me. In my last I told you Mitchell was on the threshold of the jail. He has now passed the threshold and is fairly cag'd. Wm. is traversing the country with a Hocus-Pocus man in a poor scurvy plight playing the clarinet. The gentleman who discovered the bones of which I spoke of is a Mr. Kenzie, who was sinking a well for his paper mill in a swamp supposed formerly to have been the bed of a small creek that runs near.

6 feet from the surface, under a stratum of sand 4 inches deep, they found several bones apparently belonging to the tail, 6 inches in breadth, with part of a leg-bone measuring upwards of 7 inches diameter at the joint, part of a rib 4 feet long, and many fragments in a decayed state. For want of hands no further search has yet been made, but it is intended to obtain the head and teeth if possible. The greatest curiosity in this State is the falls at Paterson where the river which is about 40 yards broad, flows along a bed of solid rock. A sudden earthquake or some great convulsion has split this rock assunder across the whole breadth of the river, 6 or 8 feet apart and upwards of 70 deep, down which the whole river roars with a noise like thunder. This place is but 8 miles distant, and I went alone on Saturday to see it. The cotton works are completely deserted. I looked in at the weaving shops and saw nothing but hens roosting on the breast beams, and everything desolate. While I was in York a teacher there offered me his school-room benches, &c., with all the scholars, amounting to 40 or 45, for 60 dollars cash, as he wished to decline the business. It is needless to add that I declined the honor of the bargain. The school-house in which I teach is situated at the extremity of a spacious level plain of sand thinly covered with grass. In the centre of this plain stands a newly erected stone meeting-house, 80 feet by 60, which forms a striking contrast with my sanc-tum sanctorum, which has been framed of logs some 100 years ago, and looks like an old sentry box. The scholars have been accustomed to great liberties by their former teacher. They used to piss and put stones in his pocket, &c., &c. I was told that the people did not like to have their children punished, but I began with such a system of terror as soon established my authority most effectually. I succeed in teaching them to read, and I care for none of their objections. The following anecdote will give you an idea of the people's character. A man was taken sick a few weeks ago and got deranged. It was universally said that he was bewitched by an old woman who lived adjoining. This was the opinion of the Dutch Doctor who attended

him & at whose request a warrant was procured from the Justice for bringing the witch before the sick man, who, after tearing the old woman's flesh with his nails till the blood came, sent her home and afterwards recovered. This is a fact. The Justice who granted the warrant went thro' among the people with me. I intend to visit the poor woman myself & publish it to the world in the Newark newspapers for the amusement of the enlightened people of N. Jersey. My Dear Orr, I trust to your friendship for the intelligence I mentioned; write me fully as I will you on receipt. I left my great-coat with a Mr. —— in Wrightstown, where Davidson and I lodged. Davidson will tell you his name. I wish you would write for it without letting Davidson know anything of the matter. I left it in the stable. I owed him nothing. I shall be much obliged if you drop a line to him that it may be sent to Philada., and this will be your warrant. Farewell. I shall write more fully next time.

Yours most sincerely,
ALEX. WILSON

⟦ XLI ⟧

NLS, GROSART

To Charles Orr.

Bloomfield, 7 August 1801.

My Dear Friend,

I received yours yesterday. I entreat you keep me on the rack no longer. Can you not spare *one* day to oblige me so much? Collect every information you can, but drop not a hint that you know any-thing of me. If it were possible you could see *her* or any one who *had*, it would be an unspeakable satisfaction to me. My Dear Orr, the world is lost for ever unto me and I unto the world. No time nor distance can ever banish her image from my mind. It is for ever present with me, and my heart is broken with the most melancholy reflexions. Whatever you may think of me, My Dear Friend, do not refuse me this favour to know how she is. Were your situation mine, I declare from the bottom of my soul I would hazard everything to oblige you. I leave the management of it to yourself. But do not forget me. Jas. Mitchell's debts amount, as I have been informed, to 2 or 300 £. Wm. is weaving in an old cellar in Elizabeth Town. My school increases; it is now 40. I have done nothing yet toward visiting the supposed witch. Some day soon I shall make it my business. There is a copper mine about 300 yards from my schoolhouse which was lately wrought and many tons of ore obtained from it. It is now neglected. Among the other effects of superstition here there lives just beside me a man who, being the seventh son, has power to cure the most inveterate King's Evil by simply laying his hands on it. He has had three patients since my coming, and tells me he has cured hundreds. He says he can feel the disorder ascending his arms, and commonly is indisposed while performing a cure on his patients. They have come 100 miles to him. He is now a man of 45, and has practised this "Laying on of hands" since he was a boy. The people with whom I live are the veriest zealots in Religion, in Praying, Singing Psalms and Hymns. I was urged to ask Blessing at Table the first day and refused, but was insisted on till through mere shame I was obliged to perform, and am obliged to officiate every evening. God forgive me, for my heart is as distant from my lips then as from you to me. I consider it a monstrous hardship. I read the few lines of poetry you sent me to the old fellow, who wanted me to find out a tune for them that he might have the godly comfort of singing them by way of hymn, which shall certainly be done. As for myself, I have recourse to a thousand expedients to unburden my mind. I am really sometimes almost distracted on seeing how and where I am situated. Sometimes I try to turn it over to diversion, as in the following verses which I wrote this morning, and enclose without preface or apology, as you know my situation:

Here oxheaded Ignorance gapes & is courted,
And curst Superstition with vision distorted;
Sweet Science and Truth, while these monsters they cherish,
Like the Babes of the Wood are abandoned to perish.

Here ten times a day they are Hymning and Praying,
And "glory to God" most religiously paying;
Should Mis'ry implore, that's a quite different story.
They lock up the cash, but to God give the glory.

Young Venus ne'er lent to our Females her graces,
Like a duck's is their gait, like old pumpkins their faces;
No heart winning looks to decoy or to charm us,
Their teeth like corruption—their [?], O enormous!

Here old wither'd witches crawl round ev'ry cabin,
And butter from churns are eternally grubbing;
Ghosts, wizzards, seventh sons, too, to cure the King's Evil,
One touch of their hand and 'tis gone to the Devil.

Here the grim Man of God, with a voice like a trumpet,
His pulpit each Sunday bestampt and bethumpet;
On all but his own pours damnation and ruin,
And heaves them to Satan for roasting and stewing.

There lonely & sad in his centry box sitting,
The windows unglazed, & the floor all beshitten;
A wretched exile murmurs A.B.C. grieving,
In sounds slow & solemn from Morning to Even.

Before you write, take a walk up to my niece's as if to enquire for me, and try if you can get any information there. I know that she used sometimes to go and see her. Forgive me, my dear friend, if in anything I have offended you. The more of mankind I see, the more sincerely I value your friendship, and trust it shall only disolve when time to me shall be no longer.

ALEX. WILSON[1]

1. This letter in the Wilson collection at the NLS is not in Wilson's hand and is marked "Copy." There are notes by a previous editor including the insertion at the commencement of the verses, "The first and last stanzas are too coarse for transcription" and the first line of verse is written: "Here (at Bloomfield) oxheaded Ignorance gapes & is courted."

XLII

NLS

To Charles Orr.

Bloomfield, 14 September 1801.

My Dear Friend,

The last letter I wrote you I fondly thought would be answered, but I have waited now 3 weeks in vain. It was directed to you at M'Phail's China Store, Dock Street. I conjure you, My Dear Friend, by all that Friendship which I always flattered myself you had for me that you will write me on receipt of this. Jas. Mitchell's Father arrived here last week from Scotland and found his 2 sons, one in Drunkenness and poverty, the other in a Jail. Think with yourself what were the feelings of the poor old man on this occasion. Jas. is since liberated. I remain here perfectly secluded from the world. Your letters were all my company and amusement, but you have deprived me of even that. As I have now no hopes of ever being in Philada., I ask it as a last favour that you would go out to the House. where I lodged and request them to bring my trunk into Philada. that you may send it to me to Newyork. If my nephew has written me it will be in Mr. M'Innes', where I wish you would enquire. I again implore you to let me know how the Family I mentioned are doing. You promised you would, and I shall take it as the utmost kindness. Orr, I wish it were possible for you and I to unite our talents and exertions as we have often thought of doing. Would it not do by making a bold push? I can engage the Reading, Grammatical, and what other parts we should agree on—you the rest. I will with pleasure join you if you are willing, for if I must teach I will strain every effort to make something of it. This would be the best moment to attempt it. Think on the Business, and I shall dispose of my Horse, and unite with you to rise or fall together. There are hardly

2 on earth better acquainted with each other, and I think in Conscience, without boasting of myself or flattering you, that we would
do well. It is want of Confidence alone that has kept us from both
fame and fortune in our respective pursuits. At all events, write me
per Return of Post. A French Gentleman from St. Domingo has been
with me to-day from Newark to teach him English. He is almost
unintelligible. I have amused myself since I came here with writing
detached Pieces of Poetry for the Newark Centinel, and have grown
into some repute with the Editor and his Readers. A song entitled
My Landlady's Nose has been reprinted in a Newyork Paper, &
in a periodical Publication called the Museum. Please to let the circumstances of the Mitchells be confined to your own breast. You
may let Robert know of the old gentleman's arrival. Once more I
ask you to oblige me with an answer to this, and to excuse the hurried way in which it has been scribbled in return for your next, I will
send you something more entertaining. I am so uneasy to know how
you come on, that I am every night conversing with you in my sleep.

I am, my Dear Friend, yours most sincerely,

ALEXANDER WILSON

NLS

To Charles Orr.

7 February 1802.

Mr. Orr,

I have no faults to reproach you with. If I had a consciousness of
the number of my own would justly impose silence on me. My
disposition is to love those who love me with all the warmth of
enthusiasm, but to feel with the keenest sensibility the smallest

appearance of neglect or contempt from those I regard. Of your friendship I have a thousand times been truly proud, have boasted of your intimacy with me and your professional abilities, almost wherever I went. I have poured out my Soul into your bosom. If I have met, or only supposed that I have in the moments of anxiety and deep mental perturbation met with cold indifference from the only quarter where I expected the sweets of Friendship they little know my heart who would expect it to make no impression on me. But Mr. Orr you can never make me your enemy and alas I have Friendship for no one. Distress preys continually on my mind—I have no friend, I ask for none. No friend on earth can ever remove my source of misery and my acquaintance with you would but distress you. I wish you every happiness possible and I doubt not but much is reserved for you. Above all I wish you to banish from your mind all suspicions of disesteem—I entertain none—I know there are people who are happy in insinuating their ideas to you, but I regard *their* love or hatred with equal indifference. I think so much necessary as explanation, but no more. You shall always share the good wishes and regard of

A L E X A N D E R   W I L S O N

❦[XLIV]❧

N L S

To Charles Orr.

14 February 1802.

Dear Sir,

It is too much—I cannot part from you after what you have said. I renounce with pleasure every harsh thought I hastily entertained of you. From this moment let all past grievances be eternally forgotten. For myself, I give them to the winds. I know the value of a

Friend & of such a Friend, too well to hope ever again for another on losing you. What is the world to that solitary Being whose
happiness only glads his own Bosom and who weeps neglected? Its
joys to such an insulated wretch are tasteless—its sad reverses almost
insupportable. Friendship sweetens the most common occurrences
of Life, multiplies all our pleasures, lightens all our losses. When
the Sun of our prosperity sinks even in the deepest midnight of misfortune Friendship sheds its cheering radiance around the unhappy
wanderer—fills his heart with serenity, and points to happier prospects. I hope My Dear Sir you will excuse the melancholy turn my
letter has taken. I cannot help it. It is always so, this some time. I
never spent 10 weeks more unhappy than these have been, and it
will be some time before my mind recovers itself. Past hopes, present difficulties and a gloomy futurity have almost deranged my
ideas and too deeply affected me. The conduct and conversation of
those who perhaps think me a Dependent for residence is such that
my spirit can never assimilate with. Amidst all these, your friendship returns to me once more like the blessed beams of Heaven after
a night of Clouds and Darkness. Let us now Dear Sir mutually forgive and henceforth enjoy the sweet interchange of conversation
and unreserved sociability. Rocks and islands may separate for a
while the stream that has long been united but these pass, the congenial waters will again meet mingle and be blended together. A
small accident may break a bone but once judiciously reunited it is
stronger than ever; *so be our friendship.* I shall leave this at your
Lodgings to-night and to-morrow Evening after nine shall call on
you and take a walk together. On the 25th of this month I remove
to the SchoolHouse beyond Gray's Ferry to succeed the present
Teacher there. I shall recommence that painful profession once more
with the same gloomy sullen resignation that a prisoner re-enters
his Dungeon or a Malefactor mounts the Scaffold; Fate urges him,
necessity me. The agreement between us is, they engage to make
the School equal to 100 Dlls per quarter, but not more than 50 are

to be admitted. The present pedagogue is a noisy, outrageous fat old Captain of a ship, who has taught these 10 years in different places you may hear him bawling 300 yards off. The Boys seem to pay as little regard to it as Ducks to the rumbling of a stream under them. I shall have many difficulties to overcome in establishing my own Rules and authority. But perseverance overcometh all things.

I am, with sincere esteem,

Your still affectionate Friend,

ALEX. WILSON

P.S. Your coming up this afternoon has altered my resolution of not calling on you till to-morrow evening. Let it be this afternoon or evening. I am a little engaged till then.

A.W.

GROSART

To Charles Orr.[1]

Gray's Ferry, 15 July 1802.

My Worthy Friend,

I expected you all last Sunday, and walked out towards the ferry several times to meet you. I hope you were entertained more to your satisfaction than you could have been in the company of an insignificant country dominie rendered peevish and melancholy by the daily cares and confinement of a most consuming employment. However, as I once told you before, I have a variety of resources in times of irritation and perplexity, but in none have I found consolation, such as to banish every pedantic pesteration, as in renewing my old pursuit of the Muses. My harp is new strung, and my soul glows with

1. "At Mr. Dixon's, Dock Street."

more ardour than ever to emulate those immortal bards who have
gone before me. I have transcribed a variety of old pieces that have
never been published, at least not in my book, which gave me the
most exquisite sensations, not from their excellence, but by recall-
ing ideas, and interesting ones too, that have been, I may say, forgotten ever since my arrival in America. I have also collected all my
productions since '94; these I intend to polish and improve occasionally, and to add to them all those contained in my last edition which
I think meritorious, and to copy the whole when corrected to my
mind in one volume. I have an irresistible desire, which seems to
come from inspiration alone, to attempt some Scots pastorals descriptive of the customs and rural manners of our native country,
interspersed with scenes of humour, love, and tenderness. In Burns,
Ferguson, Ramsay, and all our Scottish songs, these are the charms
that captivate every heart. I believe a Scotsman better fitted for
descriptions of rural scenes than those of any other nation on earth.
His country affords the most picturesque and striking scenery; his
heart and imagination warm and animated, strong and rapid in its
conceptions, its attachments, and even prejudices, his taste is highly
improved by the numberless pathetic ballads and songs handed
down from generation to generation. There is not an ignorant
ploughman in Scotland but who has a better taste and relish for a
pastoral, particularly if interwoven with a love intrigue, than most
of the pretended literati of America. Where is the country that has
ever equalled Scotland in the genuine effusion of the pastoral muse,
or where so many tears of joy, sympathy, and admiration have been
shed by the humblest peasants over her bewitching strains? Had
Thomson not possessed this ardent spirit of enthusiasm his Seasons
would never have seen that immortality to which they are so justly
entitled; but he was a Scotsman and glow'd with all their energy of
enthusiasm while ranging o'er the beauties of nature. But both
Thomson and Burns, Ramsay and Ferguson, with all who have yet
followed them, have left a thousand themes unsung, equally inter-

esting with the best of their descriptions, a thousand pictures of rustic felicity that will yet be pourtrayed by the striking pencil of some future genius. My heart swells, my soul rises to an elevation I cannot express, to think I may yet produce some of these glowing wilds of rural scenery—some new Paties, Rogers, Glauds, and Simons, that will rank with these favourites of my country when their author has mixed with his kindred clay; that my name will be familiar in farms and cottages, in circles of taste and at scenes of merriment five hundred years hence, when the statues of bloody ambition are mouldered and forgotten. By heavens! the idea is transporting, and such a recompense is worth all the misfortunes, penury, and deprivations here that the most wretched sons of science have ever suffered. But I beg pardon for occupying so much of your time. Come out on Saturday or Sunday morning. Leave that cursed town at least one day. It is the most striking emblem of purgatory, at least to me, that exists. No poor soul is happier to escape from Bridewell than I to smell the fresh air and gaze over the green fields after a day or two's residence in Philadelphia, were it not attended by the regret of parting from my friend, whose obliged and unalterable brother I am while

ALEX. WILSON

XLVI

GROSART

To William Duncan.

Gray's Ferry, 30 October 1802.

Dear Billy,

I was favoured with your despatches a few hours ago, through the kindness of Colonel Sullivan, who called on me for that purpose. I have read and re-read, over and over again, their contents; and shall devote the remainder of this evening, to reply to you, and the rest of the family, now joint tenants of the woods. By the arrival of John F. here, in August last, I received one letter from my brother David, one from Thomas W[itherspoon] and one for Alexander from David Wilson; and last week another packet arrived from Belfast, containing one letter from your father to myself; and to your mother, brother and brother-in-law, and yourself, one each, all of which I have herewith sent, and hope they may amuse a leisure hour. F. has been wofully disappointed in the expectations he had formed of his uncle. Instead of being able to assist him, he found him in the depth of poverty, and fast sinking under a severe fever. Probably the arrival of a relation contributed to his recovery; he is now able to crawl about. F. has had one child born and buried since his arrival. He weaves with Robertson, but neither likes the situation nor employment. He is a stout, active and ingenius fellow, can turn his hand to almost anything, and wishes as eagerly to get up to the lakes as ever a saint longed to get to heaven. He gives a most dismal description of the situation of the poor people of Scotland in 1800.

Your letters, so long expected, have at length relieved me from much anxiety. I am very sorry that your accommodations are so few, for my sister's sake, and the children's; a fire-place and comfortable house for the winter must, if possible, be got up without delay. If masons are not to be had, I would attempt to raise a temporary one myself, I mean a fire-place—but surely they may be had, and lime and stones are also attainable by dint of industry. These observations are made not from any doubts of your doing every thing in your power to make your mother as comfortable as possible, and as your means will enable you, but from a solicitude for a sister's health, who has sustained more distress than usual. I know the rude appearance of the country, and the want of many usual conveniences, will for some time affect her spirits; let it be your pleasure and study to banish these melancholy moments from her as much as possible. Whatever inconveniences they may for a while experience, it was well they left this devoted city. The fever, that yellow genius of destruction, has sent many poor mortals to their long homes since you departed; and the gentle man who officiates as steward to the Hospital informed me yesterday evening that it rages worse this week than at any former period this season, though the physicians have ceased reporting. Every kind of business has been at a stand these three months, but the business of death.

You intimate your design of coming down next Spring. Alexander seems to have the same intention. How this will be done, consistent with providing for the family, is not so clear to me. Let me give my counsel on the subject. You will see by your father's letters that he cannot be expected before next July, or August perhaps, a time when you must of necessity be at home. Your coming down, considering loss of time and expenses, and calculating what you might do on the farm, or at the loom, or at other jobs, would not clear you more than twenty dollars difference, unless you intended to remain here five or six months, in which time much might be done by you and Alexander on the place. I am sorry he has been so soon discouraged with farming. Were my strength but equal to my spirit, I would abandon my school for ever for such an employment. Habit will reconcile him to all difficulties. It is more healthy, more independent and agreeable, than to be cooped up in a subterraneous dungeon, surrounded by gloomy damp, and breathing an unwholesome air from morning to night, shut out from Nature's fairest scenes and the pure air of heaven. When necessity demands such a seclusion, it is noble to obey; but when we are left to choice, who would bury themselves alive? It is only in Winter that I would recommend the loom to both of you. In the month of March next I shall, if well, be able to command two hundred dollars cash *once more*. Nothing stands between me and this but health, and that I hope will continue at least till then. You may then direct as to the disposal of this money—I shall freely and cheerfully yield the whole to your management. Another quarter will enable me to settle John M.'s account, about the time it will be due; and, instead of

wandering in search of employment five or six hundred miles for a
few dollars, I would beg of you both to unite in putting the place and
house in as good order as possible. But Alexander can get nothing
but wheat and butter for this *bagging and slashing*! Never mind, my
dear namesake, put up awhile with the rough fare and rough clothing of the country. Let us only get the place in good order, and you
shall be no loser by it. Next Summer I will assuredly come up along
with your father and George, if he comes as I expect he will, and
every thing shall flourish.

My dear friend and nephew, I wish you could find a leisure hour
in the evening to give the children, particularly Mary, some instruction in reading, and Alexander in writing and accounts. Don't be
discouraged though they make but slow progress in both, but persevere a little every evening. I think you can hardly employ an hour
at night to better purpose. And make James read every convenient
opportunity. If I live to come up beside you, I shall take that burden
off your shoulders. Be the constant friend and counsellor of your
little colony, to assist them in their difficulties, encourage them in
their despondencies, to make them as happy as circumstances will
enable you. A mother, brothers, and sisters, in a foreign country,
looking up to you as their best friend and supporter, places you in a
dignified point of view. The future remembrance of your kind duty
to them now, will, in the hour of your own distress, be as a healing
angel of peace to your mind. Do every thing possible to make your
house comfortable—fortify the garrison in every point—stop every
crevice that may let in that chilling devil, the roaring blustering
northwest—heap up fires big enough for an Indian war-feast—keep
the flour-barrel full—bake loaves like Hamles' Head[1]—make the
loom thunder, and the pot boil; and your snug little cabin re-echo
nothing but sounds of domestic felicity. I will write you the moment
I hear of George. I shall do every thing I have said to you, and never

1. The name of a rock which stood in the river Cart near Wilson's birthplace
in Seedhills, Paisley (Grosart).

lose sight of the eighteenth of March; for which I shall keep night-school this Winter, and retain every farthing but what necessity requires—depend upon me. These are the outlines of *my* plan. If health stand it, all will be well; if not, we cannot help it. Ruminate on all this, and consult together. If you still think of coming down, I hope you would not hesitate for a moment to make my neighbourhood your home. If you come I shall be happy to have you once more beside me. If you resolve to stay on the farm, and put things in order as far as possible, I will think you have done what you thought best. But I forget that my paper is done.

Robb, Orr, &c., have escaped as yet from the pestilence; but Robb's three children have all had the ague. Rabby Rowan has gone to *Davie's Locker* at last: he died in the West Indies. My brother David talks of coming to America, and my father, poor old man, would be happy to be with you, rough and uncomfortable as your situation at present is. As soon as I finish this, I shall write to your mother and Alexander. There is a letter for John M., which he is requested to answer by his father-in-law. I hope John will set a firm resolute heart to the undertaking, and plant a posterity in that rich, western country, to perpetuate his name for ever. Thousands here would rejoice to be in his situation. How happy may you live thus united together in a free and plentiful country, after so many years of painful separation, where the bare necessaries of life were all that incessant drudgery could procure, and even that but barely. Should even sickness visit you, which God forbid, each of you is surrounded by almost all the friends in the world, to nurse you, and pity and console you; and surely it is not the least sad comfort of a deathbed, to be attended by affectionate relatives. Write me positively by post, two or three times. My best love to my sister, to Isabella, Alexander, John, the two Maries, James, Jenny, little Annie. God Almighty bless you all.

Your ever affectionate Friend,
ALEX. WILSON

⁕[XLVII]⁕

GROSART

To Mr. Alexander Duncan.

31 October 1802.

Dear Alexander,

I have laughed on every perusal of your letter. I have now deci-phered the whole, except the blots, but I fancy they are only by the way of *half mourning* for your doleful captivity in the backwoods, where there is nothing but wheat and butter, eggs and gammon, for *hagging* down trees. Deplorable! what must be done? It is a good place, you say, for a man who has a parcel of *weans*! . . .

But forgive this joking. I thank you, most heartily, for this your *first letter* to me; and I hope you will follow it up with many more. I shall always reply to them with real pleasure. I am glad that your chief objection to the country is want of money. No place is without its inconveniences. Want of the necessaries of life would be a much greater grievance. If you can, in your present situation, procure sufficient of these, though attended with particular disadvantages, I would recommend you to persevere where you are. I would wish you and William to give your joint labours to putting the place in as good order as possible. A farm of such land, in good cultivation, is highly valuable. It will repay all the labour bestowed upon it a hun-dred-fold; and contains within it all the powers of plenty and inde-pendence. These it only requires industry to bring forth, and a small stock of money to begin with. The money I doubt not of being able to procure, next Summer, for a year or two, on interest, independent of two hundred dollars of my own, which I hope to possess on or before the middle of March next. C.S. is very much attached to both your brother and me; and has the means in his power to assist us— and I know he will. In the meantime, if you and William unite in the undertaking, I promise you, as far as I am concerned, to make it the best plan you could pursue.

Accustom yourself, as much as you can, to working out. Don't despise *bagging* down trees. It is hard work, no doubt; but taken moderately, it strengthens the whole sinews, and is a manly and independent employment. An old weaver is a poor, emaciated, help-less being, shivering over rotten yarn, and groaning over his empty flour barrel. An old farmer sits in his arm chair before his jolly fire, while his joists are crowded with hung beef and gammons, and the bounties of Heaven are pouring into his barns. Even the article of health is a consideration sufficient to make a young man prefer the labours of the field: for health is certainly the first enjoyment of human life. But perhaps weaving holds out advantages that farming does not. Then blend the two together; weave in the depth of Win-ter, and work out the rest of the year. We will have it in our power, before next Winter, to have a shop, looms, &c., provided. Consider all I have said, and if I have a wrong view of the subject, form your own plans, and write me without delay. . . .

❧[XLVIII]❧

GROSART

To William Duncan.

Gray's Ferry, 23 December 1802.
. . . The two Mr. Purdies popped into my school, this afternoon, as unexpected as they were welcome, with news from the promised land. I shall detain them with me all night, on purpose to have an opportunity of writing you a few lines. I am glad you are all well. I hope that this is the last devilish slough of despond which you will have to struggle in for some time. I will do all that I said to you, in

my last, by the middle of March; so let care and sorrow be forgotten; and industry, hope, good-humour and economy, be your bosom friends. . . .

I succeed tolerably well; and seem to gain in the esteem of the people about. I am glad of it, because I hope it will put it in my power to clear the road a little before you, and banish despondency from the heart of my dearest friend. Be assured that I will ever as cheerfully contribute to your relief in difficulties, as I will rejoice with you in prosperity. But we have nothing to fear. One hundred bushels of wheat, to be sure, is no great marketing; but has it not been expended in the support of a mother, and infant brothers and sisters, thrown upon your bounty in a foreign country? Robert Burns, when the mice nibbled away his corn, said:

> I'll get a blessin' wi' the lave,
> And never miss't.

Where he expected one, you may a thousand. Robin, by his own confession, ploughed up his mice out of *ha' and hame*. You have built for your little wanderers a *cozie bield*, where none dare molest them. There is more true greatness in the affectionate exertions which you have made for their subsistence and support, than the bloody catalogue of heroes can boast of. Your own heart will speak peace and satisfaction to you, to the last moment of your life, for every anxiety you felt on their account. Colonel Sullivan talks with pride and affection of you.

I wish Alexander had written me a few lines of the old German text. I laugh every time I look at his last letter: its a perfect antidote against the spleen. Well, Alexander, which is the best *fun*, handling the shuttle, or the ax? When John M. comes down, write me largely. And, dear sister, let me hear from you also. . . .

I would beg leave to suggest to you the propriety of teaching the children to behave with good manners, and dutiful respect to yourself, each other, and every body.

You must excuse me for any thing I may have said amiss, or any thing I may have omitted to mention.

I am, with sincere attachment,

Your affectionate Friend,

ALEX. WILSON

THAYER

To William Bartram.

Monday noon 4 March [*1803*].

Dear Sir,

This Bird I take to be the female Yellow Rump. I suppos'd it on first sight to be some other. If Miss Bartram thinks it worth drawing it is at her service. I have this moment rec'd yours, which like all the letters you have honoured me with are to me as valuable as Bank Notes to a Miser.

Yours

ALEX. WILSON

THAYER

To William Bartram.[1]

[*1803.*]

My Dear Friend,

I send with more diffidence than on any former occasion some further attempts. If from the rough draughts here given you can

1. "Botanist."

discover what Birds they are, please to give me their names. Any advice for their amendment from you will be truly welcome.

With sincere esteem and affection,

I am, Dear Sir,

Your's

ALEX. WILSON

CRICHTON 1819

[*To a friend in Paisley.*]

1 June 1803.

. . . Close application to the duties of my profession, which I have followed since November, 1795, has deeply injured my constitution, the more so, that my rambling disposition was the worst calculated of anyone's in the world for the austere regularity of a teacher's life. I have had many pursuits since I left Scotland, Mathematics, the German Language, Music, Drawing, &c., and I am now about to make a collection of all our finest birds.

THAYER

To William Bartram.

30 October 1803.

Dear Sir,

I have been attempting the Shrub you pointed out to me last week. Will you be so obliging as to mark with a pencil its Linnaean and Vulgar names at the bottom of the Drawing and tell me in what parts I may retouch it. I fear you will think it but a feeble imitation but your kind advice and encouragement will soon enable me to do better.

With real esteem I am, Dear Sir,
Your obliged Servt.
ALEX. WILSON

UOP

To William Bartram.

10 November 1803.

Dear Sir,

I have murdered your Rose. I traced the outlines with great patience but in colouring and shading I got perfectly bewildered. After I have gained a little more practice I shall make one desperate attempt more on these Roses. I hope you will excuse my present failure. I am most respectfully

Dear Sir
Your sincere friend
ALEX. WILSON

THAYER

To William Bartram.

17 November 1803.

Dear Sir,

I have taken the liberty of sending you another Specimen of attempts to imitate your beautiful Engravings, presuming on your goodness. I have to request that you would present my best Compliments to Miss Bartram and prevail with her to select me one more from among the Collection and send it by Flora. I know the nature of your present engagements will not permit you to lose time and the choice of your amiable Niece will certainly not lessen my enthusiasm in endeavouring to execute the Task.

Yours most sincerely
ALEX. WILSON

CRICHTON 1819

To William Bartram.

20 November 1803.

I have attempted two of those prints, which Miss Nancy your niece, has so obligingly, and with so much honour to her own taste, selected for me. I was quite delighted with the Anemone, but fear I have made but bungling work of it. Such as they are I send them for your inspection and opinion. Neither of them is quite finished. For your kind advice towards my improvement, I return my most grateful acknowledgements.

The duty of my profession will not admit me to apply to this study with the assiduity and perseverance I could wish. Chief part of what I do is sketched by candle-light; and for this I am obliged to sacrifice the pleasures of social life, and the agreeable moments which I might enjoy in company with you, and your amiable friend. I shall finish the other some time this week, and shall be happy if what I have done merit your approbation.

LVI

BLC

To William Bartram.

19 December 1803.

My Dear Friend,

The Book Binder having disappointed me I must apologize to you for not being able to send the plates home as yet but expect to have the satisfaction of sending them over some day this week. If you pass this way soon I beg you would give me a call that I may have the pleasure of shewing you *Buonaparte* alive and in good health whom I captured as prisoner of war one day last week in your woods. I want you to tell me his true pedigree and what Tribe of the Buonapartes he belongs to. He seems to delight as much in Carnage and to split up sculls and carcases with as little ceremony as his celebrated Namesake did on the plains of Italy or at the Battle of Marengo. The little poetical piece you were pleased to commend I have alter'd and somewhat improved and hope you will so far honor me as to accept of it as a memento of our Friendship and the pleasure I have had in your Company

Yours sincerely

ALEX. WILSON

LVII

THAYER

To Mr. Lawson, Engraver.
Philada.

Gray's Ferry, 12 March 1804.

Dear Sir,

I dare say you begin to think me very ungenerous and unfriendly in not seeing you for so long a time. I will simply state the cause, and I know you will excuse me. 6 days in one week I have no more time than just to swallow my meals, and return to my Sanctum Sanctorum. 5 days the following week are occupied in the same routine of pedagoguing matters and the other 2 are sacrificed to that itch for drawing, which I caught from your honourable self. I never was more wishful to spend an afternoon with you. In 3 weeks I shall have a few days' vacancy, and mean to be in town chief part of the time. I am most earnestly bent on pursuing my plan of making a collection of all the birds in this part of North America. Now I don't want you to throw cold water, as Shakspeare says, on this notion, Quixotic as it may appear.[1] I have been so long accustomed to the building of airy castles and brain windmills, that it has become one of my earthly comforts, a sort of a rough bone that amuses me when sated with the dull drudgery of life.

The roads have been generally so bad that we must mutually excuse each other for past omissions and by our own future sociability prevent the Chain of Friendship from getting rusty. Compts. to Mr. Jones etc.

I remain,

[ALEX. WILSON][2]

LVIII

THAYER

To William Bartram.

29 March 1804.

My Dear Friend,

Three months have passed away since I had the pleasure of seeing you; and 3 dark and heavy months they have been to your fam-

1. Wilson suggested the publication of his *Ornithology* as a joint venture with Lawson but the engraver thought the risk too great. In his biographical sketch of Wilson, 1819, Crichton mentions Wilson's determination to proceed on his own and, without indicating the occasion, quoted Wilson as saying or writing: "I shall at least leave a small beacon to point out where I perished."

2. The signature has been cut off this letter.

ily. My heart has shared in your distress, and sincerely sympathises with you for the loss you have sustained [Bartram's nephew's death] but Time, the great curer of every grief, will gradually heal those wounds he has inflicted and many years of happiness and tranquility are, I sincerely hope, reserved for you both.

I have been prevented from seeing you so long by the hurry of a crowded school which occupied all my hours of daylight, and frequently half the others. The next quarter will leave me time enough and there is no man living in whose company I have more real satisfaction and I hope you will excuse me if I now and then steal a little of your leisure.

I send for your amusement a few attempts at some of our indigenous birds hoping that your good nature will pardon their deficiences while you point them out to me. I intended to have come up with them myself but having so many little accts. to draw up before to-morrow that must be my excuse. I am almost ashamed to send you these drawings but I know your generous disposition will forgive weakness where you perceive a sincere and eager wish to do well. They were chiefly coloured by candle-light.

I have now got my Collection of Native Birds considerably enlarged and shall endeavour, if possible, to obtain all the smaller ones this summer. Be pleased to mark the names of each with a pencil as except 3 or 4, I do not know any of them. I shall be extremely obliged for every hint from you that will assist me in this agreeable amusement.

I am extremely anxious to see the performances of your fair pupil and beg you would assure her from me that any of the birds I have are heartily at her service and surely Nature is preferable, to copy after before even the best masters, though perhaps more difficult; for I declare the face of an owl and the back of a lark, have put me to my ne plus ultra and if Miss Nancy will be so obliging as to try her hand on the last mentioned I will furnish her with one in good order and will copy her drawing with the greatest pleasure

having spent almost a week on 2 different ones and afterwards destroyed them both, and got pretty nearly in the slough of despond
altogether. My Compts. to Mr. James

and I am

Dear Sir,

Yours sincerely,

ALEX. WILSON

[LIX]

GROSART

To William Bartram.

Kingsessing, 31 March 1804.

. . . I take the first few moments I have had since receiving your
letter, to thank you for your obliging attention to my little attempts
at drawing; and for the very affectionate expressions of esteem with
which you honour me. But sorry I am, indeed, that afflictions so
severe, as those you mention, should fall where so much worth and
sensibility reside, while the profligate, the unthinking and unfeel-
ing, so frequently pass through life, strangers to sickness, adversity,
or suffering. But God visits those with distress whose enjoyments
He wishes to render more exquisite. The storms of affliction do not
last for ever; and sweet is the serene air, and warm sunshine, after a
day of darkness and tempest. Our friend has, indeed, passed away,
in the bloom of youth and expectation; but nothing has happened
but what almost every day's experience teaches us to expect. How
many millions of beautiful flowers have flourished and faded under
your eye; and how often has the whole profusion of blossoms, the

hopes of a whole year, been blasted by an untimely frost. He has gone only a little before us; we must soon follow; but while the feelings of nature cannot be repressed, it is our duty to bow with humble resignation to the decisions of the great Father of all, rather receiving with gratitude the blessings He is pleased to bestow, than repining at the loss he thinks proper to take from us. But allow me, my dear friend, to withdraw your thoughts from so melancholy a subject, since the best way to avoid the force of any overpowering passion, is to turn its direction another way.

That lovely season is now approaching, when the garden, woods and fields, will again display their foliage and flowers. Every day we may expect strangers, flocking from the south, to fill our woods with harmony. The pencil of Nature is now at work, and outlines, tints, and gradations of lights and shades, that baffle all description, will soon be spread before us by that great Master, our most benevolent Friend and Father. Let us cheerfully participate in the feast he is preparing for all our senses. Let us survey those millions of green strangers, just peeping into day, as so many happy messengers come to proclaim the power and munificence of the Creator. I confess that I was always an enthusiast in my admiration of the rural scenery of Nature; but, since your example and encouragement have set me to attempt to imitate her productions, I see new beauties in every bird, plant, or flower, I contemplate; and find my ideas of the incomprehensible First Cause still more exalted, the more minutely I examine His work.

I sometimes smile to think that while others are immersed in deep schemes of speculation and aggrandizement—in building towns and purchasing plantations, I am entranced in contemplation over the plumage of a lark, or gazing like a despairing lover, on the lineaments of an owl. While others are hoarding up their bags of money, without the power of enjoying it, I am collecting, without injuring my conscience, or wounding my peace of mind, those beautiful specimens of Nature's works that are for ever pleasing. I have had live crows, hawks, and owls—opossums, squirrels, snakes, lizards, &c., so that my room has sometimes reminded me of Noah's ark; but Noah had a wife in one corner of it, and in this particular our parallel does not altogether tally. I receive every subject of natural history that is brought to me, and though they do not march into my ark from all quarters, as they did that of our great ancestor, yet I find means, by the distribution of a few five-penny bits, to make them find the way fast enough. A boy, not long ago, brought me a large basket full of crows. I expect his next load will be bull-frogs, if I don't soon issue orders to the contrary. One of my boys caught a mouse in school, a few days ago, and directly marched up to me with his prisoner. I set about drawing it that same evening, and all the while the pantings of its little heart showed it to be in the most extreme agonies of fear. I had intended to kill it, in order to fix it in the claws of a stuffed owl, but happening to spill a few drops of water near where it was tied, it lapped it up with such eagerness and looked in my face with such an eye of supplicating terror, as perfectly overcame me. I immediately untied it, and restored it to life and liberty. The agonies of the prisoner at the stake, while the fire and instruments of torture are preparing, could not be more severe than the sufferings of that poor mouse; and, insignificant as the object was, I felt at that moment the sweet sensations that mercy leaves on the mind when she triumphs over cruelty.

My dear friend, you see I take the liberty of an old acquaintance with you, in thus trifling with your time. You have already raised me out of the slough of despond, by the hopes of your agreeable conversation, and that of your amiable pupil. Nobody, I am sure, rejoices more in her acquisition of the beautiful accomplishments of drawing than myself. I hope she will persevere. I am persuaded that any pains you bestow upon her will be rewarded beyond your expectations. Besides, it will be a new link in that chain of friendship and consanguinity by which you are already united; though I fear it will be a powerful addition to that attraction which was fully sufficient before, to make even a virtuoso quit his owls and opossums, and think of something else.[1]

ALEXANDER WILSON

GROSART, ORD

To William Bartram.

... I send you a few more imitations of birds for your opinion, which I value beyond that of anybody else, though I am seriously apprehensive that I am troublesome. These are the last I shall draw for some time, as the employment consumes every leisure moment, leaving nothing for friendship, or those rural recreations which I so much delight in. Even poetry, whose heavenly enthusiasm I used to glory in, can hardly ever find me at home, so much has this bewitching amusement engrossed all my senses.

Please to send me the names of the birds. I wish to draw a small flower, in order to represent the Humming-bird in the act of feeding: will you be so good as to send me one suitable, and not too large? The legs and feet of some are unfinished; they are all miserably imperfect, but your generous candour I know to be beyond all their defects.[2]

ALEXANDER WILSON

1. I received from Humphrey A. Olsen a transcript he had made of this letter many years ago. It added a closing sentence: "I shall be unavoidably engaged these few days in settling Accounts &c but shall take the first Opportunity of calling over to see you all meantime believe me sincerely Your Affectionate friend." As I had not the opportunity to collate the original manuscript, which could not be found at the repository to which I was directed, I have adhered to the Ord/Grosart version.

2. Grosart has 1 May 1804 as the date of this letter while Ord gives 21 May 1804.

FIGURE 8. View of the city of Philadelphia, taken from Kensington. Drawn by Mr. Birch and engraved by M. Marigot for James Cundee's *The Stranger in America* (London, 1807).

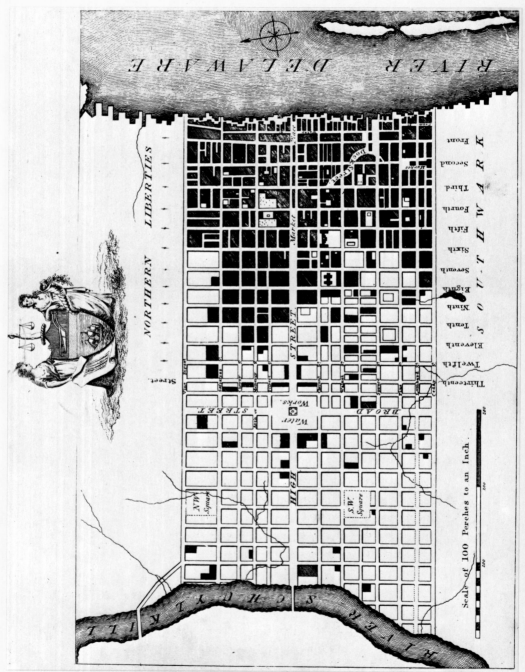

Scale of 100 Perches to an Inch.

FIGURE 10. High Street, Philadelphia. From James Cundee's *The Stranger in America* (London, 1807).

FIGURE 11. Wilson's schoolhouse at Kingsessing.

FIGURE 12. An early print of Old Swedes Church, Philadelphia.
Wilson's burial place is in the foreground.

RESIDENCE OF JOHN BARTRAM,

BUILT WITH HIS OWN HANDS, A.D. 1730.

FIGURE 13. William Bartram's house in the botanical gardens created by his father, John Bartram. The gardens were Wilson's favorite haunt and at the house there was the stimulation of Bartram's encouragement.

FIGURE 14. George Ord.

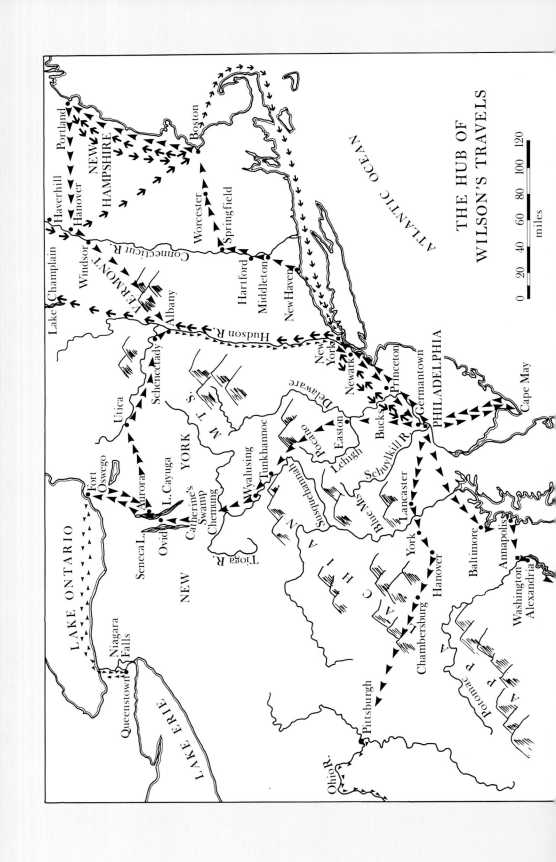

THE HUB OF
WILSON'S TRAVELS

miles

0   20   40   60   80 100 120

ATLANTIC OCEAN

LAKE ONTARIO

LAKE ERIE

NEW HAMPSHIRE

VERMONT

Portland

Haverhill

Hanover

Windsor

Lake Champlain

Connecticut R.

Worcester

Springfield

Boston

Hartford

Middleton

New Haven

Albany

Schenectady

Hudson R.

Utica

Fort Oswego

Aurora

Seneca L.

Ovid

L. Cayuga

Catherine's Swamp

Chemung

Tioga R.

NEW YORK

M T S.

Wyalusing

Tunkhannoc

Susquehanna

Pocono

Delaware

Easton

Lehigh

Blue Mts.

Schuylkill R.

Lancaster

York

Newark

New York

Princeton

Germantown

Bucks

PHILADELPHIA

Cape May

Hanover

Chambersburg

Baltimore

Annapolis

Washington

Alexandria

Potomac

Pittsburgh

Ohio R.

Niagara Falls

Queenstown

P E N N S Y L V A N I A

Wilson's Principal Ornithological Travels
Using the place-names he gives in his writings
(*see map opposite*)

JOURNEY 1. Winter 1804 to Niagara Falls. From Philadelphia via Germantown, Chestnut Hill, Springhouse Tavern. Bucks, over Northampton Heights, through Durham Vale. Then to Easton and the Lehigh River, Blue Mountains, Delaware River, the Poconos, Wiomi, Susquehanna River, Keeler's Ferry, across the Tunkhannock River, to Wyalusing, Pennsylvania, Spanish Hill, Chemung, New York, the Tioga River, Newtown, and Great Catherine's Swamp to Ovid, New York. From there up Lake Cayuga in the skiff *Niagara* and down the Oswego River to Fort Oswego, Lake Ontario. From there sailed to Queenstown for Niagara. The route of that part of the return journey from Niagara to Cayuga is uncertain, but it is likely that they sailed back to Fort Oswego. Parted with Billy Duncan on 20 November 1804 at Aurora on the shores of Lake Cayuga as Billy was returning to Ovid. Via Utica to Schenectady, then by stage to Albany. Down the Hudson River in a sloop to New York. Walked to Philadelphia which he reached 7 December 1804. Wilson is said to have covered 1,200 to 1,300 miles, mostly on foot.

JOURNEY 2. 21 September 1808. Philadelphia to Princeton, Elizabethtown, Newark, and New York. By packet to New Haven, Connecticut. Then to Middletown on the Connecticut River, to Hartford, then through Springfield and Worcester to Boston. To Portland, Maine, then via Dartmouth College, in Hanover, New Hampshire, to Windsor, Vermont, and Albany to New York City. Home to Philadelphia.

JOURNEY 3. By horse, winter 1808–1809. Philadelphia to Baltimore, then via Annapolis to Washington (where he met Jefferson). To Georgetown, Alexandria, Richmond, Norfolk, and Suffolk, in Virginia, to Wilmington, North Carolina, and Charleston, South

Carolina (which he reached February 1809). Then to Savannah, Georgia, from which he sailed back to New York. By coach to Philadelphia.

JOURNEY 4. Set out 30 January 1810. From Philadelphia to Lancaster, to Columbia, and across the Susquehanna River to York. Next to Hanover, Chambersburg, and over the Allegheny Mountains to Pittsburgh. Left Pittsburgh 24 February 1810. Having bought a rowboat, he sailed down the Ohio River and reached Louisville, Kentucky, on 17 March 1810, a distance of 720 miles (as he estimated it). Walked to Shelbyville, then to Frankfort (the capital of Kentucky), and on to Lexington. Bought a horse in Lexington and rode to Nashville via Mammoth Cave, Kentucky (north of Bowling Green). Continued to Natchez via the spot where Meriwether Lewis died ("72 miles from Nashville"—Wilson's letter of 18 May 1810 to Alexander Lawson). At Natchez he had a pleasant interlude, staying for a few days with William Dunbar at his home in the forest. From Natchez, journeyed down the Mississippi to New Orleans. Returned by sea to New York and en route landed on some of the islands in the Gulf of Mexico. Reached New York 2 August 1810. By coach to Philadelphia.

JOURNEY 5. May 1812. Month-long expedition to Cape May, New Jersey, from Philadelphia. He visited Cape May several times on ornithological sorties.

JOURNEY 6. August–September 1812. Journey into New England. Philadelphia to New York. Up the Hudson River and across "rugged country" to Lake Champlain. Then over mountains to the Connecticut River, to Haverhill, Massachusetts, and Hanover, New Hampshire. Across country to Boston. From Boston to Portland, Maine, and back. Home via Boston and New York to Philadelphia.

OVID FARM. Between Seneca and Cayuga lakes, New York. Bought by Wilson and his nephew as family base. He visited Ovid on more than one occasion.

⁕[LXI]⁕

MCZ

To William Bartram.[1]

Union School, 22 May 1804.

My Dear Friend,

I truly sympathize, tho' not without a smile, at the undeserv'd treatment you have experienced from your busy Colony. Recollection of the horrible fate of their fathers smotherd with Sulphur or perhaps a presentiment of what awaits themselves might have urg'd them to this outrage but had they known you, my dear friend, as well as I do, they would have distill'd their honey into your lips instead of poison and circl'd around you humming gratefull acknowledgements to their benevolent benefactor who spreads such a luxuriance of blossoms for their benefit. Accept my thanks for the trouble I put you to yesterday. Mrs. Leech requests me to send Miss Bartram 2 Birds and thinks they would look best drawn so that the pictures may hang their length horizontaly. I send a small scroll of Drawing paper for Miss Nancy. She will oblige me by accepting it & as soon as I get some Letter paper worthy your acceptance which will be to-morrow I shall be happy of the opportunity of supplying you.

There is some observations in your last which I would remark on but am hurry'd at the present moment. Farewell.

Yours Sincerely,

ALEX. WILSON

---

1. "Botanist at Bartram's Gardens."

HSP

To William Bartram.

15 June 1804.

My dear Friend,

I send you 3 Birds, one of them I take to be the one you spoke of last evening. I have no doubt but Nancy will do compleat justice to the little warblers.

I have arrang'd my business for our little journey and if tomorrow be fair I shall have the Chair ready for you any time in the morning, say seven o'clock. Or if you think any hour more suitable please to let me know by the Bearer and I shall make it answerable to me.

I am

Dear Sir

Yours truly

ALEX. WILSON

HSP

To William Bartram.

16 June 1804.

My Dear Friend,

I believe we had better put off our intended Jaunt untill some more auspicious day:

> Clouds, from Eastern regions driv'n,
>   Still obscure the gloomy skies;
> Let us yield since angry Heav'n
>   Frowns upon our enterprise.
>
> Haply some unseen disaster
>   Hung impending o'er our way

Which our kind almighty Master
   Saw, and sought us thus to stay.

By and by, when fair Aurora
   Bids the drowsy fogs to fly
And the glorious god of Flora
   Rises in a cloudless sky.

Then, in whirling Chariot seated,
   With my friend I'll gladly go
With his converse richly treated—
   Happy to be honoured so.

ALEX. WILSON

P.S. excuse this hasty scrap. I shall call up and see you this evening.

A. WILSON

LXIV

THAYER

18 June 1804.

The Beechen Bower[1]

O dear to my heart in this deep shaded Bower
This snug little seat and this smooth Beechen Tree

1. This dated holograph poem has not been printed in any collection of Wilson's poems. It is included here because the reference to Anna is, there can be little doubt, to William Bartram's niece, Nancy (Ann) Bartram. Too much should not be read into it despite phrases like "Maid of my bosom" and "how dearly I love her." The poem is in the manner of Wilson's poetic master, Robert Burns, who often, in his songs, expressed affection in terms of adoring love as in "O, Wert Thou in the Cauld Blast," in appreciation of kindness and friendship; or "The Lass o' Ballochmyle," in quest of patronage. I surmise that "The Beechen Bower" is simply Wilson's poetic tribute to a charming companion. A subsequent forty-four verse poem entitled "A Rural Walk" dated by Wilson, 10 August 1804, appeared in the *Literary Magazine* and is set in Bartram's Garden. It is a tribute to William Bartram and his niece, referred to as Anna, with warm testimony to both.

These old hoary Cliffs through the bushes that tower
   And bend o'er the pool their resemblance to see
The fountains the Grotto the Laurels sweet blossom
   The streamlet that warbles so soothing and free
Green solitude! dear to the Maid of my bosom
   And so for her sake ever charming to me.

Here seated with Anna what bliss so transporting
   I wish every moment an age were to be
Her taste so exalted—her humour so sporting
   Her heart full of tenderness virtue and glee
Each evening sweet Bow'r round thy cliffs will I hover
   In hopes her fair form thro' the foliage to see
Heav'n only can witness how dearly I love her
   How sweet Beechen Bower thy shades are to me.

A. WILSON

GROSART

To Alexander Lawson.

14 August 1804.

Dear Sir,

Enclosed is a copy of the "Solitary Tutor," which I should like to see in the "Literary Magazine" of this month, along with the other poem which I sent the editor last week. Wishing, for my future benefit, to call the public attention to these pieces, if, in the editor's opinion, they should seem worthy of it, I must request the favour of you to converse with him on this subject. You know the numerous pieces I am in possession of, would put it in my power to support tolerably well any recommendation he might bestow on these; and while they would not, I trust, disgrace the pages of his valuable publication, they might serve as my introduction to the literary world, and as a sort of inspiration to some future and more finished attempts. Knowing that you will freely pardon the *quantum* of vanity that suggests these hints.

I remain, with real regard, &c.,
ALEXANDER WILSON

THAYER

To William Bartram.

16 *August 1804.*

My dear Sir,

I send for your amusement some further account of the Baron Humboldt page much more pleasing to me than the noisy and virulent harangues of political parties which at present engross so much of our daily publications.

I have been drawing Woodpeckers this sometime. Pray be so good as inform me if there is not 4 different species besides the Fliccer in these parts. The common redheaded, the speckled hairy and small speckled hairy Woodpecker and another speckled one with a crimson coloured throat. I suppose that none of the large red Crested Ones can be found within 20 miles of Philada I would not begrudge 2 days sacrificed in getting possession of One. I lately discovered a new and most extraordinary Blackheaded Woodpecker on the trunk of a large tree in your woods of a perfect nondescript species. The largest of my Hawks was a mere Tom Tit to it. I was under the tree before I was aware and on looking up was perfectly astonished at the sight above me, as I don't doubt but you yourself or any other Naturalist would have been. It seemed, like our other Woodpeckers, attracted by the dry dead limbs and made them crackle like thorns under a pot. Before I could return with my gun it was gone—with what Genus to class it I am totaly ignorant. One thing I am positive of, that it was a *Woodpecker*, a *black-headed* one and a very expert one too.

You will receive with this a very neat & correct painting of some Species of Beetle which I have frequently seen. I found it in the Number of the Magazine you had last. I suppose it the production of the Dr's pencil. My best wishes for the health and happiness of the family and with sentiments of unalterable regard

I remain

Dear Sir

Yours

ALEX. WILSON

 LXVII

HSP

To Col. [Joshua] Sullivan, Frankford.
Gray's Ferry, 17 September 1804.

Dear Sir,

Your letter was put into my hand this morning having been in Town till late yesterday. I read it with regret and shared with you in that affectionate solicitude you so feelingly express for the future fate and conduct of your Boy. Your letter to David I read with tears —it was impossible for me to restrain them. I view'd the affair in the same serious light you yourself have done and in the most solemn and earnest manner with the most affectionate expressions for his future welfare. I laid down the enormity of disobedience and ingratitude to a parent who had done so much for him and whose soul was bound up in him and in the hopes of his future honour and respectability.

All that my esteem for the Father and my anxious wishes for the happiness of the Child could suggest was repeated on the occasion and I trust he will never forget the impressions of this morning's interview nor the promises so repeatedly made amid a flood of tears of future amendment and I doubt not but whatever anxieties he may cost you now that he will one day be an honour to your Name and the pride of his parents and every one related to him.

But these propensities must be nipt in the bud by kind remonstrances and determined Authority, by securing as much as possible from vicious Company and inflaming his mind, if possible, with a desire of excelling in learning and be assured, My dear Sir, that I will in these points be the constant and faithfull Guide of your Children as far as my abilities can go while they are under my care.

Charles is a most amiable Boy. They both request me to declare to you that they will never do so any more and David at my direction is now about to sit down to acknowledge his fault and ask your forgiveness which I shall let him do entirely in his own words.

                         I am
                     Dear Sir
                         Your ever affectionate Friend
                             ALEX. WILSON

LXVIII

HSP

To *William Bartram*.

                     Union School, 17 September 1804.

My dear Friend,

The second vol. of Pinkerton has at length made its appearance; and I take the freedom of transmitting it, and the Atlas, for your amusement. To condemn or approve of so extensive a work before a reperusal, and without taking into consideration all the difficulties that were to be surmounted, is, perhaps, not altogether fair. Yet we almost always form our judgment from the first impressions, and this judgment is very seldom relinquished. You will, therefore, excuse me if I give you some of the impressions made on myself by a cursory perusal.

Taking it *all in all*, it is certainly the best treatise on the subject hitherto published; tho' had the author extended his plan, and instead of 2, given us 4 volumes, it would not frequently have laid him under the necessity of disappointing his reader by the bare mention of things that required greater illustration; and of compressing the natural history of whole regions into half a page but might have fully gratified his curiosity by narrative and description. 34 pages only allotted to the whole United States! This is *brevity* with a vengeance. I had indeed expected from the exertions of Dr. Barton, as compleat an account of the natural history of this part of the world as his means of information, and the limits of the work, would admit. I have been miserably disappointed; and you will pardon me when I say that his omitting entirely the least reference to your researches in Botany and Natural History, and seeming so solicitous to let us know of his own productions, bespeak a narrowness of mind, and self-consequence and is an ungrateful and unpardonable omission. Every man acquainted with you both, would have confidently trusted that he would have rejoiced in the opportunity of making the world better acquainted with a man whose works show such a minute and intimate knowledge and attention to these subjects and from whose superior abilities and experience he had himself received so many obligations and much information. But no —All is silent not even the slightest allusion, lest posterity might discover that there existed, at this time, in the United States, a man of Genius and information superior to himself. My dear sir, I am a Scotchman, and don't love my friends with that cold icy selfish prudence that I see in some; and if I offend in thus speaking from the fulness of my heart, I know you will forgive me.

Mr. Pinkerton has, indeed, furnished us with many curious particulars unknown, or, at least, unnoticed, by all former geographers;
and also with other items long since exploded as fabulous and ridiculous; such is his account of the Upas or poisonous tree; and of children having been lost in some of our American swamps, and of
being seen many years afterwards, in a wild savage state ha! ha! ha!
But he very gravely tells his readers that the people of Scotland
eat little or no pork from a prejudice they have against swine, the
Devil having taken possession of some of them 2 thousand years
ago! What an enlightened people these Scots must be; and what
a delicate taste they must be possessed of! Yet I have traversed
nearly ¾ths of that country, and mixed much with the common
people, and never heard of such an objection before. Had the learned
Author told his readers that, until late years, Scotland, though
abounding in rich pastures, even to its mountain tops, was yet
but poorly productive in grain, fruit, &c., the usual food of hogs,
and that on this account innumerable herds of sheep, horses, and
cattle, were raised, and but very little pork, he would then have
stated the simple facts; and not subjected himself to the laughter of
every native of that part of Britain.

As to the pretended antipathy and dislike to eels, because they
resemble snakes, it is equally ridiculous and improbable; ninety-
nine out of a hundred of the natives never saw a snake in their lives.
The fact is, it is as usual to eat eels there, where they can be
got, as it is in America; and altho' I have frequently heard such
objections made to the eating of eels here, where snakes are so common, yet I do not remember to have heard the comparison made in
Scotland. I have taken notice of these two observations of his, because they are applied generally to the Scots, making them appear a
weak squeamish stomached set of beings, infected with all the prejudices and antipathies of children.

These are some of my objections to this work, which, however,
in other respects, does honour to the talents, learning, and industry

of the compiler. The Atlas pleases me and indeed far surpasses what I expected. The Maps though small and minutely correct at least far more than any I have ever seen. Among the whole those executed by our friend Lawson are very conspicuous for neatness of engraving. But I fear I have worn out your patience where I only meant to amuse by a few remarks. Wishing you, My Dear Friend a long continuation of Health peace and happiness. I bid you affectionately Farewell.

ALEX. WILSON

LXIX

THAYER

To William Bartram.

12 December 1804.

Mr. Wilson's affectionate Compliments to Mr. Bartram and sends for his amusement some Newspapers from the interior—Some moss like plants from the Sulphur Springs, a pair of Mockasons made by a Tuscarora Squaw but not finished and a Number of the Literary Magazine. Perhaps the plants might be better examined after being steeped in water. They were quite yellow with sulphur when gathered and covered with a species of small bluish coloured Caterpillar. Some other particulars respecting these Springs shall form the subject of a fireside chat some evening soon.

LXX

CRICHTON 1819

To William Bartram.

Gray's Ferry, 15 December 1804.

Dear Sir,

Though now snug at home, looking back in recollection on the long circuitous journey which I have at length finished, through trackless snows, and uninhabited forests; over stupendous mountains, and down dangerous rivers; passing over, in a course of thirteen hundred miles, as great a variety of men and modes of living, as the same extent of country can exhibit in any part of North America. Though in this tour I have had every disadvantage of deep roads and rough weather; hurried marches, and many other inconveniences to encounter, yet so far am I from being satisfied with what I have seen, or discouraged by the fatigues which every traveller must submit to, I feel more eager than ever to commence some more extensive expedition, where scenes and subjects entirely new, and generally unknown, might reward my curiosity, and where perhaps my humble acquisitions might add something to the stores of knowledge. For all the hazards and privations incident to such an undertaking, I feel confident in my own spirit and resolution. Without a family to enchain my affections, no ties but those of friendship, and the most ardent love of my adopted country; with a constitution which hardens amidst fatigues, and a disposition sociable and open, which can find itself at home by an Indian fire in the depth of the woods, as well as in the best apartment of the civilised. For these, and some other reasons that invite me away, I am determined to be a traveller. But I am miserably deficient in many acquirements absolutely necessary for such a character. Botany, mineralogy, and drawing, I most ardently wish to be instructed in, and with these I should fear nothing. Can I yet make any progress in botany, sufficient to enable me to be useful, and what would be the most proper way to proceed? I have many leisure moments that should be devoted to this pursuit, provided I could have hopes of succeeding. Your opinion on this subject will confer an additional obligation on Your affectionate friend.

ALEX. WILSON

LXXI

GROSART

To William Duncan.

Gray's Ferry, 24 December 1804.

. . . You have no doubt looked for this letter long ago, but I wanted to see how matters would finally settle with respect to my school before I wrote; they remain, however, as uncertain as before; and this quarter will do little more than defray my board and firewood. Comfortable intelligence truly, methinks I hear you say; but no matter. . . .

I shall begin where you and I left off our story, viz., at Aurora, on the shores of the Cayuga. The evening of that day, Isaac and I lodged at the outlet of Owasco Lake, on the turnpike, seven or eight miles from Cayuga bridge; we waded into the stream, washed our boots and pantaloons, and walked up to a contemptible dram-shop, where, taking possession of one side of the fire we sat, deafened with the noise and hubbub of a parcel of drunk tradesmen. At five next morning we started; it had frozen, and the road was in many places deep and slippery. I insensibly got into a hard step of walking; Isaac kept groaning a rod or so behind, though I carried his gun. . . . We set off again, and we stopped at the outlet of Skaneateles Lake, ate some pork-blubber and bread, and departed. At about two in the afternoon we passed Onondaga Hollow, and lodged in Manlius Square, a village of thirty houses, that have risen like mushrooms in two or three years, having walked this day thirty-four miles. On the morning of the 22d we started as usual by five—road rough—and Isaac grunting and lagging behind. This day we were joined by another young traveller, returning home to his father's on the Mohawk; he had a pocket bottle, and made frequent and long applications of it to his lips. The road this day bad, and the snow deeper than before. Passing through Oneida Castle, I visited every house within three hundred yards of the road, and chatted to the copper-coloured tribe. In the evening we lodged at Lard's tavern, within eleven miles of Utica, the roads deplorably bad, and Isaac and his disconsolate companion groaning at every step behind me, so that, as drummers do in battle, I was frequently obliged to keep before, and sing some lively ditty, to drown the sound of their "ohs!" and "ahs!" and "O Lords!" The road for fifteen or twenty miles was knee deep of mud. We entered Utica at nine the next morning. This place is three times larger than it was four years ago; and from Oneida to Utica is almost an entire continued village. This evening we lodged on the east side of the Mohawk, fifteen miles below Utica, near which I shot a bird of the size of a Mocking-bird, which proves to be one never yet described by naturalists. I have it here in excellent order. From the town called Herkimer we set off through deep mud and some snow; and about mid-day, between East and West Canada Creeks, I shot three birds of the Jay kind, all of one species, which appears to be undescribed. Mr. Bartram is greatly pleased at the discovery; and I have saved two of them in tolerable condition. Below the Little Falls the road was excessively bad, and Isaac was almost in despair, in spite of all I could do to encourage him. We walked this day twenty-four miles; and early on the 25th started off again through deep mud, till we came within fifteen miles of Schenectady, when a boat coming down the river, Isaac expressed a wish to get on board. I walked six miles afterwards by myself, till it got so dark that I could hardly rescue myself from the mud-holes. The next morning I entered Schenectady, but Isaac did not arrive in the boat till noon. Here we took the stage-coach for Albany, the roads being excessively bad, and arrived there in the evening. After spending two days in Albany, we departed in a sloop, and reached New York on Saturday, at noon, the first of December. My boots were now reduced to legs and upper leathers, and my pantaloons in a sad plight. Twelve dollars were expended on these two articles. . . .

On Friday, the 7th December, I reached Gray's Ferry, having walked forty-seven miles that day. I was absent two months on this journey, and I traversed in that time upwards of twelve hundred miles.

The evening of my arrival I went to L—h's, whose wife had got twins, a boy and a girl. The boy was called after me; this honour took six dollars more from me. After paying for a cord of wood, I was left with only *three-quarters* of a dollar. . . .

❦[LXXII]❦

THAYER

To William Bartram.

Union School, 24 December 1804.

My dear Sir,

I have perused Dr. Barton's publication[1] and return it with many thanks for the agreeable and unexpected treat it has afforded me. The description of the Falls of Niagara is in some places a just, though faint delineation of that stupendous cataract. But many interesting particulars are omitted and much of the writer's reasoning

---

1. *The Philadelphia Medical and Physical Journal*, vol. 1 (Grosart).

on the improbability of the wearing away of the precipice and consequent recession of the Falls, seems contradicted by every appearance there and many other assertions are incorrect. Yet on such a subject everything, however trifling, seems to attract attention. The readers imagination supplying him with scenery in abundance even amidst the poverty and barrenness of the meanest writer's description.

After this article I was most agreeably amused and diverted with "Anecdotes of an American Crow," written in such a pleasing style of playfull humour as I have seldom if ever seen surpassed & forms a perfect antidote against the spleen abounding at the same time with observations and reflexions not unworthy of the most refined philosophers.

The sketch of your father's life with the extracts from his letters I read with much pleasure. They will remain lasting monuments of the worth and respectability of the father as well as of the talents and filial affection of the son.

The description of the Choctaw Bonepickers is a picture so horrible as I think nothing can exceed. Many other pieces in this work are new and interesting. It cannot fail to promote the knowledge of Natural History and deserves on this account every support and encouragement.

I send you a pod of seeds used as a substitute for Coffee in the Western parts of Pennsylvania presented to me yesterday by Jn. Pearson of Darby and am as usual

Your sincere Friend,
ALEX. WILSON

 LXXIII

BLC

To William Bartram.

26 December 1804.

Dear Sir,

I send for your amusement the Literary Magazine for Sept. in which you will find a well written and except in a few places a correct Description of the Great Falls of Niagara. I yesterday saw a Drawing of them taken in 68 and observe that many large rocks that used formerly to appear in the rapids above the Horseshoe falls are now swept away and the form of the Curve considerably altered the consequence of its gradual retrogression. I hope this Account will entertain you as I think it by far the most complete I have yet seen.

Your Sincere friend

ALEX. WILSON

 LXXIV

GROSART

To William Duncan.

Kingsessing, 20 February 1805.

... I received yours of January 1, and wrote immediately; but partly through negligence, and partly through accident, it has not been put into the post-office; and I now sit down to give you some additional particulars. ...

This winter has been entirely lost to me, as well as to yourself. I shall on the twelfth of next month be scarcely able to collect a sufficiency to pay my board, having not more than twenty-seven scholars. Five or six families, who used to send me their children, have been almost in a state of starvation. The rivers Schuylkill and Delaware

are still shut, and waggons are passing and repassing at this moment upon the ice.

The solitary hours of this winter I have employed in completing
the poem which I originally intended for a description of our first
journey to Ovid. It is now so altered as to bear little resemblance to
the original; and I have named it the *Foresters*. It begins with a
description of the Fall or Indian Summer, and relates minutely our
peregrinations and adventures until our arrival at Catherine Landing, occupying ten hundred and thirty lines. The remainder will
occupy nearly as much; and as I shall, if ever I publish it, insert
numerous notes, I should be glad if, while you are on the spot, you
would collect every interesting anecdote you can of the country, and
of the places which we passed through. Hunting stories, &c., peculiar to the [Indians] would be acceptable. I should be extremely
glad to spend one afternoon with you for the benefit of your criticisms. I lent the poem to Mr. ——, our senator, who seems to
think it worth reading; and —— has expressed many flattering
compliments on my labours; but I don't value either of their opinions half as much as I would yours. I have bestowed more pains upon
this than I ever did upon any former poem; and if it contain nothing
really good, I shall for ever despair of producing any other that
will. . . .

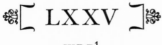

❦[LXXV]❦

WRF[1]

To William Bartram.

4 March 1805.

My Dear Friend,

This day the heart of every Republican, of every good man within
the immense limits of our happy Country, will leap with joy.

1. The original of this letter is owned by Mrs. William R. Funck of Geneva,
Ohio, a descendant of Robert Carr.

The re-appointment and continuance of our beloved Jefferson to superintend our national executive, is one of those distinguished Blessings whose beneficent effects extend to Posterity; and whose value our hearts may feel, but can never express.

I congratulate you, my dear friend, on this happy event. The enlightened philosopher—the distinguished naturalist—the first statesman on earth, the friend, the ornament of science, is the father of our Country, the faithful guardian of our liberties. May the precious fruits of such pre-eminent talents long, long be ours; and the grateful effusions of Millions of freemen, at a far distant period, follow their aged and honoured patriot to the peaceful tomb. These I know are the ardent wishes of my worthy friend as they are of
this fellow Citizen
ALEX. WILSON

P.S. I am at present engaged in drawing the two Birds I brought from the Mohock; which, if I can finish to your approbation, I intend to transmit to our excellent President, as the child of an amiable parent presents some little flower to its affectionate father as a token of its esteem.

❦[LXXVI]❦

LOC

To Thomas Jefferson.

Kingsessing, 18 March 1805.

Sir,

I beg your acceptance of a small trifle in Natural History which though imperfectly executed is offered with all the sincerity of affection to the best Friend and brightest ornament of this happy Country. If It afford you a moments amusement I shall think myself amply rewarded.

On my return from a visit to the Falls of Niagara in October last I killed two Birds on the shores of the Mohawk river and conceiving them to be little known, particularly the Jay, I have taken the liberty of transmitting under favour of Mr. Bartram as faithfull a sketch of them as I was capable of taking. The Jay approaches nearly to the *Corvus Canadensis* of Linnaeus and *Le Geay brun* of Buffon differing however in the colour and article of crest so much as to seem to be a distinct species. From several other Birds found while on the same Tour I am inclined to believe that many subjects still remain to be added to our Nomenclature in the Ornithology of the middle and northern states.

Permit me now to ask your Excellency's forgiveness for this intrusion. Rejoicing with a gratefull Country in the prospects of reaping the fruits of your preeminent services for many years I implore Heaven to bless and preserve a life so honourable to Science and so invaluable to the republican institutions of a great and rapidly increasing Empire and beg leave to Subscribe myself With the deepest veneration Your Excellencys sincere Friend and humble Servt

ALEX. WILSON

LOC

To Thomas Jefferson.[1]

18 March 1805.

Sir,

I have taken the liberty to cover a Letter for your Excell'y from Mr. Alexander Wilson accompanying a fine and accurate drawing of two rare birds which he lately procured when on a tour through the Nᵒr. eastern parts of the State of New York to view the Cataract of Niagara. Mr. Willson shewed me the birds well preserved. The Jay seems to differ from Mr. Pennant's Corvus cinorius Arct. Zool. And the Butcher Bird Lanius Excubitor Linn. Mr. Wilson, excited

1. This is the letter which William Bartram sent to Thomas Jefferson with Wilson's letter of 18 March 1805.

by motives of benevolence from a high opinion of your personal & public character, requests me to convey to you his offering as a testimony of his esteem & affection.

Some time past your worthy friend Doct. Barton, soon after his return home from Virginia informed us that it was your wish to have the horns of the Stone Buck (Capra Gorvicapra). I am directed by my brother to assure you that you are perfectly wellcome to them, and should have sent them, but living so remote from Philadelphia, have not yet found a safe mode of conveyance.

We have a horn of a species of Cervus from the coast of Hudson's Bay brought and presented to my father by Capt. Swain, who many years since made a voyage thither when on a discovery of the N. Western passage across our Continent. Tho' this horn appears to have belonged to an adult, it is singularly small & light & must have shaded the brow of a very small animal. I beg leave to repeat that you are wellcome to both these specimens, and wish for an opportunity of safe conveyance.

I sincerely unite with my friend W. and every True American in congratulations for your reelection to the Presidency of U. States.

An wishing You a long and happy Life, beg leave to subscribe
Your Excellency's
Sincere Friend
WILLIAM BARTRAM

⁘[LXXVII]⁘

GROSART

To William Duncan.

Gray's Ferry, 26 March 1805.

. . . I received your letter of January 1, sometime about the beginning of February, and wrote the same evening very fully; but have heard nothing in return. Col. S. desires me to tell you to be in no uneasiness, nor part with the place to a disadvantage on his account. His son has been with me since January. I told you in my last of the thinness of my school: it produced me the last quarter only twenty-six scholars; and the sum of fifteen dollars was all the money I could raise from them at the end of the term. I immediately called the trustees together, and, stating the affair to them, proposed giving up the school. Two of them on the spot offered to subscribe between them one hundred dollars a-year rather than permit me to go; and it was agreed to call a meeting of the people: the result was honourable to me, for forty-eight scholars were instantly subscribed for; so that the ensuing six months my school will be worth pretty near two hundred dollars. So much for my affairs. . . .

I have never had a scrap from Scotland since last summer; but I am much more anxious to hear from you. I hope you have weathered this terrible winter; and that your heart and limbs are as sound as ever. I also most devoutly wish that matters could be managed so that we could be together. This farm must either be sold or let; it must not for ever be a great gulf between us. I have spent most of my leisure hours this winter in writing the "Foresters," a poem descriptive of our journey. I have brought it up only to my shooting expedition at the head of the Seneca Lake, and it amounts already to twelve hundred lines. I hope that when you and I meet, it will afford you more pleasure than any of my productions has ever done. The two nondescript birds which I killed on the Mohawk, attracted the notice of several naturalists about Philadelphia. On the 4th of March, I set to work upon a large sheet of fine drawing paper, and in ten days I finished two faithful drawings of them, far superior to any that I had before. In the background, I represented a view of the Falls of Niagara, with the woods wrought in as finely as I possibly could do. Mr. Lawson was highly pleased with it, and Mr. Bartram was even more so. I then wrote a letter to that best of men, Mr. Jefferson, which Mr. Bartram enclosed in one of his, (both of which, at least copies of them I shall show you when we meet,) and sent off the whole, carefully rolled up, by the mail on the 20th inst., to Monticello, in Virginia. The Jay I presented to Mr. Peale, at his request; and it is now in the Museum. I have done but few other drawings, being so intent on the poem. I hope if you find any curious birds, you will attempt to preserve them, or at least their skins; if a small bird be carefully skinned, it can easily be set up at any time. I still intend to complete my collection of drawings; but the last will be by far the best. . . .

The poor of Philadelphia have suffered extremely this winter, the river having been frozen up for more than two months, yet the ice went away without doing any damage. I must again request that you and Alexander would collect the skins of as many birds as you have not seen here. . . . The process of skinning the birds may amuse you; and your collections will be exceedingly agreeable to me. In the meantime, never lose sight of getting rid of the troublesome farm, if it can be done with advantage, so that we may once more be together; and write to me frequently.

I have now nothing more to say, but to give my affectionate compliments to your mother and all the family, and to wish you every comfort that the state of society you are in can afford. With the great volume of Nature before you, you can never, while in health, be without amusement. Keep a diary of every thing you meet with that is curious. Look out, now and then, for natural curiosities as you traverse your farm; and remember me as you wander through your woody solitudes.

﹇ LXXVIII ﹈

LOC

To Alexander Wilson.
Monticello, 7 April 1805.

I recieved here yesterday your favor of Mar. 18. with the elegant drawings of the new birds you found on your tour to Niagara, for which I pray you to accept my thanks. The Jay is quite unknown to me. From my observations, while in Europe, on the birds & quadrupeds of that quarter, I am of opinion there is not in our continent a single bird or quadruped which is not sufficiently unlike all the members of it's family there to be considered as specifically different. On this general observation I conclude with confidence that your Jay is not a European bird.

The first bird on the same sheet I judge to be a Muscicapa from it's bill, as well as from the following circumstance. Two or three days before my arrival here a neighbor killed a bird, unknown to him & never before seen here as far as he could learn. It was brought to me soon after I arrived; but in the dusk of the evening, & so putrid that it could not be approached but with disgust. But I retain a sufficiently exact idea of it's form & colours to be satisfied it is the same with yours. The only difference I find in yours is that the white on the back is not so pure, and that the one I saw had a little of a crest. Your figure, compared with the white bellied Gobemouche 8. Buff. 342 Pl. enlum 566. shews a near relation. Buffon's is dark on the back.[1]

As you are curious in birds there is one well worthy your attention, to be found or rather heard in every part of America, & yet scarcely ever to be seen. It is in all the forests, from spring to fall, and never but on the tops of the tallest trees from which it perpetually serenades us with some of the sweetest notes, & as clear as those of the nightingale. I have followed it miles without ever but once getting a good view of it. It is of the size & make of the Mockingbird, lightly thrush-coloured on the back, & a greyish-white on the breast & belly. Mr Randolph, my son in law, was in possession of one which had been shot by a neighbor. He pronounces this also a muscicapa, and I think it much resembling the Moucherolle de la Martinique 8. Buffon 374. Pl. enlum. 568. As it abounds in all the

---

1. Georges Louis Leclerc, Comte de Buffon (1707–1788), French naturalist.

neighborhood of Philadelphia, you may perhaps by patience & per-severance (of which much will be requisite) get a sight, if not a possession of it. I have for 20. years interested the young sportsmen of my neighborhood to shoot me one, but as yet without success. Accept my salutations & assurances of respect.

TH: JEFFERSON

H S P

To William Bartram.

18 April 1805.

My dear Sir,

By Mr. Jefferson's condescending and very intelligent letter to me, which I enclose for your perusal, it appears that our Jay is an entire new, or rather undescribed bird, who met me on the banks of the Mohawk, to do me the honour of ushering him into the world. This duty I have conscientiously discharged, by introducing him to two naturalists: the one endeared to me and every lover of science by the benevolence of his heart and the meekness of his many virtues who like his own humble rose bushes contents himself with the shelter'd scene of rural retirement diffusing to his friends a pleasing serenity by the mildness of his manners. The other ordained by heaven to move in a distinguished orbit—an honour to the human race—the patron of science, and best hope of republicans! I say that no bird, since Noah's days, could boast of such distinguished honour.

Mr. Jefferson speaks of a very strange bird. Please let we know what it is. I shall be on the look-out, & he must be a sly fellow if he escape me. I shall watch his motions and the sound of his serenade pretty closely, to be able to transmit to our worthy President a faithful sketch of a bird which he has been so long curious to possess.[1]

I am with esteem

Your ever affect. friend

ALEX. WILSON

To William Duncan.

Gray's Ferry, 8 May 1805.

I am glad to understand that the plantation is increasing so fast in value, but more so that it is not either sold or otherwise disposed of at the low rate at which we would have once thrown it away; yet it is the perpetual cause of separating us, which I am very sorry for. I am living a mere hermit, not spending one farthing, to see if I possibly can reimburse ——, who I can see is not so courteous and affable as formerly. I hope to be able to pay him one hundred dollars, with interest, next October, and the remainder in the Spring. We shall then be clear of the world, and I don't care how many privations I suffer to effect that. I associate with nobody; spend my leisure hours in drawing, wandering through the woods, or playing upon the violin.

I informed you in my last of sending Mr. Jefferson drawings of the Falls, and some birds, which I found on the Mohawk, and which it seems have never been taken notice of by any naturalist. He returned me a very kind and agreeable letter, from Monticello, expressing many obligations for the drawings, which he was highly

1. Attached to this letter is a drawing, with notes of measurements, of a blue jay; it differs from that used for plate 1 of the *Ornithology*.

pleased with; and describing to me a bird, which he is very desirous of possessing, having interested the young sportsmen of his neighbourhood, he says, these twenty years, to shoot him one, without success. It is of the size and make of the Mocking-bird, lightly thrush-coloured on the back, and grayish-white on the breast; is never heard but from the tops of the tallest trees, whence it continually serenades us with some of the sweetest notes, and as clear as those of the nightingale. Mr. Bartram can give no account of this bird, except it be the Wood Robin, which I don't think it is; for Mr. Jefferson says, *"it is scarcely ever to be seen"*; and "I have followed it for miles without ever, but once, getting a good view of it." I have been on the look-out ever since, but in vain. If you can hear of such a bird, let me know. I wish you also to look for the new bird which I discovered. It is of the size of the Blue Jay; and is of that genus—of a dull lead colour on the back—the forehead white—black on the back of the neck—the breast and belly a dirty, or brownish white, with a white ring round its neck—its legs and bill exactly the Jay's. Pray inquire respecting it, and any other new bird. If they could be conveyed to me, drawings of them, presented to the same dignified character, might open the road to a better acquaintance, and something better might follow. Alexander and you, will, I hope, be on the look-out with the gun, and kill every bird that comes in your way; and keep written descriptions, or the skins, if possible, of those you don't know. Were I able, I would undertake another journey up to you through the woods, while the birds are abundant; and nothing would give me so much pleasure as to make another extensive tour with you for this purpose; for I am persuaded that there are many species yet undescribed; and Mr. Jefferson is anxious to replenish his museum with the rare productions of his country. . . .

＃[LXXXI]＃

GROSART

To William Duncan.

Gray's Ferry, 31 May 1805.

Yesterday evening I was finishing a Hanging-bird in my silent mansion, musing upon a certain affair, when Mr. L. popped his head in at the window, with a letter. I instantly laid down my pencil, and enjoyed a social *crack* with my distant friend; and was heartily and truly pleased with the upshot. In everything relative to this land business, you have acted amidst difficulties and discouragements with prudence and discretion. In refusing to engage with —— you acted well; and I doubt not but you will be equally circumspect in making a transfer of the property, so that the Yankee will not be able, even if he were willing, to take you in. More than half of the roguery of one-half of mankind is owing to the simplicity of the other half. You have my hearty concurrence in the whole affair, for I impatiently wish you beside me, not only to enjoy your society and friendship, but to open to you the book of knowledge, and enable you, in your turn, to teach it to others. In plain language, I wish you to prosecute your studies with me a few months; a school will soon be found, and you can then pursue them without expense, and I trust with pleasure. The business has indeed its cares, but affords leisure for many amusements; and is decent and reputable when properly discharged. I am living in solitude; spending nothing; diligently attending to the duties of the day; and filling up every leisure moment with drawing and music. I have bought no clothes, nor shall I, this Summer; therefore if you settle the matter with —— as you have agreed, we can discharge our obligations to [Sullivan], and be in a state to go on with your studies for at least six months. Mr. [Sullivan] was here yesterday, and expressed many acknowledgements for the rapid progress [David] is making, for indeed I have exerted myself to pay my obligations to the father by my attentions to the son.

I wrote you respecting the letter I had from the President. I have never been able to get a sight of the bird he mentions. I hope you will not neglect to bring your gun with you, and look out as you come along.

I have done no more to the *Foresters*. The journey is brought up to my expedition upon the Seneca Lake. I am much in want of notes of the first settlement, and present state, of the different places that we passed, as we went up the Susquehannah; every thing of this kind, with hunting anecdotes, &c., I wish you to collect on your way down. The remainder of the poem will, I hope, be superior to what is already written, the scenery and incidents being more interesting; and will extend to at least another fifteen hundred lines, which will make in all about three thousand. The notes will swell it to a tolerable size.

The *Rural Walk*, which I published last summer in the *Literary Magazine* has been lately republished in the Port Folio with many commendations on its beauties. The *Solitary Tutor* met with much approbation. But I reserve my best efforts for the remainder of the *Foresters*. . . .

I have not mentioned anything of the sale of the land, nor shall I until the business is finally concluded. I shall expect to hear from you at least twice yet before you arrive; and I hope you will make no unnecessary delay in returning. As you cut a pretty ragged appearance at present, and want something to laugh at, suppose you set your muse to work upon your tatterdamalian dishabille. The former neatness of your garb, contrasted with the present squalidness, would make a capital subject for a song, not forgetting the causes. But you are in the dress of the people you live among; you are therefore in character. B. had a hat on when I was up in your quarter, the rim of which had been eaten off, close to his head, by the rats, or perhaps cut off to make soles to his shoes; yet it was so common as to escape observation. I saw another fellow, too, at the tavern, who had pieces cut out of his *behind*, like a swallow's tail. . . .

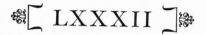

✤[LXXXII]✤

POEMS 1816

To Alexander Wilson, Sr.

1 June 1805.

. . . I have nothing more to say but to wish you all the comforts that your great age, and respectable and industrious life, truly merit. In my conduct toward you, I may have erred, but my heart has ever preserved the most affectionate veneration for you, and I think on you frequently with tears. In a few years, if I live so long, I shall be placed in your situation, looking back on the giddy vanities of human life, and all my consolations in the hopes of a happy futurity. . . .

✤[LXXXIII]✤

GROSART

To William Bartram.

Union School, 2 July 1805.

. . . I dare say you will smile at my presumption, when I tell you that I have seriously begun to make a collection of drawings of the birds to be found in Pennsylvania, or that occasionally pass through it: twenty-eight, as the beginning, I send for your opinion. They are,

I hope, inferior to what I shall produce, though as close copies of the originals as I could make. One or two of these I cannot find either in your nomenclature, or among the seven volumes of Edwards. I have never been able to find the bird Mr. Jefferson speaks of, and begin to think that it must be the Wood Robin, though it seems strange that he should represent it as so hard to be seen. Any hint for promoting my plan, or enabling me to execute better, I will receive from you with much pleasure. I have resigned every other amusement, except reading and fiddling, for this design, which I shall not give up without making a fair trial.

Criticise these, my dear friend, without fear of offending me—this will instruct, but not discourage me. For there is not among all our naturalists one who knows so well what they are, and how they ought to be represented. In the mean time accept of my best wishes for your happiness—wishes as sincere as ever one human being breathed for another. To your advice and encouraging encomiums I am indebted for these few specimens, and for all that will follow. They may yet tell posterity that I was honoured with your friendship, and that to your inspiration they owe their existence.

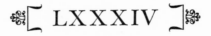

❦[LXXXIV]❧

LOC

To Thomas Jefferson.

Kingsessing, 30 September 1805.

Sir

I had the honour last spring of presenting your Excellency with drawings of two Birds which I suppos'd to be both non descripts untill the receipt of your very condescending Letter to me of Ap. 7th. referring to 8 Buffon 342. Pl. enlum. 566. which I find to contain a Bird of the same Species with one of those sent but unnoticed by me before. Allow me Sir as an atonement for this mistake once more to beg your acceptance of another Sheet of Drawings being my poor efforts to represent faithfully 4 of our most capital Songsters among which is (I believe) the Bird[1] so particularly and accurately described in your Excellency's Letter to me. This being the only Bird I can find among all our Songsters corresponding in every respect with the description there given. The clearness and plaintive Sweetness of its notes—its shy solitary disposition—continually serenading us from the tops of the tallest trees—its colour size and resemblance to the Moucherolle de la Martinique of Buffon, as observed by your Excellency, designate this, (and my friend Mr Bartram is of the same opinion) to be the Bird so justly esteemed by your Excellency.

Finding, as I do, an innocent and delightfull retreat from the sometimes harrassing business of Life in our Rural Solitudes I have employed some of my leisure hours in Drawing many of these charming Songsters of the Grove with a view at some future day of publishing in a more finished manner all the Birds resident in or which Emigrate to the United States from the South & north. May I hope that your Excellency will not think meanly of my feeble attempts or of the motives which have induced me to intrude at this time on your precious hours devoted to the Interests and happiness of an immense Country. These motives are, The most affectionate regard and veneration for your Excellency as the friend of Science and the *"best hope"* of virtuous Republicans; and the fond but humble hope of meriting your esteem.

Your Excellency's devoted friend and humble servt

ALEX. WILSON

---

1. Wilson's note: See the uppermost figure in the drawing.

❦[LXXXV]❦

CRICHTON 1819

To William Bartram.

29 November 1805.

Dear Sir,

I have been amusing myself this some time in attempting to etch; and now send you a proof-sheet of my first performance in this way. Be so good as communicate to me your own corrections, and those of your young friend and pupil, and I will receive them as a very kind and particular favour. The drawings, which I also send, that you may compare them together, were done from birds in full plumage, and in the best order. My next attempt in etching will perhaps be better, everything being new to me in this. I will send you the first impression I receive, after I finish the plate.

Yours, Ec.

ALEX. WILSON

❦[LXXXVI]❦

CRICHTON 1819

To William Bartram.

Saturday 4 January 1806.

Mr. Wilson's affectionate compliments to Mr. Bartram, and sends for his amusement and correction another proof of his Birds of the United States. The colouring being chiefly done last night, must soften criticism a little. Will be thankful for my friend's advice and correction. Mr. Wilson wishes his beloved friend a happy new year, and every blessing.

❦[LXXXVII]❦

APS

To William Bartram.

27 January 1806.

My Dear Friend

Being in town on Saturday I took the opportunity of calling on Mr. Ronaldson, Typefounder who in 1804 went down the Ohio to St. Louis with one companion in a small Batteau where they purchased a quantity of lead and returned by sea. They sometimes proceeded 70 miles in 24 hours going often night and day—had an awning and generally slept on Board with out even catching cold or any inconvenience by Musquitoes except when in the neighborhood of swamps. He describes the Country as exceedingly Beautifull.

The object of their journey being trade they had neither gun nor fishing tackle and paid little or no attention to Natural subjects, but the general scenery. He says the navigation of a Batteau is perfectly easy and attended with no hazard whatever. One solitary adventurer passed them in a small boat going by himself to New Orleans from Wheeling. If my dear friend we should be so happy as to go together what would you think of laying our design before Mr. Jefferson with a view to procure his advice and recommendation to influential characters in the route. Could we procure his approbation and patronage, they would secure our success. Perhaps he might suggest some improvements in our plan. Had we a good companion intimately acquainted with Mineralogy who would submit to our economical plan of proceeding it would certainly enhance the value of the expedition. However this I have no hope of.

I see by the papers that Mr. Jefferson designs to employ persons to explore the shores of the Mississippi the ensuing summer. Surely our exertions would promote his wishes. I write these particulars that you may give them the consideration they deserve and will call up to deliberate further on the affair.[1]

Am as Ever

Yours Truly

ALEX. WILSON

LXXXVIII

GROSART

To William Bartram.

3 February 1806.

. . . The enclosed sketch of a letter is submitted for your opinion, and, if approved, I must request of you the favour to enclose it in one of your own to Mr. Jefferson. You see I am serious in my design of traversing our southern wildernesses. Disappointed in your company, I have no hopes in another's that would add any value to the Ohio tour. I am therefore driven to this expedient, and I hope it will succeed. Please to let me hear your sentiments on this affair to-morrow morning; and oblige yours, &c. . . .

1. I did not find the manuscript of this letter. The Library of the American Philosophical Society possesses what seems to be a copy of the original among some papers apparently used by Grosart for his book on Wilson. In the body of his book Grosart reprinted Ord's incomplete version; however, in the Introduction he said he had lately received a complete and faithful copy from Mr. James Grant of Philadelphia; he gave the missing words, but did not change a few grammatical alterations made by Ord. I have assumed the APS copy to be that from Grant and have used it.

❧[LXXXIX]❧

GROSART

To William Bartram.

5 February 1806.

I am infinitely obliged to you, my dear friend, for your favourable opinion of me, transmitted to the President. Should an engagement be the consequence, I will merit the character which you have given of me, or perish in the endeavour to deserve it. Accept my assurances of perpetual affection and esteem.

The letter go off to-morrow. . . .

❧[XC]❧

ORD

To Thomas Jefferson.

Kingsessing, 6 February 1806.

Sir,

Having been engaged, these several years, in collecting materials, and furnishing drawings from nature, with the design of publishing a new Ornithology of the United States of America, so deficient in the works of Catesby, Edwards, and other Europeans, I have traversed the greater part of our northern and eastern districts; and have collected many birds undescribed by these naturalists. Upwards of one hundred drawings are completed; and two plates in folio already engraved. But as many beautiful tribes frequent the Ohio, and the extensive country through which it passes, that probably never visit the Atlantic States; and as faithful representations of these can only be taken from living nature, or from birds newly killed; I had planned an expedition down that river, from Pittsburg to the Mississippi, thence to Neworleans, and to continue my researches by land in return to Philadelphia. I had engaged as companion and assistant Mr. William Bartram of this place, whose knowledge of Botany, as well as Zoology, would have enabled me to make the best of the voyage, and to collect many new specimens in both those departments. Sketches of these were to have been taken on the spot; and the subjects put in a state of preservation to finish our drawings from, as time would permit. We intended to set out from Pittsburgh about the beginning of May; and expected to reach Neworleans in September.

But my venerable friend, Mr. Bartram, taking into more serious consideration his advanced age, being near seventy, and the weakness of his eye-sight; and apprehensive of his inability to encounter the fatigues and deprivations unavoidable in so extensive a tour; having to my extreme regret, and the real loss of science, been induced to decline the journey; I had reluctantly abandoned the enterprise, and all hopes of accomplishing my purpose; till hearing that your Excellency had it in contemplation to send travellers this ensuing summer up the Red River, the Arkansaw and other tributary streams of the Mississippi; and believing that my services might be of advantage to some of these parties, in promoting your Excellency's design; while the best opportunities would be afforded me of procuring subjects for the work which I have so much at heart. Under these impressions I beg leave to offer myself for any of these expeditions; and can be ready at a short notice to attend your Excellency's orders.

Accustomed to the hardships of travelling; without a family; and an enthusiast in the pursuit of Natural History, I will devote my whole powers to merit your Excellency's approbation; and ardently wish for an opportunity of testifying the sincerity of my professions, and the deep veneration with which I have the honour to be,[1]

Sir,

Your obedient servant,

ALEX. WILSON

ANS

To [*Joshua Sullivan*].

Gray's Ferry, 21 February 1806.

Dear Sir,

I recd. per David your very friendly Note which is so like that benevolent openess of heart which I have contemplated so often in you that I rejoice to find that neither cares nor prosperity nor a multiplicity of new and much more meritorious acquaintance has deprived me of the friendship of one to whom I have been so much obliged and whom I so truly value. I am accustomed to be poor but not to be in debt and I shall take good care that nothing of the kind shall come between us to interrupt our friendship. I expected before this to have let you know the Presidents determination with regard to our Journey but matters of infinitely more consequence no doubt has prevented him from replying to our Letters of the 8th Inst. Enclosed is a Letter from David which he says is the real sentiments of his heart and I as really believe them to be so. I thank you most sincerely for your kind offers. I hope to be able in my next to com-

1. This letter, to which Wilson received no reply, has not been found among the Jefferson Papers in The Library of Congress, thus adding weight to the theory that it was withheld from Jefferson. Whatever the reason, it does not seem to have been received by the President. The first printing of this letter was in Ord's Biographical Sketch, *American Ornithology*, Vol. IX, 1814.

municate the purport of Mr. Jefferson's Letter and my own ultimate designation. I had expected to have paid you a visit on Sunday but will not be able this time.

How happy should I be if such sentiments as David has here express'd would continue to be Clear to him in more advanced years. I should then think that the precepts of a Tutor and the Example of a virtuous and affectionate parent were abundantly repaid in preserving such a promising plant from the blasting influence of a vicious world. Compts. to Mrs. Sullivan and best wishes for the happiness of the family from

Your much obliged friend
ALEX. WILSON

GROSART

To William Duncan.

Gray's Ferry, 26 February 1806.

. . . Notwithstanding the great esteem I have for your judgment, in preference, many times, to my own, yet I believe we are both wrong in the proposed affair of Saturday week. I have not the smallest ambition of being considered an orator; and would it not, by some, be construed into vanity, or something worse, for me to go all the way from this place to deliver a political lecture at Milestown? Politics has begot me so many enemies, both in the old and new world, and has done me so little good, that I begin to think the less you and I harangue on that subject the better. I do not say this from any doubt I have of being able to say something on the subject, but much question the policy and prudence of it. If you and I attend punctually to the duties of our profession, and make our business our pleasure, and the improvement of our pupils, with their good government, our chief aim, honour and respectability, and success, will assuredly attend us, even if we never open our lips on politics.

These have been some of my reflections since we parted. I hope you will weigh them in your own mind, and acquiesce in my resolution of not interfering in the debate on Saturday, as we talked of. At the same time, I am really pleased to see the improvement the practice has produced in you, and would by no means wish to dissuade you from amusing and exercising your mind in this manner; because I know that your moderation in sentiment and conduct will always preserve you from ill will on any of these scores. But as it could add nothing to my fame, and as they have all heard me often enough on different subjects about Milestown, and as it would raise no new friends to you, but might open old sores in some of your present friends, I hope you will agree with me that it will be prudent to decline the affair. And as you have never heard me deliver any of my own compositions in this way, I will commit a speech to memory which I delivered at Milestown in the winter of 1800, and pronounce it to you when we are by ourselves in the woods, where we can offend nobody.

I have heard nothing from Washington yet, and I begin to think that either Mr. Jefferson expects a brush with the Spaniards, or has not received our letters; otherwise, he would never act so unpolitely to one for whom he has so much esteem as for Mr. Bartram. No hurry of business could excuse it. But if affairs are not likely to be settled with Spain, very probably the design of sending parties through Louisiana will be suspended. Indeed, I begin to think that if I should not be engaged by Mr. Jefferson, a journey by myself, and at my own expense, at a time too when we are just getting our heads above water, as one may say, would not be altogether good policy. Perhaps in another year we might be able, without so much injury, to make a tour together through part of the south-west countries, which would double all the pleasures of the journey to me. I will proceed in the affair as you may think best, notwithstanding my eager wishes and the disagreeableness of my present situation. I write this letter in the schoolhouse—past ten at night—L.'s folks all gone to roost—the flying squirrels rattling in the loft above me, and the cats squalling in the cellar below. Wishing you a continuation of that success in teaching which has already done you so much credit, I bid you for the present good-night. . . .

❦[XCIII]❦

ANS

To William Bartram.

Philadelphia, 22 April 1806.

My Dear Friend,

I take the liberty of informing you that, having been importuned to engage as assistant editor of that comprehensive and voluminous work, Rhees' new Cyclopaedia, now publishing here, and a generous salary offered me, I have now accepted of the same, and will commence my new avocation on Monday next.

This engagement will, I hope, enable me in more ways than one to proceed in my intended Ornithology, to which all my leisure moments will be devoted. In the meantime, I anticipate, with diffidence, the laborious and very responsible situation I am soon to be placed in, requiring a much more general fund of scientific knowledge and stronger powers of mind than I am possessed of; but all these objections have been overruled, and I am engaged, in conjunction with Mr. Samuel F. Bradford, to conduct the publication. In this pursuit I will often solicit your advice, and be happy to communicate your observations to posterity. Shut up from the sweet scenes of rural nature, so dear to my soul, conceive to yourself the pleasures I shall enjoy in sometimes paying a visit to your charming Retreat, and you cannot doubt of frequently seeing Your very sincere friend

ALEX. WILSON

ᨏ[XCIV]ᨏ

GROSART

To Mr. [?] Wilson.[1]

Philadelphia, 8 July 1806.

Dear Sir,

This will be handed to you by Mr. Michaux, a gentleman of an amiable character, and a distinguished naturalist, who is pursuing his botanical researches through North America, and intends visiting the Cataract of Niagara. The kindness I received from your family in 1804 makes me desirous that my friend, Mr. Michaux, should reside with you during his stay at Niagara; and any attention paid to him will be considered as done to myself, and suitable acknowledgements made in person by me on my arrival at Niagara, which I expect will be early next Spring.

You will be so good as give Mr. Michaux information respecting the late rupture of the rock at the Falls, of the burning spring above, and point out to him the place of descent to the Rapids below, with any other information respecting the wonderful scenery around you.

In the short stay I made, and the unfavourable weather I experienced, I was prevented from finishing my intended sketch equal to my wishes; but I design to spend several weeks with you, and not only take correct drawings, but particular descriptions of every thing relating to that stupendous Cataract, and to publish a more complete and satisfactory account, and a better representation of it, than has been yet done in the United States.

I had a rough journey home through the Genessee country, which was covered with snow to the depths of fifteen inches, and continued so all the way to Albany. If you know of any gentlemen in your neighbourhood acquainted with botany, be so good as introduce Mr. Michaux to them. . . .

1. "at The Falls of Niagara."

❦[XCV]❦

P M A

To Alexander Wilson, Sr.

Philadelphia, 24 August 1806.

My Dear Father,

I hear so seldom from you and from Scotland, my native country, that it would seem as some interdiction were laid by your Government on correspondence to America, this being the second letter since I received yours. On the first of April last, I resigned a very troublesome business after teaching nearly ten years, and was engaged by Messrs. Bradford & Co., booksellers in this city, to officiate as assistant editor of a very elegant edition of Rees New Cyclopaedia, to be comprehended in 22 quarto volumes, which they are now publishing, and which, in point of printing, engravings, &c., will, I doubt not, fully equal the original. My business consists in reading the work previous to its going to press, making additions and selections, to render the articles respecting America more full and interesting, to correct the sheets as they come from the press, visit the engravers, &c., &c., for which I am to be paid a salary of 900 dollars per annum. Having been so long accustomed to reside in the country, and particularly delighted with its rural charms, I felt considerable regret to exchange it for the confines of a crowded city, where the inhabitants are almost yearly put to the route by that terrible scourge the yellow fever; but when judgment approves habit soon reconciles us to almost any change, and, though I occasionally visit the country with a kind of enthusiasm, I am yet satisfied to sacrifice even this pleasure for the hopes of independence. The city is as healthy at present as in winter, and all fears of a visit from the fever this season is over. Everything is in abundance, particularly fruits and vegetables. A water melon that measured 13 inches in diameter by 20 inches, and weighed upwards of

30 pounds, was last night purchased by the lady of the house where I board for nine cents, or about fivepence British currency. Cucumbers have been actually sold for less than sixpence British per bushel; and peaches, apples, pears, &c., are also extremely cheap. These, in this country, form part of the necessaries of life. Flour rates about 7½ dollars per barrel. I heard from John Finlayson on Sunday last that all the family were well and I had the pleasure of receiving from him about 6 weeks ago some of the finest pinks I ever saw, and which were greatly admired by our American florists here. I did not omit this opportunity of raising their admiration of the *Flora* of my native country, by assuring them that these were but specimens of the inferior sort, and far surpassed by others of larger size and richer colours, which the gardens of a little village called the Seedhills of Paisley produces in the greatest luxuriance. I heard a few weeks ago from my sister Mary, who resides with her three youngest children in Ovid. James, who is now 13 or 14, supports his mother, and she writes me that she lives very comfortably. All the rest are in or near this city. William, by indefatigable application, has acquired a good education, is well versed in mathematics, and writes very superior to what I have ever been able to do. He has been engaged since October as teacher of Milestown School where I resided so long, and he has attained the character of an excellent teacher and a worthy man, which he truly merits. He will write to you soon himself; at least, he promised so to me when I saw him last. His brother lives in the neighbourhood and follows weaving, and goes occasionally to school to his brother, as I am extremely anxious he should rise above his present humble drudgery. We hear nothing of their father; his conduct furnishes an instance of parental depravity unexampled by anything I have known or read of, in rearing a most promising family, transporting them to a foreign country, and leaving them there to perish, while he himself cohabits with guilt, poverty, and infamy in Ireland. But I have no doubt the lash of remorse has already severely punished his unparalleled inhumanity, and I wish never to see him. If you know where Mr.

Charles Orr is, or have any opportunity of seeing him, I wish you would inform him of the following particulars, viz., that Miss Mary Robb is married to a Captain Campbell; that poor Briden, the carpenter, has been struck with the palsy; that Mr. Todd and Mr. ———, his old landlord, died of the yellow fever; and that the whole of the beautiful range of buildings where he lived in Dock Street have been destroyed by fire; that Logan, the stonecutter, died of a consumption; that Edwin and Lawson, the engravers, are both married and that I board at the very house where I parted from him on his return to Britain. These circumstances, though uninteresting to you, will be otherwise to him and I know of no other way of communicating them, as he has never written me, and as I have no idea of where he is, or whether he be alive or dead. I am extremely anxious to hear from you, and David I hope, will not neglect to write, particularly on the receipt of this. I had promised myself much pleasure from David's correspondence but neither he nor any of my relations or friends in Scotland have written me these two years except yourself. You could not oblige me more then inform me of the changes that have taken place among my old acquaintances in Paisley and the Seedhills, and the state and improvements of my native town. Next to the welfare of yourself and my step-mother, these particulars would be extremely agreeable. Several of my old friends, I understand, have been talking of coming to America, but wish persuasion and advice from those on this side of the Atlantic. But this is a matter of so much delicacy, that those who have once done it effectually will seldom ever do it again and yet I do not know a single industrious Scotsman in the country but is in much better circumstances than he ever experienced in Britain. The mischief is they have generally difficulties to surmount on their first arrival which together with the prepossession in favour of their native country and its habits, customs, &c., so natural to man, contribute to embitter their enjoyments and to make them feel little gratitude to those by whose persuasion they left their homes. There are many exceptions, however, and the best way is for every man to make this a matter of such conscience for himself. Nothing could give me more pleasure than to spend a few weeks in Paisley, where, however, I fear I would find that time, death, absence, &c., had made me a greater stranger and less known than in Philadelphia. Please to present my affectionate compliments to my brother David, to Thomas Witherspoon, to John Bell and Duncan Wright, to sisters Peggy, Jean and Janet, and particularly to my step-mother. I am happy to understand that William Urie is doing so well, and settled so near you. He and I might meet at the Cross of Paisley, I am persuaded, and not have the least recollection of each other. What havock time, war, oppression, &c., &c., makes on mankind . . . and depriving them of what constitutes the sweetest enjoyments of human life—the social intercourse of dear-loved friends, parents, and relations. You may calculate on soon hearing from me again more particularly which nothing shall prevent me from but want of health. Business requires my close and constant attendance. I keep little or no company, and to hear from my aged father will to me be the greatest happiness. Please to direct to the care of Mr. Samuel F. Bradford, Bookseller, Third Street, Philadelphia.

I remain,

my dear father,

Your ever affectionate Son,

ALEXANDER WILSON

❦[XCVI]❦

HSP

To Mr. Charles W. Peale.

Philadelphia, 18 December 1806.

Dear Sir,

Along with this you will receive the curious literary relict of which we spoke yesterday, and which was presented to me, a few weeks ago by Mr. Samuel F. Bradford, bookseller of this city.

From every internal evidence it appears to be, "The first seven *Proof Sheets* of Mr. Pope's works, containing the *author's written corrections."*

Mr. Bradford cannot, at this time, recall to recollection when or from whom he received it, or by what circumstances it came into his possession; it is therefore, with his approbation, deposited in your Museum, as a place of safety; where it will afford more general gratification than if confined to the cabinet of any private individual, and from whence, should circumstances hereafter render it necessary, it may be reclaimed.

Happy in being the means of contributing anything to your already magnificent Collection, I offer you the assurance of my affectionate esteem.[1]

ALEX. WILSON

GROSART, ORD

To William Bartram.

Philadelphia, 8 April 1807.

. . . Enclosed is a proof-sheet of our prospectus; as soon as the impressions are thrown off on fine paper, I will transmit one for Mr. L. This afternoon Mr. Lawson is to have one of the plates completely finished; and I am going to set the copper-plate printer at work to print each bird in its natural colours, which will be a great advantage in colouring, as the black ink will not then stain the fine tints. We mean to bind in the prospectus at the end of the next half volume, for which purpose twenty-five hundred copies are to be thrown off; and an agent will be appointed in every town in the Union. The prospectus will also be printed in all the newspapers, and everything done to promote the undertaking.

1. This is a typewritten copy.

I hope you have made a beginning, and have already a collection of heads, bills, and claws, delineated. If this work should go on, it will be a five years' affair; and may open the way to something more extensive; for which reason I am anxious to have you with me to share the harvest.

I started this morning, by peep of day, with my gun, for the purpose of shooting a nuthatch. After jumping a hundred fences, and getting over the ancles in mud, (for I had put on my shoes for lightness), I found myself almost at the junction of the Schuylkill and Delaware, without success, there being hardly half an acre of woodland in the whole *neck*; and the nuthatch generally frequents large-timbered woods. I returned home at eight o'clock, after getting completely wet, and in a profuse perspiration, which, contrary to the maxims of the doctors, has done me a great deal of good; and I intend to repeat the dose, except that I shall leave out the ingredient of the wet feet, if otherwise convenient. Were I to prescribe such a remedy to Lawson, he would be ready to think me mad. Moderate, nay, even pretty severe exercise, is the best medicine in the world for sedentary people, and ought not to be neglected on any account. . . .[1]

❦[XCVIII]❦

GROSART

To William Bartram.

Philadelphia, 29 April 1807.

My Dear Sir,

The receipt of yours of the 11th inst., in which you approve of my intended publication of American Ornithology, gave me much satis-

---

1. Grosart gives the addressee as William Bartram while Ord assigns it to William Duncan. On the internal evidence of this letter and that which follows, I have decided to accept Grosart's attribution.

faction; and your promise of befriending me in the arduous attempt commands my unfeigned gratitude. From the opportunities I have lately had, of examining into the works of Americans, who have treated of this part of our natural history, I am satisfied that none of them have bestowed such minute attention on the subject as you yourself have done. Indeed, they have done little more than copied your nomenclature and observations, and referred to your authority. To have you, therefore, to consult with in the course of this great publication I consider a most happy and even auspicious circumstance; and I hope you will, on all occasions, be a rigid censor, and kind monitor, whenever you find me deviating from the beauties of nature, or the truth of description.

The more I read and reflect upon the subject, the more dissatisfied I am with the *specific* names which have been used by almost every writer. A name should, if possible, be expressive of some peculiarity in colour, conformation, or habit; if it will equally apply to two different species, it is certainly an improper one. Is *migratorious* an epithet peculiarly applicable to the robin? Is it not equally so to almost every species of *turdus* we have? *Europea* has been applied by Pennant to our large *sitta* or nuthatch, which is certainly a different species from the European, the latter being destitute of the black head, neck, and shoulders of ours. Latham calls it *carolinensis*, but it is as much an inhabitant of Pennsylvania and New York as Carolina. The small red-bellied *sitta* is called *canadensis* by Latham, a name equally objectionable with the other. Turdus *minor* seems also improper; in short I consider this part of the business as peculiarly perplexing; and I beg to have your opinion on the matter, particularly with respect to the birds I have mentioned, whether I shall hazard a new nomenclature, or, by copying, sanction what I do not approve of.

I hope you are in good health, enjoying in your little Paradise the advances of the Spring, shedding leaves, buds and blossoms, around her; and bringing in her train choirs of the sweetest songsters that earth can boast of; while every zephyr that plays around you breathes fragrance. Ah! how different my situation in this delightful season, immured among musty books, and compelled to forego the harmony of the woods for the everlasting din of the city; the very face of the blessed heavens involved in soot, and interrupted by walls and chimney-tops. But if I don't launch out into the woods and fields oftener than I have done these twelve months, may I be transformed into a street musician. . . .

ＸＣＩＸ

ANS

To William Bartram.

Philadelphia, 22 May 1807.

Dear Sir,

With this you will receive V.4 part 1st of the Am. Cyclopaedia. It would have been sent a week ago but for want of an opportunity.

By the impressions of my two first plates that accompany this you will see that I have a request to make to Miss Bartram if the state of her health will permit. We want well-coloured Specimens of the plates to be sent to Boston Charleston New York etc. and as my time will not permit me to do them myself I have presumed to apply to her to colour the . . . impressions that are sent with this, according to the Specimens that accompany them, for which I shall make any return. Perhaps Mary Leech might be set to some parts of them with safety which would lessen the drudgery.

If this request should be considered as disagreeable you will not, I am sure impute it to any motives but those of the highest esteem for those to whom I make it, and the impressions may be returned tomorrow by any safe conveyance with perfect good nature on both sides.

In washing the blue Jay the most difficult part of the process is to lay on the colour without being streaked (which you will see I have not succeeded in) and in giving the true tint which I think is nearly approached in the specimen. Nothing but a wash is necessary as the engraving must be seen thro' the colour.

But you know the whole affair ten times better than I can pretend to and as I shall be engaged in Drawing on Sunday I beg you would drop me a line tomorrow by Mr. Leech.

With sincere and affectionate wishes for your happiness and that of the family I remain as ever

Dear Sir
Your much obliged friend
ALEX. WILSON

P.S. The yellow bird has been coloured with a too dull yellow and the *breast* of the hanging bird may be more of a vermilion.

A P S

To Dr. Benjamin S. Barton, M.D.

Philadelphia, 18 June 1807.

Sir,

Dr. Green having expressed a wish to see an account of the *Natural Bridge* introduced into the Cyclopaedia, and having offered to furnish the article himself, I wrote him the enclosed note, and received, in return, his answer, on the back of the same. On application to you, Mr. Bradford was referred to Mr. Conrad, who has sent me the description contained in the 2d Vol. of the Literary Magazine, p.441, which accompanies this, but which Dr. Green says is none of his. Anxious to procure as correct and interesting an account as possible of this natural curiosity, I have to request you would inform me where the *Journal* referred to is to be found, or by what means I can procure it. I am sorry to put you to so much trouble, but I hope the circumstances of the case, will, in your mind, justify the application.

I offer you the assurances of my respectful esteem,

ALEX. WILSON

ANS

To [*Samuel F. Bradford*].

New York, 2 October 1807.

Dear Sir,

I have visited the whole Booksellers of New York, distributed your letters and exhibited the specimens of the Ornithology, called on a number of gentlemen to whom I had been recommended and having done every thing here for both works that I have been able, I shall leave New York to-morrow and pass slowly through N. Jersey so as to be home some time early next week.

Messrs. Brisbane and Brannan declined engaging for any number of copies of the Ornithology but reserved their offers until the first number should be published. The specimens attracted general admiration and few or no subscribers. When I called on Dr. Miller there were two other gentlemen of the faculty with him who desired me to put down one Subscription for the College and two or three other gentlemen have subscribed. I have called on Dr. Mitchill three different times but have not seen him. Dr. Miller, however, with whom I breakfasted yesterday has promised to make respectful mention of the Ornithology in the Medical Journal. As soon as the steam boat returned from Albany I called on Mr. Fulton and mentioned some particulars in the article, Canal, which I was anxious he should see before its publication, gave him your address and presented [him with] a specimen of the Ornithology, letterpress, etc. with which he was much pleased and will call on you some time next week to examine what they have said of himself in our "Canal" etc., and if not too late to add what observations may seem necessary. His steam boat which threatens to deprive all the other passage boats and stages of business arrived yesterday forenoon after a passage of 160 miles in 27 hours carrying upwards of 60 passengers at 7 dollars each besides other goods, and set off this forenoon at ten o'clock with a heavy sea and strong gale approaching to a storm right in her teeth as we usually say. The wharves and vessels were crowded with spectators many of them dubious of his meeting such a sea but so soon as the machinery was put in motion she shot through the water as steady and level as a line amidst the shouting of the multitude.

I am with sincere esteem
Dear Sir
Yours
ALEX. WILSON

 **CII**

LOC

To Alexander Wilson.

Washington, 9 October 1807.

Th: Jefferson having a few days ago only received a copy of the printed proposals for publishing a work on American ornithology by Mr Wilson, begs leave to become a subscriber to it, satisfied it will give us valuable new matter as well as correct the errors of what we possessed before. He salutes Mr Wilson with great respect.

LOC[1]

TO THE LOVERS OF NATURAL HISTORY.

A New and Superb Work . . . Being the first of the kind
ever published in America.

1. Since this prospectus is addressed, like a letter, to the Lovers of Natural History and as it has not previously been printed in any of the major studies of Wilson by Ord, Grosart, or Cantwell, I have thought it right to include it. My transcription is from the copy Wilson sent to Thomas Jefferson. Although it is dated 6 April 1807, Jefferson does not seem to have received his copy of the proposals for publication by subscription until the autumn. See Jefferson's order, letter CII, above, 9 October 1807.

The prospectus announced that the work would be issued in numbers, with three plates each, at $2 per number, the numbers to be continued regularly every two months, but this seems to have been impracticable. Subsequent advertisements referred to publication by Bradford and Inskeep at $12 per volume, or $120 per set of ten volumes. The Library of the American Philosophical Society has copies of two of Wilson's advertisements for the first volume, and supporting editorial material, which appeared in the *Albany Gazette* of 3 November 1808 and *Charleston Courier* of 16 February 1809. The following extracts reveal that the publication had become much more ambitious.

It is now upwards of a year since the Prospectus of this work was first issued, but owing to a train of unforseen events, its publication has been retarded to the present time. During this temporary suspension the Author has had leisure to review and reconsider his plans & to new model it in such a manner as will render the work in point of elegance not inferior to any of the kind that has appeared in Europe.

The first volume is described as bound in half morocco and

printed on a superb vellum paper, and contains nine plates, engraved by Lawson and Murray, on which are represented thirty-eight of our native birds, richly coloured after nature. The letter press, which contains 160 odd pages, is executed in a style equal to any specimen of typography we have seen from Europe.

The prospectus is an interesting example of the romantic movement in American literature. Samuel Taylor Coleridge, Wordsworth, and others had been influenced by William Bartram's *Travels through North and South Carolina* . . . (1791), and Wilson too, in his own distinctive way, was proving an eager disciple. Here Wilson is seen as one in the long line of writers who have marveled at the miracle of nature which, for him, was sufficient religious experience. The study of nature was his theology. He is also shown to have been a clever publicist setting forth his wares to the best advantage.

PROPOSALS
FOR PUBLISHING BY SUBSCRIPTION,
BY SAMUEL F. BRADFORD, PHILADELPHIA,
IN IMPERIAL QUARTO,
AMERICAN ORNITHOLOGY
OR,
THE NATURAL HISTORY OF THE BIRDS OF
THE UNITED STATES,
COMPREHENDING
THOSE RESIDENT WITHIN OUR TERRITORY,
AND
THOSE THAT MIGRATE HITHER FROM OTHER REGIONS:
AMONG WHICH
WILL BE FOUND A GREAT NUMBER OF LAND AND
WATER BIRDS HITHERTO UNDESCRIBED SPECIFYING
THE CLASS, ORDER AND GENUS TO WHICH EACH
PARTICULAR SPECIES BELONGS. FOLLOWING WITH
A FEW EXCEPTIONS, THE ARRANGEMENT OF LATHAM.
Describing their Size, Plumage, Places of Resort, General Habits,
Peculiarities, Food, Mode of Constructing their Nests,
Term of Incubation, Migration, &c. &c.

BY ALEXANDER WILSON

CONDITIONS:

The work will be printed in large Imperial Quarto, on a rich vellum paper, and issued in Numbers, price Two Dollars each, payable on delivery. . . . Three plates, 13 inches by 10, will accompany each Number, containing at least ten Birds, engraved and coloured from original drawings, taken from Nature. . . . The Numbers to be continued regularly once every two months, until the whole be completed.

THE study of Natural History is certainly the most pleasing, as well as the most rational and sublime amusement, that can occupy the mind of man. To whatever portion of the vast chain of created beings we direct our research, the wisdom, power, and benificence of the Deity, in its formation, in the harmony of its parts, and in the provident care exercised for its preservation, fill us with wonder, delight, and awful veneration. These sensations encrease on every re-examination; and the mind once habituated to the contemplation of these manifestations of the Divinity, opens for itself a never failing source of enjoyment and instruction. In our social walks and rural excursions, every where surrounded by the wonders of creation, we seem, as it were, to hold converse with the great Author of the Universe, through the medium of his works, and with hearts glowing with devotion, to "Look through Nature up to Nature's God."

The garden, the fields, the depth of the forest, the most solitary and unfrequented regions, furnish the naturalist with a perpetual fund of amusement. . . . He hears around him the mingled warblings of the feathered tribes, and recognizes, with the joy of an old acquaintance, the peculiar notes of every particular species, and, by a charming association of ideas, a thousand interesting circumstances, connected with, and relating to, their different manners, economy, migrations, &c. On this hand he beholds one species just returned from the orange groves of Guiana and Surinam, to charm him with its simple melody. . . . On that, a second, who has abandoned the shores of the Amazon or Orinoco, to trace his shallow streams and rivulets. . . . Around him sweeps another, who has skimmed, in a few hours, over a space equal to one fourth of the globe, to glide along the surface of his ponds, and seek a shelter under his roof; while a brilliant and numerous family, in green, blue and glowing scarlet, that but lately caught the eye of the sun-burnt savage of Brazil, amidst his native woods, now flutter through our orchards, or fill our groves with melody. Impelled by the powerful impressions of love, and the dictates of nature, all of them have winged their way to our more temperate and abundant regions, to rear their young in safety, and conduct a joyous progeny back to southern climes, and far distant countries.

To such pleasing ideas as these does an acquaintance with, and contemplation of, this gay and beautiful, this innocent and sportive part of the creation, give rise. A thousand new subjects for wonder and delight present themselves to our view, which before were entirely unseen or overlooked; in each of which we behold fresh evidences of a great, a good, and all-upholding Creator: and surely these are enjoyments far beyond the idle prattle of novels, . . . the noisy discord of politics . . . the

short-lived joys of scandal, ambition, avarice or debauchery. From these
destroyers of the health, morals and tranquillity of the human race, how
noble, how exquisitely pleasing, to retire to where the great Book of
Nature is spread before us . . . . ever open and inviting . . . . replete with
a divine and inexhaustible store of pleasure and instruction!

To promote the study of this branch of Natural History, so friendly
to virtue and piety, and so congenial to innocence, by exhibiting to the
eye, a faithful representation of the numerous, and richly adorned families of the feathered race, that tenant the woods and waters of this peaceful, highly favoured and happy country . . . to rescue this part of American history, from the obscurity in which the mistakes, the prejudices, and
circumscribed situation of foreigners have involved it, and to furnish his
fellow-citizens with an elegant and rational amusement, and with additional motives for self-congratulation and love of country, are the great
designs of this publication.

Much as we are indebted to the efforts of the naturalist, to whatever
nation he may belong, it is yet a mortifying truth to our literary pride,
that by foreigners alone, has not only this, but almost every other branch
of our natural history been illustrated. Nothing similar to the present undertaking has ever been attempted in America; and, indeed, if we except
the efforts of a few distinguished individuals, the annals of our literary
history present a long and melancholy void in this most interesting and
instructive department of science. It remains now with Americans themselves to decide, whether they will still send across the Atlantic for an
account of the productions of their own country, or become, like every
other enlightened people, the proper historians of their own territories.

To enter into an examination of all the different European publications
on the Ornithology of this part of North America, would lead us far from
our purpose, and might seem invidious, as they have appeared under the
sanction of names highly and justly esteemed. Catesby, Edwards, Buffon,
and others, have respectively published splendid and voluminous works
on this subject. But a century has now nearly elapsed, since the first of
these gentlemen visited our country, and the others derived their figures
and descriptions chiefly from *dried subjects*, and from the reports of tran-
sient travellers. With all due deference, therfore, to such names, the
author will be pardoned for believing that much remains yet to be done,
that half of our birds have not been figured by any of these writers; and
that a more full and faithful publication than has ever yet appeared on

this subject is due to *America*, and to the *World* in which the glare of false and gaudy colouring, and the extravagant distortion of posture will not be substituted for the simplicity of truth and nature. Let the abilities of the painter be what they may, if he has nothing but stuffed skins, or dried specimens to draw from, he can no more give the true tints, form and air of the living original, than he could delineate the native features, the genuine character, and soft expression of the soul, from the shrunk and shrivelled visage of an Egyptian mummy.

The author of the work now proposed to the public, has enjoyed advantages which many of those above-mentioned were deprived of. With the means of consulting many of the ablest writers who have treated on the subject, he has, during thirteen years, resided chiefly in the country, where he had the best opportunities of pursuing this his favourite study. He has traversed several thousand miles of the interior in the same pursuit, and has neither drawn nor described a single species before examining several individuals of the same kind; and collecting, from personal observation, facts relative to their history. And, that full justice may be done to the drawings, the publisher has engaged two eminent artists, Messrs. Lawson and Murray, to finish the whole of the engravings, whose abilities are a sufficient guarantee for the execution of this part of the work.

Upwards of 150 of the drawings are already finished, and the plates for the first number nearly ready; which, if sufficient encouragement offer, will be published early this ensuing Autumn. Each number will contain ten birds, carefully coloured after the originals, and accompanied by appropriate descriptions; and though the nature of the plan precludes the possibility of them succeeding each other in generic order, yet the order, genus, and specific name of each will be particularly given, as well as those by which they are known in different parts of the country. Where the plumage of the male and female is nearly alike, the former only will be figured; but where the difference is considerable, both will be represented, in order to correct the numerous errors into which European naturalists have fallen, in describing the male and female of the same nest, as two males of two separate species. . . . in mistaking the *male* of others for the *female*, and vice versa; and in considering a periodical change of plumage, to which many of our birds are subject as marks of an entire different species.

The extent of the work cannot at present be precisely ascertained:

it is conjectured, however, that one hundred plates may comprehend the whole, forming two handsome volumes. The drawings will be made with the most scrupulous adherence to nature, the engravings will be executed, and the impressions coloured, under the eye of the author. . . . the type for the letter-press is entirely new, and of singular beauty: and the public may rest assured, that no pains or expense will be spared, in any department of the work, to render it, in point of accuracy and elegance, worthy their support.
Philadelphia, April 6th, 1807

SUBSCRIPTIONS RECEIVED BY S. F. BRADFORD, NO.4, SOUTH THIRD STREET, PHILADELPHIA.
& also by D. Rapine, Capitol Hill.

 C I I I

HSP

[Note on a daddy long legs.]

28 August 1808.

On the morning of the 28th of March I took from the leaves of a lemon tree in Messrs. Bartrams Gardens a species of Acaris vulgarly called long legs—Grandady etc. etc. the body of which is nearly globular and the legs 8 in number from 1¼ to 3 inches in length—each having two joints near their middle [parts] ¼ to ½ inch apart—these *legs* after being torn from the body of the insect and laid upon paper in a room were agitated by sudden and violent motions which often raised them from the paper and they continued in that jerking or palpitating state for upwards of 30 minutes—the motion at first being almost incessant in each but gradually diminishing or rather the intervals between each convulsive agitation increasing from a quarter of a second to a minute or two; and even after some of them seemed entirely dead, on being touched a little with the finger they seemed to revive and started about as violent as ever—These convulsive motions if they may be so called seemed to originate in the joints and what is very singular each leg before its final cessation seemed to suffer expiring agonies starting about more violent than ever for a second or two, after which no attempts with the finger could restore it. To some of the legs a small fragment of the body adhered—others had snapt short—the latter seemed to outlive the former contrary to what might have been expected. Whether these extraordinary phenomena were occasioned by Galvanism electricity or were the mere convulsive vibrations of the nerves must be left to the practical entomologist to discover and determine—The same experiment I have tried twice before with this insect with the like effects. Mr. Wm. Bartram and his niece Miss Ann Bartram witnessed this singular exhibition.[1]

A. WILSON

GROSART

To William Bartram.

Philadelphia, 21 September 1808.

. . . In a few minutes I set out for the Eastern States, through Boston to Maine, and back through the State of Vermont, in search of birds and subscribers. I regret that I have not been able to spend an evening with you before my departure. But I shall have a better stock of adventures to relate after my return.

I send a copy of the prospectus, and my best wishes for the happi-

---

1. Although signed, this is not a letter but a note prepared for publication.

ness of the whole family. I leave my horse behind, and go by the stage coach, as being the least troublesome. I hope to make discoveries in my tour, the least agreeable of which will, I fear, be—that I have bestowed a great deal of labour and expense to little purpose. But all these things will not prevent me from enjoying, as I pass along, the glorious face of Nature, and her admirable productions, while I have eyes to see, and taste and judgment to appreciate them. . . .

CRICHTON 1819

[*To a friend.*]

Boston, 10 October 1808.

. . . I have purposely avoided saying anything either good or bad, on the encouragement I have met with. I shall only say, that among the many thousands who have examined my book, and among these were men of the first character for taste and literature, I have heard nothing but expressions of the highest admiration and esteem. If I have been mistaken in publishing a work too good for the country, it is a fault not likely to be soon repeated, and will pretty severely correct itself. But whatever may be the result of these matters, I shall not sit down with folded hands, whilst anything can be done to carry my point, since God helps them who help themselves. I am fixing correspondents in every corner of these northern regions, like so many piquets and outposts, so that scarcely a *wren* or *tit* shall be able to pass along, from New York to Canada, but I shall get intelligence of it. . . .

❦[CVI]❦

THAYER

To Daniel H. Miller, Ironmonger.
North Second Street.
Between Arch & Race Streets, Philadelphia.

Boston, 12 October 1808.

Dear Sir,

I arrived here on Sunday last, after various adventures, the particulars of which, as well as the observations I have had leisure to make upon the passing scenery around me, I shall endeavour, as far as possible, to compress into this letter, for your own satisfaction, and that of my friends in Philadᵃ who may be interested for my welfare. My company in the stage coach to N. York were all unknown to me, except Col. Simonds who was on his route to Fort Oswego, on Lake Ontario, to take command of the troops intended to be stationed on that part of the frontier, to prevent evasions of the embargo law. The sociable disposition and affability of the Colonel made this part of the journey pass very agreeably, for both being fond of walking, whenever the driver stopt to water, or drink grog, which was generally every 6 or 8 miles, we set out on foot, and sometimes got on several miles before the coach overhauled us. By this method we enjoyed our ride with more satisfaction and with some little saving of horseflesh, which I know you will approve of. At Princeton I bade my fellow passengers good bye, as I had to wait upon the reverend doctors of the college. I took my book under my arm, put a number of prospectus into my pocket, and walked up to this spacious sanctuary of literature. I could amuse you with some of my reflections on this occasion, but room will not permit. Dr. Smith, the President, and Dr. M'Lean, Professor of Natural History, were the only two I found at home. The latter invited me to tea, and both were much pleased and surprised with the appearance of the work. I expected to receive some valuable information from M'Lean, on the ornithology of the country, but I soon found, to my astonishment, that he scarcely knew a *sparrow* from a *woodpecker*. At his particular request, I left a specimen of the plates with him; and from what passed between us, I have hopes that he will pay more attention to this department of his profession than he has hitherto done. I visited several other literary characters; and about half-past 8 the Pilot coming up, I took my passage in her to New Brunswick. In the corner of the carriage I heard the snoring of two animals but whether four or two legged I could not tell. We reached Brunswick about 12 at night where I immediately went to bed.

The next morning and afternoon were spent in visiting the few gentlemen here likely to patronise my undertaking. I had another siege of the same kind at Elizabethtown; and, without tiring you with details that would fill a volume, I shall only say that I reached Newark that day, having gratified the curiosity and feasted the eyes of a great number of people who repaid me with the most extravagant compliments, which I would have very willingly exchanged for a few simple *subscriptions*. I spent nearly the whole of Saturday in Newark, where my book attracted as many starers as a bear or a mammoth would have done, and I arrived in New York the same evening. Early on Monday morning I waited on Dr. Sam Mitchill who received me with great kindness and seemed highly gratified at seeing the Book. I staid with him to breakfast, presented his lady with a copy of one of my poems which by some means or other she had heard of and at the Drs. request left my volume with him for that day as he wished to write a review of it for his Medical Repository. During the remainder of this day I wrote 4 or 5 letters. These were partly delivered the same day. In the afternoon of Tuesday I took my book under my arm and waited on each of these gentlemen to whom I had written the preceding day. Among these

I found some friends, but more admirers. The professors of Columbia College expressed much esteem for my performance. The professor of languages, being a Scotchman, and also a *Wilson*, seemed to feel all the pride of national partiality so common to his countrymen; and would have done me any favour in his power. I spent the whole of this week traversing the streets, from one particular house to another, till, I believe, I became almost as well known as the public crier, or the clerk of the market, for I could frequently perceive gentlemen point me out to others as I passed with my book under my arm.

Time now urging me to go, I engaged a Mr. Hardy, Author of American Biography in 4 volumes and one of the city commissioners, to be my agent here in collecting subscribers. Hardy had been very obliging and useful to me and from his energy and general knowledge of the trade I expect something may be done. I spent part of Saturday in viewing the different curiosities in and about New York. On Governor's Island I found Mr. Sowder who introduced me to his partner and conducted me through the whole works erecting and erected there. Of these it is impossible for me within the bounds of this letter and unacquainted as I am with the science of fortification to give you an adequate account. The face of this island was formerly very irregular consisting of heights and hollows, the shore in some places precipitous in others heaped with large stones, so that though a strong Fort is situated in the center of the island many places were completely covered from its fire. To prevent all possibility of this the whole surface is now forming into a gradual slope from the Fort to the sea on all sides; so that, as Sowder observed to me, they will be able with their grape shot and 18 pounders to *brush the shoes* of every invader the moment he sets his foot on it. In addition to this they are now erecting on the West point of the island a circular battery or castle of such prodigious strength and constructed with a degree of judgement that seems to have provided for every possible emergency that I think it may defy not only the

fury of the waves but the whole vengeance of those insolent &
presumptious beings who imperiously boast of being *Rulers of the
Waves*. It is forming of vast masses of hewn stone dove-tailed into
each other and united by a strong cement composed of lime mixed
with cannon borings. It will contain three tier of guns 26 on the
lower, 33 on the next and as many as they please on the upper and
two thousand years hence will, I doubt not, stand a lasting monument of the skill and abilities of the builders. Sowder seems to have
a genius excellently suited for this kind of work and has got his
head as full of bombs, embrasures, ravellins and cannon balls as
mine has sometimes been with Tom-tits, Catbirds and Woodpeckers. On the other extremity of the island upwards of 200 men
were engaged in carrying an enormous chain from a vessel to the
shore, the bars of each link were as thick as a man's arm and two feet
in length. They had already several hundred feet of it piled up on
shore, how much remained on board I know not. This chain is to be
stretched from Governor's to Bedloes Island which is also forti-
fying. Returning to New York I examined the new City Hall erecting there. It is 250 feet by 175 according to my measurement with
projecting wings and a portico supported by 8 columns and as many
more as you enter the inner doors. The wings as well as front are
adorned with pilasters. The ground story of a reddish colored
stone, the north front of the same, all the tops of the outward parts
of white marble highly polished and ornamented with elegant but
simple sculpture, and is by far the most beautiful piece of architecture I have ever seen in America. The work owing to some cause or
other progressing with a snail's pace, tho' they have 35 or 40 stone
cutters, and 10 or 12 mason's constantly at work. The second story
exclusive of the ground one is nearly up.

The market of New York is also worthy of a few observations.
This is situated in the lowest and filthiest part of the whole city in
a street called Fly [?] Market. The market place is supported by
brick pillars similar to ours in the middle of the street immediately

over a large common sewer which occasions it to be elevated by a wooden floor three or four feet above the level of the street. Into this dark and gloomy place where even at mid-day a lantern would sometimes be a useful attendant, you ascend by means of steps. The stalls on each side are formed of enormous wooden chests, the tops or lids of which are occasionally scraped but the ends and sides are never cleaned and are sufficient to turn the stomach of a Hottentot. Into these precious repositories which fill up almost the whole sides of the market and shut every ray of light, are thrown sheep heads, cow and calves heads and such *nice* fragments as remain from the sales of the day, which in summer must produce a most fragrant odour. The butchers are nearly as dirty as their stalls, and the gutters which descend into the common sewer below the market pass among the feet of the sellers of vegetables who occupy one side of the street. The whole market by the intersection of two streets is divided into three parts, the first has 13 pillars a side, the next 7 and the last 8, from which you may judge of the length of the whole. The fish market comprehended in the scheme, contained 28 stalls well filled. In apples, pears and peaches of which there were considerable quantities and very good, they nearly rival us; but the noise, confusion, filth and irregularity of the whole would soon disgust you and nothing but habit could reconcile people to such wretched slovenliness. In the evening I went to the theatre and saw Cooper in *Romeo*. The inside of the house looks rather gayer than ours and the scenery is much superior; but the eternal clankings of the box door latches during the performance by loungers passing out and in; and a shrill piercing whistle three or four times repeated from one of the upper side boxes at every shifting of the scenes are extremely disagreeable to a stranger. I have many other things to say of New York but I must proceed to tell you that on Sunday morning, Oct. 2ᵈ, I went on board the packet for New Haven, distant 90 miles. The wind was favourable, and carried us rapidly thro' Hellgate, (a place I had no intention of calling at in my tour) on the other side of which we found upwards of 60 vessels beating up for a passage. The Sound here, between Long Island and the main, is narrowed to less than half a mile, and filled with small islands, and enormous rocks under water, among which the tide roars and boils violently and has proved fatal to many a seaman. At high water it is nearly as smooth as any other place, and can then be safely passed. The country, on the New York side, is ornamented with several handsome country seats, painted white, and surrounded by great numbers of Lombardy poplars. The breeze increasing to a gale we were borne thro' the water on the wings of the wind, a cataract roaring at our bow and two torrents of foam sweeping her sides and in 8 hours from the time we set sail the high red-fronted mountain of New Haven rose to our view. In two hours more we landed; and, by the stillness and solemnity of the streets, recollected we were in New England, and that it was Sunday, the latter of which circumstances had been almost forgotten on board.

This town is situated on a sandy plain; the streets are shaded with elm trees and poplars crossing each other at right angles. In a large park or common covered with grass, and crossed by two streets, and several foot paths, stands the church & church-yard, the State house and College building, which last are 180 yards in front. From these rise 4 or 5 wooden spires or steeples which, in former time, as one of the professors informed me, were so infested by woodpeckers, which bored them in all directions, that to preserve their steeples from destruction, they were obliged to set people, with guns, to watch and shoot these irreverend invaders of the sanctuary. Just about the town the pasture-fields & corn look well, but a few miles off, the country is poor and ill cultivated.

The literati of New Haven received me with politeness and respect; and after making my usual rounds, which occupied a day and a half I commissioned the principal Bookseller, an active intelligent man and my friend to be my representative leaving him papers and specimens of the plates. I set off for Middletown the next day

22 miles distant. The country through which I passed was generally flat and sandy, in some places whole fields were entirely covered with sand, not a blade of vegetation to be seen, like some parts of New Jersey. Round Middletown the country, however, is really beautiful and the ground rich; and here I first saw Connecticut river ½ mile wide, stretching along the east side of the town, which consists of one very broad street, with rows of elms on each side. On entering I found the streets filled with troops, it being muster-day; and I counted 250 horse, and 600 foot, all in uniform. The legislature of Connecticut have passed a law or laws imposing very heavy fines for non attendance and exempting from every species of poll tax those who equip themselves with uniform etc., which I have been told has had excellent effects. The sides of the street were chocked up with waggons, carts, and wheel-barrows, filled with bread, roast beef, fowls, cheese and liquor, barrels of cyder, and rum bottles. Some were singing out, "Here's the best brandy you ever put into your head!" others in dozens shouting, "Here's the round & sound gingerbread! most capital gingerbread!" In one place I observed a long row of 20 or 30 country girls, drawn up with their backs to a fence, and two young fellows supplying them with rolls of bread from a neighbouring stall, which they ate with a hearty appetite, keeping nearly as good time with their grinders, as the militia did with their musquets. In another place the crowd had formed a ring, within which they danced to the catgut scrapings of an old negro. The spectators looked on with as much gravity as if they were listening to a sermon; and the dancers laboured with such hard working seriousness, that it seemed more like a pennance imposed on the poor devils, for past sins, than mere frolic or amusement. After seeing the troops go through a great number of evolutions which ended in the representation of a battle all which they performed very respectably, I waited on a Mr. Alsop of this town, to whom I had been recommended. By him I was introduced to a number of others. He also furnished me with a

good deal of information respecting the birds of New England, being himself a great sportsman—a man of fortune and education— and had a considerable number of stuffed birds, some of which he also gave me, besides letters to several gentlemen of influence in Boston. I endeavoured to recompense him in the best manner I could, and again pursued my route to the N.E. The country between this and Hartford is extremely beautiful, much resembling that between Philada. and Frankford. The road is hard sandy soil; and in one place I had an immense prospect of the surrounding country, nearly equal to that which we saw returning from Easton, but less covered with woods. On reaching Hartford, which also lies on the Connecticut river and has a good many vessels belonging to it I waited on Mr. Goodrich, a member of Congress, who recommended me to several others, particularly a Mr. Wadsworth, a gentleman of taste and fortune, who was extremely obliging. It is impossible for me to mention particulars; the publisher of a newspaper here expressed the highest admiration of the work, has since paid many handsome compliments to the publication in his newspaper as three other editors did in New York. This is a species of currency that will neither purchase plates, nor pay the printer; but, nevertheless, it is gratifying to the vanity of an author—*when nothing better can be got*. My journey from Hartford to Boston, through Springfield, Worcester, &c., 128 miles, it is impossible for me to detail at this time. From the time I entered Massachusetts until within ten miles of Boston which is nearly two-thirds the length of the whole State, the universal features of the country were stony mountains, rocky pasture fields and hills and swamps adorned with pines. The fences in every direction composed of strong stone walls—mosses, with turf cut for fuel—not an orchard in ten mile, unless a few struggling self-planted stunted apple trees. Every 6 or 8 miles you come to a meeting-house, painted white, with a spire and a few houses. I could perceive little difference in the form or elevation of all their steeples.

The people here make no distinction between town and township; and passengers frequently asked the driver, "What town are we now in?" when perhaps we were on the top of a miserable barren mountain, several miles from a house. It is in vain to reason with them on the impropriety of this—custom makes every absurdity proper. There is scarcely any currency in this country but paper, and I solemnly declare that I do not recollect having seen one dollar since I left New York. Bills even of 25 and 50 cents of a hundred different banks, whose very names one has never heard of before, are continually in circulation. The jargon of kume, kaw, kaunt etc., for come, cow, count—is also general in this country. Their boasted schools, if I may judge from the state of the school-houses, are no better than our own. Their politics except in some few districts *bitterly* federal.

Lawyers swarm in every town, like locusts. Almost every door has the word *Office* painted over it, which, like the web of a spider, points out the place where the spoiler lurks for his prey. There is little or no improvement in agriculture; in 50 miles I did not observe a single grain or stubble field, though the country has been cleared and settled these 150 years. In short, the *steady habits* of a great portion of the inhabitants of those parts of New England through which I passed, seem to be laziness, law bickerings, and religious hypocrisy. A man here is as much ashamed of being seen walking the streets on Sunday, unless in going and returning from church, as many honester fellows would be of being seen going to a bawdy house.

As you approach Boston the country improves in its appearance; the stone fences give place to posts and rails; the road becomes wide and spacious; and everything announces a better degree of refinement and civilization. It was dark when I entered Boston, of which I shall give you some account in my next. I have visited the celebrated *Bunker's Hill,* and no devout pilgrim ever approached the sacred tomb of his Holy Prophet with more awful enthusiasm, and profound veneration, than I felt in tracing the grass-grown entrenchments of this hallowed hill, made immortal by the bravery of those heroes who defended it, whose ashes are now mingled with its soil, and of whom a mean, beggarly pillar of bricks is all the memento! My dear friend my paper compels me to conclude. Remember me to all our mutual friends. Tell Benny & Ronaldson I have got on the scent of Antimony, said to be found on Saco River, in the District of Maine—further particulars in my next.

Yours very Sincerely,
ALEX. WILSON

GROSART

To Daniel H. Miller.

Windsor, Vermont, 26 October 1808.

Dear Sir,

I wrote you two or three weeks ago from Boston, where I spent about a week. A Mr. S., formerly private secretary to John Adams, introduced me to many of the first rank in the place, whose influence procured me an acquaintance with others; and I journied through the streets of Boston with my book, as I did at New York and other places, visiting all the literary characters I could find access to.

I spent one morning examining Bunker's Hill, accompanied by Lieutenant Miller and Sergeant Carter, two old soldiers of the revolution, who were both in that celebrated battle, and who pointed out to me a great number of interesting places. The brother of General Warren, who is a respectable physician of Boston, became very much my friend, and related to me many other matters respecting the engagement.

I visited the University of Cambridge, where there is a fine library, but the most tumultuous set of students I ever saw.

From the top of Bunker's Hill, Boston, Charlestown, the ocean, islands, and adjacent country, form the most beautiful varied prospect I ever beheld.

The streets of Boston are a perfect labyrinth. The markets are dirty; the fish market is so filthy that I will not disgust you by a description of it. Wherever you walk, you hear the most hideous howling, as if some miserable wretch were expiring on the wheel at every corner; this, however, is nothing but the draymen shouting to their horses. Their drays are twenty-eight feet long, drawn by two horses, and carry ten barrels of flour. From Boston I set out for Salem, the country between swampy, and in some places the most barren, rocky, and desolate in nature. Salem is a neat little town. The wharves were crowded with vessels. One wharf here is twenty hundred and twenty-two feet long. I stayed here two days, and again set off for Newburyport, through a rocky, uncultivated, sterile country. . . .

I travelled on through New Hampshire, stopping at every place where I was likely to do any business; and went as far east as Portland in Maine, where I staid three days, and the Supreme Court being then sitting, I had an opportunity of seeing and conversing with people from the remotest boundaries of the United States in this quarter, and received much interesting information from them in regard to the birds that frequent these northern regions. From Portland I directed my course across the country, among dreary savage glens, and mountains covered with pines and hemlocks, amid whose black and half-burnt trunks the everlasting rocks and stones, that cover this country, "grinned horribly." One hundred and fifty-seven miles brought me to Dartmouth College, Newhampshire, on the Vermont line. Here I paid my addresses to the reverend fathers of literature, and met with a kind and obliging reception. Dr. Wheelock, the president, made me eat at his table, and the professors vied with each other to oblige me.

I expect to be in Albany in five days, and if the Legislature be sitting, I shall be detained perhaps three days there. In eight days more I hope to be in Philadelphia. I have laboured with the zeal of a knight errant in exhibiting this book of mine, wherever I went, travelling with it, like a beggar with his bantling, from town to town, and from one country to another. I have been loaded with praises—with compliments and kindnesses—shaken almost to pieces in stage coaches; have wandered among strangers, hearing the O's and Ah's, and telling the same story a thousand times over—and for what? Ay, that's it! You are very anxious to know, and you shall know the whole when I reach Philadelphia. . . .

THAYER

To Alexander Lawson.[1]

Albany, 3 November 1808.

Dear Sir,

Having a few leisure moments at disposal, I will devote them to your service in giving you a sketch of some circumstances in my long literary pilgrimage, not mentioned in my letters to Mr. Miller. And in the first place, I ought to thank you for the thousands of compliments I have rec'd for my birds, from persons of all descriptions, which were chiefly due to the taste and skill of the engraver. In short, the book, in all its parts, so far exceeds the ideas and expectations of the first literary characters in the eastern parts of the United States, as to command their admiration and respect. The only objection has been the 120 dollars, which, in innumerable

1. "Pine Street, Between 9th and 10th Streets Philadelphia."

instances, has risen like my evil genius between me and my hopes. Yet I doubt not but when those subscribed for are delivered, and the book a little better known, the whole number will be disposed of, and perhaps encouragement given to go on with the rest. To effect this, to me, most desirable object, I have encountered the hardships and fatigues of a long, circuitous unproductive and expensive journey, with a zeal that has increased with increasing difficulties and sorry I am to say that the whole number of subscribers which I have obtained amount only to 41!

While in New York I had the curiosity to call on the celebrated author of the "Rights of Man." He lives in Greenwich, a short way from the city. In the only decent apartment, I believe, of a small indifferent-looking frame house, I found this extraordinary man, sitting wrapt in a night gown, the table before him covered with newspapers, with pen and ink beside them. Paine's face would have excellently suited the character of *Bardolph*; but the penetration and intelligence of his eye bespeak the man of genius, and of the world. He complained to me of his inability to walk, an exercise he was formerly fond of; examined the book, leaf by leaf, with great attention—desired me to put his name as a subscriber, and, after inquiring particularly for Mr. Peale and Mr. Benny, wished to be remembered to both.

My journey through almost the whole of New England has rather lowered the Yankeys in my esteem. Except a few neat academys, I found their schoolhouses equally ruinous and deserted as our own—fields and mountains covered with stones—stone fences & pasture fields—scrubby oaks and pine trees—a meeting house and steeple painted white every 4 or 5 miles—wretched orchards —scarce one grain field in 20 miles—the taverns along the road dirty, and filled with loungers, bawling about law suits and politics— the people snappish, and extortioners, lazy, and 200 years behind the Pennsylvanians in agricultural improvements. I traversed the country bordering the Connecticut river for nearly 200 miles.

Mountains rose on either side, sometimes 3, 6, or 8 miles apart, the space between almost altogether alluvial; rich and fertile plains, but not half cultivated. From some projecting headlands I had immense prospects of the surrounding countries, every where clothed in pine, hemlock, and scrubby oak.

It was late in the evening when I entered Boston, and, whirling through the narrow, lighted streets, or rather lanes, I could form but a very imperfect idea of the town and that not much to its credit. Early the next morning, resolved to see where I was, I sought out the way to beacon hill, the highest part of the town, and from whence you look down on the roofs of the houses—the bay interspersed with islands—the ocean—the surrounding country, & distant mountains of New Hampshire; but the most singular objects are the long wooden bridges, of which there are 5 or 6, some of them three-quarters of a mile long, uniting the towns of Boston and Charlestown with each other, and with the main land. I looked round with an eager eye for the eminence so justly celebrated in the revolutionary history of the United States, *Bunker's Hill*, but I could see nothing that I could think deserving of the name, till a gentleman, who stood by, pointed out a white monument on a height beyond Charlestown, which he said was the place. I explored my way thither, without paying much attention to other passing objects; and, in tracing the streets of Charlestown, was astonished and hurt at the indifference with which they directed me to the place. I inquired if there were any person still living here who had been in the action, I was directed to a Mr. Miller, who was a lieutenant in this memorable affair. He is a man of about 60—stout, remarkably fresh colored, with a benign and manly countenance. I introduced myself without ceremony—shook his hand with sincere cordiality, and said, with some warmth, that I was proud of the honour of meeting with one of the heroes of Bunker's Hill—the first unconquerable champions of their country. He looked at me, pressed my hand in his, and the tears instantly glistened in his eye, which as instantly called up corresponding ones in my own. We were long acquaintances in a moment. On our way to the place, he called on a Mr. Carter, who, he said, was also in the action, and might recollect some circumstances which he had forgotten. With these two veterans I spent three hours, the most interesting to me of any of my life. As they pointed out to me the route of the British—the American entrenchments—the spot where the greatest slaughter was made—the spot where Warren fell, and where he was thrown amid heaps of the dead, I felt as though I could have encountered a whole battalion myself in the same glorious cause. But perhaps the sight of a few heads arms and legs flying about might have altered the matter. The old soldiers were highly delighted with my enthusiasm! we drank a glass of wine *to the memory of the illustrious dead*, and parted almost with regret.

From Boston to Portland, in the District of Maine, you are almost always in the neighbourhood, or within sight of, the Atlantic. The country may be called a mere skeleton of rocks, and fields of sand, in many places entirely destitute of wood, except a few low scrubby junipers, in others covered with pines of a diminutive growth. On entering the tavern in Portland, I took up the newspaper of the day, in which I found my song of *Freedom and Peace*, which I afterwards heard read before a numerous company (for the Supreme Court was sitting), with great emphasis, as a most excellent song; but I said nothing on the subject. This Town is about equally divided in politics, the more wealthy however are bitterly federal, most maliciously inveterate against the present administration and in the constant habit of evading embargo laws—three vessels went out loaded during the time I staid there—their destination Canada.

From Portland I steered across the country for the northern parts of Vermont, among barren, savage, pine-covered mountains, through regions where Nature has done little and art infinitely less to make it a fit residence for man than any country I ever traversed. Among these dreary tracts I found winter had already commenced, and the snow several inches deep. I called at Dartmouth College, the president of which, as well as of all I visited in N. England, subscribed. Though sick with a severe cold, and great fatigue, I continued my route to this place, passing and calling at great numbers of small towns on my way.

The Legislature is at present in session—the Newspapers have to-day noticed my book, and inserted my advertisement—I shall call on the principal people and employ an agent among some of the booksellers in Albany, and return home by New York.

I have thought of you and Mrs. Lawson often since my departure. I most sincerely hope you are both perfectly recovered. I had no idea of being so long absent and am ashamed to have left the care and expenses of my horse on Mr. Miller without leaving funds for the purpose. Remember me to all our friends. I was out this morning at the house which Jones talks of roughcasting—they seem to have had it lately painted and the bricks interlined. I have not yet seen the proprietors. In my enquiries for Messrs. Benny and Ronaldson I have unfortunately been unsuccessful notwithstanding all my exertions but perhaps I may enable them to trace this mineral to its native spot. I inserted notices in several country papers to that purpose and I have not a doubt but that it exists both in Massachusetts & Vermont. But travelling in Stages is not the way to procure information as you can only go *as* they go and *where* they go. With the most sincere regard I remain

Dear Sir—

Yours affectionately

ALEX. WILSON

Please to communicate the within to our mutual friend. A.W.

CRICHTON 1819

Journal Extracts

Arrived at —— waited on Dr. —— Principal of the Seminary.[1] It was near dusk before I could see him, and our conversation, which was held on the steps leading to his house occupied about five minutes. He considered the volume as too expensive for any class of reader about this town. He behaved with cold indifference—turned over a few leaves without any seeming interest, and said, that as far as he could see, (for it was nearly dark) it looked well. He returned the volume and we parted. If, as Principal of this college, this literary luminary shed no more cheerful influence over the exertions of his pupils than he did on the author of the American Ornithology I do not much wonder that storms and tempests should desolate this seminary, and damp the energies of the inhabitants.

Arrived at ——, called on the Governor of the Health Office; there were several gentlemen in company. He turned over a few leaves very carelessly, asked some trifling questions, and then threw down the book saying, "I don't intend to give a hundred and twenty dol-

1. These extracts are not from a letter but come, it is believed, from Wilson's private journal or diary and refer to his journey through the eastern states covered by his letters to Daniel Miller and Alexander Lawson of October and November 1808. This journal has not been seen since Ord quoted from it in 1814, with further extracts in 1828. It is possible only to conjecture how Crichton was able to give these paragraphs in 1819. When Ord died in 1866 the diary was not among the large collection of books bequeathed by him to the College of Physicians in Philadelphia. These were very much working notes, not intended for publication, and the diary appears to have been Wilson's safety valve as in these and later extracts he reveals a touch of acerbity.

lars for the knowledge of birds." Taking up a newspaper he began to read. I lifted the book, and without saying a word, walked off with a smile of contempt for this very polite, and very learned Governor. If science depended on such animals as these, the very name would long ere now have been extinct.

The city Recorder declared, that he never read or bought books on animals, fishes, plants or birds—he saw no use in them. Yet this same reptile could not abstain from acknowledging the beauty of the plates of the Ornithology.

LOC

To Thomas Jefferson.

Saturday noon 17 December 1808.

Alexander Wilson, author of *American Ornithology*, would be happy to submit the first volume of this work to the inspection of Mr. Jefferson, if he knew when it would be convenient for the President.

A. WILSON[1]

UOV

To Richard Fitzhugh esquire.

Washington, 19 December 1808.

Dear Sir

You will perhaps recollect the having spoken to me of a Mr Coffer[2] in your neighborhood who had made himself very partic-

1. At the meeting which resulted from this letter Jefferson gave Wilson a letter of introduction to a friend, Richard Fitzhugh. The letter is not only evidence of the president's interest in ornithology, but of his good will towards Wilson.

2. Joshua Coffer of Fairfax County, Virginia. He became a subscriber to the *American Ornithology* and is mentioned by Wilson in his essay on the hummingbird (vol. 2, pp. 29–30).

ularly acquainted with the history & habits of the different birds of our country, & that I often expressed a wish to obtain a communication of his knolege. My object in this was to forward it to a Mr. Wilson, whom I knew to be engaged in a work on the birds of our country. Mr. Wilson having come to this place with the first volume of his work, I mentioned yourself & Mr. Coffer to him as persons who I thought could communicate to him more original information as to his subject than perhaps any other persons. On this he sollicited an introduction to you, and hopes through you to be made known to Mr. Coffer. he is accordingly the bearer of this letter and on behalf of the world for whose information he is writing I sollicit your favorable attention to him, and your good offices with Mr. Coffer, and that you will both be so kind as to communicate to him the observations you have made on the birds of our country; in this way your information will be preserved, and will be the more valuable as the opportunities of obtaining such are very rare. With my best respects to Mrs. Fitzhugh. I salute you with friendship & respect.

TH. JEFFERSON

Rich.ᵈ Fitzhugh esq.

❦[CXI]❧

LOC

To Thomas Jefferson.

Washington, 24 December 1808.

Sir,

The person who is the Bearer of this, has in his possession specimens of *Copper Ore* found in Orange County, State of Virginia, which he is solicitous to show to the President. Considering this discovery (if the facts be as he states) highly important at this interesting crisis[1] I have advised him to wait on you without delay—

I have succeeded, tolerably, among the gentlemen here, in procuring subscriptions to my Publication; and leave this place to-day. I shall remit you an account of my interview with Coffer, and am, with considerations of high respect,

Sir,

Your obedt Humble sert
ALEX. WILSON

UOV

To Daniel H. Miller.

Washington, D.C., 24 December 1808.

Dear Sir

Having an opportunity by a son of Mr. Amies[2] of Philada., I cheerfully sit down, before leaving this place, to give you a few particulars of my expedition. I shall begin with my horse, he I am happy to inform you is in good health, and *sees* as well, and I believe sometimes much better, and farther, than his Master. I spent nearly a week in Baltimore, with tolerable success, having procured 16 subscribers there. In Annapolis, I passed my book through both

1. The "interesting crisis" is a reference to effects of the Embargo Act of 22 December 1807. It was calamitous for the North American shipping interests and had the effect of frustrating lawful commerce with other nations by preventing U.S. ships from sailing to foreign ports. Wilson was in Washington when the pressures on Jefferson must have been considerable, and a supply of pure copper, while not a solution to the crisis, would have had substantial commercial benefits. The Act was repealed in March 1809.

2. Mr. Amies was an eminent papermaker. He supplied the special paper for the plates of the *American Ornithology*.

Houses of the Legislature. The wise men of Maryland stared and gapt, from bench to bench; but having never heard of such a thing as 120 Dlls for a Book, the *Ayes* for subscribing were NONE & so it was unanimously determined in the negative. Noways discouraged by this sage decision, I pursued my route through the tobacco fields, sloughs and swamps, of this illiterate corner of the State, to Washington, distant 38 miles; and on my way opened 55 gates! I was forewarned that I should meet with many of these embarrassments, and I opened 22 of them with all the patience and philosophy I could muster, but when I still found them coming thicker and faster, my patience and philosophy both abandoned me, and I saluted every new Gate, which obliged me to plunge into the mud to open it, with perhaps less Christian resignation than I ought to have done. The negroes *there*, are very numerous, and most wretchedly clad. Their whole covering, in many instances, assumes the appearance of neither coat, waistcoat, nor breeches, but a motley mass of coarse, dirty woolen rags, of various colours, gathered up about them. When I stopped at some of the negro huts to inquire the road, both men and women huddled up their filthy bundles of rags around them, with both their arms, to cover their nakedness, and came out, very civilly, to show me the way. I cannot pretend within the bounds of a letter to give you a complete description of Washington. It consists of a great extent of unfenced commons, one half of which is nearly level and little higher than the Potomack; the other parts, on which the Capitol and President's Home are built, are high and commanding. The site is much better than I expected to find it; and is certainly a noble place for a great Metropolis. I saw one brick house building, which is the whole improvements of that kind going on at present. The taverns and boarding houses are crowded with an odd assemblage of Characters. Fat placemen—Expectants—Contractors—Petitioners—Office Hunters—Lumber dealers—Salt Manufacturers and numerous adventurers. Among the rest are deputations from different Indian nations, along our distant frontiers, who are come here to receive their last *alms* from the President, previous to his retirement—

The President received me very kindly. I asked for nobody to introduce me, but merely sent him in a line that I was there; when he ordered me to be immediately admitted. He has given me a letter to a gentleman in Virginia, who is to introduce me to a person there, who, Mr. Jefferson says, has spent his whole life hitherto in studying the manners of our Birds; and from whom I am to receive a whole load of facts and information. The President intended to have sent for him himself, and to have taken down, from his mouth, what he knows on the Subject; thinking it a pity, as he says, that the knowledge he possesses should die with him; but he has entrusted the business to me, and I have promised him an account of our interview. Mr. Madison, Gen. Wilkinson, Gallatin, Eppes, Quincy, Giles, Lloyd, Granger, & Smith of the Navy Department, have subscribed. All I have gleaned here amount to 17. I shall set off, on finishing this letter, to Georgetown and thence to Alexandria. I will write you or some of my friends from Richmond. Remember me affectionately to all our friends. I wish them a happy Christmas and shall drink their health to-morrow, *Solus.*

Your very sincere friend
ALEX. WILSON

THAYER

To Daniel H. Miller.

Charleston, 22 February 1809.

Dear Sir,

I have passed through a considerable extent of country since I wrote you last; and met with a variety of adventures, some of which may perhaps amuse you. Norfolk turned out better than I expected. I left that place on one of the coldest mornings I have experienced since leaving Philada.

I left it with a heavy heart, on account of some circumstances which I shall relate for the satisfaction of my nephew Mr. Duncan and his father's family. In the year 1801, George Duncan, a lad of 14 entered on board the ship Haro, at Greenock in Scotland as an apprentice, merely I believe that he might by this means reach his brother and me. The ship was bound for Norfolk where she arrived on the 17th of September, but the boy was never heard of. On my arrival in Norfolk I stated the circumstances in an advertisement which I inserted in all the papers but without effect. Early on the morning of my departure, however, the following note was handed to me by the physician of the Hospital, "George Duncan was received into the Marine Hospital of Norfolk on the 4th day of October 1801, and died of yellow fever on the seventh of the same month." I instantly went to the Hospital and sought out the Nurse who was then and is now the Matron of the Hospital. Her relation left no doubt in my mind that my poor friend had died unknown and unpitied here. He was buried with the rest of the unfortunates who died that year in the court or yard before the Hospital. I walked among the crowds of graves a while with sensations that I need not describe. A tear or two was all I could pay to his memory and I soon after left town as I have before stated. But let us change the subject.

I mentioned to you in my last that the streets of Norfolk were in a most disgraceful state; but I was informed that some time before they had been much worse; that at one time the news-carrier delivered his papers from a boat which he poled along through the mire; and that a party of sailors, having nothing better to do, actually launched a ship's long-boat into the streets, rowing along with four oars through the mud, while one stood at the bow, heaving the lead, and singing out the depth.

I passed through a flat, pine covered country, from this to Suffolk,

24 miles distant, and lodged in a planter's house, 10 miles beyond this, who informed me that every year regularly in August
and September, almost all his family are laid up with the fever;
that at one time 40 of his people were sick; and that of 13 children only 3 were living. Two of these, with their mother, appeared likely not to be long tennants of this world. 30 miles farther, I came to a small place on the Nottaway river, called Jerusa-
lem. Here I found the river swelled to such an extraordinary height,
that the oldest inhabitant had never seen the like. After passing
along the bridge, I was conveyed in a *flat* a mile and three-quarters
through the woods, where the torrent sweeping along in many
places rendered this sort of navigation rather disagreeable. I proceeded on my journey, passing through solitary pine woods, perpetually interupted by swamps that covered the road with water
two and three feet deep, frequently half a mile at a time, looking
like a long river or pond. These in the afternoon were surmountable;
but the weather being exceedingly severe, they were covered every
morning with a sheet of ice, from half an inch to an inch thick, that
cut my horse's legs and breast. After passing a bridge, I had many
times to wade, and twice to swim my horse, to get to the shore. I
attempted to cross the Roanoke at three different ferries, 35 miles
apart, and at last succeeded at a place about 15 miles below Halifax.
A violent snow storm made the roads still more execrable.

The productions of these parts of North Carolina are hogs, turpentine, tar, and apple brandy, a tumbler of this last is usually their
morning's beverage, as soon as they get out of bed. So universal is
this, that the first thing you find them engaged in, after rising, is
preparing the brandy toddy. You can scarcely meet a man whose
lips are not parched and chopped or blistered with drinking this
poison. Those who dont drink it, they say, are sure of the ague. I,
however, escaped. The pine woods have a singular appearance, every tree being stripped, on one or more sides, of the bark, for 6 or
7 feet up. The turpentine covered these parts in thick masses. I

saw the people, in different parts of the woods, mounted on benches, chopping down their sides; leaving a trough or box in the tree for the turpentine to run into. Of hogs they have immense multitudes; one person will sometimes have 500. The leaders have bells round their necks; and every drove knows their particular call, whether it be a conch-shell, or the bawling of a negroe, though half a mile off. Their owners will drive them sometimes for 5 days to a market, without once feeding them.

The taverns are the most desolate and beggarly imaginable. Bare, bleak, and dirty walls; one or two old broken chairs, and a bench, form all the furniture. The white females seldom or ever make their appearance; and every thing must be transacted through the medium of negroes. At supper, you sit down to a meal, the very sight of which is sufficient to deaden the most eager appetite; and you are surrounded by half-a-dozen dirty, half-naked negroes and negresses, whom any man of common scent might smell a quarter of a mile off. The house itself is raised upon props, 4 or 5 feet; and the space below is left open for the hogs, with whose charming vocal performance the wearied traveller is serenaded the whole night long, till he is forced to curse the hogs, the house, and every thing about it.

I crossed the Taw river at Washington, for Newbern, which stands on a sandy plain, between the Trent and Neuse rivers, both of which abound with alligators. Here I found the shad fishery begun, on the 5th inst.; and wished to have had some of you with me to assist in dissecting some of the finest shad I ever saw. From thence to Wilmington was my next stage, 100 miles, with only one house for the accommodation; two of the landlords having been broken up with the fever.

The general features of North Carolina, where I crossed it, are immense, solitary, pine savannahs, through which the road winds among stagnant ponds, swarming with alligators; dark, sluggish creeks, of the colour of brandy, over which are thrown high wooden bridges, without railings, and so crazy and rotten as not only to

alarm the horse, but his rider, and to make it a matter of thanks-
giving with both when they get fairly over, without going through
or being precipitated into the gulf below as food for the alligators.
Enormous cypress swamps, which, to a stranger, have a striking,
desolate, and ruinous appearance. Picture to yourself a forest of
prodigious trees, rising, as thick as they can grow, from a vast flat
and impenetrable morass, covered for ten feet from the ground with
reeds. The leafless limbs of the cypresses are clothed with an extraordinary kind of moss, from two to 10 feet long, in such quantities that 50 men might conceal themselves in one tree. Nothing
in this country struck me with such surprise as the prospect of several thousand acres of such timber, hanging, as it were, with many
million tons of tow, waving in the wind. I attempted to penetrate
several of these swamps, with my gun, in search of something new;
but, except in some chance places found it altogether impracticable.
I coasted along their borders, however, in many places, and was
surprised at the great profusion of evergreens, of numberless sorts;
and a variety of berries that I knew nothing of. Here I found multitudes of birds that never winter with us in Pennsylvania, living in
abundance. Though the people told me that the alligators are so
numerous as to destroy many of their pigs, calves, dogs, &c., yet I
have never been able to get my eye on one yet, though I have
been several times in search of them with my gun. In Georgia, they
tell me, they are ten times more numerous, and I expect some sport
among them. I saw a dog at the Santee river, who swims across
when he pleases, in defiance of these voracious animals; when he
hears them behind him, he wheels round, and attacks them, often
seizing them by the snout. They generally retreat, and he pursues
his route again, serving every one that attacks him in the same manner. He belongs to the boatman; and, when left behind, always takes
to the water.

    As to the character of the North Carolinians, were I to judge it by
the specimens I met with in taverns, I should pronounce them to
be the most ignorant, debased and indolent as well as dissipated,

portion of the Union. But I met with a few such noble exceptions, that, for *their* sakes, I am willing to believe they are all better than they seemed to be.

Wilmington contains about 3000 souls; and yet there is not one cultivated field within miles of it. The whole country, on this side of the river, is heaps of sand, into which you sink up to the ancles; and hardly a blade of grass is to be seen. All about is pine barrens. I called on the person who keeps the Register of Wills to enquire after that of Peter Bradas, according to your request. The wills are arranged alphabetically and the gentleman and I examined all the *B*s without finding it. I also conversed with a number of elderly people of the town who have been long in public business, but could hear nothing of him.

From Wilmington I rode through the same solitary pine savannahs, and cypress swamps; sometimes 30 miles without seeing a hut, or human being. On arriving at the Wackamaw, Pedee, and Black rivers I made long zigzags among the rich nabobs there, who live on their rice plantations, amidst large villages of negroe huts. One of these gentlemen told me that he had something better than 600 head of blacks. These excursions detained me greatly. The roads to their Plantations were so long, so difficult to find, and so bad, and their hospitality such, that I could scarcely get away again. I ought to have told you that the deep sands of South Carolina had so worn out my horse, that, with all my care, I found he would give up. Chance led me to a planter, named Vereen, about 40 miles north of the Wackamaw river, where I proposed to bargain with him, and to give up my young blood horse for another in exchange; giving him at least as good a character as he deserved. He asked 20 dollars to boot, and I 30. We parted, but I could perceive that he had taken a liking to him; so I went on. He followed me to the sea beach, about 3 miles, under pretence of pointing me out the road; and there, on the sands, amidst the roar of the Atlantic, we finally bargained; and I found myself in possession of a large, well formed and elegant, sorrel horse, that ran off with me at a canter for 15 miles along the sea shore; and travelled the same day 42 miles, with nothing but a few mouthfuls of rice straw, which I got from a negroe. If you have ever seen the rushes with which carpenters sometimes smooth their work, you may form some idea of the common fare of the S. Carolina horse. I found now that I had got a very devil before my chair; the least sound of the whip made him spring half a rod at a leap; no road, however long or heavy, could tame him. Two or three times he had nearly broke my neck, and chair to boot; and at Georgetown ferry he threw one of the boatmen into the river. But he is an excellent traveller, and for that one quality I forgive him all his sins, only keeping a close rein, and a sharp look out.

On arriving at Charleston I took the earliest opportunity of seeking out Mr. Porter and I. Drummond the persons against whom I had Acc^{ts} from Mr. Foering, and but for the suspense Drummond has kept me in I should have wrote you 5 days ago. It would occupy too much time & paper to detail all the particulars of my agency in this business. There is no dependence on a word Drummond says. He has promised me 20 barrels of rice for a week past, and there is no probability of getting it this month, if ever. Porter says he has treated him in like manner. The suit it is expected will be concluded & judgement given in May or June perhaps in 3 years. I have tried every art with him—he says he cannot pay the money & has nothing but this rice, which he pretends is coming to him down the river & which he is willing to give & I as willing to take, at market price, as part payment—the action still good for the remainder. I have been after him 5 times this afternoon; should it be delivered while I am here I shall take care to secure it for Mr. Foering by the first vessel sailing; if not Porter as soon as it is delivered will do this. Mr. Porter appears an honest well meaning fellow but cannot, he says raise money to pay off *his* acc^{t} I had a long conversation with him this morning when he at last contrived to give me a check for 50 dollars, which I thought best to accept. Mr. Foering may draw on me for the sum if he pleases by presenting this to Mr. Bradford. Drummond is a prevaricating shuffling fellow. I have been these two days perpetually after him. Should he deliver this rice to-morrow I shall mention it in the postscript.

I should now give you some account of Charleston, with the streets of which I am as well acquainted as I was with those of New York and Boston; but I reserve that till we meet. I shall only say, the streets cross each other at right angles—are paved on the sides —a low bed of sand in the middle; and frequently in a state fit to compare with Norfolk. The town, however, is neat—has a gay appearance—full of stores; has a market place, which far surpasses that of Philadelphia for cleanliness, and is an honour to the city. Many of the buildings have 2, 3, and 4 ranges of piazzas, one above another, with a great deal of gingerbread work about them. The streets are crowded with negroes; & their quarrels often afford amusement to the passengers. In a street called Broad street, I every day see a crowd of wretchedly clad blacks, huddled in a corner for sale: people handling them like black cattle. Here are female chimney sweeps; stalls with roasted sweet potatoes for sale; and on the wharves clubs of blacks, men and women, sitting round fires, amid heaps of oyster-shells—these seem the happiest mortals on earth. The finest groups for a comic painter might every day be found here that any country can produce. They cook victuals here among the oyster heaps and boil homini while others are eating it.

The ladies of Charleston are drest with taste; though far inferior to those of Philad.ª for their pale and languid countenances and coarse features by no means correspond with their figures. One might say that Bartolozzi had formed the one and Jamie Aitken the other. They [appear?] the most sickly looking useless things on earth, fit only to go [to] bed. I went one night to the Theatre— Cooper performed as usual excellently and Webster also, as usual, twisted his mouth and writhed himself like a man in the pangs of the Colick. The theatre is far inferior to that of Philad.ª

To-morrow afternoon I shall set off for Savannah. You must not

expect to hear from me till I return. I have collected 125 subscribers
since leaving home.

I shall sail from Savannah. Compliments to our friends.

Yours

ALEX. WILSON

P.S. As I expected the 20 Barrels of rice have dwindled to 10 which
he offers on condition that the suit is raised. On consulting our lawyer who thinks it may be 2 years before judgement is finally obtained we have proposed that if he will deliver this rice at the market
price, give notes for the payment of the ballance, one half in May
and the rest in September, with approved endorsing, and pay the
costs of suit, we will consent to raise the action. To this he has at
last consented. The dispute now is only about the price of the rice
which he refuses to deliver in to-day contrary to my earnest wish—
for he is so irritated at me for sticking so close to him, that we have
been almost at buffets. The endorsers he has named are well known
to Porter, and, as he says, perfectly good. I suppose the whole will
be settled to-morrow and Porter will write instantly the result to
Mr. Foering. People here are so universally indolent that they want
a little of our Northern spirit to stir them up to action.[1]

A.W.

1. At a late stage in the preparation of this book, I found an earlier version
of this letter in Wilson's hand, dated 15 February 1809, at the Library of the
University of Virginia. Many of the phrases are identical with those of the
later letter but, as it proceeds, there are indications, in content and handwriting,
that Wilson had come to treat it as a first draft. Wilson also realized that his
commission on behalf of Foering was still at an early stage on 15 February and
as Foering was an important public figure in Philadelphia, and a subscriber to
the *American Ornithology*, he wanted to give him the result of his efforts to get
a firm commitment from Porter and Drummond, in which he had some success.
There are a few portions in the early draft not repeated in the letter that ultimately went to Miller, but they are not significant.

❈[CXIV]❈

GROSART

To Daniel H. Miller.

Savannah, 5 March 1809.

Dear Sir,

I have now reached the *ne plus ultra* of my peregrinations, and shall return home by the first opportunity. Whether this shall be by land or water, depends on circumstances; if the former, I shall go by Augusta, where I am told twelve or fifteen subscribers may be procured. These, however, would be insufficient to tempt me that way, for I doubt whether my funds would be sufficient to carry me through.

The innkeepers in the Southern States are like the vultures that hover about their cities, and treat their guests as the others do their *carrion*: are as glad to see them, and pick them as bare. The last letter I wrote you was on my arrival in Charleston. I found greater difficulties to surmount there than I had thought of. I solicited several people for a list of names, but that abject and disgraceful listlessness, and want of energy, which have unnerved the whites of all descriptions in these States, put me off from time to time, till at last I was obliged to walk the streets, and pick out those houses, which, from their appearance, indicated wealth and taste in the occupants, and introduce myself. Neither M., Dr. R., nor any other that I applied to, gave me the least encouragement, though they promised, and knew I was a stranger. I was going on in this way, when the keeper of the library, a Scotsman, a good man, whose name had been mentioned to me, made me out a list from the directory; and among these I spent ten days. The extreme servility, and superabundance of negroes, have ruined the energy and activity of the white population. M. appears to be fast sinking into the same insipidity of character, with a pretty good sprinkling of rapacity. In Charleston, however, I met with some excellent exceptions among the first ranks of society; and the work excited universal admiration. Dr. D. introduced it very handsomely into the Courier. On hearing of General Wilkinson's arrival, I waited on him. He received me with kindness—said he valued the book highly—and paid me the twelve dollars; on which I took occasion to prognosticate my final success on receiving its *first fruits* from him.

I will not tire you by a recital of the difficulties which I met with between Charleston and Savannah, by bad roads and the extraordinary flood of the river Savannah, where I had nearly lost my horse, he having, by his restiveness, thrown himself overboard; and, had I not, at great personal risk, rescued him, he might have floated down to Savannah before me.

I arrived here on Tuesday last, and advertised in the *Republican*, the editors of which interested themselves considerably for me, speaking of my book in their Thursday's paper with much approbation. The expense of advertising in the Southern States is great; but I found it really necessary. I have now seen every person in this place and neighbourhood, of use to be seen. Here I close the list of my subscriptions, obtained at a price worth more than five times their amount. But, in spite of a host of difficulties, I have gained my point; and should the work be continued in the style it has been begun, I have no doubt but we may increase the copies to four hundred. I have endeavoured to find persons of respectability in each town, who will receive and deliver the volumes, without recompense, any further than allowing them to make the first selection. By this means the rapacity of *some* booksellers will be avoided.

The weather has been extremely warm these ten days, the thermometer stood in the shade on Friday and Saturday last, at 78° and 79°. I have seen no frost since the 5th of February. The few gardens here are as green and luxuriant as ours are in summer—full of flowering shrubbery, and surrounded with groves of orange trees, fifteen and twenty feet high, loaded with fruit. The streets are deep beds of heavy sand, without the accommodation of a foot pavement. I most sincerely hope that I may be able to return home by water; if not, I shall trouble you with one letter more. . . .

⁂[CXV]⁂

GROSART

To William Bartram.

Savannah, 5 March 1809.

Three months, my dear friend, are passed since I parted from you in Kingsess. I have been travelling ever since; and one half of my journey is yet to be performed—but that half is homewards, and through old Neptune's dominions, where I trust I shall not be long detained. This has been the most arduous, expensive, and fatiguing expedition I ever undertook. I have, however, gained my point in procuring two hundred and fifty subscribers, in all, for my Ornithology; and a great mass of information respecting the birds that winter in the Southern States, and some that never visit the Middle States; and this information I have derived personally, and can therefore the more certainly depend upon it. I have, also, found several new birds, of which I can find no account in Linnaeus. All these things we will talk over when we meet. . . .

I visited a great number of the rich planters on the rivers Santee and Pedee, and was much struck with the miserable swarms of negroes around them. In these rice plantations, there are great numbers of birds, never supposed to winter so far north, and their tameness surprised me. There are also many here who never visit Pennsylvania. Round Georgetown I also visited several rich planters, all of whom entertained me hospitably. I spent ten days in Charleston, still, in every place where I stopped a day or two, making excursions with my gun.

On the commons, near Charleston, I presided at a singular feast. The company consisted of two hundred and thirty-seven carrion crows (*vultur atratus*), five or six dogs, and myself, though I only kept order, and left the eating part entirely to the others. I sat so near to the dead horse, that my feet touched his, and yet at one time I counted thirty-eight vultures on and within him, so that hardly an inch of his flesh could be seen for them. Linnaeus and others have confounded this vulture with the turkey buzzard, but they are two very distinct species.

As far north as Wilmington, in North Carolina, I met with the ivory-billed woodpecker. I killed two, and winged a male, who alarmed the whole town of Wilmington, screaming exactly like a young child crying violently, so that everybody supposed I had a baby under the apron of my chair, till I took out the bird to prevent the people from stopping me. This bird I confined to the room I was to sleep in, and in less than half-an-hour he made his way through the plaster, the lath, and partly through the weather boards; and would have escaped, if I had not accidently come in. The common people confound the *P. principalis* and *P. pileatus* together. . . .

I am utterly at a loss in my wood rambles here, for there are so many trees, plants, shrubs, and insects, that I know nothing of. There are immense quantities of elegant butterflies, and other singular insects. I met with a grasshopper so big that I took it for a bird; it settles upon trees and bushes. I have kept a record of all the birds which I have seen or shot since I left home.

This journey will be of much use to me, as I have formed acquaintance in almost every place, who are able to transmit me information. Great numbers of our summer birds are already here; and many are usually here all winter.

There is a Mr. Abbot here, who has resided in Georgia thirty-three years, drawing insects and birds. I have been on several excursions with him. He is a very good observer, and paints well. He has published, in London, one large folio volume of the Lepidopterous insects of Georgia. It is a very splendid work. There is only one vessel here bound to New York; she sails some time next week, and I shall take my passage in her. I caught a fever here by getting wet; I hope the sea air, and sea-sickness, will carry it off. . . .

ANS

To [Samuel F. Bradford].[1]

Savannah, 8 March 1809.

Dear Sir,

Having now visited all the towns within one hundred miles of the Atlantic, from Maine to Georgia, and done as much for this bantling book of mine as ever author did for any progeny of his brain, I now turn my wishful eye towards *Home, Home*! There is a charm, a

1. Grosart indicates that this letter of 8 March 1809 was to William Bartram. Although the ANS original does not give the name, the content suggests that it was to Samuel F. Bradford, not Bartram. At the twentieth Annual General Meeting of the Wilson Ornithological Club held at the Carnegie Museum, Pittsburgh, on 28–29 December 1934, a loan collection of Alexander Wilson material was exhibited; in a brief description of this in the Museum of Comparative Zoology at Harvard University (Wilsoniana) is included a letter to Samuel F. Bradford said to have been written from Charleston, South Carolina, dated 5 March 1809 and concluding with a list of subscribers. This, of course, is at odds with the letters to Lawson and Bartram, dated "Savannah 5th March, 1809." Long searching has not unearthed a letter of 5 March 1809 to Bradford but it is not inconceivable that the letters to Bradford of 5 and 8 March 1809 are one and the same.

melody, in this little word home, which only those know, who have forsaken it to wander among strangers, exposed to dangers, fatigues, insults and impositions, of a thousand nameless kinds. Perhaps I feel the force of this idea rather more at present than usual, being indisposed with a slight fever these three days, which a dose of sea-sickness will, I hope, rid me of. The weather since my arrival in this place has been extremely warm for the season. The wind generally S.W., and the thermometer ranging between 75° and 82°. To me it feels more intolerable than our summer heat in Philad? The streets of Savannah are also mere beds of burning sand, without even a foot pavement; and until one learns to traverse them with both eyes and mouth shut, both are plentifully filled with showers and whirlwinds of sand. I was longer detained in Charleston than I expected, partly on account of the races, which occupied the minds of many I wished to visit, to the exclusion of every thing else. At 9 they were in bed; at 10 breakfasting—dressing at 11—gone out at 12, and not visible again, at least to me, until 9 or ten next morning. I had also great difficulty in procuring a list of names—Dr. Ramsay promised but never performed—Morford [?] was more honest for he absolutely refused under pretence of ignorance and after repeated disappointments I at length thought of the keeper of the Public Library, Mr. Davidson, who furnished me with a list that kept me 8 days employed pacing the streets.

The indolence, want of energy, and dissipation, of the wealthy part of the community in that place, are truly contemptible. The superabundance of negroes in the Southern States has destroyed the activity of the whites. The carpenter, bricklayer, and even the blacksmith, stand with their hands in their pockets, over looking their negroes. The planter orders his servant to tell the overseer to see my horse fed and taken care of; the overseer sends another negro to tell the driver to send one of his hands to do it. Before half of this routine is gone through, I have myself stript, rubbed down, and fed my horse. Everything must be done through the agency of these slovenly blacks and a gentleman here can hardly perform the services of Cloacina without half a dozen negroes to assist him. These, however, are not one-tenth of the curses slavery has brought on the Southern States. Nothing has surprised me more than the cold, melancholy reserve of the females, of the best families, in S. Carolina and Georgia. Old and young, single and married, all have that dull frigid insipidity, and reserve, which is attributed to solitary old maids. Even in their own houses they scarce utter anything to a stranger but yes or no, and one is perpetually puzzled to know whether it proceeds from awkwardness or dislike. Those who have been at some of their balls say that the ladies hardly even speak or smile, but dance with as much gravity, as if they were performing some ceremony of devotion. On the contrary, the negro wenches are all sprightliness & gaiety; and if report be not a defamer, on them are lavished, in secret, those caresses from the first dawnings of manhood to impotent old age, that render them callous to all the finer sensations of love and female excellence.

I will not detain you by a recital of my journey from Charleston to Savannah—in crossing the Savannah river at a place called the Two Sisters' Ferry; my horse threw himself into the torrent, and had I not, at the risk of my own life, rescued him, would have been drowned. All the rivers have been extremely high this season. I have visited every person in and about this place from whom I can expect anything. I set up my horse and chair at Venden [?] this forenoon but could not sell them without too great a sacrifice. This evening I have sold them both for 170 dollars exactly the money they cost me but this is to be paid in Sea Island Cotton at 29 cents per lb. With the first vessel that sails for Philad.ª or N. York I will take my passage home. The following names you will please order to be added to the former list. They are *all*, I believe, good. I would write you more but am really unwell.

James Shoolbred,   Charleston   Charleston Library Society
                                        1 copy
Dr. Alexander Baron   Do.   Medical Society of S. C.
                                        1 copy
Thomas Heyward Junr.   Do.   Isaac Neufville,   Charleston
Dr. M. Irvine   Do.   Langdon Cheves   Do.
E. P. M. Izard   Do.   David Bailey   Do.
J. Blake Esqr.   Do.   Benjamin Ferrand
                                        172 Pearl St. N. York
Gen. Wm. Washington   Do.   Samuel Davis—Richmond
                                        Virginia
Wm. Loughton Smith   Do.   Wm. B. Bulloch   Savannah
John Cripps   Do.   Dr. John Grimes   Do.
Charles Richardson   Do.   Savannah Library
                                        1 copy
Thomas Cochran   Do.   Matthew McAlister   Do.
Genl. Van der Horst   Do.   W. Stephens   Do.
Gabl. Manigault   Do.   Dr. White   Savannah
L. C. Radcliffe   Joseph Stiles   Do.
Willm. Drayton Esqr.   Do.   Thomas Young   Do.
M. Miller   Savannah   John Bolton   Do.
D. B. Mitchell   Do.   James Jackson   Do.
James M. Wayne   Do.   James Ronalds   No. 188
John P. Williamson   Do.   Pearl St. N. York
Joseph P. McKinnie   Do.

Hazen Kimball   Do.
Dr. John Cumming   Do.
E. Woodruff   Do.
Thos. Telfair   Do.
John B. Rittenhouse, Georgetown
    Dist. Columbia.

I am with sentiments of sincere regard & friendship
                    Dear Sir
                    Yours
                        ALEX. WILSON

 CXVII

PMA

To Alexander Wilson, Sr.[1]

Philadelphia, 15 June 1809.

Dear Father,

Mr. David Brown having informed me of his intention of sailing for Scotland, I have transmitted to you by him the first volume of my American Ornithology, just publishing, and shall, if I live to finish it, send you regularly the remaining nine volumes as they appear. In giving existence to this Work, I have expended all I had been saving since my arrival in America. I have also visited every town within 150 miles of the Atlantic coast, from the river St. Lawrence to St. Augustine in Florida, from whence I returned about two months ago. Whether I shall be able to realize a fortune by this publication, or recover first costs, or suffer the sacrifice of my little all is yet doubtful. I met with a most honourable reception among many of the first characters in the United States, and have collected such a mass of information on this branch of Natural History, as will entitle the work to the merit of originality at least.

I called on John Finlayson yesterday at his rural retreat in a charming hollow, sheltered with apple trees, where, "hens on the midden, ducks in dibs are seen," and a clear brook rins wimplin by his yard. John is an active, industrious fellow, and much esteemed in his neighbourhood; has a fine family of children, hives of bees, a ewe with 3 lambs, 4 looms, and many other comforts and curiosities about him. We went to a neighbouring farmer together, to see a flock of the merino breed of sheep, which are now multiplying in the United States beyond all belief. My nephew, W. Duncan, and his brother, have commenced manufacturing at Milestown, with considerable success. Their sister Mary keeps house for them and they

1. "Seedhills of Paisley, N. Britain."

live very happily. I have heard nothing of my sister in Gennesee these 12 months. I wrote her lately respecting the death of her son George, who fell a victim to the yellow fever three weeks after his arrival in America. He was received into the marine hospital at Norfolk, Virginia, on the 3rd of October, and died on the 5th. I examined the nurse and sexton, and visited the place where the multitude of that year (chiefly strangers,) were buried, and would have placed a humble stone over his grave had it been possible to ascertain the spot.

William Mitchell, formerly of Williamsburgh, who had been supposed dead these several years, is living and in good health at New Orleans—as a common soldier. During my journey through Virginia & the Carolinas, I made every inquiry respecting Bowman, formerly writing-master, but could hear nothing of him. John Rowan still continues in the honourable profession of making bitters, and prescribing in certain disorders. Robert Shaw and family were well last March. Mr. Brown can inform you respecting their situation.

I am still under engagements to Mr. Bradford as assistant editor of the Cyclopaedia. This, with the Ornithology, and other occasional things in the poetical way, keep me from the sin of idleness, which I have been pretty well preserved from for these 15 years. Joseph Roger died about 10 months ago in Schenectady—I saw his widow there in October last. I could have wished to have seen William Morrison and Nelly, but my time would not permit. Thomas Wotherspoon, once my most particular friend and companion, has, I suppose, altogether forgot me—remember my respects to Jean and him. I shall most probably never see either them, or any of my friends, or Paisley, more—but

> While remembrance' power remains,
>   Those native scenes shall meet my view;
> Dear—long lost friends!—on foreign plains
>   I'll sigh, and shed a tear for you.

All my relations in and about Philad? are well. I should be happy to hear from John Bell and Jean, and would willingly give 100 dollars to spend a few days with you all in Paisley, but like a true bird of passage, I would again wing my way across the western waste of waters, to the peaceful and happy regions of America.

What has become of David that I never hear from him? Let me know, my dear father, how you live, and how you enjoy your health at your advanced age. I trust the publication I have now commenced, and which has procured for me reputation & respect, will also enable me to contribute to your independence and comfort, in return for what I owe to you. To my stepmother, sisters, brothers, and friends, I beg to be remembered affectionately,

Your grateful son,
ALEX. WILSON

CXVIII

GROSART

To *William Bartram.*

Philadelphia, 4 August 1809.

Dear Sir

The second volume of "American Ornithology" being now nearly ready to go to press, and the plates in considerable forwardness, you will permit me to trespass on your time, for a few moments, by inquiring if you have anything interesting to add to the history of the following birds, the figures of which will be found in this volume....

I have already said everything of the foregoing that my own observations suggested, or that I have been enabled to collect from those on whom I could rely. As it has fallen to my lot to be the biographer of the feathered tribes of the United States, I am solicitous to do full justice to every species; and I would not conceal one good quality that any one of them possesses. I have paid particular attention to the mocking-bird, humming-bird, king-bird and cat-bird; all the principal traits in their character I have delineated in full. If you have anything to add on either of them, I wish you would communicate it in the form of a letter, addressed particularly to me. Your favourable opinion of my work (if such you have) would, if publicly known, be of infinite service to me, and procure me many friends.

I assure you, my dear friend, that this undertaking has involved me in many difficulties and expenses which I never dreamt of; and I have never yet received one cent from it. I am, therefore, a volunteer in the cause of Natural History, impelled by nobler views than those of money. The second volume will be ready for delivery on the first of January next. I have received communications from many different parts of the United States, with some drawings, and offers of more. But these are rarely executed with such precision as is necessary for a work of this kind.

Let me know if you have ever seen the nest of Catesby's *cowpen-bird*. I have every reason to believe that this bird never builds itself a nest, but, like the cuckoo of Europe, drops its eggs into the nests of other birds, and leaves the result to their mercy and management. I have found no less than six nests this season, with each a young cow-bird contained in it. One of these, which I had found in the nest of the Maryland yellow-throat, and which occupied the whole nest, I brought home, and put it into the cage of a crested red-bird, who became its foster father, and fed, and reared it, with great affection. It begins to chant a little.

I have just heard from our old friend M. He has not yet published the first number of his work; and Bonaparte has been so busy with cutting throats, and building bridges, in the forests of Austria, that the *Inspector of the Forests of France* has not yet received his appointment. . . .

 ᴄ CXIX ᴐ

THAYER

To William Bartram.[1]

11 October 1809.

Dear Sir,

Thanks for your bird, so neatly stuffed, that I was just about to skin it. It is the Rallus virginianus of Turton, and agrees exactly with his description. The one in company was probably the female. Turton mentions 4 species as inhabitants of the United States. I myself have seen 6. Mr. Abbot of Savannah showed me two new species. I found the *Sora*, as the Virginians call it, in the rice flats near Savannah, in March. Gen. Wilkinson told me that the *Sora* was in multitudes at Detroit. Query—don't you think they breed in the north, like the rice-birds? Are not the European naturalists mistaken in saying that the reed-bird and rice-bird pass from the Island of Cuba, in September, to Carolina? All the Spaniards I have conversed with say that these birds are only seen in Cuba early in the Spring and again in October. And the people of the district of Maine and all the New England States, and those who have lived on the Illinois river, declare that these birds breed there in vast numbers.

I have many times been told that our small snow-bird breeds in the Great Swamp, which I can hardly believe. When I was in Williamsburg, Virginia, Bishop Madison told me of a mountain, in the interior of that State, where they bred in multitudes. I have lately had the most positive assurances from a gentleman, who lived on the ranges of the Alleghany about 250 miles distant on the west branch of the Susquehannah that he saw them there 4 months ago; and that they built their nests almost every where among the

1. "Kingsess Botanick Garden."

long grass. He said he took particular notice of them, as he had heard it said down here, that they changed to sparrows in summer. What think you of these matters?

Yours

ALEX. WILSON

To William Bartram.[1]

Philadelphia, 25 October 1809.

Dear Sir,

With an anxious wish to make the second volume of American Ornithology as acceptable as I can, I have increased the number of figures to 50, occupying nine plates. In doing this I have introduced several species that I think necessary to inform you of, that if you are acquainted with anything remarkable in their history you may be so obliging as communicate it to me for publication.

I have lately received a present from our old friend at Paris, Mr. Michaux of nine large folio plates superbly printed in colours, the subjects Botany. Had I an opportunity I would send them out for your examination. Do you know anything relative to the mode of breeding, eggs, etc., etc. of the small Pigeon Hawk, dark brown above the tail barred with dull white, 10[?] inches in leng., streaked on the belly and breast with brown—the thigh feathers remarkably long.

Or of the SMALL HAWK, commonly though improperly called the Sparrow Hawk, above of a bright red body beautifully crossed with black particularly the tail, the head blue. crown red cheeks spotted

1. "pr favor Major Carr."

with black—10½ [?] inches—streaked laterally below with brown —vent white.

Both these birds are described as having *yellow* eyes—All the specimens I have yet met with had the eyes dusky.

I have frequently shot a smaller Hawk than this last with very long slender legs and blue wings much like the preceding but certainly a different species—that had yellow eyes. Pray tell me what you know of these two Birds.

What bird do you mean by the little chocolate-breasted Titmouse mentioned in your Volume?

Rose breasted Grosbeak	Chipping Sparrow
Pigeon Hawk	Small field Sparrow
Small Hawk	Tree Sparrow
Snow bird	Song Sparrow—Query your
Pine finch—much like F. tristis	passer palustris
but smaller; feeds on Pinus	Cowpen Bunting Male
Canadensis	Female and young

When you find leisure be so good as let me hear from you.

Your very sincere friend

ALEX. WILSON

CXXI

GROSART

To William Bartram.

Philadelphia, 11 November 1809.

Dear Sir,

Since I parted from you yesterday evening, I have ruminated a great deal on my proposed journey; I have considered the advantages and disadvantages of the three modes of proceeding: on horseback—in the stage-coach, and on foot. Taking everything into view,

I have at length determined to adopt the last, as being the cheapest, the best adapted for examining the country we pass through; the most favourable to health; and, in short, except for its fatigues, the best mode for a scientific traveller or naturalist, in every point of view. I have also thought that by this determination I will be so happy as to secure your company, for which I would willingly sustain as much hardship, and as many deprivations, as I am able to bear.

If this determination should meet your approbation, and if you are willing to encounter the hardships of such a pedestrian journey, let me know as soon as is convenient. I think one dollar a day, each, will be fully sufficient for our expenses, by a strict regard, at all times, to economy. . . .

❦[CXXII]❦

GROSART

To Alexander Lawson.

Pittsburgh, 22 February 1810.

Dear Sir,

From this first stage of my Ornithological pilgrimage, I sit down with pleasure, to give you some account of my adventures since we parted. On arriving at Lancaster, I waited on the Governor, Secretary of State, and such other great folks as were likely to be useful to me. The Governor received me with civility, passed some good natured compliments on the volumes, and readily added his name to my list. He seems an active Man, of plain good sense, and little ceremony. By Mr. Leech I was introduced to many members of both houses, but I found them, in general, such a pitiful, squabbling, political mob, so split up, and justling about the mere formalities of legislation, without knowing any thing of its realities, that I abandoned them in disgust. I must, however, except from this censure a few intelligent individuals, friends to Science, and possessed of taste, who treated me with great kindness. On Friday evening I set out for Columbia, where I spent one day in vain. I crossed the Susquehannah on Sunday forenoon, with some difficulty, having to cut our way through the ice for several hundred yards; and passing on to York, paid my respects to all the literati of that place without success. Five miles north of this town lives a very extraordinary character, between 80 and 90 years of age, who has lived by trapping Birds and animals these 30 years. Dr. Fisher carried me out in a sleigh to see him, and presented me with a Tolerable good full length figure of him; he has also promised to transmit to me such a collection of facts relative to this singular Original, as will enable me to draw up an interesting narrative of him for the Port Folio. I carried him a half a pound of snuff, of which he is insatiably fond, taking it by handfuls. I was much diverted with the astonishment he expressed on looking at the plates of my work—he could tell me anecdotes of the greater part of the subjects of the first volume, & some of the second. One of his traps, which he says he invented himself, is remarkable for ingenuity, and extremely simple. Having a letter from Dr. Mulenburgh to a clergyman in Hanover, I passed on through a well-cultivated country, chiefly inhabited by Germans, to that place, where a certain Judge *Hustetter* took upon himself to say, that such a book as mine ought not to be encouraged, as it was not within the reach of the commonality; and therefore inconsistent with our Republican institutions! By the same mode of reasoning, which I did not dispute, I undertook to prove him a greater culprit than myself, in erecting a large, elegant, three story brick house, so much beyond the reach of the *Commonality*, as he called them, and consequently grossly contrary to our Republican institutions. I harangued this Solomon of the Bench more seriously afterwards, pointing out to him the great influence of Science on a young rising

Nation like ours, & particularly the science of Natural History, till he began to show such symptoms of *intellect*, as to seem ashamed of what he had said.

From Hanover I passed through a thinly-inhabited country, and crossing the North Mountain, at a pass called Newman's Gap, arrived at Chambersburgh, whence I next morning returned to Carlisle, 30 miles, to visit the reverend Doctors of the College. During my stay here, which was two days, I examined a remarkable Cave about a mile from the town. About 300 yards from the spot is a farm house, where I halted to procure a candle and with that, and a brand of fire, I arrived at the mouth of the cave, which is at the bottom of a perpendicular clift of limestone rocks of 40 or 50 feet in height. The entrance is about 9 feet high & rather more in breadth—the roof nearly horizontal, the floor, dry and smooth, was studded with numerous transparent pillars of ice from three to 4 feet high, & 6 or 8 inches in diameter, occasioned by the droppings from above—Twas early in the morning. One solitary *Winter Wren* had taken possession of the place, who with some reluctance gave way to me. I lighted the candle and with that in one hand and the firebrand in the other, I began slowly to explore the confines of this silent and gloomy cavern. In some places the roof rose to the height of 20 feet; in others it was so low that I was forced to stoop. I was obliged to thrust my lights into every crevice to observe its appearance. In this manner I advanced, sometimes winding, once or twice turning at right angles, for upwards of 300 yards till I came to a place where the cave seemed to separate into several paths—the walls were wet and miry and at my feet were several springs of water perfectly clear, standing in little hollows, but not running ones. Here I stuck down my lights and sat down on a shelving part of the bottom to indulge in a train of solemn and melancholy contemplations, that forc'd themselves on my mind in this gloomy & silent recess. On my return I picked up several Bats that hung in a seeming torpid state from the sides of the cave, and wrapping them in my handkerchief put them in my pocket. On reaching the tavern I was relating to several people in the barroom, my mornings expedition, when two of the Bats, feeling influence of the stove, had disengaged themselves from my handkerchief, & were flying round the room to the surprise of the company.

The towns of Chambersburgh and Shippensburgh produced me nothing. Sunday the 11th I left the former of these places in the stage; and in 15 miles began to ascend the alpine regions of the Alleghany mountains, where *above, around, & below* us, nothing appeared but prodigious declivities, covered with woods; and the weather being fine, such a profound silence prevailed among these aerial solitudes, as imprest the soul with awe, and a kind of fearful sublimity. Something of this arose from my being alone, having left the stage several miles below. These high ranges continued for more than one hundred miles to Greensburgh, 32 miles from Pittsburgh; from thence the country is nothing but an assemblage of steep hills and deep valleys descending rapidly till you reach within 7 miles of this place, where I arrived on the 15th. We were within two miles of Pittsburgh, when suddenly the road descends a long and very steep hill, where the Alleghany river is seen at hand on the right stretching along a rich bottom, and bounded by a high ridge of hills on the west. After following this road, parallel with the river, & about a quarter of a mile from it through a rich low valley, a cloud of black smoke, at its extremity announced the town of Pittsburgh. On arriving at the town, which stands on a low flat and looks like a collection of Blacksmith's shops, Glass houses, Breweries, Forges and Furnaces, the Monongahela opened to the view on the left running along the bottom of a range of hills so high that the sun at this season sets to the town of Pittsburgh at a little past four. This range continues along the Ohio as far as the view reaches. The ice had just begun to give way in the Monongahela, and came down in vast bodies for the three following days. It has now begun in the Alleghany, and at the moment I write it is one white Mass of rushing ice.

The country beyond Ohio to the west appears a mountainous & hilly region. The Monongahela is lined with Arks, usually called Kentucky Boats, waiting for the rising of the river & the absence of the ice, to descend. A perspective view of the town of Pittsburgh at this season, with the numerous arks and covered keel boats preparing to descend the Ohio; the grandeur of its hills, and the interesting circumstance of its three great rivers—the pillars of smoke rising from its Furnaces, Glass-works etc. would make a noble picture. I began a very diligent search in this place, the day after my arrival, for subscribers and continued it for four days. I succeeded beyond expectation, having got 19 names of the most wealthy & respectable part of the inhabitants. The industry of this town is remarkable; everybody you see is busy; & as a proof of the prosperity of the place an eminent lawyer told me that there has not been one suit instituted against a mercht. of the town these three years!

The Glass Houses, of which there are 3, have more demands for Glass than they are able to answer. Mr. Bakewell the proprietor of the best, shewed . . . yesterday a chandelier of his manufacture highly ornamented . . . for which he received 300 dollars. It would ornament the . . . in Philada. and is perfectly transparent.

Gentlemen here assure me that the road to Chilicothe is impassable on foot by reason of the freshe[t]s. I have resolved to navigate a small Batteau, which I have bought, & named the ORNITHOLOGIST, down to Cincinatti, 528 miles myself; intending to visit five or 6 towns that lie in my way. From Cincinatti I will cross over to the opposite shore, & abandoning my boat make my way to Lexington, where I expect to be ere your letter can reach that place. Had I gone by Chilicothe, I would have missed five towns, equally large as it. Some say I ought not to attempt going down by myself—others think I may—I am determined to make the experiment, the expense of hiring a rower being considerable. As soon as the ice clears out the Alleghany, and the weather will permit, I shall shove off, having everything in readiness. I have ransacked the woods and fields here without finding a single bird new to me, or indeed any thing but a few snow birds and sparrows. I expect to have something interesting to communicate in my next.

Please send me finished proof of the plate you have begun, and while it is absent begin another. Direct to me at the Post Office Lexington. If Conrad will allow me to publish those birds of Clarks I wish you to begin that next.

My friends will please accept through you my best wishes and kindest respects, and I regret that while the grand spectacle of enormous mountains, regions of expanded forests, glittering towns, & noble rivers are passing in rapid succession before my delighted view they are not beside me to enjoy the varying scenery; but as far as my pen will enable me I will freely share it with them, and remember them affectionately until I forget myself.[1]

Yours most sincerely,
ALEX. WILSON

Friday 23   My Baggage is on board I have just to despatch this and set off. The weather is fine & I have no doubt of piloting my Batteau in safety to Cincinatti. Farewell! God bless you.

A.W.

1. This letter has been collated with an article in the *Penn Monthly* (June 1879), pp. 248–251: "Private letters of Wilson, Ord, and Bonaparte," by Dr. Elliott Coues, adding approximately five hundred words to the Ord and Grosart versions.

❧[CXXIII]❧

GROSART

To Alexander Lawson.

Lexington, 4 April 1810.

My Dear Sir,

Having now reached the second stage of my bird-catching expedition, I willingly sit down to give you some account of my adventures and remarks since leaving Pittsburgh; by the aid of a good map, and your usual stock of patience, you will be able to listen to my story, and trace all my wanderings. Though generally dissuaded from venturing by myself on so long a voyage down the Ohio in an open skiff, I considered this mode, with all its inconveniences, as the most favourable to my researches and the most suitable to my funds, and I determined accordingly. Two days before my departure, the Alleghany river was one wide torrent of broken ice, and I calculated on experiencing considerable difficulties on this score. My stock of provisions consisted of some biscuit and cheese, and a bottle of cordial presented me by a gentleman of Pittsburgh; my gun, trunk, and great-coat, occupied one end of the boat; I had a small tin occasionally to bale her, and to take my beverage from the Ohio with; and bidding adieu to the smoky confines of Pittsburgh, I launched into the stream, and soon winded away among the hills that every where enclose this noble river. The weather was warm and serene, and the river like a mirror except where floating masses of ice spotted its surface, and which required some care to steer clear of; but these to my surprise, in less than a day's sailing, totally disappeared. Far from being concerned at my new situation, I felt my heart expand with joy at the novelties which surrounded me; I listened with pleasure to the whistling of the Red-bird on the banks as I passed, and contemplated the forest scenery as it receded, with increasing delight. The smoke of the numerous sugar camps, rising lazily among the mountains, gave great effect to the varying landscape; and the grotesque log-cabins, that here and there opened from the woods, were diminished into mere dog-houses by the sublimity of the impending mountains. If you suppose to yourself two parallel ranges of forest-covered hills, whose irregular summits are seldom more than three or four miles apart, winding through an immense extent of country, and enclosing a river half a mile wide, which alternately washes the steep declivity on one side, and laves a rich flat forest-clad bottom on the other, of a mile or so in breadth, you will have a pretty correct idea of the appearance of the Ohio. The banks of these rich flats are from twenty to sixty and eighty feet high, and even these last were within a few feet of being overflowed in December, 1808.

I now stripped, with alacrity, to my new avocation. The current went about two and a half miles an hour, and I added about three and a half miles more to the boat's way with my oars. In the course of the day I passed a number of arks, or, as they are usually called, Kentucky boats, loaded, with what it must be acknowledged are the most valuable commodities of a country; viz. men, women and children, horses and ploughs, flour, millstones, &c. Several of these floating caravans were loaded with store goods for the supply of the settlements through which they passed, having a counter erected, shawls, muslins, &c. displayed, and every thing ready for transacting business. On approaching a settlement they blow a horn or tin trumpet, which announces to the inhabitants their arrival. I boarded many of these arks, and felt much interested at the sight of so many human beings, migrating like birds of passage to the luxuriant regions of the south and west. The arks are built in the form of a parallelogram, being from twelve to fourteen feet wide, and from forty to seventy feet long, covered above, rowed only occasionally by two oars before, and steered by a long and powerful one fixed above, as in the annexed sketch.

The barges are taken up along shore by setting poles, at the rate of twenty miles or so a day; the arks cost about one hundred and

ARK.

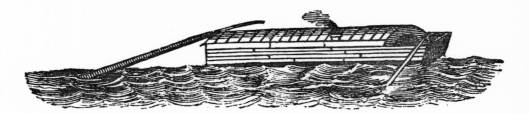

BARGE FOR PASSING UP STREAM.

fifty cents per foot, according to their length; and when they reach their places of destination, seldom bring more than one-sixth their original cost. These arks descend from all parts of the Ohio and its tributary streams, the Alleghany, Monongahela, Muskingum, Sciota, Miami, Kentucky, Wabash, &c., in the months of March, April, and May particularly, with goods, produce and emigrants, the two former for markets along the river, or at New Orleans, the latter for various parts of Kentucky, Ohio, and the Indiana Territory. I now return to my own expedition. I rowed twenty odd miles the first spell, and found I should be able to stand it perfectly well. About an hour after night I put up at a miserable cabin, fifty-two miles from Pittsburgh, where I slept on what I supposed to be cornstalks, or something worse; so preferring the smooth bosom of the Ohio to this brush heap, I got up long before day, and, being under no apprehension of losing my way, I again pushed out into the stream. The landscape on each side lay in one mass of shade, but the grandeur of the projecting headlands and vanishing points, or lines, was charmingly reflected in the smooth glassy surface below. I could only discover when I was passing a clearing, by the crowing of cocks; and now and then, in more solitary places, the big-horned owl made a most hideous hollowing, that echoed among the mountains. In this lonesome manner, with full leisure for observation and reflection, exposed to hardships all day, and hard berths all night, to storms of rain, hail and snow, for it froze severely almost every night, I persevered from the 24th of February to Sunday evening, March 17th, when I moored my skiff safely in Bear-Grass Creek, at the Rapids of the Ohio, after a voyage of seven hundred and twenty miles. My hands suffered the most; and it will be some weeks yet before they recover their former feeling and flexibility. It would be the task of a month to detail all the particulars of my numerous excursions, in every direction from the river. In Steubenville, Charlestown, and Wheeling, I found some friends. At Marietta I visited the celebrated remains of Indian fortifications, as they are improperly called, which cover a large space of ground on the banks of the Muskingum. Seventy miles above this, at a place called Big-Grave Creek, I examined some extraordinary remains of the same kind there. The Big Grave is three hundred paces round at the base, seventy feet perpendicular, and the top, which is about fifty feet over, has sunk in, forming a regular concavity, three or four feet deep. This tumulus is in the form of a cone, and the whole, as well as its immediate neighbourhood, is covered with a venerable growth of forest, four or five hundred years old, which gives it a most singular appearance. In clambering around its steep sides, I found a place where a large white oak had been lately blown down, and had torn up the earth to the depth of five or six feet. In this place I commenced digging, and continued to labour for about an hour, examining every handful of earth with great care, but except some shreds of earthen ware, made of a coarse kind of gritty clay, and considerable pieces of charcoal, I found nothing else; but a person of the neighbourhood presented me with some beads, fashioned out of a kind of white stone, which were found in digging on the opposite side of this gigantic mound, where I found the hole still remaining. The whole of an extensive plain a short distance from this is marked out with squares, oblongs and circles, one of which comprehends several acres. The embankments by which they are distinguished are still two or three feet above the common level of the field. The Big Grave is the property of a Mr. Tomlinson, or Tumblestone, who lives near, and who would not expend three cents to see the whole sifted before his face. I endeavoured to work on his avarice, by representing the probability that it might contain valuable matters, and suggested to him a mode by which a passage might be cut into it level with the bottom, and by excavation and arching, a most noble cellar might be formed for keeping his turnips and potatoes. "All the turnips and potatoes I shall raise this dozen years," he said, "would not pay the expense." This man is no antiquary, or theoretical farmer, nor much of a practical one either I fear; he has about two thousand acres of the best land, and just makes out to live. Near the head of what is called the Long Reach, I called on a certain Michael Cressap, son to the noted Colonel Cressap, mentioned in Jefferson's Notes on Virginia. From him I received the head of a Paddle fish, the largest ever seen in the Ohio, which I am keeping for Mr. Peale, with various other curiosities. I took the liberty of asking whether Logan's accusation of his father having killed *all* his family, had any truth in it; but he replied that it had not. Logan, he said, had been misinformed; he detailed to me all the particulars, which are too long for repetition, and concluded by informing me that his father died early in the revolutionary war, of the camp fever, near New York.

Marietta stands on a swampy plain, which has evidently once been the ancient bed of the Muskingum, and is still occasionally inundated to the depth of five or six feet. A Mr. Putnam, son to the old general of Bunker's Hill memory, and Mr. Gillman and Mr. Fearing, are making great exertions here, in introducing and multiplying the race of merinos. The two latter gentlemen are about establishing works by steam, for carding and spinning wool, and intend to carry on the manufacture of broadcloth extensively. Mr. Gillman is a gentleman of taste and wealth, and has no doubts of succeeding. Something is necessary to give animation to this place, for since the building of ships has been abandoned here, the place seems on the decline.

The current of the Muskingum is very rapid, and the ferry boat is navigated across in the following manner. A strong cable is extended from bank to bank, forty or fifty feet above the surface of the river, and fastened tight at each end. On this cable are two loose running blocks; one rope from the bow of the boat is fastened to the first of these blocks, and another from the after part of the boat to the second block, and by lengthening this last a diagonal direction is given to the boat's head, a little up stream, and the current striking forcibly and obliquely on her aft, she is hurried forward with amazing velocity without any manual labour whatever. I passed Blannerhasset's island after night, but the people were burning brush, and by the light I had a distinct view of the mansion house, which is but a plain frame of no great dimensions. It is now the property of a Mr. Miller from Lexington, who intends laying it chiefly in hemp. It is nearly three miles long, and contains about three hundred acres, half of which is in cultivation; but like all the rest of the numerous islands of the Ohio, is subject to inundations. At Galliopolis, which stands upon a high plain, and contains forty or fifty scattered houses, I found the fields well fenced and well cultivated, peach and apple orchards numerous, and a considerable appearance of industry. One half of the original French settlers have removed to a tract of land opposite to the mouth of Sandy River. This town has one shop and two taverns; the mountains press in to within a short distance of the town. I found here another Indian mound planted with peach trees. On Monday, March 5th, about ten miles below the mouth of the great Sciota, where I saw the first flock of paroquets, I encountered a violent storm of wind and rain, which changed to hail and snow, blowing down trees and shrubs in all directions; so that for immediate preservation I was obliged to steer out into the river, which rolled and foamed like a sea, and filled my boat nearly half full of water; and it was with the greatest difficulty I could make the least headway. It continued to snow violently until dusk, when I at length made good my landing at a place on the Kentucky shore, where I had perceived a cabin; and here I spent the evening in learning the art and mystery of bear-treeing, wolf-trapping, and wild-cat hunting, from an old professor. But notwithstanding the skill of the great-master, the country here is swarming with wolves and wild-cats, black and brown; according to this hunter's own confession he had lost sixty pigs from Christmas last, and all night long the distant howling of the wolves kept the dogs in a perpetual uproar of barking. This man was one of those people called squatters, who neither pay rent nor own land, but keep roving on the frontiers advancing as the tide of civilized population approaches. They are the immediate successors of the savages, and far below them in good sense and good manners, as well as comfortable accommodation. An engraved representation of one of their cabins would form a striking embellishment to the pages of the Port Folio, as a specimen of the *first* order of *American Architecture*.

Nothing adds more to the savage grandeur, and picturesque effect, of the scenery along the Ohio, than these miserable huts of human beings, lurking at the bottom of a gigantic growth of timber, that I have not seen equalled in any other part of the United States. And it is truly amusing to observe how dear and how familiar habit had rendered those privations, which must have been first the offspring of necessity. Yet none pride themselves more on their possessions. The inhabitants of these forlorn sheds will talk to you with pride of the richness of their soil, of the excellence and abundance of their country, of the healthiness of their climate, and the purity of their waters; while the only bread you find among them is of Indian corn, coarsely ground in a horse-mill, with half of the grains unbroken; even their cattle are destitute of stables and hay, and look like moving skeletons; their own houses worse than pigsties; their clothes an assemblage of rags; their faces yellow, and lank with disease; and their persons covered with filth, and frequently garnished with the humours of the Scotch fiddle; from which dreadful disease by the mercy of God, I have been most miraculously preserved. All this is the effect of laziness. The corn is thrown into the ground in the Spring, and the pigs turned into the woods, where they multiply like rabbits. The labour of the squatter, is now over till Autumn, and he spends the Winter in eating pork, cabbage, and hoe-cakes. What a contrast to the neat farm, and snug cleanly habitation, of the industrious settler, that opens his green fields, his stately barns, gardens and orchards, to the gladdened eye of the delighted stranger!

At a place called Salt Lick I went ashore to see the salt-works, and to learn whether the people had found any further remains of an animal of the ox kind, one of whose horns, of a prodigious size, was discovered here some years ago, and is in the possession of Mr. Peale. They make here about one thousand bushels weekly, which sells at one dollar and seventy-five cents per bushel. The wells are from thirty to fifty feet deep, but nothing curious has lately been dug up. I landed at Maysville, or Limestone, where a considerable deal of business is done in importation for the interior of Kentucky. It stands on a high, narrow plain between the mountains and the river, which is fast devouring the bank, and encroaching on the town; part of the front street is gone already, and unless some effectual means are soon taken, the whole must go by piecemeal. This town contains about one hundred houses, chiefly log and frames. From this place I set out on foot for Washington. On the road, at the height of several hundred feet above the present surface of the river, I found prodigious quantities of petrified shells, of the small cockle and fanshaped kind, but whether marine remains or not am uncertain. I have since found these petrified concretions of shells universal all over Kentucky, wherever I have been. The rocks look as if one had collected heaps of broken shells, and wrought them up among clay, then hardened it into stone. These rocks lie universally in horizontal strata. A farmer in the neighbourhood of Washington assured me, that from seven acres he reaped at once eight thousand weight of excellent hemp, fit for market.

Amidst very tempestuous weather I reached the town of Cincinnati, which does honour to the name of the old Roman, and is the neatest and handsomest situated place I have seen since I left Philadelphia. You must know that during an unknown series of ages, the river Ohio has gradually sunk several hundred feet below its former bed, and has left on both sides, occasionally, what are called the first or nearest, and the second or next, high bank, the latter of which is never overflowed.

The town of Cincinnati occupies two beautiful plains, one on the first, and the other on the second bank, and contains upwards of five hundred houses, the greater proportion of which are of brick. One block-house is all that remains of Fort Washington. The river Licking comes in from the opposite shore, where the town of Newport, of forty or fifty houses, and a large arsenal and barracks, are lately erected. Here I met with Judge Turner, a man of extraordinary talents, well known to the literati of Philadelphia. He exerted himself in my behalf with all the ardour of an old friend. A large Indian mound in the vicinity of this town has been lately opened by Doctor Drake, who showed me the collection of curiosities which had been found in that and others. In the centre of this mound he also found a large fragment of earthen ware, such as I found at the Big Grave, which is a pretty strong proof that these works had been erected by a people, if not the same, differing little from the present race of Indians, whose fragments of earthen ware, dug up about their late towns, correspond exactly with these. Twenty miles below this I passed the mouth of the Great Miami, which rushes in from the north, and is a large and stately river, preserving its pure waters uncontaminated for many miles with those of the Ohio, each keeping their respective sides of the channel. I rambled up the banks of this river for four or five miles, and in my return shot a turkey. I also saw five or six deer in a drove, but they were too light-heeled for me.

In the afternoon of the 15th I entered Big-Bone Creek, which being passable only about a quarter of a mile, I secured my boat, and left my baggage under the care of a decent family near, and set out on foot five miles through the woods for the Big-bone Lick, that great antediluvian rendezvous of the American elephants. This place, which lies "far in the windings of a sheltered vale," afforded me a fund of amusement in shooting ducks and paroquets, (of which last I skinned twelve, and brought off two slightly wounded,) and in examining the ancient buffalo roads to this great licking-place. Mr. Colquhoun, the proprietor, was not at home, but his agent and manager entertained me as well as he was able, and was much amused with my enthusiasm. This place is a low valley, everywhere surrounded by high hills; in the centre, by the side of the creek, is a quagmire of near an acre, from which, and another smaller one below, the chief part of these large bones have been taken; at the latter places I found numerous fragments of large bones lying scattered about. In pursuing a wounded duck across this quagmire, I had nearly deposited my carcass among the grand congregation of mammoths below, having sunk up to the middle, and had hard struggling to get out. As the proprietor intends to dig in various places this season for brine, and is a gentleman of education and intelligence, I have strong hopes that a more complete skeleton of that animal called the mammoth, than has yet been found, will be procured. I laid the strongest injunction on the manager to be on the look-out, and to preserve every thing; I also left a letter for Mr. Colquhoun to the same purport, and am persuaded that these will not be neglected. In this neighbourhood I found the Columbo plant in great abundance, and collected some of the seeds. Many of the old stalks were more than five feet high. I have since found it in various other parts of this country. In the afternoon of the next day I returned to my boat, replaced my baggage, and rowed twenty miles to the Swiss settlement, where I spent the night. These hardy and industrious people have now twelve acres closely and cleanly planted with vines from the Cape of Good Hope. They last year made seven hundred gallons of wine, and expect to make three times as much the ensuing season. The houses are neat and comfortable, they have orchards of peach and apple trees, besides a great number of figs, cherries, and other fruits, of which they are very curious. They are of opinion that this part of the Indian Territory is as well suited as any part of France to the cultivation of the vine, but the vines they say require different management here from what they were accustomed to in Switzerland. I purchased a bottle of their last vintage, and drunk to all your healths as long as it lasted, in going down the river. Seven miles below this I passed the mouth of Kentucky river, which has a formidable appearance. I observed twenty or thirty scattered houses on its upper side, and a few below, many of the former seemingly in a state of decay. It rained on me the whole of this day, and I was obliged to row hard and drink healths to keep myself comfortable. My birds' skins were wrapt up in my great coat, and my own skin had to sustain a complete drenching, which, however, had no bad effects. This evening I lodged at the most wretched hovel I had yet seen. The owner, a meagre diminutive wretch, soon began to let me know of how much consequence he had formerly been; that he had gone through all the war with General Washington—had become one of his *life-guards*, and had sent many a British soldier to his long home. As I answered him with indifference, to interest me the more he began to detail anecdotes of his wonderful exploits; "One Grenadier," said he, "had the impudence to get up on the works, and to wave his cap in defiance; my commander [General Washington I suppose]¹ says to me, 'Dick,' says he, 'can't you pepper that there fellow for me?' says he 'Please

1. The brackets here and elsewhere are as given by Grosart and Ord. It has, however, been necessary to simplify their confusing use of inverted commas in this letter.

your honour,' says I, 'I'll try at it;' so I took a fair, cool and steady aim, and touched my trigger. Up went his heels like a turkey! down he tumbled! one buckshot had entered *here*, and another *here*, [laying a finger on each breast] and the bullet found the way to his brains right through his forehead. By God he was a noble looking fellow!'' Though I believed every word of this to be a lie, yet I could not but look with disgust on the being who uttered it. The same miscreant pronounced a long prayer before supper, and immediately after called out, in a splutter of oaths, for the pine splinters to be held to let the gentleman see. Such a farrago of lies, oaths, prayers, and politeness, put me in a good humour in spite of myself. The whole herd of this filthy kennel were in perpetual motion with the itch; so having procured a large fire to be made, under pretence of habit I sought for the softest plank, placed my trunk and great coat at my head, and stretched myself there till morning. I set out early and passed several arks. A number of turkeys which I observed from time to time on the Indiana shore, made me lose half the morning in search of them. On the Kentucky shore I was also decoyed by the same temptations, but never could approach near enough to shoot one of them. These affairs detained me so, that I was dubious whether I should be able to reach Louisville that night. Night came on, and I could hear nothing of the Falls; about eight I first heard the roaring of the Rapids, and as it increased I was every moment in hopes of seeing the lights of Louisville; but no lights appeared, and the noise seemed now within less than half a mile of me. Seriously alarmed, lest I might be drawn into the suction of the Falls, I cautiously coasted along shore, which was full of *snags* and *sawyers*, and at length with great satisfaction, opened Bear-Grass Creek, where I secured my skiff to a Kentucky boat, and loading myself with my baggage, I groped my way through a swamp up to the town. The next day I sold my skiff for exactly half what it cost me; and the man who bought it wondered why I gave it such a droll Indian name (the *Ornithologist*) "some old chief or warrior I sup-

pose," said he. This day I walked down along shore to Shipping-
port, to take a view of those celebrated Rapids, but they fell far
short of my expectation. I should have no hesitation in going down
them in a skiff. The Falls of Oswego, in the state of New York,
though on a smaller scale, are far more dangerous and formidable in
appearance. Though the river was not high, I observed two arks
and a barge run them with great ease and rapidity. The Ohio here is
something more than a mile wide, with several islands interspersed;
the channel rocky, and the islands heaped with drift wood. The
whole fall in two miles is less than twenty-four feet. The town of
Louisville stands on a high *second* bank, and is as large as Frankfort,
having a number of good brick buildings and valuable shops. The
situation would be as healthy as any on the river, but for the numerous swamps and ponds that intersect the woods in its neighbourhood. These from their height above the river might all be drained
and turned into cultivation; but every man here is so intent on making of money, that they have neither time nor disposition for improvements, even where the article health is at stake. A man here
told me that last Fall he had fourteen sick in his own family. On
Friday the 24th, I left my baggage with a merchant of the place to be
forwarded by the first wagon, and passed through Middletown and
Shelbyville, both inconsiderable places. Nine-tenths of the country
is forest; the surface undulating into gentle eminences and declivities, between each of which generally runs a brook, over loose flags
of limestone. The soil, by appearance, is of the richest sort. I observed immense fields of Indian corn, high excellent fences, few
grain fields, many log houses; and those of the meaner sort. I took
notice of few apple orchards, but several very thriving, peach ones.
An appearance of slovenliness is but too general about their houses,
barns, and barn-yards. Negroes are numerous; cattle and horses
lean, particularly the former, who appear as if struggling with starvation for their existence. The woods are swarming with pigs, pigeons, squirrels and woodpeckers. The pigs are universally fat, ow-

ing to the great quantity of mast this year. Walking here in wet weather is most execrable, and is like travelling on soft soap; a few days of warm weather hardens this again almost into stone. Want of bridges is the greatest inconvenience to a foot-traveller here. Between Shelbyville and Frankfort, having gone out of my way to see a pigeon roost, (which by the by is the greatest curiosity I have seen since leaving home) I waded a deep creek called Benson, nine or ten times. I spent several days in Frankfort, and in rambling among the stupendous cliffs of Kentucky river. On Thursday evening I entered Lexington. But I cannot do justice to these subjects at the conclusion of a letter, which, in spite of all my abridgments, has far exceeded in length what I first intended. My next will be from Nashville. I shall then have seen a large range of Kentucky, and be more able to give you a correct delineation of the country and its inhabitants. In descending the Ohio, I amused myself with a poetical narrative of my expedition, which I called *"The Pilgrim,"* an extract from which shall close this long, and I am afraid tiresome letter. . . .

THAYER

To Alexander Lawson.[1]

Lexington, 6 April 1810.

Dear Sir,

I have this instant recd. yours enclosing the etching, which to me is most acceptable. The Owl is admirably done, and the Lark most sweetly and freely managed. The little black and white Creeper may be dug up as deep as you please only leaving the necessary lights, and the breast of the pine Creeper below may increase pretty con-

1. "At Mr. Wm. Jones N⁰ 45 George Street, [Southern?] Philadelphia."

siderably in depth of colour from the throat onward to the tree, as it is of a dirty yellow there. What would you think of shading the ground gradually & fully under the Lark? The Owls eyes I am afraid will not bear much work as they are extremely brilliant & I do not know but the tail may be . . . to a . . . by deepening the work gradually . . . row of white . . . also behind the ear [words not clear]. But these are only suggestions of mine which I leave to your superior judgement. When the plate is finished and letter'd, send me a proof, also if you have been able to get a proof of the *next* send both enclosed to me at St. Louis, Louisiana Ter. near the mouth of the Missouri, where I expect to be about the middle of May. I am preparing more work for you but cannot at present send the Drawings I have made for want of small birds to fill up the groups, but as Spring is now commencing I hope to be able to send you a packet of skins and drawings from Nashville. I want Mr. Rider to ascertain how many plates are wanted to make up 400 copies of each volume and to get them printed, hot pressed, and coloured, and present his accounts as was agreed on. I can implicitly rely on Mr. Rider, and nothing that I can do for him in return shall be wanting. I did not think Mr. Peale would have acted as he has done. I sincerely believe that the publication of these 3 of Clark's Birds in the Amer. Orn. would be advantageous to his work; but if they think otherwise and prefer Peale's drawings, I am satisfied. I shall find subjects enough on the vast regions I have yet to traverse. I will not beg from Man what the God of Nature has scattered around me in such abundance. I have melancholy news for Barallet. Poor Beck is sinking in fortune and in spirits every day. He says there is nothing for him to do & he pays 300 dollars rent. To complete his misfortunes, Mrs. Beck has been in a state of mental derangement and close confinement these two months, produced he thinks by their situation and prospects. As my baggage has not yet arrived from Louisville, I cannot say what encouragement I shall meet with here—It shall not be my fault if I do not succeed. I propose after finishing here to send my trunk etc.

on to Nashville before me and follow with one of the volumes & a few necessaries in a budget.

It is a mistaken idea that this country is earlier in the parallels of latitude than the Atlantick states. There is scarcely a single bird of prey in the woods, not a single flower (except the Sanguinaria Canadensis) making its appearance. Whereas I have seen near Philad^a. the woods thickening about the 10th of April. I have to pass through an extensive untimbered country along Green river, called Barrens, which is represented as abounding with birds and being beyond every thing beautiful which I expect will produce something new. In your next let me know how you come on at your Country retreat. I beg to be remembered to Mrs. Lawson and shall be glad if anything I have here written furnish her and yourself with an hour's amusement. Compts. to my nephew and to my good friends at No. 45 George Street.

Good bye

ALEXR. WILSON

Mr. Bradford wishes the annexed matter as early as possible.[2]

CXXV

GROSART

To Alexander Lawson.[1]

Nashville, Tennessee, 28 April 1810.

My Dear Sir,

Before setting out on my journey through the wilderness to Natchez, I sit down to give you, according to promise, some account

2. A scribbled note at the foot of the letter. Probably written by Wilson.

1. The long letters to Alexander Lawson, penned in the middle of a formidable journey, were written for more than Wilson's immediate friends and in the knowledge that, suitably edited, they would appear in *The Port Folio*. Wilson never seems to have considered writing a fuller narrative of his expeditions but at least we have these uninhibited impressions.

of Lexington, and of my adventures through the State of Kentucky. These I shall be obliged to sketch as rapidly as possible. Neither my time nor my situation enables me to detail particulars with any degree of regularity; and you must condescend to receive them in the same random manner in which they occur, altogether destitute of fanciful embellishment; with nothing but their novelty, and the simplicity of truth, to recommend them.

I saw nothing of Lexington till I had approached within half-a-mile of the place, when the woods opening, I beheld the town before me, on an irregular plain, ornamented with a small white spire, and consisting of several parallel streets, crossed by some others; many of the houses built of brick, others of frame, neatly painted; but a great proportion wore a more humble and inferior appearance. The fields around looked clean and well fenced; gently undulating, but no hills in view. In a hollow between two of these parallel streets, ran a considerable brook, that, uniting with a larger a little below the town, drives several mills. A large quarry of excellent building stone also attracted my notice as I entered the town. The main street was paved with large masses from this quarry, the foot path neat, and guarded by wooden posts. The numerous shops piled with goods, and the many well dressed females I passed in the streets; the sound of social industry, and the gay scenery of "the busy haunts of men," had a most exhilarating effect on my spirits, after being so long immured in the forest. My own appearance, I believe, was to many equally interesting; and the shopkeepers and other loungers interrogated me with their eyes as I passed, with symptoms of eager and inquisitive curiosity. After fixing my quarters, disposing of my arms, and burnishing myself a little, I walked out to have a more particular view of the place.

This little metropolis of the western country is nearly as large as Lancaster in Pennsylvania. In the centre of the town is a public square, partly occupied by the court-house and market place, and distinguished by the additional ornament of the pillory and stocks.

The former of these is so constructed as to serve well enough, if need be, occasionally for a gallows, which is not a bad thought; for as nothing contributes more to make *hardened villains* than the pillory, so nothing so effectually rids society of them as the gallows; and every knave may here exclaim, "My *bane* and *antidote* are both before me."

I peeped into the court-house as I passed, and though it was court day, I was struck with the appearance its interior exhibited; for, though only a plain square brick building, it has all the gloom of the Gothic, so much admired of late, by our modern architects. The exterior walls, having, on experiment, been found too feeble for the superincumbent honours of the roof and steeple, it was found necessary to erect, from the floor, a number of large, circular, and unplastered brick pillars, in a new order of architecture, (the thick end uppermost), which, while they serve to impress the spectators with the perpetual dread that they will tumble about their ears, contribute also, by their number and bulk, to shut out the light, and to spread around a reverential gloom, producing a melancholy and chilling effect; a good disposition of mind, certainly, for a man to enter a court of justice in. One or two solitary individuals stole along the damp and silent floor; and I could just descry, elevated at the opposite extremity of the building, the judges sitting, like spiders in a window corner, dimly distinguishable through the intermediate gloom. The market place, which stands a little to the westward of this, and stretches over the whole breadth of the square, is built of brick, something like that of Philadelphia, but is unpaved and unfinished. In wet weather you sink over the shoes in mud at every step; and here again the wisdom of the police is manifest; as nobody at such times will wade in there unless forced by business or absolute necessity; by which means a great number of idle loungers are, very properly, kept out of the way of the market folks.

I shall say nothing of the nature or quantity of the commodities which I saw exhibited there for sale as the season was unfavourable to a display of their productions; otherwise something better than a few cakes of black maple sugar, wrapt up in greasy saddle-bags, some cabbage, chewing tobacco, catmint and turnip tops, a few bags of meal, sassafras-roots, and skinned squirrels cut up into quarters —something better than all this, I say, in the proper season, certainly covers the stalls of this market place, in the metropolis of the fertile country of Kentucky.[2]

The horses of Kentucky are the hardiest in the world, not so much by nature as by education and habit. From the commencement of their existence they are habituated to every extreme of starvation and gluttony, idleness and excessive fatigue. In Summer they fare sumptuously every day. In Winter, when not a blade of grass is to be seen, and when the cows have deprived them of the very bark and buds of every fallen tree, they are ridden into town, fifteen or twenty miles, through roads and sloughs that would become the graves of any common animal, with a fury and celerity incomprehensible by you folks on the other side of the Alleghany. They are there fastened to the posts on the side of the streets, and around the public square, where hundreds of them may be seen, on a court day, hanging their heads from morning to night, in deep cogitation, ruminating perhaps on the long expected return of Spring and green herbage. The country people, to their credit be it spoken, are universally clad in plain homespun; soap, however, appears to be a scarce article; and Hopkins's double cutters would find here a rich harvest, and produce a very improving effect. Though religion here has its zealous votaries, yet none can accuse the inhabitants of this flourishing place of bigotry, in shutting out from the pale of the church or church-yard any human being, or animal whatever. Some of these sanctuaries are open at all hours, and to every visitor. The birds of heaven find a hundred passages through the broken panes; and the cows and hogs a ready access on all sides. The wall of separation is broken down

2. See below, pp. 353–355.

between the living and the dead; and dogs tug at the carcase of the horse, on the grave of his master. Lexington, however, with all its faults, which a few years will gradually correct, is an honourable monument of the enterprise, courage, and industry of its inhabitants. Within the memory of a middle-aged man, who gave me the information, there were only two log huts on the spot where this city is now erected; while the surrounding country was a wilderness, rendered hideous by skulking bands of bloody and ferocious Indians. Now numerous excellent institutions for the education of youth, a public library, and a well endowed university, under the superintendence of men of learning and piety, are in successful operation. Trade and manufactures are also rapidly increasing. Two manufactories for spinning cotton have lately been erected; one for woollen; several extensive ones for weaving sail cloth and bagging; and seven rope-walks, which, according to one of the proprietors, export, annually, ropeyarn to the amount of 150,000 dollars. A taste for neat, and even elegant, buildings is fast gaining ground; and Lexington, at present, can boast of men who do honour to science, and of females whose beauty and amiable manners would grace the first circles of society. On Saturday, April 14th, I left this place for Nashville, distant about 200 miles. I passed through Nicholasville, the capital of Jessamine county, a small village begun about ten years ago, consisting of about twenty houses, with three shops and four taverns. The woods were scarcely beginning to look green, which to me was surprising, having been led by common report to believe that Spring here is much earlier than in the lower parts of Pennsylvania. I must further observe, that instead of finding the woods of Kentucky covered with a profusion of flowers, they were, at this time, covered with rotten leaves and dead timber, in every stage of decay and confusion; and I could see no difference between them and our own, but the magnitude of the timber, and superior richness of the soil. Here and there the white blossoms of the *Sanguinaria canadensis*, or red root, were peeping through the withered leaves; and the buds of the buckeye, or horse chestnut, and one or two more, were beginning to expand. Wherever the hackberry had fallen, or been cut down, the cattle had eaten the whole bark from the trunk, even to that of the roots.

Nineteen miles from Lexington I descended a long, steep, and rocky declivity, to the banks of Kentucky river, which is here about as wide as the Schuylkill; and winds away between prodigious perpendicular cliffs of solid limestone. In this deep and romantic valley the sound of the boat horns, from several Kentucky arks, which were at that instance passing, produced a most charming effect. The river, I was told, had already fallen fifteen feet; but was still high. I observed great numbers of uncommon plants and flowers, growing among the cliffs; and a few solitary bank swallows were skimming along the surface. Reascending from this, and travelling for a few miles, I again descended a vast depth to another stream called Dick's river, engulfed among the same perpendicular masses of rock. Though it was nearly dark I found some curious petrifications, and some beautiful specimens of mother-of-pearl on the shore. The roaring of a mill-dam, and the rattling of the mill, prevented the ferryman from hearing me till it was quite night; and I passed the rest of the road in the dark over a rocky country, abounding with springs, to Danville. This place stands on a slight eminence, and contains about eighty houses, chiefly log and frame buildings, disposed in two parallel streets, crossed by several others. It has two ropewalks and a woollen manufactory; also nine shops and three taverns. I observed a great many sheep feeding about here, amidst fields of excellent pasture. It is, however, but a dull place. A Roman Catholic chapel has been erected here, at the expense of one or two individuals. The shopkeepers trade from the mouth of Dick's river down to New Orleans, with the common productions of the country, flour, hemp, tobacco, pork, corn, and whiskey. I was now one hundred and eighty miles from Nashville, and I was informed, not a town or village on the whole route. Every day, however, was pro-

ducing wonders in the woods, by the progress of vegetation. The
blossoms of the sassafras, dogwood, and red bud, contrasted with
the deep green of the poplar and buckeye, enriched the scenery on
every side; while the voices of the feathered tribes, many of which
were to me unknown, were continually engaging me in the pursuit.
Emerging from the deep solitude of the forest, the rich green of the
grain fields, the farm house and cabins embosomed midst orchards
of glowing purple and white, gave the sweetest relief to the eye. Not
far from the foot of a high mountain, called Mulders Hill, I overtook
one of those family caravans so common in this country, moving to
the westward. The procession occupied a length of road, and had a
formidable appearance, though, as I afterwards understood, it was
composed of the individuals of only a single family. In the front went
a wagon drawn by four horses, driven by a negro, and filled with
implements of agriculture; another heavy-loaded wagon, with six
horses, followed, attended by two persons; after which came a numerous and mingled group of horses, steers, cows, sheep, hogs, and
calves with their bells; next followed eight boys mounted double,
also a negro wench with a white child before her; then the mother
with one child behind her, and another at the breast; ten or twelve
colts brought up the rear, now and then picking herbage, and trot-
ting ahead. The father, a fresh good-looking man, informed me that
he was from Washington county in Kentucky, and was going as far
as Cumberland river; he had two ropes fixed to the top of the wagon,
one of which he guided himself, and the other was entrusted to his
eldest son, to keep it from oversetting in ascending the mountain.
The singular appearance of this moving group, the mingled music
of the bells, and the shoutings of the drivers, mixed with the echoes
of the mountain, joined to the picturesque solitude of the place, and
various reflections that hurried through my mind, interested me
greatly; and I kept company with them for some time, to lend my
assistance if necessary. The country now became mountainous, perpetually ascending and descending; and about forty-nine miles from

Danville I passed through a pigeon roost, or rather breeding place, which continued for three miles, and, from information, extended in length for more than forty miles. The timber was chiefly beech; every tree was loaded with nests, and I counted, in different places, more than ninety nests on a single tree. Beyond this I passed a large company of people engaged in erecting a horse-mill for grinding grain. The few cabins I passed were generally poor; but much superior in appearance to those I met with on the shores of the Ohio. In the evening I lodged near the banks of Green river. This stream, like all the rest, is sunk in a deep gulf, between high perpendicular walls of limestone; is about thirty yards wide at this place, and runs with great rapidity; but, as it had fallen considerably, I was just able to ford it without swimming. The water was of a pale greenish colour, like that of the Licking, and some other streams, from which circumstance I suppose it has its name. The rocky banks of this river are hollowed out in many places into caves of enormous size, and of great extent. These rocks abound with the same masses of petrified shells so universal in Kentucky. In the woods, a little beyond this, I met a soldier, on foot, from New Orleans, who had been robbed and plundered by the Choctaws as he passed through their nation. "Thirteen or fourteen Indians," said he, "surrounded me before I was aware, cut away my canteen, tore off my hat, took the handkerchief from my neck, and the shoes from my feet, and all the money I had from me, which was about forty-five dollars." Such was his story. He was going to Chilicothe, and seemed pretty nearly done up. In the afternoon I crossed another stream of about twenty-five yards in width, called Little Barren; after which the country began to assume a new and very singular appearance. The woods, which had hitherto been stately, now degenerated into mere scrubby saplings, on which not a bud was beginning to unfold, and grew so open that I could see for a mile through them. No dead timber or rotting leaves were to be seen, but the whole face of the ground was covered with rich verdure, interspersed with a variety of very beautiful flowers, altogether new to me. It seemed as if the whole country had once been one general level; but that from some unknown cause, the ground had been undermined, and had fallen in, in innumerable places, forming regular, funnel-shaped, concavities of all dimensions, from twenty feet in diameter, and six feet in depth, to five hundred by fifty, the surface or verdure generally unbroken. In some tracts the surface was entirely destitute of trees, and the eye was presented with nothing but one general neighbourhood of these concavities, or, as they are usually called, sink-holes. At the centre, or bottom of some of these, openings had been made for water. In several places these holes had broken in, on the sides, and even middle of the road, to an unbroken depth; presenting their grim mouths as if to swallow up the unwary traveller. At the bottom of one of those declivities, at least fifty feet below the general level, a large rivulet of pure water issued at once from the mouth of a cave about twelve feet wide and seven high. A number of very singular sweet smelling lichens grew over the entrance, and a pewee had fixed her nest, like a little sentry-box, on a projecting shelf of the rock above the water. The height and dimensions of the cave continued the same as far as I waded in, which might be thirty or forty yards, but the darkness became so great that I was forced to return. I observed numbers of small fish sporting about, and I doubt not but these abound even in its utmost subterranean recesses. The whole of this country from Green to Red River, is hollowed out into these enormous caves, one of which, lately discovered in Warren County, about eight miles from the Dripping Spring, has been explored for upwards of six miles, extending under the bed of the Green River. The entrance to these caves generally commences at the bottom of a sinkhole; and many of them are used by the inhabitants as cellars or spring-houses, having generally a spring or brook of clear water running through them. I descended into one of these belonging to a Mr. Wood, accompanied by the proprietor, who carried the light. At first the darkness was so intense that I could scarcely see a few feet beyond the circumference of the candle; but, after being in for five or six minutes, the objects around me began to make their appearance more distinctly. The bottom, for fifteen or twenty yards at first was so irregular, that we had constantly to climb over large masses of wet and slippery rocks; the roof rose in many places to the height of twenty or thirty feet, presenting all the most irregular projections of surface, and hanging in gloomy and silent horror. We passed numerous chambers or off-setts, which we did not explore; and after three hours' wandering in these profound regions of glooms and silence, the particulars of which would detain me too long, I emerged with a handkerchief filled with bats, including one which I had never seen described; and a number of extraordinary insects of the Gryllus tribe, with anten-nae upwards of six inches long, and which I am persuaded had never before seen the light of day, as they fled from it with seeming terror, and I believe were as blind in it as their companions the bats. Great quantities of native glauber salts are found in these caves, and are used by the country people in the same manner, and with equal ef-fect, as those of the shops. But the principal production is saltpetre, which is procured from the earth in great abundance. The cave in Warren county above-mentioned, has lately been sold for three thousand dollars, to a saltpetre company, an individual of which in-formed me that, from every appearance, this cave had been known to the Indians many ages ago; and had evidently been used for the same purposes. At the distance of more than a mile from the entrance, the exploring party, on their first visit, found the roof blackened by smoke, and bundles of half-burnt canes lying scattered about. A bark mockasin, of curious construction, besides several other Indian ar-ticles, were found among the rubbish. The earth, also, lay piled in heaps, with great regularity, as if in preparation for extracting the saltpetre.

Notwithstanding the miserable appearance of the timber on these barrens, the soil, to my astonishment, produced the most luxuriant fields of corn and wheat I had ever before met with. But one great disadvantage is the want of water, for the whole running streams, with which the surface of this country once abounded have been drained off to a great depth, and now murmur among these lower regions, secluded from the day. One forenoon I rode nineteen miles without seeing water, while my faithful horse looked round, but in vain, at every hollow, with a wishful and languishing eye, for that precious element. These barrens furnished me with excellent sport in shooting grouse, which abound here in great numbers; and in the delightful groves that here and there rise majestically from these plains, I found many new subjects for my Ornithology. I observed all this day, far to the right, a range of high rocky detached hills, or knobs, as they are called, that skirt the barrens, as if they had been once the boundaries of the great lake that formerly covered this vast plain. These, I was told, abound with stone, coal, and copperas. I crossed Big Barren River in a ferry boat, where it was about one hundred yards wide; and I passed a small village called Bowling Green, near which I rode my horse up to the summit of one of these high insulated rocky hills, or knobs, which overlooked an immense circumference of country, spreading around bare and leafless, except where the groves appeared, in which there is usually water. Fifteen miles from this, induced by the novel character of the country, I put up for several days, at the house of a pious and worthy Presbyterian, whence I had excursions, in all directions, through the surrounding country. Between this and Red River the country had a bare and desolate appearance. Caves continued to be numerous; and report made some of them places of concealment for the dead bodies of certain strangers who had disappeared there. One of these lies near the banks of the Red River, and belongs to a person of the name of ——, a man of notoriously bad character, and strongly suspected, even by his neighbours, of having committed a foul murder of this kind, which was related to me with all its minutiae of horrors. As this man's house stands by the road side, I was induced, by motives of curiosity, to stop and take a peep of him. On my arrival I found two persons in conversation under the piazza, one of whom informed me that he was the landlord. He was a dark mulatto, rather above the common size, inclining to corpulency, with legs small in proportion to his size, and walked lame. His countenance bespoke a soul capable of deeds of darkness. I had not been three minutes in company when he invited the other man (who I understood was a traveller) and myself, to walk back and see his cave, to which I immediately consented. The entrance is in the perpendicular front of a rock, behind the house; has a door with a lock and key to it, and was crowded with pots of milk, placed near a running stream. The roof and sides of solid rock were wet and dropping with water. Desiring —— to walk before with the lights, I followed with my hand on my pistol, reconnoitering on every side, and listening to his description of its length and extent. After examining this horrible vault for forty or fifty yards, he declined going any farther, complaining of a rheumatism; and I now first perceived that the other person had staid behind, and that we two were alone together. Confident in my means of self-defence, whatever mischief the devil might suggest to him, I fixed my eye steadily on his, and observed to him, that he could not be ignorant of the reports circulated about the country relative to this cave. "I suppose," said I, "you know what I mean?" "Yes, I understand you," returned he, without being the least embarrassed, "that I killed somebody and threw them into this cave—I can tell you the whole beginning of that damned lie," said he; and, without moving from the spot, he detailed me a long story, which would fill half my letter, to little purpose, and which, with other particulars, I shall reserve for your amusement when we meet. I asked him why he did not get the cave examined by three or four reputable neighbours, whose report might rescue his character from the suspicion of having committed so horrid a crime. He acknowledged it would be well enough to do so, but did not seem to think it worth the trouble; and we returned as we advanced, —— walking before with the lights. Whether this man be guilty or not of the transaction laid to his charge I know not; but his manners and aspect are such as by no means to allay suspicion.

After crossing Red River, which is here scarce twenty yards broad, I found no more barrens. The timber was large, and the woods fast thickening with green leaves. As I entered the State of Tennessee, the face of the country became hilly, and even mountainous. After descending an immense declivity, and coursing along the rich valley of Manskers creek, where I again met with large flocks of paroquets, I stopt at a small tavern to examine, for three or four days, this part of the country. Here I made some interesting additions to my stock of new subjects for the Ornithology. On the fourth day I crossed the Cumberland, where it is about two hundred and fifty yards wide, and of great depth, bounded as usual, with high precipitous banks, and reached the town of Nashville, which towers like a fortress above the river. Here I have been busily employed these eight days; and send you the enclosed parcel of drawings,[3] the result of every moment of leisure and convenience I could obtain. Many of the birds are altogether new; and you will find along with them every explanation necessary for your purpose.

You may rest assured of hearing from me by the first opportunity after my arrival at Natchez. In the meantime I receive with much pleasure the accounts you give me of the kind inquiries of my friends. To me nothing could be more welcome; for whether journeying in this world, or journeying to that which is to come, there is something of desolation and despair in the idea of being forever forgotten in our absence, by those whom we sincerely esteem and regard. . . .

GROSART

"This letter,[4] it should seem, gave offence to some of the inhabitants of Lexington; and a gentleman residing in that town, solici-

3. The loss of these drawings was to prove a serious setback to Wilson.
4. With the letter of 28 April 1810 to Alexander Lawson, printed above, Grosart printed the letter of 16 July 1811, preceded by this note.

tous about its reputation, undertook, in a letter to the Editor of the *Port Folio*, to vindicate it from strictures which he plainly insinuated were the offspring of ignorance, and unsupported by fact.

After a feeble attempt at sarcasm and irony, the letter-writer thus proceeds:

'I have too great a respect for Mr. Wilson, as your friend, not to believe he had in mind some other market house than that of Lexington, when he speaks of it as "unpaved and unfinished." But the people of Lexington would be gratified to learn what your ornithologist means by "skinned squirrels cut up into quarters," which curious anatomical preparations he enumerates among the articles he saw in the Lexington market. Does Mr. Wilson mean to joke upon us? If this is wit we must confess that, however abundant our country may be in good substantial matter-of-fact salt, the attic tart is unknown among us.

I hope, however, soon to see this gentleman's American Ornithology. Its elegance of execution, and descriptive propriety, may assuage the little pique we have taken from the author.'

The Editor of the *Port Folio* having transmitted this letter to Wilson, previous to sending it to press, it was returned with the following note'':

To the Editor of The "Port Folio."
Bartram's Gardens, July 16, 1811.
Dear Sir,

No man can have a more respectful opinion of the people of Kentucky, particularly those of Lexington, than myself; because I have traversed nearly the whole extent of their country, and witnessed the effects of their bravery, their active industry, and daring spirit for enterprise. But they would be gods, and not men, were they faultless.

I am sorry that truth will not permit me to retract, as mere jokes, the few disagreeable things alluded to. I certainly had no other market-place in view, than that of Lexington, in the passage above-mentioned. As to the circumstance of "skinned squirrels, cut up into quarters," which seems to have excited so much sensibility, I candidly acknowledge myself to have been incorrect in that statement, and I owe an apology for the same. On referring to my notes taken at the time, I find the word "halves," not quarters; that is, those "curious anatomical preparations," (skinned squirrels) were brought to market in the form of a saddle of venison; not in that of a leg or shoulder of mutton.

With this correction, I beg leave to assure your very sensible correspondent, that the thing itself was no joke, nor meant for one; but, like all the rest of the particulars of that sketch, "good substantial matter of fact."

If these explanations, or the perusal of my American Ornithology should assuage the "little pique" in the minds of the good people of Lexington, it will be no less honourable to their own good sense, than agreeable to your humble servant, &c. Port Folio for August, 1811.

❊[CXXVI]❊

M C Z

To Miss Sarah Miller,
Milestown.
Care of Mr. Daniel Miller, Ironmonger,
North Second St., Philadelphia.

Nashville, 1 May 1810.

My dear friend,

Nine hundred miles distant from you sits Wilson, the hunter of birds' nest and sparrows, just preparing to enter on a wilderness of 780 miles, most of it the territory of Indians, *alone*, but in good spirits, and expecting to have every pocket crammed with skins of

new and extraordinary birds before he reach the City of New Orleans. I daresay you have long ago accused me of cruel forgetfulness
in not writing as I promised, but *that*, I assure you, was not the
cause. To have forgot my friends in the midst of strangers, and to
have forgot *you* of all others, would have been impossible. But I still
waited until I should have something very interesting to amuse you
with, and am obliged at last to take up the pen without having anything remarkable to tell you of. Yet I don't know but a description
of the *fashions* of Kentucky would be almost as entertaining as those
of London and Paris. What would you think of a blanket Riding
Dress, a straw side saddle, and a large mule with ears so long that
they might almost serve for reins? I have seen many such fashionable figures in Kentucky. Or, what would you think of a beau who
had neither been washed or shaved for a month, with three yards of
coarse blue cloth wrapt round his legs by way of boots, a ragged
greatcoat, without coat, jacket or neckcloth, breathing the rich perfume of corn whisky? Such figures are quite fashionable in Kentucky.
This is a charming country for ladies. From the time they are first
able to handle a cowskin, there is no amusement they are so fond of
as flogging their negroes & negro wenches. This they do with so
much coolness and seeming satisfaction, that it really gives them an
air of great dignity and manliness. The landlady of the tavern where
I lodge is a great connoisseur at this sort of play and while others
apply their cowskin only to the back, she has discovered that the
shins, elbows, and knuckles are far more sensible, and produce more
agonising screams and greater convulsions in the black devils, as
she calls them, than any other place. My heart sickens at such barbarous scenes, and, to amuse you, I will change to some more agreeable subject.

　　In passing from Lexington to Nashville—a distance of 200 miles
—I overtook on the road a man mending his stirrup leathers, who
walked round my horse several times & observed that I seemed to
be *armed*. I told him I *was* well armed with gun and pistols, but I
hoped he was not afraid to travel with me on that account, as I

FIGURE 15A. Audubon's original drawing of the Mississippi Kite in the collection of the New-York Historical Society. Audubon has noted that the drawing was made June 28, 1821.

FIGURE 15B. Havell's engraving, plate CXVII, to which another bird, described as a female, has been added.

FIGURE 15C. The bird added to "B" is a mirror image of this male Kite drawn by Wilson and published in Vol. III (1811) of his *American Ornithology*. There are other apparent instances of Audubon's use of Wilson's *American Ornithology* as a source book in addition to those illustrated.

1. *Picus Auratus.* Gold-winged Woodpecker. 2. *Emberiza Americana.* Black-throated Bunting.

3. *Motacilla Sialis.* Blue Bird.

FIGURE 16A. Vol. I, plate 3 (1808) of the *American Ornithology* illustrates the Gold-winged Woodpecker.

FIGURE 16B. Audubon's drawing of the same bird (Yellow-shafted Flicker), Havell plate No. XXXVII, has had five inches of paper pasted on, apparently to allow the artist to add the two male birds at the bottom. They, and the other partly hidden bird, bear a remarkable resemblance to Wilson's illustration.

FIGURE 17A. Wilson's Red-winged Starling bird No. 1 of Vol. IV, plate 30 (1811).

FIGURE 17B. Audubon's plate of the same bird (Red-winged Blackbird), Havell plate no. LXVII. The adult male bird at the top resembles Wilson's drawing and the young bird on the bottom twig is strikingly similar to that perched on the bottom left of Wilson's drawing.

MICO CHLUCCO the LONG WARIOR
or KING of the SIMINOLES

W. Bartram Delin. J.Trenchard Sculp.

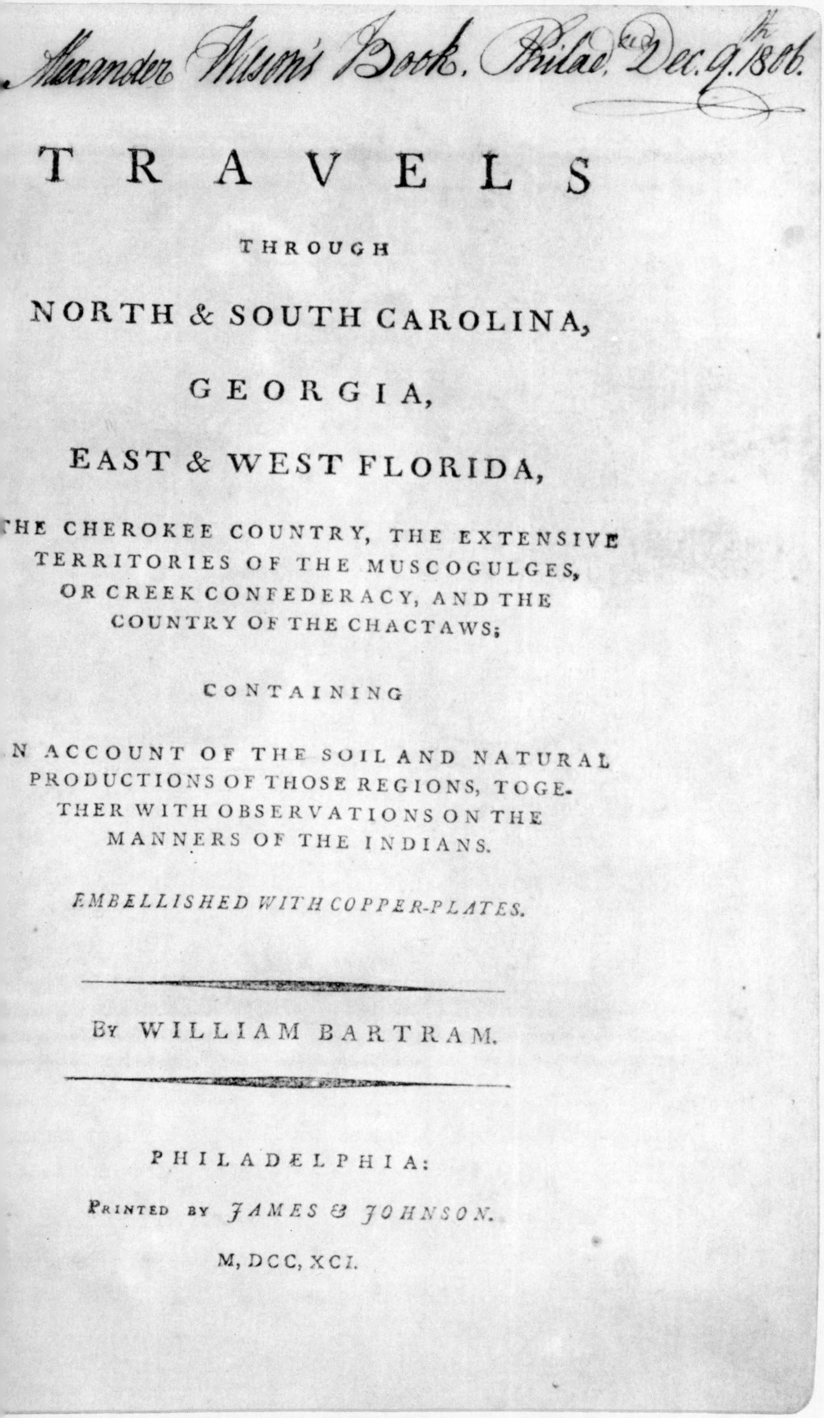

Alexander Wilson's Book. Philadª Dec. 9th 1806.

TRAVELS

THROUGH

NORTH & SOUTH CAROLINA,

GEORGIA,

EAST & WEST FLORIDA,

THE CHEROKEE COUNTRY, THE EXTENSIVE
TERRITORIES OF THE MUSCOGULGES,
OR CREEK CONFEDERACY, AND THE
COUNTRY OF THE CHACTAWS;

CONTAINING

AN ACCOUNT OF THE SOIL AND NATURAL
PRODUCTIONS OF THOSE REGIONS, TOGE-
THER WITH OBSERVATIONS ON THE
MANNERS OF THE INDIANS.

EMBELLISHED WITH COPPER-PLATES.

By WILLIAM BARTRAM.

PHILADELPHIA:

PRINTED BY *JAMES & JOHNSON.*

M, DCC, XCI.

FIGURE 18. The frontispiece and title page of Alexander Wilson's copy of
William Bartram's Travels, bearing his mature signature. This is pictorial
evidence of Wilson's relationship with William Bartram; his guide,
philosopher, and friend.

FIGURE 19

Plaster medallion of Alexander Wilson
after Alfred Joseph Stothard.

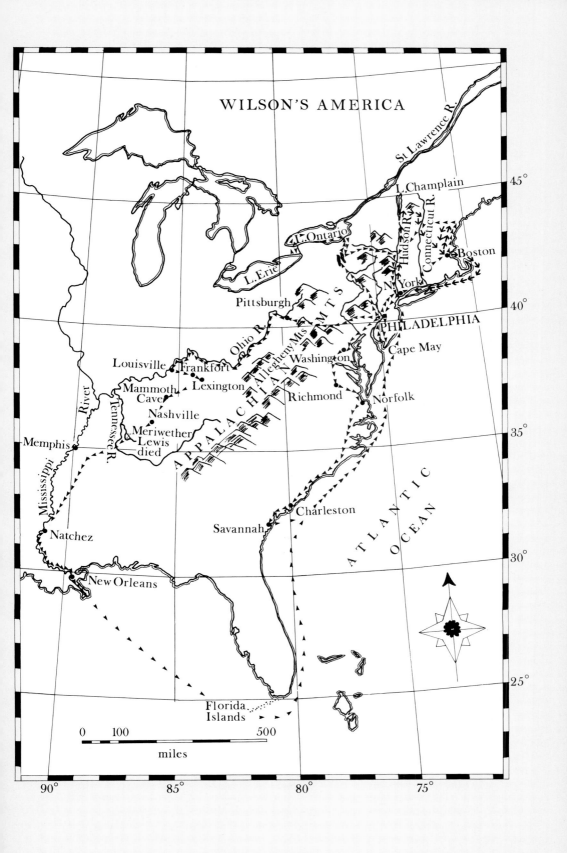

WILSON'S AMERICA

St Lawrence R.

L.Champlain

45°

L.Ontario

Hudson R.

Connecticut R.

Boston

L.Erie

Pittsburgh

N.York

40°

PHILADELPHIA

Ohio R.

Allegheny Mts

Washington

Cape May

Louisville

Frankfort

Louisville

Mammoth
Cave

Lexington

Richmond

Norfolk

River

Tennessee R.

Nashville

35°

Memphis

Meriwether
Lewis
died

A P P A L A C H I A N   M T S

Charleston

A T L A N T I C

Natchez

Savannah

O C E A N

30°

New Orleans

25°

Florida
Islands

Mississippi

0   100   500

miles

90°   85°   80°   75°

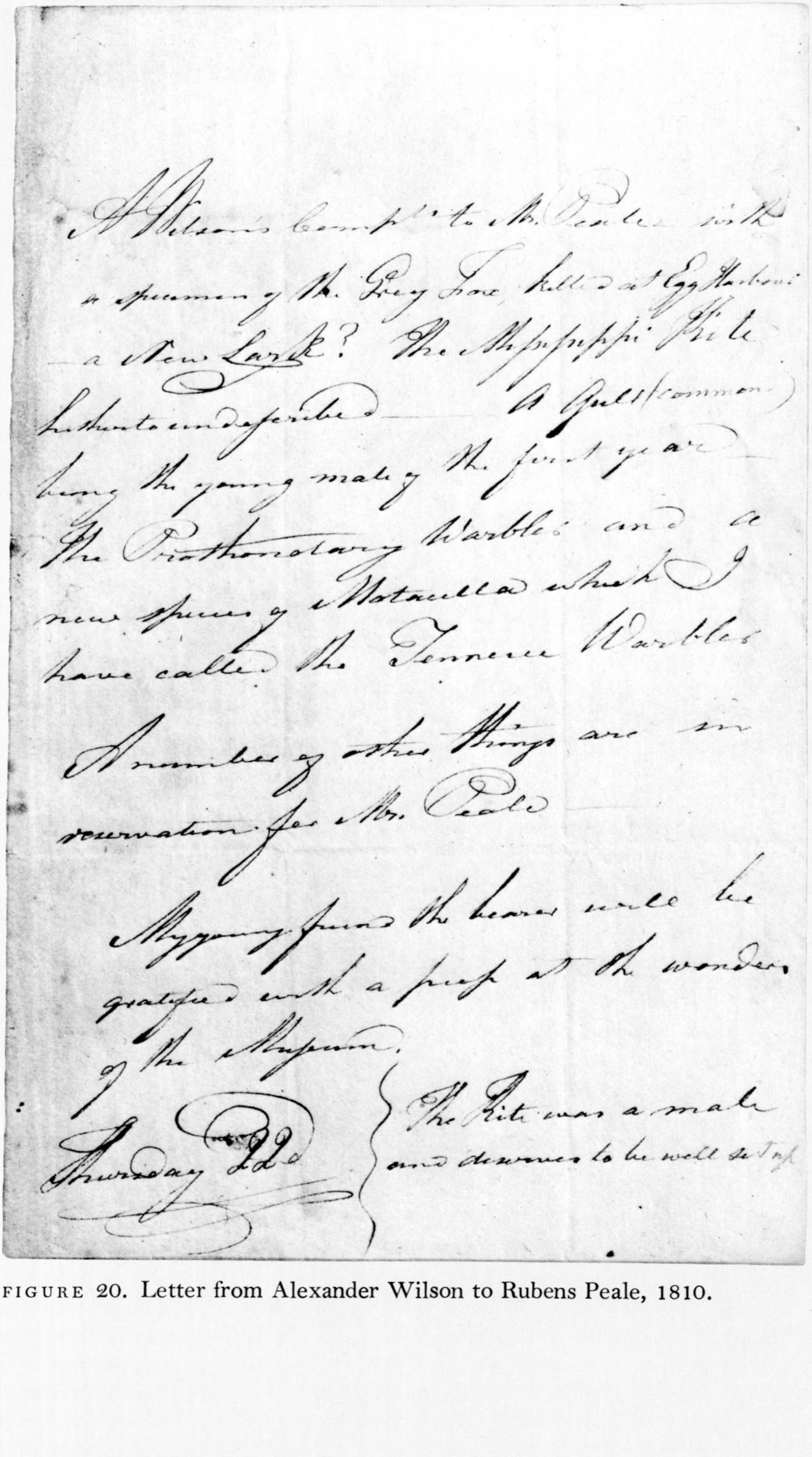

FIGURE 20. Letter from Alexander Wilson to Rubens Peale, 1810.

should be better able to assist in defending him as well as myself if attacked. After understanding the nature of my business, he consented to go on with me, and this man furnished me with as much amusement as Strap did to Roderick Random. He was a most zealous Methodist, and sung Hymns the first day almost perpetually: finding that I should be obliged to bear with this, I got him to try some of them to good old song tunes, and I then joined with him, as we rode along, with great piety. I found one in his book that very nearly answered to Jone's song of The Vicar and Moses, and that soon became a favourite air with us. He laboured with so much earnestness to make me a convert, preaching sometimes with great vehemence that I had no other resource but on such occasions to ride hard down hill, which, the preacher being unable to do I generally broke the thread of his discourse by this means. He was, however, very usefull to me taking charge of my horse while I went into the woods after strange Birds, and got so attached to me that he waited two days for me in a place where I had some drawings to make. I stopt five days in the Barrens of Kentucky, exploring that extraordinary country, in the house of a good presbyterian, who charged me nothing, and would have kept me a month for some lessons in drawing which I gave his two daughters. Here my psalm-singing Methodist left me. These Barrens are almost without wood, and the whole face of the ground seemed to be covered with blossomed strawberries. They must be in immense quantities here in the proper season. Great numbers of beautiful flowers that I have never seen before were seen in every direction, some of them extremely elegant. Many of the inhabitants keep their milk in caves 100 feet below the surface of the ground, and these caves extend so far underground that they have never ventured to their extremities. Frightful stories are told of some tavern keepers, who are suspected of destroying travellers and secreting their bodies in these caves. If I were not afraid to give you the horrors, I would relate an adventure I had in one of the most frightful of these caves with the fellow to whom it belongs, and who is strongly suspected of being a murderer, even by his neighbours. The town I am now in is the capital of the State of Tennessee, and is built on the top of a rocky mountain above the Cumberland river, which is about as large as the Schuylkill, but much deeper. The people are now planting in their cotton fields, and it is curious to see the seeds lying like rags of tattered cotton along in the trenches. Apropo of rags, I have been obliged to throw a good many of mine overboard since I purchased a horse. My handkerchiefs are reduced to three, & other articles in proportion. By the time I reach New Orleans, I expect to carry all the remainder on my back. My Perokeet is my faithful companion yet, and I shall try hard to bring him home with me. He creeps into my pocket when I ride, and when I alight he comes out to amuse the people where I stop.

Please present my respectful compliments to your Mother & father, and don't be offended at anything I have said. If I hear or see any ghosts or hobgoblins between this and Natchez, or anything worth telling, you may depend on hearing from me.

Compliments to sister Jones, &c., &c., &c., and believe me to be, Yours affectionately,

ALEX. WILSON

Compts. to your Brother. I would willingly write to him at present, but must postpone it for a week or two longer.

CXXVII

GROSART

To Alexander Lawson.

Natchez, Mississippi Territory, 18 May 1810.
Dear Sir,

About three weeks ago I wrote to you from Nashville, enclosing three sheets of drawings, which I hope you have received. I was at that time on the point of setting out for St. Louis; but being detained a week by constant and heavy rains, and considering that it would add four hundred miles to my journey, and detain me at least a month; and the season being already far advanced, and no subscribers to be expected there, I abandoned the idea, and prepared for a journey through the wilderness. I was advised by many not to attempt it alone; that the Indians were dangerous, the swamps and rivers almost impassable without assistance, and a thousand other hobgoblins were conjured up to dissuade me from going alone. But I weighed all these matters in my own mind; and attributing a great deal of this to vulgar fears and exaggerated reports, I equipped myself for the attempt. I rode an excellent horse, on which I could depend; I had a loaded pistol in each pocket, a loaded fowling-piece belted across my shoulder, a pound of gunpowder in my flask, and five pounds of shot in my belt. I bought some biscuit and dried beef, and on Friday morning, May 4th, I left Nashville. About half-a-mile from town I observed a poor negro with two wooden legs, building himself a cabin in the woods. Supposing that this journey might afford you and my friends some amusement, I kept a particular account of the various occurrences, and shall transcribe some of the most interesting, omitting every thing relative to my Ornithological excursions and discoveries, as more suitable for another occasion. Eleven miles from Nashville I came to the Great Harpath, a stream of about fifty yards wide, which was running with great violence. I could not discover the entrance of the ford, owing to the rains and inundations. There was no time to be lost, I plunged in, and almost immediately my horse was swimming. I set his head aslant the current, and being strong, he soon landed on the other side. As the weather was warm, I rode in my wet clothes without any inconvenience. The country to-day was a perpetual succession of steep hills and low bottoms; I crossed ten or twelve large creeks, one of which I swam with my horse, where he was near being entangled among some bad drift wood. Now and then a solitary farm opened from the woods, where the negro children were running naked about the yards. I also passed along the north side of a high hill, where the whole timber had been prostrated by some terrible hurricane. I lodged this night in a miner's who told me that he had been engaged in forming no less than thirteen companies for hunting mines, all of whom had left him. I advised him to follow his farm, as the surest vein of ore he could work. Next day (Saturday) I first observed the cane growing, which increased until the whole woods were full of it. The road this day winded along the high ridges of mountains that divide the waters of the Cumberland from those of the Tenessee. I passed few houses to-day; but met several parties of boatmen returning from Natchez and New Orleans; who gave me such an account of the road, and the difficulties they had met with, as served to stiffen my resolution to be prepared for every thing. These men were as dirty as Hottentots; their dress a shirt and trowsers of canvass, black, greasy, and sometimes in tatters; the skin burnt wherever exposed to the sun; each with a budget, wrapt up in an old blanket; their beards, eighteen days old, added to the singularity of their appearance, which was altogether savage. These people came from the various tributary streams of the Ohio, hired at forty or fifty dollars a trip, to return back on their own expenses. Some had upwards of eight hundred miles to travel. When they come to a stream that is unfordable, they coast it for a fallen tree; if that cannot be had, they enter with their budget on their head, and when they lose bottom, drop it on their shoulders, and take to swimming. They have sometimes fourteen or fifteen of such streams to pass in a day, and morasses of several miles in length, that I have never seen equalled in any country. I lodged this night at one Dobbins's, where ten or twelve of these men lay on the floor. As they scrambled up in the morning, they very generally complained of being unwell, for which they gave an odd reason, lying within doors, it being the first of fifteen nights they had been so indulged. Next morning (Sunday) I rode six miles to a man's, of the name of Grinder, where our poor friend Lewis perished. In the same room where he expired, I took down from Mrs. Grinder the particulars of that melancholy event, which affected me extremely. This house or cabin is seventy-two miles from Nashville, and is the last white man's as you enter the Indian country. Governor Lewis, she said, came hither about sunset, alone, and inquired if he could stay for the night; and, alighting, brought the saddle into the house. He was dressed in a loose gown, white, striped with blue. On being asked if he came alone, he replied that there were two servants behind, who would soon be up. He called for some spirits, and drank a very little. When the servants arrived, one of whom was a negro, he inquired for his powder, saying he was sure he had some powder in a canister. The servant gave no distinct reply, and Lewis, in the meanwhile, walked backwards and forwards before the door, talking to himself. Sometimes, she said, he would seem as if he were walking up to her; and would suddenly wheel round, and walk back as fast as he could. Supper being ready he sat down, but had eaten only a few mouthfuls when he started up, speaking to himself in a violent manner. At these times, she says, she observed his face to flush as if it had come on him in a fit. He lighted his pipe, and drawing a chair to the door sat down, saying to Mrs. Grinder, in a kind tone of voice, "Madam, this is a very pleasant evening." He smoked for some time, but quitted his seat and traversed the yard as before. He again sat down to his pipe, seemed again composed, and casting his eyes wistfully towards the west, observed what a sweet evening it was. Mrs. Grinder was preparing a bed for him; but he said he would sleep on the floor, and desired the servant to bring the bearskins and buffalo robe, which were immediately spread out for him; and it being now dusk, the woman went off to the kitchen, and the two men to the barn, which stands about two hundred yards off. The kitchen is only a few paces from the room where Lewis was, and the woman being considerably alarmed by the behaviour of her guest could not sleep, but listened to him walking backwards and forwards, she thinks, for several hours, and talking aloud, as she said, "like a lawyer." She then heard the report of a pistol, and something fall heavily on the floor, and the words—"O Lord!" Immediately afterwards she heard another pistol, and in a few minutes she heard him at her door calling out "O madam! give me some water, and heal my wounds." The logs being open, and unplastered, she saw him stagger back and fall against a stump that stands between the kitchen and room. He crawled for some distance, and raised himself by the side of a tree, where he sat about a minute. He once more got to the room; afterwards he came to the kitchen-door, but did not speak; she then heard him scraping the bucket with a gourd for water; but it appeared that this cooling element was denied the dying man! As soon as day broke and not before—the terror of the woman having permitted him to remain for two hours in this most deplorable situation —she sent two of her children to the barn, her husband not being at home, to bring the servants; and on going in they found him lying on the bed; he uncovered his side, and showed them where the bullet had entered; a piece of the forehead was blown off, and had exposed the brains, without having bled much. He begged they would take his rifle and blow out his brains, and he would give them all the money he had in his trunk. He often said, "I am no coward; but I am so strong, so hard to die." He begged the servant not to be afraid of him, for that he would not hurt him. He expired in about two hours, or just as the sun rose above the trees. He lies buried close by the common path, with a few loose rails thrown over his grave. I gave Grinder money to put a post fence round it to shelter it from the hogs, and from the wolves; and he gave me his written promise he would do it. I left this place in a very melancholy mood, which was not much allayed by the prospect of the gloomy and savage wilderness which I was just entering alone. . . .

I was roused from this melancholy reverie by the roaring of Buffalo River, which I forded with considerable difficulty. I passed two or three solitary Indian huts in the course of the day, with a few acres of open land at each; but so wretchedly cultivated, that they just make out to raise maize enough to keep in existence. They pointed me out the distances by holding up their fingers. This is the country of the Chickasaws, though erroneously laid down in some maps as that of the Cherokees. I slept this night in one of their huts. The Indians spread a deer skin for me on the floor. I made a pillow of my portmanteau, and slept tolerably well. An old Indian laid himself down near me. On Monday morning, I rode fifteen miles, and stopt at an Indian's to feed my horse. The sight of my paroquet brought the whole family around me. The women are generally naked from the middle upwards; and their heads, in many instances, being rarely combed, look like a large mop. They have a yard or two of blue cloth wrapt round by way of petticoat, that reaches to the knees. The boys were generally naked; except a kind of bag of blue cloth, by way of fig-leaf. Some of the women have a short jacket, with sleeves, drawn over their naked body, and the rag of a blanket is a general appendage. I met to-day two officers of the United States' army, who gave me a better account of the road than I had received. I passed through many bad swamps to-day; and at about five in the evening, came to the banks of the Tennessee, which was swelled by the rains, and is about half-a-mile wide thirty miles below the Muscle Shoals, and just below a long island laid down in your small map. A growth of canes of twenty and thirty feet high covers the low bottoms, and these cane swamps are the gloomiest and most desolate-looking places imaginable. I hailed for the boat as long as it was light, without effect. I then sought out a place to encamp, kindled a large fire, stript the canes for my horse, eat a bit of supper, and lay down to sleep, listening to the owls, and the Chuck-Wills-Widow—a kind of Whip-poor-Will that is very numerous here. I got up several times during the night to recruit my fire, and see how my horse did, and but for the gnats, would have slept tolerably well. These gigantic woods have a singular effect by the light of a large fire, the whole scene being circumscribed by impenetrable darkness except that in front, where every leaf is strongly defined and deeply shaded. In the morning, I hunted until about six, when I again renewed my shoutings for the boat; and it was not until near eleven that it made its appearance. I was so enraged at this delay that, had I not been cumbered with baggage, I believe I should have ventured to swim the river. I vented my indignation on the owner of the boat, who is a half-breed, threatening to publish him in the papers, and advise every traveller I met to take the upper-ferry. This man charges one dollar for man and horse, and thinks because he is a chief he may do in this way what he pleases. The country now assumed a new appearance—no brushwood, no fallen or rotten timber. One could see a mile through the woods, which were covered with high grass fit for mowing. These woods are burnt every Spring, and thus are kept so remarkably clean that they look like the most elegant noblemen's parks. A profusion of flowers altogether new to me, and some of them very elegant, presented themselves to my view as I rode along. This must be a heavenly place for the botanist. The most observable of these flowers was a kind of Sweet William, of all tints, from white to the deepest crimson; a suberb Thistle, the most beautiful I had ever seen; a species of Passion flowers, very beautiful; a stately plant of the Sunflower family—the button of the deepest orange, and the radiating petals bright carmine, the breadth of the flower about four inches; a large white flower like a deer's tail; great quantities of the Sensitive plant, that shrunk instantly on being touched, covered the ground in some places. Almost every flower was new to me, except the Carolina Pink-root and Columbo, which grew in abundance on every side. At Bear Creek, which is a large and rapid stream, I first observed the Indian boys with their blow-guns. These are tubes of cane, seven feet long, and perfectly straight when well made. The arrows are made of slender slips of cane, twisted, and straightened before the fire, and covered for several inches at one end with the down of thistles, in a spiral form, so as just to enter the tube. By a puff they can send these with such violence as to enter the body of a partridge, twenty yards off. I set several of them a-hunting birds by promise of reward, but not one of them could succeed. I also tried some of the blow-guns myself, but found them generally defective in straightness. I met six parties of boatmen to-day, and many straggling Indians, and encamped about sunset near a small brook, where I shot a turkey, and on returning to my fire found four boatmen, who stayed with me all night, and helped me to pick the bones of the turkey. In the morning I heard the turkies gobbling all round me, but not wishing to leave my horse, having no great faith in my guests' honesty, I proceeded on my journey. This day (Wednesday) I passed through the most horrid swamps I had ever seen. These are covered with a prodigious growth of canes, and high woods, which together shut out almost the whole light of day for miles. The banks of the deep and sluggish creeks that occupy the centre are precipitous, where I had often to plunge my horse seven feet down, into a bed of deep clay, up to his belly; from which nothing but great strength and exertion could have rescued him. The opposite shore was equally bad, and beggars all description. For an extent of several miles, on both sides of these creeks, the darkness of night obscures every object around. On emerging from one of the worst of these, I met General Wade Hampton, with two servants and pack-horse, going, as he said, towards Nashville. I told him of the mud campaign immediately before him. I was covered with mire and wet, and I thought he looked somewhat serious at the difficulties he was about to engage. He has been very sick lately. About half-an-hour before sunset, being within sight of the Indian's, where I intended to lodge, the evening being perfectly clear and calm, I laid the reins on my horse's neck to listen to a Mocking-bird, the first I had heard in the Western country, which, perched on top of a dead tree before the door, was pouring out a torrent of melody. I think I never heard so excellent a performer. I had alighted, and was fastening my horse, when, hearing the report of a rifle immediately beside me, I looked up, and saw the poor Mocking-bird fluttering to the ground. One of the savages had marked his elevation, and barbarously shot him. I hastened over into the yard, and, walking up to him, told him that was bad, very bad! that this poor bird had come from a far distant country to sing to him, and that, in return, he had cruelly killed him. I told him the Great Spirit was offended at such cruelty, and that he would lose many a deer for doing so. The old Indian, father-in-law to the bird-killer, understanding by the negro interpreter what I said, replied that when these birds come singing and making a noise all day near the house, somebody will surely die, which is exactly what an old superstitious German, near Hampton in Virginia, once told me. This fellow had married the two eldest daughters of the old Indian, and presented one of them with the bird he had killed. The next day I passed through the Chickasaw Bigtown, which stands on the high open plain that extends through their country three or four miles in breadth, by fifteen in length. Here and there you perceive little groups of miserable huts formed of saplings, and plastered with mud and clay. About these, are generally a few peach and plum trees. Many ruins of others stand scattered about, and I question whether there were twenty inhabited huts within the whole range of view. The ground was red with strawberries, and the boatmen were seen in straggling parties feasting on them. Now and then a solitary Indian, wrapt in his blanket, passed sullen and silent. On this plain are beds of shells, of a large species of clam, some of which are almost entire. I this day stopt at the house of a white man, who had two Indian wives, and a hopeful string of young savages, all in their fig leaves. Not one of them could speak a word of English. This man was by birth a Virginian, and had been forty years among the Chickasaws. His countenance and manners were savage and worse than Indian. I met many parties of boatmen to-day, and crossed a number of bad swamps. The woods continued to exhibit the same open luxuriant appearance, and at night I lodged at a white man's, who had also two wives, and a numerous progeny of young savages. Here I met with a lieutenant of the United States army anxiously inquiring for General Hampton. On Friday, the same open woods continued. I met several parties of Indians, and passed two or three of their hamlets. At one of these were two fires in the yard, and at each eight or ten Indians, men and women, squat on the ground. In these hamlets there is generally one house built of a circular form, and plastered thickly all over without and within with clay. This is called a hot house, and it is the general winter-quarter of the hamlet in cold weather. Here they all kennel, and, having neither window nor place for the smoke to escape, it must be a sweet place while forty or fifty of them have it in occupancy. Round some of these hamlets were great droves of cattle, horses, and hogs. I lodged this night on the top of a hill, far from water, and suffered severely from thirst. On Saturday, I passed a number of most execrable swamps. The weather was extremely warm, and I had been attacked by something like the dysentery, which occasioned a constant burning thirst, and weakened me greatly. I stopt this day frequently to wash my head and throat in the water, to allay the burning thirst, and, putting on my hat without wiping, received considerable relief from it. Since crossing the Tennessee, the woods have been interspersed with pine, and the soil has become more sandy. This day I met a Captain Hughes, a traveller on his return from Santa Fee. My complaint increased so much that I could scarcely sit on horseback, and all night my mouth and throat were parched with a burning thirst and fever. On Sunday, I bought some raw eggs, which I ate. I repeated the dose at mid-day, and towards evening, and found great benefit from this simple remedy. I inquired all along the road for fresh eggs, and for nearly a week made them almost my sole food, till I completed my cure. The water in these cane swamps is little better than poison; and under the heat of a burning sun, and the fatigues of travelling, it is difficult to repress the urgent calls of thirst. On the Wednesday following, I was assailed by a tremendous storm of rain, wind, and lightning, until I and my horse were both blinded by the deluge, and unable to go on. I sought the first most open place, and, dismounting, stood for half-an-hour under the most profuse heavenly shower-bath I ever enjoyed. The roaring of the storm was terrible; several trees around me were broken off and torn up by the roots, and those that stood were bent almost to the ground. Limbs of trees of several hundred weight flew past within a few yards of me, and I was astonished how I escaped. I would rather take my chance in a field of battle than in such a tornado again.

On the fourteenth day of my journey, at noon, I arrived at this place, having overcome every obstacle alone, and without being acquainted with the country; and, what surprised the boatmen more, without whisky. On an average, I met from forty to sixty boatmen every day returning from this place and New Orleans. The Chickasaws are a friendly, inoffensive people; and the Choctaws, though more reserved, are equally harmless. Both of them treated me with civility, though I several times had occasion to pass through their camps where many of them were. The paroquet which I carried with me was a continual fund of amusement to all ages of these people; and as they crowded around to look at it, gave me an opportunity of studying their physiognomies without breach of good manners.

In thus hastily running over the particulars of this journey, I am obliged to omit much that would amuse and interest you; but my present situation, a noisy tavern, crowded in every corner, even in the room where I write, with the sons of riot and dissipation, prevents me from enlarging on particulars. I could also have wished to give you some account of this place, and of the celebrated Mississippi, of which you have heard so much. On these subjects, however, I can at present only offer you the following sketch, taken the morning after my arrival here.

The best view of this place and surrounding scenery, is from the old Spanish fort on the south side of the town, about a quarter of a mile distant. From this high point, looking up the river, Natchez lies on your right, a mingled group of green trees, and white and red houses, occupying an uneven plain, much washed into ravines, rising as it recedes from the bluff or high precipitous bank of the river. There is, however, neither steeple, cupola, nor distinguished object to add interest to its appearance. The country beyond it to the right is thrown up into the same irregular knolls; and at the distance of a mile in the same direction you have a peep of some cultivated farms, bounded by the general forest. On your left, you look down, at a depth of two or three hundred feet, on the river winding majestically to the south, the intermediate space exhibiting wild perpendicular precipices of brown earth. This part of the river and shore is the general rendezvous of all the arks or Kentucky boats, several hundreds of which are at present lying moored there, loaded with the produce of the thousand shores of this noble river. The busy multitudes below present a perpetually varying picture of industry; and the noise and uproar, softened by the distance, with the continual crowing of the poultry, with which many of those arks are filled, produce cheerful and exhilarating ideas. The majestic Mississippi, swelled by his ten thousand tributary streams, of a pale brown colour, half a mile wide, and spotted with trunks of trees, that show the different threads of the current and its numerous eddies, bears his depth of water past in silent grandeur. Seven gun boats, anchored at equal distances along the stream, with their ensigns displayed, add to the effect. A few scattered houses are seen on the low opposite shore, where a narrow strip of cleared land exposes the high gigantic trunks of some deadened timber that bound the woods. The whole country beyond the Mississippi, from south round to west and north, presents to the eye one universal ocean of forest, bounded only by the horizon. So perfect is this vast level, that not a leaf seems to rise above the plain, as if shorn by the hands of heaven. At this moment, while I write, a terrific thunder storm, with all its towering assemblage of black alpine clouds, discharging lightning in every direction, overhangs this vast level, and gives a magnificence and sublime effect to the whole.[1]

Extracts from Journal

March 9—Visited a number of the literati and wealthy of Cincinnati, who all told me that they would think of it, viz., subscribing. They are a very thoughtful people.

March 17—Rained and hailed all last night. Set off at eight o'clock, after emptying my boat of the deluge of water. Rowed hard all day. At noon recruited myself with some biscuits, cheese, and American wine. Reach the Falls—night sets in—hear the roaring of the Rapids. After excessive hard work arrive at Bear-grass Creek, and fasten my boat to a Kentucky one. Take my baggage, and grope my way to Louisville—put up at the Indian Queen Tavern, and gladly sit down to rest myself.

March 18—Rose quite refreshed. Found a number of land speculators here. Titles to lands in Kentucky subject to great disputes.

March 19—Rambling round the town with my gun. Examined Mr. ——'s drawings in crayons. Very good. Saw two new birds he had —both Motacillae.

March 20—Set out this afternoon with the gun. Killed nothing new. People in taverns here devour their meals. Many shopkeepers board in taverns; also, boatmen, land speculators, merchants, &c. No naturalist to keep me company.

March 21—Went out this afternoon shooting, with Mr. A. Saw a number of Sandhill cranes. Pigeons numerous.

March 23—Packed up my things, which I left in the care of a mer-

---

1. The letter suddenly breaks off here in both Grosart and Ord and is followed by extracts from the lost diary or journal. There is no doubt that Grosart was indebted to Ord for both letter and diary extracts.

chant here to be sent on to Lexington; and having parted with great regret, with my paroquet to the gentlemen of the tavern, I bade adieu to Louisville, to which place I had four letters of recommendation, and was taught to expect much of every thing there; but neither received one act of civility from those to whom I was recommended, one subscriber, nor one new bird; though I delivered my letters, ransacked the woods repeatedly, and visited all the characters likely to subscribe. Science or literature has not one friend in this place. Every one is so intent on making money that they can talk of nothing else; and they absolutely devour their meals that they may return the sooner to their business. Their manners correspond with their features.

Good country this for lazy fellows; they plant corn, turn their pigs into the wood, and in the autumn feed upon corn and pork—they lounge about the rest of the year.

March 24—Weather cool. Walked to Shelbyville to breakfast. Passed some miserable log-houses in the midst of rich fields. Called at 'Squire C.'s, who was rolling logs. Sat down beside him, but was not invited in, though it was about noon.

March 29—Finding my baggage not likely to come on, I set out from Frankfort for Lexington. The woods swarm with pigs, squirrels, and woodpeckers. Arrive exceedingly fatigued.

Wherever you go you hear people talking of buying and selling land; no readers, all traders. The Yankees, wherever you find them, are all traders. Found one here, a house carpenter, who came from Massachusetts, and brought some barrels of apples down the river from Pennsylvania to this town, where he employs the negro women to hawk them about the streets, at thirty-seven and a half cents per dozen.

Restless, speculating set of mortals here, full of lawsuits, no great readers, even of politics or newspapers.

The sweet courtesies of life, the innumerable civilities in deeds and conversation, which cost one so little, are seldom found here. Every man you meet with has either some land to buy or sell, some law-suit, some coarse hemp or corn to dispose of; and if the conversation do not lead to any of these he will force it. Strangers here receive less civilities than in any place I have ever been in. The respect due to the fatigues and privations of travellers is no where given, because every one has met with as much, and thinks he has seen more than any other. No one listens to the adventures of another, without interrupting the narrative with his own; so that, instead of an auditor, he becomes a competitor in adventure-telling. So many adventurers, also, continually wandering about here, injure the manners of the people, for avarice and knavery prey most freely and safely upon passengers whom they may never meet again.

These few observations are written in Salter White's garret, with little or no fire, wood being a scarce article here—the forests being a full half mile distant.

April 9—Court held to-day, large concourse of people; not less than one thousand horses in town, hitched to the side-posts—no food for them all day. Horses selling by auction. Negro woman sold same way: my reflections while standing by and hearing her cried, "three hundred and twenty-five dollars for this woman and boy! going! going!" Woman and boy afterwards weep. Damned, damned slavery! this is one infernal custom which the Virginians have brought into this country. Rude and barbarous appearance of the crowd. Hopkins' double cutters much wanted here.

April 10—Was introduced to several young ladies this afternoon, whose agreeable society formed a most welcome contrast to that of the lower orders of the other sex. Mrs. ——, an amiable, excellent lady; think that savage ignorance, rudeness and boorishness, were never so contrasted by female sweetness affability, and intelligence.

April 12—Went this evening to drink tea with Mr. ——; was introduced to Mrs. ——, a most lovely, accomplished and interesting woman. Her good sense and lively intelligence of a cast far superior to that of almost any woman I have ever seen. She is most unfortunately unwell with a nervous complaint, which affects her head. She told me, most feelingly, that the Spring, which brings joy to every other being, brings sorrow to her, for in Winter she is always well.

April 25—Breakfasted at Walton's, thirteen miles from Nashville. This place is a fine rich hollow, watered by a charming, clear creek, and never fails. Went up to Madison's Lick, where I shot three Paroquets and some small birds.

April 26—Set out early, the hospitable landlord, ISAAC WALTON, refusing to take anything for my fare, or that of my horse, saying—"You seem to be travelling for the good of the world; and I cannot, and will not charge you anything. Whenever you come this way, call and stay with me, you shall be welcome!" This is the first instance of such hospitality which I have met with in the United States.

Wednesday, May 23—Left Natchez,[2] after procuring twelve subscribers; and having received a kind letter of invitation from William Dunbar, Esq.,[3] I availed myself of his goodness, and rode nine miles along the usual road to his house; where, though confined to his bed by a severe indisposition, I was received with great hospitality and kindness; had a neat bed-room assigned me; and was requested to consider myself as at home during the time I should find it convenient to stay in exploring this part of the country.

2. A further brief extract from the diary indicates that Wilson safely reached the town of Natchez on 17 May, a distance of 678 miles from Lexington, and wrote in his journal, "This journey 478 miles from Nashville, I have performed alone, through difficulties, that those who have never passed the road can have no conception of" (Crichton 1819, p. 62).

3. See above, part 1, pp. 101–102.

❧[CXXVIII]❧

To William Dunbar, Esquire.
Forest near Natchez, Mississ. Terr.[1]

New Orleans, 24 June 1810.

My dear Sir,

In half an hour I sail for New York[2] and am ashamed to confess that I write this in haste. I recd. by Dr. Don your obliging letter and do assure you that on my part our correspondence will never be neglected while I can hope to enjoy yours. I most sincerely rejoiced with all that know you in the prospect of the complete restoration of your health, of which, from that energy of mind which so strongly characterized you in my eye, I never doubted—I never can forget the pleasure I enjoyed in the sweet Society of your charming family —nor the attention of your most excellent wife (pardon the familiarity of the phraze) to make my residence agreeable—I have suc-

1. On Wilson's departure from New Orleans he sent this letter of thanks and farewell to William Dunbar. It is transcribed from *Life, Letters and Papers of William Dunbar* by Mrs. Dunbar Rowland (Jackson, Mississippi, 1930). In Rowland's transcript it is signed "A. Will. Wilson"—surely an error for Wilson's usual signature, "Alex. Wilson." Dunbar died only four months later on 16 October 1810.

2. Wilson "departed from Philadelphia on the thirtieth of January, 1810 and returned on the second of August, of the same year. It is stated in his diary that the total amount of his expenses, until his arrival in New York, was the sum of four hundred and fifty-five dollars" (Ord, p. xcvii, note). If 2 August, as given by Ord, was the date of his arrival in New York, then it is supported by Wilson's letter from Philadelphia on 2 September 1810 to William Bartram in which he mentions that incessant labour since his return had prevented him calling upon Bartram. However, in his letter to his father of 25 February 1811 he said that he returned to Philadelphia on 2 September 1811, and then on 4 March 1811, writing to James Gibb, he gave the date of his return as 6 September. The seeming confusion about dates would suggest that Wilson's mind was wholly concentrated on what he termed "difficulties relative to my publication."

ceeded here in obtaining 64 subscribers to my book—men of the first respectability.

[I had intended ?] to pass through Florida, but the season is too far advanced the Birds either young or losing their plumage in this and the next month would supply me with very bad specimens & might lead me into error—I do intend in a year or two to sail for this country in January and stay till April for the sole purpose of making a complete collection of all the Aquatic tribes of birds found in your river and Bayous—I have made many excursions round this place and found a few curious & new to me. So minute and exact is Nature in her nice discriminations of different species of Birds and so general vague and incorrect are almost all the accounts of illiterate sportsmen and those unacquainted with the source that I pay little attention to any accounts received from such people relative to my pursuits. Nine times in ten they will be found altogether erroneous.

I shall make the experiment myself that you mention relative to the Turkey Buzzard, tho' I have little faith in it. The quality of its oil I would not dispute that also I shall try. Will you be so obliging as request Dr. Seip, the first time you meet with him to be so good as drop me a few lines, should any more subscribers be found at Natchez I shall always be glad to hear from that gentleman for whom as well as Dr. Brown I have a very great esteem. Dr. Brown I conclude a gentleman of very correct and discriminating talents; and the most suitable person within my knowledge to accompany you in your tours for the success [. . .] of which I am much interested. My most Respectfull compts. to Mrs. Dunbar & the young ladies.

May Heaven prosper for (I would almost say) a thousand years the health & happiness of so worthy a family—is the ardent wish of

My dear Sir

Your much obliged friend

ALEX. WILSON

P.S. I am sorry the volumes of the Ornithology have not come on as expected; but I will instantly despatch them on my arrival and take the opportunity of sending Eliza the coloured [. . .] and some drawing paper.

CXXIX

APS

To Mr. Rubens Peale.
Museum.

Philadelphia, Thursday 22 [?] 1810.

A. Wilson's Compts. to Mr. Peale with a specimen of the Grey Fox, killed at Egg Harbour—a New Lark? The Mississippi Kite hitherto undescribed—A Gull (common) being the young male of the first year—The Prothonotary Warbler and a new species of Motacilla which I have called the Tennesee Warbler.

A number of other things are in reservation for Mr. Peale—

My young friend the bearer will be gratified with a peep at the wonder of the Museum.

The Kite was a male and deserves to be well set up.

CXXX

GROSART

To William Bartram.

Philadelphia, 2 September 1810.

. . . Incessant labour since my return, to make up my loss of drawings, which were sent by post from Nashville, has hitherto prevented me from paying you a visit. I am closely engaged on my third volume. Any particulars relative to the history of the meadow lark, crow blackbird, snow bunting, cuckoo, paroquet, nonpareil, pinnated grous, or blue grosbeak, if interesting, would be received by me with much pleasure. I have lately received from Michaux a number of rich specimens of birds, printed in colours. I have since made some attempts at this kind of printing and have succeeded tolerably well.

Michaux has published several numbers of his American Sylva, in Paris, with coloured plates. I expect them here soon.

I collected a number of entire new species in my south-western tour; and in my return I visited several of the islands off the Florida shore, where I met with some very curious land birds.

Mr. Dunbar, of Natchez, remembered you very well, and desired me to carry his good wishes to you. . . .

❊[CXXXI]❊

BLY

To Mr. John L. Gardiner.
Gardiner's Island,
near the East end of Long Island, New York.
                    Philadelphia, 12 September 1810.

Dear Sir,

On my return from Louisiana, a short time since, your very obliging letter of the 5th of June was put into my hand. The circumstances of my absence will appologise for not answering your friendly communication sooner. I thank you most sincerely for the improvements you suggest, and for the interest you take in my Publication, an interest not merely verbal, but so kindly manifested by actions. I shall pay particular attention to your hints.

Your kind invitation to Gardiner's Island also demands my gratitude. Had I known of your residence, on my arrival last month at

New York from N. Orleans, I should certainly have paid you a visit. You can, however, be of great & Distinguished service to me, if matters of more moment will permit you, in procuring for me a skin of the Fishing Hawk & Bald Eagle, with such further particulars of their manners and disposition as you may be able to collect. I know of no gentleman in the United States who, from his situation, is better able to do justice to this subject than yourself. Among all our Birds none has so noble an exterior as the Bald Eagle, and none has been so miserably caricatured. These two birds I intend to exhibit in my 4th Volume, which will appear early next Spring, and if you can furnish me with the skins I shall try to do justice to both in the drawing and shall be happy to present to the public such details of their manners & characters as you may have time to collect.

The Woodpecker you mention I am already acquainted with. It is very numerous in the Southern States, and even in the Gennesee Country, where it is also called the Woodcock. There is a still larger species found in Louisiana, called the Ivory billed Woodpecker, the biggest of the whole genus, both of these will appear in Vol. IV. The particulars you give me relating to the Fishing Hawk are curious & interesting. Pray Do the Crowblackbirds occupy the lower parts of the Hawk's nest while he inhabits the upper?

If your time would permit you, you could make the History of these two noble Birds the Hawk & Eagle greatly interesting. I have already a Drawing of the Eagle done with much care from a fine living specimen, but I should like to compare and correct it once more with the original Bird, or skin. Of the Fishing Hawk I have as yet nothing. I have just written to Dr. Mitchill on the subject of the *Grouse*, a bird of Game very plenty on Long Island, and whose habits are but little known to Europeans.

You will confer a singular obligation on me by writing when convenient. The publication of my Third Volume has been retarded by my 7 month's absence, but I am getting it forward as fast as possible.

Do the *White* Snowbirds, or Snow Buntings, ever visit you in winter? And have you ever remarked a solitary bird, something less than the blue Jay, and of a rather lighter colour than the Catbird— The forehead and lower parts are of a dirty white, the back wings and tail of a dark leaden grey, the hind head is black, and the feathers on the crown are *full,* as if crested. This bird is called the Canada Jay—I am extremely desirous of procuring a specimen. If it visits you it must be only in winter.

With great respect

I am

Dear Sir

Your very humble servt.

ALEX. WILSON[1]

CXXXII

GROSART

To William Duncan.[1]

Philadelphia, 12 February 1811.

. . . So you have once more ascended the preceptor's rostrum, to wield the terrors of the taws and hickory. Trying as this situation is,

---

1. Gardiner started to scribble a draft of his reply at the foot and on the outside of this letter. He writes that he told his Indian man, who among other things is employed to shoot and keep the crows and crow blackbirds out of the Indian cornfield, to kill a fishing hawk for Wilson. Apparently only one pair was left at that season and by the next day they had gone. He promises to help Wilson and says he himself had seen an eagle, "In the act of flying away with a lamb, about ten days old, which by its struggling and my halloing it dropt when about ten foot high—but it had broken the lamb's back in the act of seizing it."

The chapters concerning the ivory-billed woodpecker, the pileated woodpecker, the white-headed eagle, and the fish hawk in volumes three and four of *American Ornithology* relate to this letter.

1. "Frankford, Pennsylvania."

and various and distracting as its avocations sometimes undoubtedly are, it is elysium to the scenes which you have lately emerged
from; and as far transcends these latter, as honourable independence
towers above despised and insulted servitude. You wish me to suggest any hints I may think proper for your present situation. Your
own experience and prudence render anything I could advise unnecessary, as it is all included in the two resolutions which you have
already taken; first, to distinguish, as clearly as possible, the whole
extent of your duty; and, secondly, to fulfil every item of that to the
best of your abilities. Accordingly, the more extensive and powerful
these are, the greater good you will be capable of doing; the higher
and more dignified will your reputation be; and the easier and
calmer will your deportment be, under every circumstance of duty.
You have but these two things to surmount, and the whole routine
of teaching will become an agreeable amusement; and every closing
day will shed over your mind that blissful tranquility, "which nothing earthly gives or can destroy."

Devote your whole time, except what is proper for needful exercise, to rendering yourself completely master of your business. For
this purpose rise by the peep of dawn; take your regular walk; and
then commence your stated studies. Be under no anxiety to hear
what people think of you, or of your tutorship; but study the improvement, and watch over the good conduct, of their children con-
signed to your care, as if they were your own. Mingle respect and
affability with your orders and arrangements. Never show yourself
feverish or irritated; but preserve a firm and dignified, a just and
energetic deportment, in every emergency. To be completely master of one's business, and ever anxious to discharge it with fidelity
and honour, is to be great, beloved, respectable and happy.

I could have wished that you had been accommodated with a room
and boarding in a more private and retired situation, where your
time and reflections would have been more your own; and perhaps
these may be obtained hereafter. Try to discover your own defects,

and labour with all your energy to supply them. Respect yourself, and fear nothing but vice and idleness. If one had no other reward for doing one's duty, but the grateful sensations arising therefrom on the retrospection, the recompense would be abundant, as these alone are able to bear us up amidst every reverse. . . .

At present I cannot enlarge further, my own mind being harrassed with difficulties relative to my publication. I have now no farther dependence on Murray; and I mean to make it consistent both with fame, and the interest, of Lawson to do his best for me. I hope you will continue to let me hear from you, from time to time. I anticipate much pleasure from the improvements which I have no doubt you will now make in the several necessary departments of your business. Wishing you every success in your endeavours to excel, I remain, with sincere regard, &c. . . .

❦[CXXXIII]❦

GROSART, POEMS 1816

To Alexander Wilson, Sr.

25 February 1811.

Dear Father,

I have made various excursions through the United States in quest of ornithological subjects. My last route was across the Alleghany mountains to Pittsburg, thence to the falls of the Ohio, 720 miles alone, in a small boat—thence through the Chickasaw, and Choctaw country, (nations of Indians) and West Florida, to New Orleans, in which journey I sustained considerable hardship, having many dangerous creeks to swim, and having to encamp for thirteen different nights in the woods alone. From New Orleans I sailed to East Florida, furnished with a letter to the Spanish Governor there, and visited a number of the islands that lie to the south of the peninsula. I returned to Philadelphia on the 2d of September last, after an absence of seven months.

In prosecuting this journey, I had sometimes to kindle a large fire; I then stript the canes for my horse, ate a bit of supper, and lay down to sleep, listening to the owls and cheekwills, and to a kind of Whip-Poor-Will, that are very numerous. I got up several times during the night to recruit my fire, and see how my horse did, and but for the gnats would have slept tolerably well. These gigantic woods have a singular effect by the light of a large fire, the whole scene being circumscribed by impenetrable darkness, except that in front, where every leaf is strongly defined and deeply shaded. On passing the ferry, the country assumed a new appearance; no brush-wood, or broken and fallen timber. One could see a mile through the woods, which were covered with high grass fit for mowing. A pro-fusion of flowers altogether new to me, and some of them very ele-gant, presented themselves to my view as I rode along. This must be a noble place for the botanist. The most noticeable of these flowers was a kind of sweet william, of all tints, from white to the deepest crimson. A superb thistle, the most beautiful I had ever seen, a species of passion flower, very beautiful, a stately plant of the sun-flower family, the button of the deepest orange, and the radiating petals, bright carmine; the breadth of the flower about four inches, a large white flower like a deer's tail, great quantities of the sensitive plant, that shrunk instantly on being touched, in some places covered the ground. Almost every flower was new to me, except the Carolina perule root, and columbo, which grows in abundance on every side.

On Saturday I passed a number of execrable swamps. The weather was extremely warm, and I had been attacked by something like the dysentery, which occasioned a constant burning thirst, and weak-ened me greatly. My complaint increased so much, that I could scarcely sit on horseback, and all night my mouth and throat were parched with a burning thirst and fever. On Sunday I bought some raw eggs, which I ate, and repeated the dose at mid-day and towards evening. I found great benefit from this simple remedy, and enquired all along the road for fresh eggs, and for nearly a week made them almost my sole food, until I completed my cure. The water in these cane swamps is little better than poison, and under the heat of a burning sun, and the fatigues of travelling, it is difficult to repress the urgent calls of thirst. On the Wednesday following, I was assailed by a tremendous storm of wind, and rain, and lightning, until I and my horse were both blinded by the deluge, and unable to go on. I sought the first open place, and dismounting, stood for half an hour under the most profuse shower-bath I had ever enjoyed. The roaring of the storm was terrible. Several trees around me were broken off, and torn up by the roots, and those that stood were bent almost to the ground. Limbs of trees flew past within a few yards of me, and I was astonished how I escaped; and I would rather take my chance in a field of battle, than in such a tornado again.

On the fourteenth day of my journey, at noon, I arrived at Natchez, Mississippi, after having overcome every obstacle alone, and without being acquainted with the country, and what surprised the boatmen more, without whisky. . . .[1]

[At this point, Grosart's version ends, but in the Life which is included in Poems 1816, there is the following extract, said to be from "a letter to his father" of "February 25th, 1811."]

The publication of the Ornithology, though it has swallowed up the little I have saved, has procured me the honour of many friends, eminent in this country, and the esteem of the public at large—for which I have to thank the goodness of a kind father, whose atten-

1. The actual letter has not been found and it will be noted that the second and third paragraphs are almost identical with a substantial portion of letter CXXVII to Alexander Lawson dated 18 May 1810. The extracts from this letter in Poems 1816 do not include the second and fourth paragraphs above and, as an editorial hotchpotch letter CXXXIII must be treated with a measure of reservation.

tions to my education in early life, as well as the books then put into my hands, first gave my mind a bias towards relishing the paths of literature, and the charms and magnificence of nature. These, it is true, particularly the latter, have made me a wanderer in life, but they have also enabled me to support an honest and respectable situation in the World, and have been the sources of almost all my enjoyments.

CXXXIV

THAYER

To Mr. James Gibb.
Near Newark, New Jersey.

Philadelphia, 4 March 1811.

My dear friend,

I received yours of Feby 25th 1810 twelve months after date, a long time for a letter to travel between Newark and Philad^a. I attributed this however to its proper cause and was extremely glad to hear from my friend once more. Mr. Miller having got an engagement at Baltimore to which place he set off yesterday rendered any exertion of mind on his behalf unnecessary. That Mrs. Gibb & you are both well pleased with your situation gives me sincere pleasure. You may depend on this that I shall never approach within 20 miles of Newark without going to see you.

The Song is at your service if I knew how to get it conveyed as the publication contains 14 or 15 more on the same subject all set to music. Miller intends to return in 3 months. If I cannot find an opportunity sooner I will send it by him. As to the Forresters it was published from time to time for 9 months in the Port Folio, with 4 plates but has never been published separately. On the 28th of Jany. 1810 I left Philad^a for Pittsburgh there I purchased a small batteau which I navigated alone to the Falls of the Ohio 720 miles, from there I set out on foot for Lexington, Kentucky 75 miles—thence to Nashville in Tennesee 200 miles, thence through the Chickasaw and Choctaw nations, Mississippi Territory & part of West Florida to New Orleans, 730 miles—I encamped 13 nights in the woods between Nashville and Natchez and carried a live Parakeet in my pocket from Big Bone Lick in Kentucky to New Orleans—from N. Orleans I sailed for Florida and visited some of the islands off the South side of the peninsula and on the 6th September arrived safe in Philad^a, having made many additions to my stock of drawings and Birds, many of them Nondescript.

I have just published my third volume of Amer. Orn. and have got nearly half of the plates of the Fourth finished. I live secluded from the rest of Mankind always poring over Birds, or pursuing them in the woods—If you could procure me a new Bird from any of your sporting friends I would be pleased to perpetuate the recollection of our friendship by stating from whom I recd. it. At any rate please to write me frequently. I had a letter from our old friend, Oliver lately, who has fixed his everlasting residence, it seems, in Scotland. I wrote a poetical description of my voyage down the Ohio, entitled The Pilgrim, which was published in the Port Folio of last July. I daresay you will find it in your neighbourhood.

Compliments to Mr. Gardner & to Mr. Tho[mpson] but in particular to your amiable partner & bosom friend, Mrs. Gibb. I do sincerely rejoice in your present agreeable situation and hope [you will not] exchange it, but for a better.

I am With Great Regard

Dear Sir

Yours

ALEX. WILSON

P.S. When at Natchez I went to Camp where I was informed by his officer that W. Mitchell died on the 10th October 1809 at Point

Coupee on the Mississippi of a Fever and Dysentry—10 perished
out of the same boat on their way up to the present Quarters of the
army—At New Orleans I accidentally met with the little Frenchman I taught at Bloomfield & Bob Ellis of Paisley, it seems, was
twice in the house in which I boarded, but he sailed for Liverpool
before I knew of the circumstance.

❦[CXXXV]❧

PBC

To Mr. David Wilson.
Seedhills of Paisley, North Britain.

Philadelphia, 6 June 1811.

Dear Brother,

I have this day recd. your letter of the 13th April, commencing,
as usual, with reproaches for not writing, *some* of which though
harsh are just; the rest shall be forgotten. The letters and package
which I sent you about 3 months ago have I hope ere this time come
to hand. By the first safe opportunity I will transmit a trifle to our
old father, whose *existence* so far from being *forgotten* is as dear to
me as my own. But David, an ambition of being distinguished in the
literary world has required sacrifices and exertions from me with
which you are perhaps unacquainted, and a wish to reach the glorious rock of *Independence* that I might from thence assist my relations who are still struggling with and buffetting the billows of
adversity has engaged me in an undertaking more laborious and
expensive than you are aware of and has occupied almost every
moment of my time these several years. I have since Feby. 1810
slept for weeks in the wilderness alone in an Indian country with my
gun and pistols in my bosom, have found myself so reduced by sick-

ness as to be scarcely able to stand when 300 miles from a white settlement and under the burning latitude of 25 degrees, have by resolution surmounted all these and other obstacles in my way to my object and I now begin to see the blue sky open around me and Independence slowly descending to give me a wag of her fist which I trust nothing but death shall separate me from.

I feel most sincerely for the distressed state of your country and for my poor sister and brother in law who have been so deeply unfortunate. If Mr. Wright is in good health able and willing to work let him not hesitate one moment to come to this country. He may perhaps find many things to dislike here but abundance to eat and drink is every ones prerogative in the United States of America. Those who wish to be happy here must abandon *for ever* their country, nor permit regrets & repinings at the loss of their old acquaintance or despair at the difficulties they will *certainly* have to meet with *for a short time* to enter their mind. Should you feel disposed to accompany him and your father be perfectly willing to part with you, write me to that effect and I will take measures to procure you a passage, and shall assist you in procuring a steady situation as far as my influence may extend. Of your Character and abilities I am not sufficiently informed to say what would be your best pursuit here—when we are sometime together I will be better able to advise you. You will please to communicate this to Mr. Wright and your father and write me by the first opportunity. Should you determine to set out before him you will immediately let me know and I will transmit you funds for that purpose.

I will write in a short time to my father, in the meantime I beg to be remembered to him our mother my sisters particularly my sister Jean and John Bell to whom I intend to write in a few weeks

I am with sincere regard
Dear Brother
Yours affectionately
ALEX. WILSON

 CXXXVI

HSP

To Mr. George Ord.
Philada.

Bartram's Gardens, 9 July 1811.

Dear Sir,

My friend Major Carr, the bearer of this, is desirous of conversing with you on the subject of Hemp, of which he has at present a
large & very promising field; and I feel happy in introducing him
to your acquaintance, as I know you will be mutually pleased with
each other. I hope you are preparing me some notes on the *Purple
Martin*; if not, I shall be sadly disappointed. My 4th Vol. is printed;
but the Engraver has not yet finished with the two last plates. I am
arranging things better for the 5th, which I hope to be able to publish in 4 months after the present.

Knowing the *charms* that the City presents at *this season*, it would
be a mere waste of words to invite you to the *Country*; particularly
to *such* a place as *this*, and to *such* a person; but *Heaven bless you*. So
prays your's,

ALEX. WILSON

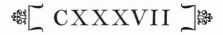 CXXXVII

HC

To [Mr. Jones].

Bartram's Garden, 9 August [1811?].

Dear Sir,

As Lawson will probably be in town to-day, I wish you would
oblige me by sending Peter out with an impression of his plate, and

I will colour it, and let Mr. Lawson know what alterations may be wanted, without delay, perhaps before he leaves the city—If I do *not* send it in before he goes, it is my wish that he should leave the plate at Browns.

Any trifling alteration of cleaning, or so, can be done here in less time than to take it out again; and I want the plate printed as soon as possible. Mr. Lawson says he sent in a Port Folio of mine to your house which Peter will put the impression in.

Yours with Sincerity
ALEX. WILSON

CXXXVIII

PMA

To Mr. Duncan Wright.
Arkleston   near Paisley   North Britain.

Philadelphia, 20 October 1811.

Dear Brother and Sister,[1]

I received by David your letter, and the present of neckcloths for which please to accept my acknowledgements and thanks. I have read your letter with attention, and heard from my brother your misfortunes, which have been severe indeed, but which must be forgotten as much as possible. The representation you give of the state of trade, and situation of tradesmen in Paisley & around, is truly deplorable. To me, it is not surprising that numbers abandon such a country. My astonishment is that anybody able to leave it should remain in it. Were the United States in the same desolation & bankruptcy, with as mournful prospects of improvement, I would no more hesitate whether I should leave it than I would a half-ruined

---

1. The brother and sister to whom this letter is written were Wilson's half-sister Janet Wilson and her husband.

house ready to tumble about my ears. The United States and its territories contain at present seven millions of souls. In 1794, when I first arrived, its population was less than *four million*. All these, generally speaking, are doing well. Do you imagine that there is not room or a fair chance left for one single family? The deficiency, if there be any, might be in the individual, not in the country, which holds out every encouragement to the active & industrious. You have frequently heard of *sea-sickness*, how disagreeable and distressing it is. There is another kind to which new-comers are sometimes subject on their arrival here, and for a few months after, called *home-sickness*, no less disagreeable while it lasts. But these maladies are generally temporary, and leave the patient better than before, with a keen appetite and renovated spirits. If you can conquer the qualms of this last kind on your first arrival, and look round you for employment, with the resolution of a *Man* determined to surmount difficulties, come when you will, you will certainly succeed. I have, however, determined with myself never to entice or persuade a man from his native country to a foreign land. These are adventures that should be undertaken on his own risk, and supported by his own resolution. But you have asked my advice with so much earnestness, that I would be acting a most unnatural part did I refuse it. There is little chance of following the employment of bleaching here; but there is an infinite number of employments besides to which your own judgment & activity may direct you. As to the precise sum of money necessary for you to have on your arrival here I am not fit to determine. Some little furniture will be necessary, and other articles, to set up housekeeping. Industry and economy will soon arrange all these matters. Robert Shaw, formerly of Seedhills, makes a good living in New York by dyeing and cleaning of clothes. He also keeps a tavern, and I do not see why something of the kind might not also do here. But of these matters, you yourself must be the judge. It is also customary here for some people to farm land on what is called *The Shares*; that is, for half the produce of the ground.

There are ten thousand avenues for industry here; every man must choose that best suited to his taste and capacity. David is well, and lives with me. He seems very well pleased with his new situation, and I shall endeavour to make it mutually advantageous to us both.

I am, with sincerity,

Dear Brother and Sister,

Affectionately yours,

ALEX. WILSON

P.S. Should you determine on coming here, I will render you every assistance in my power; but difficulties must be encountered everywhere in *this* world.

A. W.

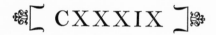

CXXXIX

CRICHTON 1819

To Thomas Crichton.

Philadelphia, 28 October 1811.

Dear Sir,[1]

I received your kind letter, of May 31, with a copy of the Library, both extremely agreeable to me, and interesting to one, who for seventeen years had heard nothing concerning you, but who had neither forgot you, nor the many friendly acts he had experienced from you. I have read your poem several times. It embraces a wide range of subjects, and contains much excellent sentiment, with several well drawn sketches, among which that of Chloe, the novel reader, is conspicuous and just. To the prayer of the last eight lines I most heartily say amen.

---

1. In the spring of 1811 Crichton said that Wilson's friend Mr. Brown (see letter CXVII) had told him that he was sending a packet to Wilson and had urged Crichton to renew his correspondence. This letter is Wilson's response.

I thank you for the information you have given me of my old friends, Neilson, Kennedy, Picken, &c. and am glad to find, that, amidst the deaths, disasters and convulsions of domestic life, your merit continues to meet its reward. The contrast between your life and mine, during the last twenty years has been great; yet, I much question, whether, with both in perspective, I should have been willing to exchange fates, and I am sure you never would; so neither of us ought to complain.

While every letter I receive from Britain acknowledges the general desolation of trade and the sufferings of its manufacturers, I see nothing around me in this happy country but peace, prosperity, and abundance. Our merchants indeed have experienced great embarrasments, but generally speaking the country is flourishing. The census of our population amounts to upwards of seven millions, nearly double to what it was when I first landed in America. What nation on earth can produce a parallel to this?

My dear Sir, I cannot recal to my mind some of our social interviews without a smile. You found me in early life an enthusiastic young man, pursuing what I thought right, without waiting to consider its expediency, and frequently suffering, (and that feelingly too) for my temerity. At present, I have the same ardour in the pursuit of my object, but the object is selected with more discretion.

If you see my old friend David Brodie, (for I understand that he still treads this earth, *in propria persona*,) present him with my respects. He and I mutually studied each other's characters for some time, with the laudable design of telling each other. My report was made first, and in full detail; David's never made its appearance, and so I lost a very favourable opportunity of knowing my own faults. I suppose he found me so heterogeneous and contradictory—so confounded bad, and entangled, that he did not know at which end to begin.

My dear Sir, I shall be always glad to hear from you, when you find convenient to write, and beg you would convey my sincere respects to the surviving friends you mention, particularly to Mr. M'Gavin, and believe me, with great truth,

Dear Sir,

Your most obliged friend,
ALEX. WILSON

CRICHTON 1819

[To a Paisley friend.]

3 November 1811.

My Dear Friend,

I was a wanderer when I was in Scotland, and I have been much more so since my arrival here. Few Americans have seen more of their country than I have done, and none love it better. Fortune has not yet paid me up all her promises, after all the wild goose chase she has led me; but she begins to look a little more gracious than usual, and I am not without hope. Twenty years of disappointment have only whetted my appetite for independence. . . .

[There is a fragment quoted in Poems 1816 which may be another portion of this letter. We are told by the writer of the Life in this book that soon after the publication of the fourth volume of the *American Ornithology*, Wilson's letters to Scotland were filled with lamentations about the appearance of the approaching contest between Great Britain and America.]

I love the arts of peace as I do Heaven. . . . Everybody wishes for a good understanding with Great Britain. Of the sentiments and views of our government I can say nothing, being little conversant in these matters, and having long quitted the turbulent field of politics.

LCP

To Mr. Mordecai Churchman.
Easton, Pennsylvania.

Philadelphia, 4 November 1811.

Dear Sir

I was much delighted with yours of June 23d detailing particulars of the Chimney Swallow. Having been great part of the present Summer ranging along our Sea shores in quest of the Aquatic Birds I have been prevented from acknowledging your favour sooner. My 4th Vol. is now published and my 5th which contains the History of this Singular Swallow is now in press. I am ashamed to impose so much on your goodness but there are somethings relative to this bird which if you procure me information would make its History complete. 1. I am extremely anxious to know certainly whether there are at present Chimney Swallows in the Court House chimney in a dead living or torpid state—And secondly—Are you possessed of any authentic proofs that they ever were found there in the depth of winter—Could you procure me positive information on these two points within ten days—I should ever feel an obligation not only to you Sir but also the town of Easton which has enabled me to throw more light on the history of this Bird than any former writer has done. I will wait your answer with the fond expectation of hearing from you. I beg you to remember me to your worthy family with whom I should be happy to spend an other afternoon *once a day* as I did when I had the pleasure of being with you.

My best respects & thanks to Mr. Arnott and also to Mr. Abraham Hart who so obligingly explored the Chimney for me—I am sorry to send him on such a black errand but he could bring a good deal of light out of darkness by obliging me once more with a peep up, or down the Chimney. Truth they say sometimes lies at the bottom of a well—It may also lurk at the bottom of a Chimney—Excuse my freedom and believe me with great Sincerity

My dear Sir

your much obliged friend

ALEX. WILSON[1]

CXLII

HSP

To Hon. Samuel L. Mitchill.
Washington.

Philadelphia, 14 January 1812.

Dear Sir,

I take this liberty of introducing to you Major Robt. Carr of this city, my particular friend, and the gentleman of whom I lately transmitted you some acct. He has promised to deliver this to you in person and I most cheerfully recommend him to your attention and friendship. His business at Washington being to follow up with what influence he can procure his petition to the Secretary of War as stated to you in my last. You will not I am persuaded be the last in assisting with your counsel and advice one so deserving, and so anxious to support the honour of his Country in the arduous profession of a Soldier. I am confident Carr will never dishonour those by

---

1. This letter was brought to my attention by Mr. Humphrey A. Olsen who informed me that it was deposited at The Library Company of Philadelphia, bound in a copy of John Churchman, *The Magnetic Atlas* (Baldwin, London, 1804). In his long chapter on the chimney swallow, *American Ornithology*, vol. 5, Wilson acknowledged the assistance of Mordecai Churchman and wrote that on 20 May 1811 he spent part of the day in the town of Easton, and he referred to ". . . my respected friend Mordecai Churchman, cashier of the bank there, and one of the people called Quakers."

whom he is so much regarded—On his known bravery and intelligence his vigilance activity and high sense of honour all who know him have the highest dependance.

The 5th Vol. of my Ornithology will be ready for delivery in about 2 months—I have lately shot a number of Fine Hawks, 4 of which are altogether new to me and I believe to Europeans. One is almost totally black and of great strength and fierceness. I have also had the promise of the *Swallow tailed Hawk* from Dr. Samuel Brown of Fort Adams, Miss Ter. and of several others which frequent the Prairies with which we all are unacquainted—The United States will exhibit such a display of noble Eagles and Hawks in the 5th & 6th vols. of this Work as I think no other country can produce. The *printing* of the *present vol.* (vol. 5) surpasses any thing hitherto done in this part of the World for which I am indebted to the talents & attention of my worthy friend the bearer of this letter to whom I beg leave to refer you for particulars, and am

With very great esteem,

Dear Sir

Your Obliged humble [fd]

ALEX. WILSON

 **CXLIII**

ANS

Mr. John Abbot, Naturalist.[1]
Savannah, Georgia.

Philada., 23 January 1812.

Dear Sir,

I this day rec'd. a small box containing a roll of Drawings, 3 in number, which I myself delivered to Dr. Bartons, also a *small* pack-

---

1. John Abbot was an outstanding artist/naturalist, the illustrator of *The Natural History of the Rarer Lepidopterous Insects of Georgia*, ed. James Edward Smith, 2 vols. (1797), which contains 104 fine engraved plates.

age directed to Wm. Bartram, which has also been sent to him, and 4 Birds, viz., the Small Crow, female solitary Flycatcher, and the male and female Ground dove—all in good order. The Crow and the Flycatcher I had already figured—The other two were very welcome; you will please to draw on me thro' Mr. Oemler for the amount of these 4 & any other you may send, at the rate I mentioned, & I hereby empower him to pay you accordingly. Please to send the Chuck Wills widow, (Male) and egg, and the beautiful rare Sparrow you mention, also the Stripped Wren. I do not know the large Green-billed Woodpecker—nor any Woodpecker as large as the Wood Cocks—if you know of such, be so good as send me one. The Slate-coloured rice bird is a species of Grosbeak, about the size of the Rice bird, and the black headed Green warbler is common in the Bahamas and sometimes comes to Georgia. It is not the Hooded Warbler. The Crossbill you mention is, I suppose, the female of the Common one. It is [. . . .] When I was in the Mississippi Territory two years ago I shot the small yellow Warbler with rust coloured spots on the back.

My 5th Volume is nearly ready for publication and I have nearly got through all the Land birds. Any remarkably rare Hawks or Owls will be very welcome particularly the Swallow tailed. Be so good as mention the colour of the bill, eyes, & legs and any other fugitive parts. I shall also be glad of any anecdote relative to their Manners, nest, eggs, etc.

I will send you a list of *all* the Land & Water Birds which I have yet to draw—marking those with a *star*, that I think you can furnish me with. In the meantime, send me by the first opportunity what you can in a strong box directed to A. Wilson, care of Bradford & Inskeep, Booksellers, Philada. Let me know if there be anything here which I can do for you and I will do it with pleasure. Can you inform me of the nest or eggs etc. of the Ground Dove—I wish you could procure me any particulars of this beautiful little Dove. I presume they are migratory. I hope you will soon get quit of that distressing complaint, the *Rheumatism*—How is my friend Dr. Bald-win & what has become of him. As I will send Mr. Oemler the Volumes 3, 4 & 5 in a few weeks (5 or 6) you will be able to see the Birds I have already described. I hope you will embrace the *first opportunity* of sending me another package, and write me at the same time by post, mentioning the name of the Vessel. Compliments to Mr. Oemler, and my best wishes for your health and happiness.

With great esteem
Your sincere wellwisher
ALEX. WILSON

I can send you a Dozen Crossbills if you chose. Some red—others (the females & young) olive yellow.

A.W.

CXLIV

THAYER

To William Bartram.

Favoured by Major Carr.
Philadelphia, 12 February 1812.

My dear friend,

It has not been from neglect or forgetfullness I assure you that I have not been to see you since we parted in October. Since Mr. Wm. Duncan left me as colourist I have been obliged to sit closely at that employment myself and what with Drawing Writing my 5th volume (which is now nearly printed) and correcting the proofs I have had few moments to spare.

I lately recd. some letters from Natchez on the Mississippi giving me an account of some new Birds which I am promised particularly a Singular Hawk. I was also told by the same communications that Mr. Bradbury, an English Botanist who was sent out by the Linnean Society of London has returned from the interior of Louisiana where he has been for several years, and has brought a superb collection; as he Draws well and has found a number of Birds and has promised to my friends in Natchez to let me copy any of them, I am in hopes that on Mr. Bradbury's arrival here on his way to London I shall find something new. He comes by the way of N. Orleans. Mr. Abbot of Savannah lately sent me the male and female Ground Dove in excellent order—a beautiful specimen.

I hope to have the 5th vol. ready for delivery in three or four weeks at farthest—Early in April I hope to pitch my tent once more beside yours so that it will be dubious whether the Martin or me be your first visitor. I beg to be remembered to your brother and the family whom I trust are all well.

Since the numerous and alarming Earthquakes that have taken place in various quarters of the country commenced I have frequently thought of the repeated remarks you made towards the close of last Summer, that the weather was much like that which preceded the former Earthquake—In this your simple *Oral* Almanack has been a more faithful Prognasticator than all the profound Astronomical Ones of the country. Wishing you my dear friend peace, health and happiness till I see you and as long after that as Human Nature is capable of—I remain most sincerely,

Your's truly,
ALEX. WILSON

P.S. My nephew and Brother, all join their best respects to you and the family.

A.W.

GROSART

To Mr. F. A. Michaux.

Philadelphia, 6 June 1812.

My Dear Friend,

I had the pleasure of receiving a letter from you, dated April 10, 1812; but living at Mr. Bartram's, I have not yet seen Mr. Correa, the gentleman who brought it over. I have also had the great satisfaction of examining the plates of your four numbers of *Forest Trees*, which are beautifully executed; and I regret most sincerely that my little knowledge of the French language prevents me from perusing with equal satisfaction, the interesting particulars you relate of their history. I expected long before this to be able to congratulate you on the publication of a translation of your work here, and I announced the same in the preface of one of my volumes; but sorry I am to inform you that no steps have yet been taken to put the design in execution, and I fear none will be taken for many months to come. Unless there be an evident certainty of profit, booksellers, in general, are very indifferent to publish works of any kind, however great their merit may be; and the poor author's feelings are little regarded. Few men have known this more experimentally than myself. I have sacrificed everything to publish my *Ornithology* —have written six volumes and am engaged on the seventh [yet I have never yet received a single *cent* of its proceeds].[1]

I have frequently conversed with Mr. Bradford about publishing a translation of your *Forest Trees*; and you may rest assured that, should it be undertaken, I will use all my influence in its favour. Were you here yourself, I have no doubt but it would be undertaken, and I think with success, for all who have seen it admire it. I procured our good friend, Mr. Wm. Bartram, a sight of it, and he was greatly delighted with its appearance. One of my friends read a great part of it in English to him, and he was highly satisfied. . . .

Dr. Barton has not yet published his *General Zoology*, which he has been announcing, from time to time, for so many years. It is much easier to say these things than do them.

Mr. Wm. Bartram is still as you left him, and you are frequently the subject of our conversation at table. I have made many extensive excursions lately, and have discovered, in all, about forty new species of Land Birds, never taken notice of by any other writer. I am

1. These words are added from MCZ which has a scrap of this letter, though probably a copy.

now engaged on the Water Birds; and had just returned yesterday from the seashore when your letter was presented to me. Dr. H. and Mr. P. have both publicly announced your work, but as no translation has been yet made, it has not been reviewed by any of our writers. . . .

Wishing you all the success which is justly due to the labours, journies, and investigations you have made in behalf of Natural History, I remain, &c.

Yours sincerely
ALEX. WILSON

❧[CXLVI]❧

HSP

To Sarah Miller.[1]

Philadelphia, 7 August [1812].

My dear Sarah,

I cannot be out tomorrow as I expected Mr. B. and I having all our accounts to settle, but I will take the very first opportunity of coming out to let you know particulars. In the meantime do not be alarmed when I tell you that I must now either run the risk of losing all or make one last and very long and expensive journey to collect what is due, and see how accounts are with the agents. There is no other choice left between this and absolute ruin. You will not therefore My dearest friend object to this as on it my whole hopes of happiness depend. Mr. B. has positively refused to advance any thing untill he receives it and I have as positively told him that I will proceed no further with the work untill I am paid for what I have done.

It will be three or 4 weeks before I think of setting out I will see you many times before then. I would ask your forgiveness for all

1. "at Jacob Miller's, Esquire, near Milestown."

these disappointments but I know you are goodness itself & pity my suffering more than your own.—Keep a good heart—amuse yourself with your kind friends from Montgomery—But do not forget your ever affectionate

ALEXANDER WILSON

CXLVII

POEMS 1816

To Alexander Wilson, Sr.

16 August 1812.

The difficulties and hardships I have encountered in life have been useful to me.[1] In youth I had wrong ideas of life, imagination too often led judgment astray. You would find me much altered from the son you knew me in Paisley, more diffident of myself, and less precipitate, though often wrong. . . .

POEMS 1816

October 1812.

I am much indebted to Mr. Brown for the interest he has taken in my publication. Owing to its vast expense, this work has ill repaid me for my exertions. You will be surprised, when I assure you, that, up to this very day, I have never shared a single cent of its profits![2]

1. This series of excerpts is all that remains of Wilson's letters to his friends or relatives in Paisley during the last year of his life. We must assume that the originals have been destroyed for ten years of endeavour has failed to reveal them. Although it was now eighteen years since he had left Scotland, Wilson's correspondence with his friends there appears to have been active and indeed to have revived in the last year of his life. It is unfortunate that these few gleanings and one further very short passage are all that we have left of the letters back to Scotland as he came to the end of his life.

2. Poems 1816 quotes from a Wilson letter of October 1812 in which reference is made to a Mr. Brown and the writer of the Life appends a footnote which

CRICHTON 1819

The common changes of life pass so gradually through a neigh-bourhood, that those immediately around take little notice of them; but were a man to be told in the morning, of all the friends whom he left well around him the preceding evening, that the family of his next door neighbour were dead, one child excepted; that his rich and respectable acquaintance had become a drunkard and beggar, and his most beggarly neighbour had become rich and influential, what would be his astonishment and surprise. Such is the surprise of a man, when the accumulated casualties of eighteen years are pre-sented to his eye at once.[3]

❦[CXLVIII]❦

ORD

To George Ord.

Boston, 13 October 1812.

Dear Sir,

It is not in my power at present to give you anything more than a slight sketch of my rambles since leaving Philadelphia. My route up the Hudson afforded great pleasure, mingled with frequent re-gret that you were not along with me, to share the enjoyment. About thirty miles south of Albany we passed within ten miles of the celebrated Catskill Mountains, a gigantic group, clothed with forest

reads, "A gentleman to whose correspondence with Mr. Wilson the writer is much indebted." It is fairly certain that this is the same Mr. David Brown mentioned in Wilson's letter to his father of 15 June 1809 (CXVII).

3. This excerpt from another letter is in the reflective mood of his letters home at this time. According to Crichton it was occasioned by "a letter from a friend in which were detailed the vicissitudes of a few whom, in early life, he had been acquainted with in Paisley."

to the summits. In the river here I found our common reed (*Zizania aquatica*) growing in great abundance in shoals extending along the middle of the river. I saw flocks of Red-wings, and some Black Ducks, but no Rail, or Reed-birds . . .

From this place my journey led me over a rugged, mountainous country, to Lake Champlain, along which I coasted as far as Burlington in Vermont. Here I found the little Coot-footed Tringa or Phalarope that you sent to Mr. Peale; a new and elegantly marked Hawk; and observed some Black Ducks. The shores are alternate sandy bays, and rocky headlands running into the lake. Every tavern was crowded with officers, soldiers, and travellers. Eight of us were left without a bed; but having an excellent great-coat, I laid myself down in a corner, with a determination of sleeping in defiance of the uproar of the house, and the rage of my companions, who would not disgrace themselves by a prostration of this sort. . . .

From Lake Champlain I traversed a rude mountainous region to Connecticut river, one hundred miles above Dartmouth College. I spent several days with the gun in Groton, and Ryegate townships, and made some discoveries. From this I coasted along the Connecticut to a place called Haverhill, ten miles from the foot of Moose-hillock, one of the highest of the *White Mountains* of New Hampshire. I spent the greater part of a day in ascending to the peak of one of these majestic mountains, whence I had the most sublime and astonishing view that was ever afforded me. One immensity of forest lay below, extended on all sides to the farthest verge of the horizon; while the only prominent objects were the columns of smoke from burning woods, that rose from various parts of the earth beneath to the heavens; for the day was beautiful and serene. Hence I travelled to Dartmouth, and thence in a direct course to Boston. From Boston I passed through Portsmouth to Portland, and got some things new; my return was by a different route. I have procured three new and beautiful Hawks; and have gleaned up a stock of remarks that will be useful to me hereafter.

I hope, my dear sir, that you have been well since I left you, I have myself been several times afflicted with a violent palpitation of the heart, and want to try whether a short voyage by sea will not be beneficial.

In New England the rage of war, the virulence of politics, and the pursuit of commercial speculation, engross every faculty. The voice of Science, and the charms of Nature, unless these last present themselves in the form of *prize sugars*, *coffee*, or *rum*, are treated with contempt.

❦[CXLIX]❦

GROSART

To William Bartram.

Philadelphia, 21 April 1813.

My Dear Friend,

I have been extremely busy these several months, my colourists having all left me; so I have been obliged to do extra duty this last winter. Next week I shall publish my seventh volume; and shall send you your copy with the earliest opportunity. I am now engaged with the ducks, all of which, that I am acquainted with, will be comprehended in the eighth volume.

Since I had the pleasure of seeing you, I have hardly left the house half-an-hour; and I long most ardently to breathe once more the fresh air of the country, and gaze on the lovely face of Nature. Will it be convenient for the family to accommodate me (as I shall be alone) this summer? Please to let me know.

I lately received from the celebrated Mr. West, a proof impression of his grand historical picture of the death of Admiral Nelson— a present which I highly value.

The Philosophical Society of Philadelphia have done me the honour to elect me a member, for which I must certainly, in gratitude, make them a communication on some subject, this summer. I long very much to hear from you; and, with my best wishes for your health and happiness, am very truly

Your sincere friend,
ALEX. WILSON

POEMS 1816, CRICHTON 1819

Philadelphia, 6 July 1813.

. . . I am, myself, far from being in good health. Intense application to study has hurt me much. My 8th volume is now in the press and will be published in November. One volume more will complete the whole which I hope to be able to finish in April next.[1]

1. In his biographical sketch of 1819 Crichton wrote the following supplementary words concerning the short passage which we have from this letter: "In the last letter which he appears to have written to his friends in Paisley, he sympathises with one of the most intimate of his old companions on the loss of a son, and then alludes to the declining state of his own health." This is the final letter of which we have any record, followed only by the list of undrawn birds in Wilson's own hand dated 13 August 1813, quoted in full in Part One of this book, and his Last Will and Testament signed and dated 16 August 1813, seven days before his death. Wilson's Last Will and Testament and Inventory is printed in Part Two, Appendix IV.

APPENDIXES

The Legal Case Involving
"The Hollander, or Light Weight"[1]

DOCUMENT A

[A summons for criminal libel coupled with incitement to unrest. It is a private prosecution with concurrence of the procurator fiscal and relates to the publication of the poem "The Hollander, or Light Weight." The summons asks for penalties of £50 as damages and assythment (legal compensation or atonement) to the private prosecutor, for an apology in open court and a fine of £10 to the procurator fiscal as a deterrent, and for payment of expenses of the process. The summons is dated 10 June 1790.]

ALLAN MACONOCHIE Esquire
Advocate Sheriff Depute of the Shire of
Renfrew To

Officers Jointly & Severally specially constitute Whereas it is Humbly meant and Shewn to me by William Henry Silk Manufacturer in Newtown of Paisley with concourse of Edward Jamieson Writer in Paisley Procurator fiscal of the Sheriff Court of Renfrew and he for himself and for the public interest Against

1. The court records of the legal case involving Alexander Wilson's poem "The Hollander, or Light Weight" are here published for the first time. They are in the Manuscript Department of the National Library of Scotland, Edinburgh, and I am indebted to Mr. Henry Herron, former procurator fiscal of Paisley and then of Glasgow, for his help in arranging and elucidating the papers. The notes are by Mr. Herron.

Alexander Wilson Weaver in Seedhills of Paisley THAT WHERE by the Laws of this and of every other well governed realm The writing and printing or the causing to be written or printed Scandalous & Libellous papers in the stile of poems or otherways falsely attacking traducing Scandalizing & defaming the Character of any person whatever and throwing out reflections & insinuations against such persons honesty & integrity Or papers or libels of an incendiary nature tending to create discord betwixt a Manufacturer and his workers and to stirr up combinations opposition & violence among Servants or workers against their Master or Employers more especially in a Manufacturing Town & neighborhood And the handing about or distributing such papers or causeing the same to be so distributed through any Town or the Country around Are Crimes of a very bad tendency & Severely punishable Nevertheless true it is and of verity That the said Defender has presumed to commit and be guilty of the said crimes In so far as the said Defender having taken up a groundless Malice & ill will at the private Complainer he did in the month of February last at least within these Twelve months past maliciously write & print Or cause to be written & printed a very Scandalous ill natured & Scurrilous paper or libel in the Stile of a poem Intituld "The Hollander or light weight a poem" with a motto or quotation prefixed thereto tending to hold out the person meant as the object of the poem in a detestable point of view and industriously distributed or caused the same to be distributed among the Inhabitants of the Town of Paisley & Neighbourhood thereof wherein a most injurious attack is wantonly made upon the private Complainer's Character and reflections and insinuations are therein thrown out against his integrity honesty & fair Dealing and he is even accused of having perjured himself and threatnings are also thrown out against him and that in a dark artful & incidious manner for tho' the Complainers name is not there fully mentioned yet it is obvious from different circumstances & hints thrown out in the said paper, that the private Complainer is the person against whom such insinuations are meant & intended to apply and the said paper or libel is of an incendiary nature and has a tendency to create discord between the Complainer and his workers and to stirr up combinations & excite violence & Opposition among the private Complainers Servants against him in carrying on his business in the Manufacturing Town of Paisley and Neighbourhood thereof to his great hurt and prejudice At least within the time foresaid such a paper or libel has been maliciously published & distributed and altho' the Complainers name is not therein fully published yet it is apparent that he is the person pointed at as the object of the Satire and many persons who have read the said paper understood & believed that he was the person against whom the abuse & Scurrility therein contained was pointed at a printed copy of which paper or libel is herewith produced And the said Defender Alexander Wilson is guilty actor or art & part [aiding and abetting] of writing said libel and afterwards printing or causing it to be printed and of distributing or causing the same to be distributed to the public Wherefore the premises or part thereof being proven, the said Defender Alexander Wilson Ought and Should be Decerned and Ordained to make payment to the private Complainer of the sum of Fifty pounds Sterling in name of Damages and Assythment and he also Ought and Should be Decerned & Ordained to appear in Open Court and beg pardon of God and the Complainer and confess acknowledge and declare that the insinuations thrown out against the Complainers character in the foresaid libel are false Scandalous & injurious and the said Alexander Wilson Defender Ought also to be fined and amerciated in the sum of Ten pounds Sterling to the Procurator Fiscal of Court to deter him and Others from the Commission of such crimes in time coming And Lastly the said Defender Ought and Should be Decerned & Ordained in the expence of this process

Therefore it is my Will that ye pass and Lawfully summon Warn and Charge the said defender personally or at his dwelling place to compear before me or my substitute in a court to be held within the Tolbooth of Paisley the   day of

In the hour of Cause to Answer at the Instance of the said pursuers in the matter libelled as also to appear time and place foresaid & find sufficient Caution acted in the books of this Court that he shall attend the whole diets of Court diets of probation and for pronouncing Sentence in said cause under the pain of One hundred Merks Scots and also that ye summon such witnesses as shall be given you in a list subscribed by the pro'r fiscal as witnesses for proving the foregoing libel to appear time and place foresaid and bear leal [true] and sooth fast [trustworthy] witnessing on oath anent the Crimes Charged against the said defender each under the pain of ten pounds Scots with Certification GIVEN and SUBSCRIBED by the Clerk of Court At Paisley the tenth day of June 1790 years

ROB. WALKINSHAW

Follows a list of Witnesses to be adduced against the said defender for proving for foregoing Libel

1   John Neilson Printer & Bookseller in Paisley
2d   Samuel King son of the deceased Hugh King baker in Paisley
3d   John Mitchell Dancing master in Paisley
4th George Murdoch Merchant in Paisley
5th William Mitchell weaver in Williamsburgh near Paisley
6th Thomas Witherspoon weaver in Seedhills of Paisley
7th Andrew Clark weaver in William[sburgh] near Paisley

EDW JAMIESON
Paisley 22^d June 17[90]

Mr James Orr . . .
Actor Fiscus instructs Exco . . . of citation and a printed copy of the Poem libelled . . . with Craig . . . who gives in an incidental petition. . . . Having advised the defr's petition allows the Clerk of Court to receive the defenders own Judicial Enactment

JAMES ORR

Compeared the defender Alexander Wilson who judicially enacts himself that he shall attend the whole diets of Court diets of probation and for pronouncing sentence in this cause under the pain of one hundred merks Scots

ALEXANDER WILSON

Mr. Jas Orr . . . Paisley . . . July 1790 parties pro'rs present The def . . . gives in answers The . . . to reply to the. . . .

Paisley 15 July 1790 . . .

Mr Jas Orr . . . parties present   Replies for the . . .

R W (Clerk)
to the Sheriff Depute

DOCUMENT B

[The poem submitted to the Sheriff Court by William Henry.]

THE
HOLLANDER,
OR
LIGHT WEIGHT:
A POEM

— Unheard of tortures
Must be reserv'd for such: these herd together;
The common damn'd shun their society,
And look upon themselves as fiends less foul. — Blair.

ATTEND a' ye wha on the loom,
    Survey the shuttle jinkin',
Whase purse has aft been sucket toom
    While *Willy's* scales war clinkin.
A' ye that for some luckless hole
    Hae pay't, (though right unwilling)
To satisfy his hungry soul,
    A saxpence or a shilling
            For fine some day.
Shall black Injustice lift its head,
    An' cheat us like the devil,
Without a man to stop its speed,
    Or crush the growin' evil?
No; Here am I, wi' vengeance big,
    Resolv'd to ca'm his clashing;
Nor shall his cheeps, or pouther't wig,
    Protect him frae a lashing
            Right keen this day.
See! cross his nose he lays the Spec's
    An owre the claith he glimmers,
Ilk wee bit trifling faut detects,
    And cheeps and dolefu' yaummers.
"Dear man! that wark 'ill never do;
    "See that: ye'll no tak telling";
Syne knavish chirts his fingers through,

An' libels down a shilling
              For holes that day.
Perhaps the fellow's needin' clink,
    To ca'm some threatnin' beagle,
Whilk mak's him at sic baseness wink,
    An' for some siller wheedle.
In greetan, herse, ungracious croon,
    Aul' *Willy* granes, "I hear ye,
"But weel-a-wat our siller's doon,
    "We really canna spare ye
              "Ae doyt this day."
Health to the brave Hibernian boy,
    Who when by *Willy* cheated,
Cock'd up his hat, without annoy,
    An' spoke by passion heated:
"Upon my shoul I have a mind,
    "Ye old deceiving devil,
"To toss your wig up to the wind,
    "And teach you to be shivil
              "To me this day."
But see! anither curtain's drawn;
    Some chiel his web has finish'd,
An' *Willy* on the tither han',
    The price o't has diminish'd.
But brought before the awfu' Judge,
    To pay the regulation,
Will. lifts his arm, without a grudge,
    And swears by his salvation
              He's right that day.
Anither's been upo' the push,
    To get his keel in claith,
In certain hopes to be soon flush
    O notes an' siller baith.
Returnin' for his count at night,
    The poor impos'd on mortal,
Maun pay for puns o' clean light weight,
    Though he's maist at the portal
              O' Want that day.

In vain he pleads—Appeals to God,
   That scarce he lost an ounce;
The holy watcher o' the brod
   Cheeps out that he's a dunce.
Out frae the door he een maun come,
   Right thankfu' gin he get
Some *counterfeits*, a scanty sum,
   Brought frae the Aul' Kirk yett
              Yon preaching day.
O sirs! what conscience he contains,
   What curse maun he be dreein'!
Whase ev'ry day is mark'd wi' stains
   O' cheating and o' leein!
M'K****l, H*b, or throuther O*r,
   May swear an' seem to fash us,
But Justice dignifies their door,
   An' gen'rously they clash us
              The clink each day.
Our Hollander (gude help his saul)
   Kens better ways o' working;
For *Jock* an' him has aft a sprawl
   Wha'll bring the biggest dark in.
"Weel, *Jock*, what hast thou screwt the day?"
   "Deed father I'se no crack o't,
"Nine holes, sax ounce, or thereaway,
   "Is a' that I cou'd mak o't,
              "This live lang day."
Sic conversation aft taks place,
   When darkness bides their logic,
Like Milton's Deil, an' Sin, they trace
   For some new winning project.
Daft though they be, and unco gloyts,
   Yet they can count like scholars,
How farthings multipli'd by doyts,
   Grow up to pounds an' dollars,
              Some after day.
Forby (to gie the deil his due),
   I'll own wi' biggest won'er,

That nane can sell their goods like you,
    Or swear them up a hun'er.
Lang hackney'd in the paths o' vice,
    Thy conscience nought can scar her;
An' *tens*, an' *twalls*, can in a trice,
    Jump up twa hun'er far'er
            On ony day.
What town can thrive wi' sic a crew,
    Within its entrails crawlin'!
Muck worms that maist provoke a spew,
    To see or hear them squalin'.
Down on your knees, man, wife and wean,
    For ance implore the devil,
To harle to himsel his ain,
    An' free us frae sic evil,
            This vera day.

DOCUMENT C

[The Execution of Service of the copy summons upon Wilson by the sheriff officer, dated 12 June 1790.]

Upon the Twelfth day of June . . . and Ninety years I James Jamieson Sheriff Officer in virtue of a Libelled Summons raised before the Sheriff Depute of the Shire of Renfrew at the instance of William Henry Silk Manufacturer in Newtown of Paisley with concourse of Edward Jamieson writer in Paisley pro'r fiscal of the Sheriff Court of Renfrew and he for himself for the public interest against Alexander Wilson Weaver in Seedhills of Paisley past and Lawfully summoned warned & Charged the said Defender to Compear before the said Sheriff Depute or his Substitut in a Court to be held within the Tolbooth of Paisley on the Twenty second day of June instant In the hour of Cause to Answer at the instance of the said pursuers anent the matters libelled as also to Compear time and place foresaid and find sufficient Caution & Surety acted in the books of said Court that he shall attend the whole diets of Court diets of probation and for pronouncing sentence in said Action under the penalty of One hundred merks Scots with [Cert'n] This I did by leaving a full double of said Libelled Summons to the will with a List of witnesses to be adduced for proving thereof thereto prefixed and a Short copy of Citation thereto subjoined for the said Alexander Wilson in the hands of his Landlady within the dwelling house where he lodges & resides in Seedhills of Paisley to be given to him Because after due enquiry made by me I could not apprehend himself personally which Short copy of Citation was Signed by me contained the Date hereof and was left as aforesaid Before these witnesses William Hart Town Officer in Paisley & William Smith Sheriff Officer there who were both present thereat and are hereto Subscribing with me

JAS JAMIESON
WILLIAM HART WITNESS
WILLIAM SMITH WITNESS

DOCUMENT D

[An incidental petition by Wilson to the Court to dispense with his finding caution, dated 22 June 1790. According to the minutes of the Court (at the end of Document A), this was granted.]

22nd June] Unto the Sheriff of Renfrew
1790] The Petition of Alexander Wilson
] Weaver in Paisley

Humbly Sheweth

That a Libel is this day tabled against the petitioner at the instance of Mr. Henry Silk Manufacturer in Newtown of Paisley with concourse of the pro'r fisk for the alleged crime of defamation, and publishing scandalous libels etc. agst. the said Mr. Henry.

That the petitioner is cited to find caution dejudicis Listi, and has accordingly been at pains to get a Cautioner to enact for him but owing to the circumstance of his being a Journeyman Weaver, and consequently that any person who would become bound, would be in the same line and all depending for their support upon the manufacturers of the place, who are all concerned in the prosecution; such persons as the petitioner trusted to, have, on these accompts, refused to enact as Cautioner for the petitioner.

The petitioner is therefore obliged to apply to your Lord'p and he humbly apprehends you will see cause to dispense with the necessity of Caution in this very particular case.

   May it therefore please your Lord'p to dispense with the petitioner's finding Caution.

ALEX^R WILSON

DOCUMENT E

[The answers or defenses to the summons (Document A). They are dated 1 July 1790 and consist of a denial that the poem refers to Henry and assert that, even if it did, it is not libelous.]

1st July]   ANSWERS for Alex Wilson
1790   ]   Weaver in Seedhills of Paisley
        ]   To
              The LIBEL raised at the instance of
              Wm Henry Manufacturer in Newtown of
              Paisley with concourse of the pro'r Fisk

   The present prosecution is perhaps of as curious a nature as any that ever came before this Court; And is evidently founded upon the simple conjectures of the pursuer himself—This will appear sufficiently obvious from the Poem libelled, which, being perused in the most minute and careful manner by any disinterested person, who never heard any thing of it before, could not be said to apply to Mr. Henry, and this rule of judging of the import and meaning of the Poem is certainly the most fair and equitable. The defender, however, shall endeavour more particularly, to show this from what is after stated, and also to point out and make appear That the libel as laid is groundless and vexatious.

   1st Then. The very title of the poem, disproves every idea of its being intended to apply to the private Complainer—A *Hollander*, the defender apprehends to be an epithet only applicable to a person born in that country, which Mr. Henry will never pretend to be the case with him; and if so the term *Light Weight*, is equally inapplicable, being of the same signification as the word *Hollander*.

   2dly   It might have been of service to the Complainer, in order to support his libel, That the poem either at the beginning or end, had mentioned the place of residence of *Willy* so often used therein; and if such had been the case, and found to agree with that of Mr. Henry, then Your Lord'p would have been more able to judge whether the libel was well founded as applying to him, and whether the Author of the Poem was culpable for having published the same—No place or date, however, is mentioned, and on this accompt the Poem can as well apply to any *Willy* in Holland, and, indeed more so, than to the private Complainer.

As to the Poem itself, supposing, (but not admitting) the same to be intended for Mr. Henry, the defender does humbly submit that there is neither an attack made upon his honesty and integrity, Or is the substance thereof of such a nature, and of such a dangerous tendency as the libel so roundly holds out: Nor can the Complainer alledge that the poem has hurt or prejudiced him either in person, family or effects—It is not sufficient for him to say, That he is the person *meant* by the Poem; for as before noticed, no person unprejudiced, and a stranger to the Town of Paisley, could say That he was the *Willy* therein mentioned To maintain that he is threatened by the Poem and even accused of perjury is without all shadow of foundation; and to show this more fully, the defender shall call your Lord'ps attention to the verses of the Poem, which he apprehends the Complainer's conjectures to be grounded upon.

In the first place. The private Complainer alleges that *"Threatenings are thrown out against him"* in the Poem. In this, however, he is very far mistaken. The defender has perused the whole of the Poem and can find no such threatenings as the pursuer would insinuate. He is amazingly apprehensive and timorous; and founds, (as the defender believes,) his notion of threatening upon the second verse of the Poem, where towards the end, the following words are used "Nor shall his cheeps or pouther't wig *Protect him frae a lashing*—Right keen this day". The lashing here mentioned is not to be construed into the idea of the Author's intention of maltreating and beating the *Willy* in the Poem; but in the strain of poetical language, it is simply representing to the person that he the Author will lash him with poetry, which is seldom offensive, altho' the reverse would now seem to be the case upon the part of the private Complainer. This your Lord'p will at once see is the whole force of the term *lashing*, and consequently that the Complainers apprehensions of maltreatment are perfectly feigned, and altogether groundless.

2dly. It is again alledged in the libel, That the pursuer *"is even accused of having perjured himself."* Where, in all the four corners of the poem, Mr. Henry has any foundation for saying so, does not appear to the defender, nor indeed, can what is not therein appear to any person. Any thing said in the poem respecting the *Willy's*, swearing is in the sixth verse thereof: But a moments attention to the words of the Author in that verse must convince your Lord'p that his conduct is far from being reprehensible, or in the least censurable. The Author does by no means say that Willy perjured himself upon the occasion alluded to in the verse. He on the contrary approves of what Willy had done, and ends the verse with these two lines, "Will. lifts his arm without a grudge—And swears by his salvation—*He's right that day.*" Hence, supposing (but not admitting) that the poem was meant to apply to the Complainer, where is he accused of having *perjured* himself? This affords ground for no such assertion, and let the libel be ever so broad, it should have consisted of facts at least something plausible, which in this particular is clearly very far from being true.

Were the defender, however, to go over and comment particularly upon every verse of the Poem, he undoubtedly would tire your Lord'ps patience, and consume time to very little purpose. The above observations will in some degree tend to show Your Lord'p that the poem against whatever person the same was intended to apply is most inoffensive, and cannot have the pernicious effects set furth in the libel. If the *Willy* mentioned in the Poem is offended at the terms of it, and prosecutes accordingly, then the *Hibernian boy*, and *Jock* will commence actions also: But the first matter of enquiry is to find out who *Willy*, the *Hibernian boy*, and *Jock* are, which will be attended with most extraordinary trouble owing to the great number of these particular names & persons in every place round about.

Upon these grounds, it is not doubted but your Lord'p will see the prosecution in a wanton, illfounded, and vexatious point of view; And that you will dismiss the same accordingly with expences.

In respect whereof
JOHN CRAIG

DOCUMENT F

[This is dated 15 July 1790 and constitutes the replies to Document E. It points out that the poem can refer only to Henry and notes that Wilson "does not seem to deny that he is the Author of the poem."]

15 July REPLIES for William Henry
1790 Silk Manufacturer in Paisley
and the Pro'r fiscal
To
The Answers for Alex Wilson

The respondent in his answers, in place of showing any regret for having commited the offence with which he is charged in the Libel endeavours to justify himself & to hold out the poem Libelled on as a piece of humour & he pretends to say that there is nothing in it which applys to the character of the pursuer & would even make himself believe that there is nothing said in it which is wrong, but lightly however as the respondent himself may think of the matter it must appear at first sight to every disinterested person that if such liberties as are taken in the poem were to be countenanced that it would be attended with very dangerous and pernicious consequences to the public at large.

In the Town of Paisley the rage for defaming peoples characters by writing poems & other papers of that kind have for some time past prevailed too much and if a check was not to be put to such practices it is hard to say to what length these scandalous publications might be carried; From the way in which the Defender treats the matter now under Consideration in his Answers your Lord'p will no doubt have some ideas of the liberties which they think themselves entitled to take & when you consider how easily the minds of the working people in a manufacturing town are inflamed & particularly those about the Town of Paisley of which we have already had too many instances, it is not doubted but your Lord'p will agree with the pursuer in thinking that a cheque can not be too soon put to such proceedings.

In the beginning of the answers the Defender is pleased to say that the prosecution is founded on the simple conjectures of the pursuer and that the poem upon being perused by any disinterested person who never heard of it, could not be said to apply to Mr. Henry, but as to both of these averrments the respondent is not speaking what he thinks nor was it his intention when he wrote the poem that it should be left in so ambiguous a state for to every person that has read it who knows any thing whatever of Mr. Henry and even the respondents most intimate connections & acquaintances do not hesitate to say that when they first saw the poem it struck them that it was meant to apply Agt. Mr. Henry and it was not untill it became a subject of public conversation over the whole Town that Mr. Henry thought it worth his while to take notice of it so that it was not from his own conjectures that he was induced to raise the prosecution, but to follow the respondent in his own way of arguing the pursuer will endeavour more particularly to show from what is after stated that he has good cause to complain.

Before touching upon any part of the poem itself it may be proper here to observe that for some years previous to the pursuers settling in Paisley he had resided in Holland & for these good many years past he has carried on a very considerable Manufactury in the Town of Paisley.

In the Answers the respondent is pleased to alledge that the very title of the poem disproves every idea of its being intended to apply to the Complainer and he argues that the epithet of Hollander is applicable to a person only born in Holland & says that the term light weight is of the same signification—But with respect to the inferences which the respondent would seem to wish to be drawn from both of these Texts the pursuer has little doubt but he will be able to satisfy your Lord'p that the respondent has been rather unfortunate. That the poem in question is meant to strike at & apply to the character of a manufacturer in the Town parish or neighbourhood of Paisley there can be no doubt whatever and that the complainer is the only Manufacturer that ever resided in Holland who at present or perhaps ever did carry on business in Paisley he will have no difficulty to establish so that altho' the complainer was not actually born in Holland there can be little doubt that from the Connection with & residence he has had in that Country he is the person meant to be pointed out, As to the appellation of light weight it is the first time that (that) the pursuer has heard that it was synonimous with Hollander at any rate in the present case it is perfectly obvious where & at whom it is meant to apply but to enlarge & comment upon the subject would be spending your Lord'p time to no purpose; In a word it is plain and no person can read the poem without saying and admiting that it insinuates that the person who the poem means to point out has been guilty of cheating and deceiving by not (not) giving weight according to what they charged.

In the next paragraph of the answers the respondent seems to lay some stress upon the Circumstances of the place of Willy's residence not being mentioned but that the pursuer apprehends your Lord'p could not have expected nor would the Complainer have thought the Author worthy of being dubd'd a poet of the meanest discription had his conceptions been no greater than to conceal a circumstance of that kind on which account therefore that paragraph shall be past over in silence.

As to the next paragraph it comes rather more closely to the point and altho the Defender is there pleased to assert that allowing the poem to be intended Agt. Mr. Henry there is neither an attack made upon his character nor is the subsistance of it of an incendiary nature tending to create discord between the complainer & his workers & that he is neither thereby threatned nor accused of perjury yet the Complainer in the sequel is hopefull that from the poem itself he will be able to satisfy your Lord'p that the Defender has transgressed & been guilty in all & each of these particulars.

The Defender himself seems to be very conscious of the verses in the poem from which cause for suspicion has arisen & he in the first place as he stiles it himself points out the verse in the poem from which the suspicion arises & he there acknowledges himself that there is a threatning of some kind meant intended & given but argues that as the Author was writing in a poetical strain that nothing but a lashing with the pen in that same stile could be meant. Such lashing however the Complainer considers bad enough & whether it is meant as a lashing with the pen or with his fists he considers them equally pernicious and he leaves it with your Lord'p to Judge how far such liberties ought to be countenanced or allowed and at the same time the Complainer must beg leave to differ with the defender in thinking that the language of poetry is seldom offensive. In that verse too there is an evident attack made upon the person Agt. whom the poem is intended as to being a Cheater & deceiver & in the next verse Stronger instances cannot be figured of a wish to excite discord & discontent amongst workers if insinuations can possibly have the effect to convey an idea of Masters having wronged them. The next two verses are exactly in the same Stile & no less pains seems to have been taken to increase the flame than the former verse points out.

The next verse the Defender seems to think he has gone a little too far with and he endeavours to paliate the matter by endeavouring to show that he approves of the Conduct of the Complainer upon the occasion alluded to in the verse but how far that is consistant with the idea of any neutral or disinterested person your Lord'p is apprehended will have no difficulty whatever to discover. From the first four lines of the verse there does not remain the possibility of a doubt that the Willy there alluded to is accused of cheating his workmen out of some part of the wages which he had engaged to give & on the other hand the last four lines of the verse clearly demonstrates that he swears the worker not even out of his due but contrary to the regulation. The next three verses are equally ungenerous & ungratefull and there can be no doubt that taking the whole four together the accusation is as plain as if it had been stamp'd in Capitals in the plainest English & that the accusation is both ungenerous & unjust the Complainer can appeal to every man of faith or credit in the neighbourhood where he lives.

As to the remaining verses of the poem they are something of a piece with the others but the Complainer shall follow the Defenders example and pass them over in silence with this observation that they cannot miss to strike you Lord'p with the same ideas and perhaps much stronger ones than those which the Complainer could endeavour to point out was he to attempt it.

That the poem is composed and possesses all the different pernicious and venomous ingredients mentioned in the libel the complainer does not suppose can well be disputed and that he is the person agt whom these dark invidious insinuations are meant to apply (to apply) he apprehends there can be as little doubt. He has already mentioned that he is the only manufacturer in Paisley who ever resided in Holland & he does not suppose that there is a manufacturer in Town who has a son of the name of Jock carrying on business in the same way except himself and besides it is plain from the eight verse of the poem that (that) it is meant to apply to an elder of the Auld Kirk & that the complainer is at present not only the only manufacturer who is an Elder of that Church but even the only one of the name of Willy he will have no difficulty to ascertain. Taking therefore the whole circumstances together there can scarsely remain a doubt that the poem libelled on is of a scandalous inflamatory & incendary nature that the Complainer is the person agt. whom the object of the Satire is intended and that his character has thereby been most falsely attacked traduced Scandalized and defamed.

Therefore & upon the whole and as the Defender does not seem to deny that he is the Author of the poem it is humbly hoped your Lord'p will see good cause for repelling his defences and Decerning agt. him conform to the conclusions of the libel

In Respect Whereof
EDW JAMIESON

DOCUMENT G

[An interlocutor by Sheriff Orr, dated 10 August 1790, when the case was called on the procedure roll. The sheriff ordered Wilson to lodge duplies to Document F not later than 17 August 1790 and to state whether he admits or denies "composing, uttering or promulgating" the poem. There is a further minute by the clerk, dated 23 September 1790, that duplies for Wilson had been lodged.]

In Causa Wm. Hendry[2] & fiscal
agt. Alexr. Wilson
Paisley 10th Aug 1790

Mr. Jas. Orr Sh: Subst.
parties pro'rs present

The Sheriff Depute having considered the Libel, Answers & Replies of Parties and having signified his opinion thereon Appoints the Defender to lodge Duplies and therein to set furth whether he admits or Denies the Composing, Uttering or Promulgating the Paper Complained of, or being art and part in the Composition & Promulgating thereof and that against the seventeenth instant

JAMES ORR
Paisley 23 Sept 1790

Mr Jas Orr Sh Sub
parties pro'rs present Duplies for the Def

R W (Clerk)
to the Sheriff Dept

DOCUMENT H

[The duplies for Wilson. The document is undated but the backing sheet gives the date 23 September 1790, which is the date of the last minute in Document G above. It points out that it is for the prosecution to prove the charge. It is not for the accused to admit anything, thereby incriminating himself. Today in a criminal trial it is permissible by statute for the defense to lodge a minute of admissions. This

---

2. The spelling of the manufacturer's name is inconsistent in the court papers.

is not common and usually refers to formal evidence which is not disputed but is necessary to prove.]

DUPLIES for Alexander Wilson
defender

To

The Replies of Wm. Hendry &
Fisk pursuers

By an Interlocutor in this cause of date the 10th day of August last the defender is appointed to lodge duplies, and therein to set furth whether he admits or denies the "Composing, uttering or promulgating the paper complained of, or being art and part in the composition and promulgating thereof."

It is an established rule in all criminal prosecutions, that the pursuers are bound to prove their libel by the testimony of *witnesses*, and cannot insist upon the defender to criminate himself either by a judicial examination, or by a reference to oath of the facts contained in the libel—In the same manner, in the case now before the Court, the pursuers were impressed with the same idea, which is founded in universal practice: And they according to the form in every criminal action, serve the defender not only with a copy of the libel, but also, *with a list of witnesses to be adduced against him for proving that libel.*

The defender, therefore, humbly apprehended that the first point to determine was the relevancy of the libel, and consequently the proof to establish the libel: But in this he has been mistaken, and seeing that the pursuers have *witnesses* ready to instruct the libel, and who are annexed to the Summons, he finds himself disposed neither to admit or deny in terms of the Interlocutor altho' he entertains the highest respect for the Court: but he is ready to await the effect of the proof which the pursuers mean to bring forward, and craves a proof of all facts and circumstances tending to alleviate or exculpate agreeable to the forms of criminal proceedure.

In Respect Whereof
JOHN CRAIG

DOCUMENT I

[This is dated 21 October 1790 and is an incidental petition by Wilson. It narrates that Wilson withdraws the duplies (Document

H) and reiterates that he denies the charge as laid. The petition is signed by John Craig, presumably Wilson's procurator (or solicitor). The petition narrates that Wilson would have signed this petition but was unable to do so because of his absence in "the East Country." The solicitor gives an assurance that Wilson will subscribe the petition on his return.]

21st October]   UNTO The Honble The Sheriff
1790   ]   of Renfrewshire
                  The Petition of Alexr Wilson weaver
                  in Seedhills of Paisley
HUMBLY SHEWETH

That in the process depending before the Court at the instance of William Henry Silk Manufacturer in Newtown of Paisley, with concourse of the pro'r fisk against the petitioner, your Lord'p was pleased upon the 10th of August last to pronounce the following Interlocutor "The Sheriff Depute having considered the libel, answers, and replies of parties, and having signified his opinion thereon, Appoints the defender to lodge duplies, And therein to set furth whether he admits or denies the composing, uttering or promulgating the paper complained of, or being art and part in the composition and promulgating thereof, and that against the seventeenth instant."

In consequence of this Interlocutor the petitioner lodged Duplies, and he therein declined to admit or deny altho' he entertained the highest respect for the Court as he then was of opinion, That it was incumbent upon the pursuers to bring home the charge in the Libel to the petitioner by the testimony of witnesses. The petitioner, however, now has no objections to withdraw these duplies and in place thereof he does deny the libel as laid, which will answer and fulfill the terms of your Lord'ps Interlocutor before recited. This denial the petitioner would have signed himself but his absence in the East Country for sometime past prevents his doing so; but upon his return, his pro'r had no hesitation to say, that his Client will subscribe the petition.

MAY it therefore please your Lord'p
to receive this petition as fulfilling
the terms of the Interlo. of 10th Aug.
last.

JOHN CRAIG

DOCUMENT J

[Begins with a minute dated 21 October 1790 that defender's procurator lodges the incidental petition (Document I). There follows an interlocutor dated 16 November 1790 by Sheriff Orr allowing the duplies (Document H) to be withdrawn and appoints 23 November 1790 as the diet of trial.]

Paisley 21 Oct 1790
The Defs. Pror. gives in an
Incidl. petition

. . .

Paisley 16th Novr. 1790
Mr. Jas. Orr Sh. Subt.
parties pro'rs present

Having Considered the Incidental Petition given in for the Defender and whole Process and having advised with the Sheriff Depute thereanent Appoints the Duplies to be withdrawn as not fulfilling the terms of the Interlocutor of the Tenth of August last Holds the Denial Stated in the Incidental Petition as fulfilling said Interlocutor Finds the Libel Relevant and allows the Pursuers a proof thereof allows the Defender a Conjunct proof and a proof of all facts and circumstances tending to alleviate or Exculpate Assigns the twenty third day of November inst. for that purpose and Grants Diligence.

JAMES ORR[3]

3. This is the last document in the series. One can only speculate. The diet of trial is only a week after it was fixed although the procedure roll has been somewhat leisurely in operation. Could it be that Wilson was still in "the East Country"? He never signed the incidental petition (Document I). Was a warrant to apprehend granted on 23 November 1790 if Wilson failed to appear? If so, was it never executed? Alternatively, was nothing done on 23 November 1790? Was the action allowed to go to sleep? Or was the action settled out of court? Wilson seems to have become less recalcitrant as evidenced by the incidental petition (Document I).

Advertisement in *The Glasgow Advertiser* by Paisley Reformers

Paisley, Saracen's Head Inn,
8 February 1793.

At a numerous and respectable meeting of Delegates from the Societies of this county associated for PARLIAMENTARY REFORM, the reports of the Delegates from their respective Societies were received; when it appeared that the greatest unanimity and peace prevailed through the whole Societies; that their numbers were rapidly encreasing, and that nothing but the accomplishment of their just constitutional and united demands, could ever prevail over their firmness and perseverance.

The particulars respecting their future meetings being determined, they unanimously agreed to the following DECLARATION, which they ordered to be published in the Glasgow Advertiser, Edinburgh Gazetteer, and London Star; and that 2000 copies be printed, in the form of handbills, for the perusal of the County Societies.

I. In the name of the Societies which we represent, we declare our firm and inviolable attachment to the genuine principles of the British Constitution, as established in 1688, our veneration for the person and family of our Gracious Sovereign, and our unalterable determination to obey our country's laws, and discountenance every measure that can be reasonably deemed seditious, dangerous, or unconstitutional.

II. We are determined to persevere in every lawful exertion, till we attain the glorious end for which we have associated. Our first application may be unsuccessful, but we should think ourselves unworthy of the appellation we have assumed, if a temporary repulse could induce us to depart from the cause in which we have engaged—We disclaim the cowardly idea; we pledge ourselves to maintain the firmest perseverance, and, by the regularity of our conduct, to manifest the rectitude of our intentions, and shew to the world that we really are THE FRIENDS OF THE PEOPLE.

III. No riot nor tumult shall ever meet our countenance or approbation. If these exist any where, we pity the infatuation of such as may have been unwarily led into measures so hurtful to the cause of liberty, and so inimical to the peace and good order of society; and we abhor the diabolical designs of those who, from wicked or interested motives, may have attempted to stimulate a spirit of discontent or confusion in any part of the country. We also feel compassion for the man whose ears have been filled with fabricated stories of our disloyalty, and disaffection to government; and hope the time is approaching, when the conduct of those, who have so misrepresented us, shall be displayed in its native colours, and exposed to all the contempt and odium it so justly deserves.

We have already, in our different Societies, publicly declared, what are the objects of our association; and think it unnecessary here to recapitulate them. But in the present crisis, we cannot help expressing our serious concern at the prospect of that greatest of national calamities into which our rulers seem ready to plunge us. We cannot evade the present opportunity of declaring our disapprobation of a measure so pregnant with ruin to our dearest interests—that we look forward with horror, and anticipate the miseries that must unavoidably ensue; and that we will not consent, that the nation shall be wantonly precipitated into such an abyss of destruction. We are persuaded, that we speak the mind of every one whose breast glows with sensations of humanity, when we declare, that war is the height of wickedness, when undertaken without the most urgent necessity. If urgent necessity presses our Ministry to enter into a war at present, let them shew where that necessity is; and they may expect the concurrence and support of a brave and loyal people. But if no such necessity exists, who can fail to reprobate the measure— a measure so evidently calculated to sink us in poverty and ruin. Is it to prevent a people from enjoying the privileges nature has given them, that we are to sacrifice thousands of lives, one of which is of more importance than all the riches which ever passed the Scheldt? If the blood of one man calls for vengeance on the guilty head of his destroyer, is it a light thing to sport with the lives of thousands. Does humanity shudder at the late atrocious conduct of the French? Does our Minister wish, for the sake of human nature, that such a deed could be for ever obliterated from the page of history? and is he callous to the feelings that ought to arise from the woes of his countrymen? Does he feel no remorse at shedding the blood of multitudes—at beholding thousands of our brave citizens torn from their endearing homes, and exposed to the cruelest of deaths where no friend is near to sooth and alleviate the agonies of their last moments? Can we hear the feelings expressed by our parliament for the murder of one man, and believe it possible that they will not have similar sensations from contemplating the slaughter of thousands?

Dreadful are the calamities of war! In the present case, we have our commerce, our fortunes, our lives to lose; without the alleviating prospect of the smallest advantage. Contrary to the dictates of morality, and religion, it must be incompatible with the happiness and prosperty of nations; for "what is morally wrong, cannot be politically right." War may be profitable to individuals; but it is always the bane of national happiness.

Fellow citizens, in one voice proclaim your disapprobation of war, and your eager desire to avert it. It is of the utmost importance to your commercial interests, as well as to the GREAT CAUSE OF HUMANITY. What calamities must follow the stagnation of trade! What crowds of ideas shocking to all the feelings of nature does war excite in every susceptible breast! Can you carry your imagination to the field of battle and death! Can you behold the blood of your fellows, your countrymen, your friends, shed forth in torrents, and hesitate one moment to come forward, and declare that you will not bring upon your heads the imputation of so much guilt: *for guilty you will be, if you are silent, and suffer that silence to be construed into consent.*

THE MEETING also unanimously agreed to the following RESOLUTIONS:

I. That a Reform in the representative election of Great Britain, and a shorter duration of parliamentary delegation, are essentially necessary to the true interests of the Sovereign, and the happiness of the subject; to procure which in a peaceable and constitutional manner is the great design, and universal wish of our Associations.

II. That the Liberty of the Press, of so much importance to the safety of a free people, calls for the protection and support of all, as being the terror of villainy and corruption, the palladium of civil liberty, and the boast and glory of every free nation.

III. That Press Warrants are an insult to justice and humanity the miserable source of ruin and distress to numberless families, and a disgrace to the British Constitution.

IV. That the united thanks of the Societies are justly due to the Right Hon. Charles James Fox, for his open and animated disapprobation of involving the Nation in the miseries of unnecessary war; to the Hon. Thomas Erskine, for his noble and unwearied exertions in defence of the Liberty of the Press; to Colonel Macleod, the sincerity of whose wishes for the interests of his country, his late elegant and pathetic Address to the Societies of Scotland, will remain a perpetual monument; to Mr. Grey for the active and leading part he has always taken in the cause of the People. (The eyes of the nation are still upon him; they know his abilities, and integrity; and that, that in depending upon these, they will never be disappointed): And to all the Members of the illustrious Minority in Parliament, who, in spite of the torrent of ministerial influence, have boldly stood forth in support of the real interests of their country.

ROBERT DARROCH, President.
JAMES MITCHELL, Secretary.

Wilson's Naturalization Certificate[1]

9th June, 1804.

Be it remembered that at a Court of Common Pleas held at Philadelphia in and for the County of Philadelphia in the Commonwealth of Pennsylvania in the United States of America on the Ninth day of June in the year of our Lord One thousand eight hundred and four Alexander Wilson a native of Scotland exhibited a Petition praying to be admitted to become a Citizen of the said United States and having on his solemn Oath declared and also made full proof thereof by other testimony in the said Court that he was residing within the limits and under the jurisdiction of the United States between the twenty ninth day of January one thousand seven hundred and ninety five and the eighteenth day of June one thousand seven hundred and Ninety eight and has resided within the United States in the State of Pennsylvania ten years last past, and it appearing to the satisfaction of the said Court that during the said period the said Alexander Wilson has behaved as a man of good moral character attached to the principles of the Constitution of the United States and well disposed to the good Order and happiness of the [same]; and the said Alexander Wilson having then and there declared on his solemn Oath aforesaid that he would support the Constitution of the United States and that he absolutely and entirely renounced and abjured all allegiance and fidelity to any foreign Prince Potentate State & Sovereignty whatever and particularly to the King of the United Kingdoms of Great Britain and Ireland of whom he was before a Subject. The said Court

1. Historical Society of Pennsylvania, Philadelphia.

thereupon admitted the said Alexander Wilson to become a Citizen of
the United States and ordered all he said proceeding to be recorded by
the Prothonotary of the said Court which . . . accordingly

> In witness whereof I have hereunto set
> my hand & the seal of the Court aforesaid
> at Philadelphia the fourteenth day of June
> in the year of our Lord One thousand eight
> hundred & four
>
> [CHA. BIDDLE]

Wilson's Last Will and Testament, with Inventory[1]

I Alexander Wilson now of the City of Philadelphia do hereby make and publish my last Will and Testament respecting my worldly Goods and Estate as follows—that is to say I give and bequeath to my honoured father two copies of the "American Ornithology"

And to my Nephew William Duncan One Copy of said "American Ornithology"—And as for and concerning all the rest residue and remainder of my estate, whatsoever and wheresoever, including my right and Interest in the publication of the "American Ornithology" I do give and bequeath the same unto Sarah Miller her heirs executors Administrators and assigns forever And I do nominate and appoint Daniel H Miller & George Ord of the City of Philadelphia executors of this my last will and testament—In witness whereof I have hereunto set my hand and seal this sixteenth day of August in the year of our Lord One thousand eight hundred and thirteen.

ALEX WILSON

Signed sealed published and declared by the testator Alexander Wilson for and as his last Will and Testament in the presence of us

> HENRY L. CORYELL (scvn)　　25th Sept 1813
> SUSANNAH JONES (scvn)　　　same day

Philadelphia September 25th 1813 When personally appeared Henry L. Coryell and Susannah Jones the Witnesses to the aforegoing Will and on their solemn oaths according to Law did depose and say that they did see and hear Alexander Wilson the Testator in the said Will named sign

1. Held by the Office of the Register of Wills, Room 180, City Hall, Philadelphia (Will No. 107 of 1813, also in Will Book 5, p. 64).

seal publish and declare the said Will as and for his last Will and Testament and that at the doing thereof he was of sound mind memory and understanding to the best of their knowledge and belief

Coram

SAM BRYAN
Register

Drs   The Estate of Alexander Wilson deceased in account with Cr
      Daniel H. Miller and George Ord. Executors
1813   The said Executors claim allowance as follows viz.

September 3d		To Cash paid Hannah January bill for attending funeral for sundry articles furnished by her	Dolls.Cents 18.50
,,	,,	To ditto paid Smithers bill of cakes	4.21
,,	6	,, ditto paid Adam Short sextons fees	3
,,	,,	,, ditto paid Nicholas Collin rector of the Swedish Corporation for Mr. Wilsons grave	10
,,	,,	,, ditto paid Keran Fitzgerald for the Hearse	6
,,	,,	,, ditto paid L. Biddles bill of Crape, Gloves etc.	61.12½
,,	,,	,, ditto paid John Douglass Jnr for a coffin	24
,,	24	,, ditto paid at Registers Office for Letters Testamentary and for Citation to David Wilson	5.75
,,	,,	,, ditto paid Doct. Gallahers bill for attending Mr. Wilson	25
,,	,,	,, ditto paid Doctr. Caldwells bill for ditto	24
,,	,,	,, ditto paid for publishing Notices for settlement of accounts	3
,,	,,	,, ditto paid Sam Ewing Esqr. for professional Services in the case of David Wilson vs. the Executors of Alexr. Wilson decd.	20
			204.58½

Paid Register for examining and passing this account
and for copy seal and Certificate   3.50
                                                                    ─────────
                                                                    $208.08½
                                                                    ═════════

The said Executors charge themselves as follows viz.
By Cash found in the Pocket Book of Mr. Wilson   200
"   Sundry articles of wearing apparel Books etc. as per
     inventory but which have not yet been appraised——
     Balance due the Executors on this account so far
     as settled,   8.08½
                                                                    ─────────
                                                                    $208.08½
                                                                    ═════════

Philadelphia Nov. 1st 1816

The following are the claims against the Estate of Alexr. Wilson decd.

Assignees of Bradford & Inskeep $2284.22
David Wilson—about—   75
Alex Duncan   Do say   60
James McAlpin   31
                                   ─────────
                                   $2450.22
                                   ═════════

To pay which nothing remains in the hands of the Executors except a
few volumes of Books, sundry articles of wearing apparel etc etc as per
Inventory

The executors however are well assured that that [sic] so soon as the
remaining volumes of Ornithology which remain in the hands of the
assignees shall be sold, & the full settlement takes place, there will be
ample funds for the discharge of all legal claims against the estate of
Mr. Wilson.

The within Statement is furnished by the Subscriber and of the Executors
of the Estate of Alex Wilson decd. with the view of satisfying any of
the creditors of said estate who may be desirous of information on the
subject.

Philadelphia Novemb 1st 1816   D. H. MILLER

GLOSSARY OF SCOTTISH WORDS

beagle *lawman*
bodle *small coin*
brislt *bruised*
brod *table*
caft *bought*
cheeps *chirps*
　(*tut-tutting*)
chiel *young fellow*
chirts *squeezes*
claith *cloth*
clashing *noise*
clash us *pay us*
clink *money*
cork *small*
　manufacturer
counterfeits *false*
　money
croon *hum*
dark *day's work*
doyt *small coin*
draff *chaff*
dreein' *enduring*
fash *trouble*
forby *besides*
get *bastard*

girnan *snarling*
girnit *snarled*
gorge *devour*
granes *groans*
groat *fourpence*
harl *drag*
harle *take*
harnish *harness, the*
　web given to the
　piecework weaver
　and returned as a
　woven length of
　fabric
hole *flaw in the weave*
jinkin *moving quickly*
keel in claith *end of*
　the web
kist *chest*
limmer *loose woman*
lugs *ears*
maun *must*
neek *smoke*
noddle *head*
oe *grandson*
P--y Corse *Paisley*
　Cross

poortith *poverty*
poucht *pocketed*
reek *smoke*
sic *such*
sicker *sure*
siller *money*
spew *vomit*
sprawl *contest*
swack *whack*
throuther *unmethodical*
tither *other*
toom *empty*
twa hun'er far'er *that*
　is, better quality
　cloth
twalls *twelves*
unco gloyts *great*
　blockheads
wabsters *weavers*
war *were*
wean *child*
weel-a-wat *well I*
　never
yaummers *laments*
yett *gate*

Bibliography

MANUSCRIPTS

Crawfurd, Andrew. *The Cairn of Lochwinnoch*. Compiled by Dr. Crawfurd of Johnshill, Lochwinnoch. 46 manuscript vols. in the Paisley Central Library. For Alexander Wilson, see vols. 1, 4, 5, 6, 7.

Public Record Office, London. *State Papers XLIII*. Ref. HO102, Item Nos. 4/12. A collection of papers and reports to the Home Office in London about the unrest in Scotland 1791–1794.

THE WRITINGS OF ALEXANDER WILSON

American Ornithology—Selected Editions

Wilson, Alexander. *American Ornithology*. 9 vols. Philadelphia: Bradford and Inskeep, 1808–1814.
Contains a biographical sketch of Alexander Wilson by George Ord in vol. 9.

—— and Charles Lucien Bonaparte. *American Ornithology*. Edited by Robert Jameson. 4 vols. Edinburgh: Constable & Co., 1831.
Contains a memoir of Wilson by Rev. Dr. W. M. Hetherington.

——. *American Ornithology*. With a continuation by Charles Lucien Bonaparte. Notes and life of Wilson by Sir William Jardine. 3 vols. London: Whittaker, Treacher & Arnot; Edinburgh: Stirling & Kenny, 1832.

—— and Charles Lucien Bonaparte. *American Ornithology*. 3 vols. Philadelphia: Porter & Coates, 1871.
Contains portfolio of 103 plates.

Wilson's Poems—Selected Editions

Wilson, Alexander. *Poems.* Paisley: J. Neilson, 1790.
Contains no list of subscribers. At the end has his "Journal" for September 1789 to 2 October 1789.

——. *Poems, Humorous, Satirical and Serious.* Second edition. Edinburgh: P. Hill, 1791.
This was Wilson's own copy which I describe in the Introduction. The pagination is irregular. There are various notes in Wilson's hand. On a blank page at the end, also in his hand, is a list of his poems which are not included in the volume, e.g. "The Foresters," "Blue Bird," "King Bird," "Matilda," "Watty and Meg," etc., but excluding those which were in any way involved with his reforming activities. There is a note at the side, "about 4000 lines," and it would appear that he contemplated an American edition. Details of this book are also given in Robert Brown, *Paisley Poets*, Paisley: J. & J. Cook, 1889, vol. 1, pp. 45–46.

Poems Chiefly in the Scottish Dialect by Alexander Wilson with an Account of His Life and Writings. Paisley: J. Neilson, 1816.
Grosart states that this Life was "chiefly by Thomas Crichton." In fact the collection appears to have been made by a Dr. Whyte who died before the Life was written and the collection completed. The Life was written by Dr. Robert Watt, author of *Bibliotheca Britannica*, probably with assistance from Thomas Crichton.

The Poetical Works of Alexander Wilson. Belfast: John Henderson, 1844.
A useful source book with an "extended memoir" of Wilson's life and also the Craw portrait.

The Poetical Works of Alexander Wilson with an Extended Memoir of His Life and Writings. Belfast: J. Henderson.
No date is given, but a note on this copy by Mrs. Alice McKenzie, formerly librarian at the Paisley Central Library, indicates that it was published in 1860. Compare with above.

The Poems and Literary Prose of Alexander Wilson. Edited by the Rev. Alexander B. Grosart. 2 vols. Paisley: Alexander Gardner, 1876.
Contains a useful life but, more important, a valuable collection of Wilson's correspondence.

SECONDARY SOURCES

Books

Allen, Elsa G. *The History of American Ornithology before Audubon. Trans. Amer. Philos. Soc.*, n.s. 41, 3 (October 1951).

Audubon, John James. *The Birds of America.* 4 vols. London, 1827–1838. With 435 plates of which the first 10 were engraved by W. H. Lizars, Edinburgh, but retouched or reengraved by Robert Havell, Jr., London, who was responsible for the remaining 425 plates.

——. *The Birds of America.* With an introduction and descriptive text by William Vogt. New York: The Macmillan Company, 1937.

——. *The Original Water-Colour Paintings by John James Audubon for the Birds of America.* Introduction by Marshall B. Davidson. London: Michael Joseph Ltd., and the Connoisseur, 1966. Also in the United States by American Heritage Publishing Co., Inc..

Blair, Matthew. *The Paisley Shawl.* Paisley: Alexander Gardner, 1904. *The Paisley Thread Industry.* Paisley: Alexander Gardner, 1907.

Brodie, David, Accountant. *A Short Set of Book-Keeping by Double Entry.* Paisley: Neilson & Hay, 1831.

Brown, Robert. *Paisley Poets.* 2 vols. Paisley: J. & J. Cook, 1889.

——. *Paisley Burns Clubs 1805–1893.* Paisley: Alexander Gardner, 1893.

——. *The History of Paisley.* 2 vols. Paisley: J. & J. Cook, 1886.

Buchanan, Robert. *The Life and Adventures of John James Audubon.* Third edition. London: Sampson, Low, Son & Marston, 1869.

Burns, Robert. *Robert Burns' Literary Correspondents 1786–1796.* Alloway, Ayr: Burns Monument Trustees, 1938.

——. *Robert Burns and Mrs. Dunlop, Correspondence.* Edited by William Wallace. London: Hodder and Stroughton, 1898.

Butterfield, L. H. *John Witherspoon Comes to America.* Princeton: Princeton University Press, 1953.

Cantwell, Robert. *Alexander Wilson: Naturalist and Pioneer*. Philadelphia: J. B. Lippincott Co., 1961.
This is an important book in the Alexander Wilson story. Cantwell uncovered much new material. Court records concerning Wilson's arrest are printed in an appendix.

Catesby, Mark. *The Natural History of Carolina, Florida and the Bahama Islands: Containing the Figures of Birds, Beasts, Fishes, Serpents, Insects and Plants*. Third edition, 2 vols. London: 1771. (First edition of each volume 1731 and 1743). If Alexander Wilson was the father of American ornithology then surely Mark Catesby was the grandfather and J. J. Audubon the son!

Chancellor, John. *Audubon—A Biography*. London: Weidenfeld and Nicolson, 1978.

Collins, Varnum Lansing. *President Witherspoon*. 2 vols. Princeton: Princeton University Press, 1925.

Crawfurd, George. *The History of the Shire of Renfrew*. Continued by William Semple. Paisley: Alex Weir, 1782.

——. *A General Description of the Shire of Renfrew*. Continued by George Robertson. Paisley: J. Neilson, 1818.

Crichton, Thomas. *Memoir of the Life and Writings of John Witherspoon D. D., Late President of the College of New Jersey. Edinburgh Christian Review and Christian Instructor*, vol. 28 (October 1829).

——. *Biographical Sketch of the Late Alexander Wilson to a Young Friend*. Paisley: J. Neilson, 1819.
These sketches together with Ord's expanded *Life* and *Poems* (1816) are the best of the early memoirs of Alexander Wilson's life.

Cromek, R. H., editor. *Select Scottish Songs*. 2 vols. London: T. Cadell and W. Davies, 1810. For Alexander Wilson see vol. 2, pp. 211–225 (as given in Ms.).

Earnest, Ernest. *John and William Bartram, Botanists and Explorers*. Philadelphia: University of Pennsylvania Press, 1940.

Edwards, George. *A Natural History of Uncommon Birds, 1743–1751: Gleanings of Natural History, 1750–1764*. 7 vols. in 3. London, in 4 parts between 1743 and 1751 (1743, 1747, 1750, 1751); in 3 parts between 1758 and 1764.

Graham, Henry Grey. *The Social Life of Scotland in the Eighteenth Century*. London: Adam and Charles Black, 1964.

Hector, William. *Selections from the Judicial Records of Renfrewshire*. Paisley: J. & J. Cook, series 1, 1876; series 2, 1878.

Herrick, Francis Hobart. *Audubon the Naturalist*. 2 vols. New York: D. Appleton and Company, 1917.
An objective and definitive account of Audubon.

Hunter, Thomas. *Notes on the Literature of Paisley and District*.
A series of articles which appeared in *The Paisley and Renfrewshire Gazette*, February to November 1952. 30 to 40 copies privately printed by T.H.

Janson, Charles William. *The Stranger in America*. London, 1807.
Preface says drawings by "Mr. Birch," but the engravings are inscribed "drawn under the direction of the author and engraved by M. Marigot."

Jardine, Sir William, editor. *The Naturalist's Library*, vol. 40 (1843).
Contains "Memoir of Alexander Wilson" written by Jardine.

Kastner, Joseph. *A World of Naturalists*. London: John Murray, 1978.

Kay, John. *A Series of Original Portraits*. 2 vols. Edinburgh, 1842. Vol. 2, pp. 83–84, about John Witherspoon.

MacKean, William. *Letters Home During a Trip in America 1869*. Paisley, 1875.
Printed for family and friends.

Motherwell, William. *The Harp of Renfrewshire*. Paisley: J. Lawrence, Jr., 1819.

Murray, Norman. *The Scottish Hand Loom Weavers, 1790–1850: A Social History*. Edinburgh: John Donald, Ltd., 1978.

Ord, George. *Sketch of the Life of Alexander Wilson*. Philadelphia: Harrison Hall, 1828.
This life is substantially enlarged from that which Ord wrote for vol. 9 of the *American Ornithology*. Contains many more letters.

Oxford Companion to American History. By Thomas H. Johnston in consultation with Harvey Wish. New York: Oxford University Press, 1966.

Parkhill, John. *The History of Paisley*. Paisley: Robert Stewart, 1857.

Paton, Allan Park. *Wilson the Ornithologist: A New Chapter in His Life*. London: Longmans, Green & Company, 1863.

Picken, Ebenezer. *Poems and Epistles Mostly in the Scottish Dialect with Glossary*. Paisley: John Neilson, 1788.

Poesch, Jessie. *Titian Ramsay Peale 1799–1825 and His Journals of the Wilkes Expedition. Memoirs of the Amer. Philos. Soc.*, vol. 52. Philadelphia, 1961.

Rowland, Mrs. Dunbar. *Life, Letters and Papers of William Dunbar*. Jackson, Mississippi: Mississippi Historical Society, 1930.

Semple, David. *The Poems and Songs and Correspondence of Robert Tannahill*. Paisley: Alexander Gardner, 1876.

Sharp, Elizabeth A. *William Sharp (Fiona MacLeod)*. London: William Heinemann, 1910.

Tait, Alexander. *Poems and Songs*. Paisley, 1790.

Turnbull, Gavin. *Poetical Essays*. Glasgow: David Niven, 1788.

Wilson, Alexander. *Memoirs of Alexander Wilson*. Philadelphia: Carey & Lea, 1831.

Wilson, James Grant. *The Poets and Poetry of Scotland*. 2 vols. London: Blackie & Son, 1877.

Periodicals

Abbot, John. "Notes on My Life." Edited by C. L. Remington. *Lepidopterist News* 2, 3 (1948).

Allen, Elsa G. "John Abbot, Pioneer Naturalist of Georgia." *The Georgia Historical Quarterly* 4, 2 (1957).

Burns, Frank L. "Miss Malvinia Lawson's Recollections of Ornithologists." *The Auk*, n.s. 34 (1917): 275–282.

——. "Alexander Wilson: The Unsuccessful Lover." *The Wilson Bulletin* no. 64 (1908): 130–145.

Coues, Elliott. "Private Letters of Wilson, Ord and Bonaparte." *Penn Monthly* 10 (1879): 443–455.

Glasgow Advertiser, 1793.

Hicks, Lawrence E. "An Account of the Twentieth Annual Meeting of the Wilson Ornithological Club Held in Pittsburgh, December 28–30, 1934, with the Details of an Exhibition of Wilsoniana." *The Wilson Bulletin*, n.d.

Hunter, Clark. "Alexander Wilson: Paisley Poet and American Ornithologist." *Scotland's Magazine* 68, 6 (June 1972).

K.J. "Bi-centenary of a Naturalist: Alexander Wilson—Paisley's Most Gifted Son." *Paisley Daily Express*, 6 July 1966.

Motherwell, William, editor. *The Paisley Magazine*. Paisley: David Dick, 1828.
Published for only one year. See pages 582–585 and 632–635 for interesting contemporary views of Wilson.

Rhoads, Samuel N. "George Ord." *Cassinia* 12 (1908).

Scottish Journal of Topography, Antiquities, Traditions Etc., vol. 1 (September 1847–February 1848); vol. 2 (March–July 1848). Vol. 2, pp. 228–232 and pp. 245–247, contains the records of Wilson's trial regarding "The Shark."

Stone, Witmer. "Some Unpublished Letters of Alexander Wilson and John Abbot." *The Auk* 23, 4 (1906).

Index

In an entry, page numbers in italics indicate that a letter (or letters) to that correspondent begins on that page. Birds are listed by first letter of common name, unless several of one species occur in the text, when they are listed by species name. Those named in Latin in the text are cross-referenced in English.

Two thousand copies of
The Life and Letters of Alexander Wilson
were printed and bound at The Stinehour Press
in Lunenburg, Vermont. The illustrations were
printed at The Meriden Gravure Company in
Meriden, Connecticut.

The type face is Monotype Bell,
an accurate adaptation of a late eighteenth-
century British type design for the printer and
publisher John Bell. The paper is Rising Book
Laid. The design was by Freeman Keith.